Custom, Law, and Monarchy

Custom, Law, and Monarchy

A Legal History of Early Modern France

MARIE SEONG-HAK KIM

OXFORD
UNIVERSITY PRESS

OXFORD
UNIVERSITY PRESS

Great Clarendon Street, Oxford, OX2 6DP,
United Kingdom

Oxford University Press is a department of the University of Oxford.
It furthers the University's objective of excellence in research, scholarship,
and education by publishing worldwide. Oxford is a registered trade mark of
Oxford University Press in the UK and in certain other countries

First Edition published in 2021

Published in the United States of America by Oxford University Press
198 Madison Avenue, New York, NY 10016, United States of America

British Library Cataloguing in Publication Data
Data available

Library of Congress Control Number: 2021940040

ISBN 978–0–19–284549–8

DOI: 10.1093/oso/9780192845498.001.0001

To Jim

Acknowledgments

Over the last decade I had the privilege of spending years at several institutes in Europe, which graciously funded my various projects in Korean law. During my fellowship tenures—at the Collegium de Lyon, the Netherlands Institute for Advanced Study at Wassenaar, the Freiburg Institute of Advanced Studies, and the Käte Hamburger Kolleg Recht als Kultur at the University of Bonn—I found myself repeatedly pulled to my former interests in French history. For one thing, the immense literature on custom by European scholars convinced me there is a need for an accessible study of early modern French legal history in English; for another, my comparative work on custom as a source of law in East Asia made the French monarchy and its law appear in a new light with fresh perspectives. The present book is an outcome of the confluence of disparate intellectual endeavors that began some forty years ago in Seoul and have undergone many detours since.

Along the way I have profited from the encouragement and advice from friends and colleagues. I thank, among others, Professors Ronald G. Asch, Bernard Barbiche, Denis Crouzet, Mark Greengrass, Kjell Å Modéer, and Alain A. Wijffels, who kindly read parts of the draft at different stages. I owe a special thanks to Professor James B. Collins at Georgetown University; he read the entire manuscript more than once and helped me with the book in a way I could not have expected of anyone else. Errors in this book are of course my own. A Franklin Research Grant from the American Philosophical Society allowed me to consult the fabulous collections of French *coutumes* at the Jacob Burns Law Library at George Washington University. Also, an extended visit to the Max Planck Institute for European Legal History in Frankfurt, made possible by an MPI scholarship and a visiting professorship at the Goethe University School of Law, assuaged my otherwise perpetual interlibrary loan blues.

I wish to record here my deepest gratitude to Professor James D. Tracy, my doctoral advisor at the University of Minnesota. From the time he supervised my dissertation on Michel de L'Hôpital, he has been my single greatest source of inspiration and enlightenment, helping me find meaning in the academic journey in my adopted country. In appreciation of my lifelong debts, I dedicate this book to Jim. Finally, thanks and love as always to Christopher and John-Paul, and to Joel who made the maps in the following pages.

Contents

List of Figures and Maps

Figures

Maps

1
Introduction

This book sets forth the evolution of law in late medieval and early modern France. The state of the law in the ancien régime was rather different from what we commonly know as French law, namely, the Civil Code promulgated after the French Revolution. For some six hundred years, from the thirteenth through the end of the eighteenth century, France did not have a unified law. Legal relations of the people were governed by a disorganized amalgam of norms, including provincial and local customs (*coutumes*), elements of Roman law and canon law, royal edicts and ordinances, and judicial decisions, all coexisting with little apparent internal coherence. The multiplicity of laws and fragmentation of jurisdictions were the defining features of the monarchical era. How the legal system comprising such various sources of law functioned to meet the changing needs of society and the state presents an important question to historians and jurists alike.

A key subject in European legal history is the metamorphosis of popular custom (*consuetudo*) into customary law (*jus consuetudinarium*). The transmutation of the amorphous mass of normative expressions existing in social practices and usages into a source of law subject to doctrinal scrutiny was a feat of medieval legal science. Equally significant was the incorporation of custom into the national hierarchy of law. How to manage customary law was a common concern for late medieval and early modern kingdoms. In the late fifteenth and sixteenth centuries French kings undertook campaigns to record the *coutumes*. The collection and standardization of customs took place in different parts of the continent, but nowhere was it carried out in the same scale and intensity as in France. The main focus of this book is on the royal enterprise of customary law redaction, which encompassed not just the exercise of power by public authorities but concerted efforts by an array of individual actors, ranging from royal commissioners who supervised the local assemblies that drew up the *coutumes*, to doctrinal authors who commented on them in learned treatises, and to legal practitioners who argued them in the courtroom.

As the French monarchy consolidated territorial holdings in the Late Middle Ages, in particular in the aftermath of the Hundred Years War (1337–1453), the creation of a more effective judicial system became urgent. Most critical was to reduce the cumbersome processes of proving the law in litigation. In the absence of written texts, the parties had to proffer and substantiate the custom each time their cases were heard before the court, which entailed much confusion, not to mention serious delays and expenses. In 1454, Charles VII (r. 1422–1461) issued

Custom, Law, and Monarchy: A Legal History of Early Modern France. Marie Seong-Hak Kim, Oxford University Press.
 DOI: 10.1093/oso/9780192845498.003.0001

his famous Ordinance of Montils-lès-Tours and ordered the recording of customs, usages, and procedures of different regions. Louis XI (r. 1461–1483) professed his desire to reduce rampant lawsuits. Charles VIII (r. 1483–1498) commanded that the redaction of customs take place in the assembly of the three estates of each locality, presided over by royal commissioners. The *coutumes* drawn up in the assembly were promulgated through the solemn process of homologation.[1] They became a formal body of laws like royal laws. Invoking customs different from the ones in the official texts was prohibited.

The reign of Louis XII (r. 1498–1515) saw the publication of some twenty-five provincial *coutumes*. Another fifteen *coutumes* were compiled under Francis I (r. 1515–1547). After a brief lull, a new phase of the campaign began in the late 1550s under Henry II (r. 1547–1559), this time focusing on reforming the *coutumes* that had already been published but proved incomplete or inadequate. The crowning achievement was the reformation of the custom of Paris in 1580 under Henry III (r. 1574–1589), originally published in 1510. It was followed by several more redactions through the end of the Valois dynasty. At the closing of the sixteenth century, there were sixty-five general customs (*coutumes générales*) and some three hundred local customs (*coutumes locales*) across the kingdom.[2] Under Henry IV (r. 1589–1610) and his successors of the Bourbon dynasty, the recording of customs took place only sporadically. The authorized *coutumes* provided for more stable and predictable norms, securely incorporated into the state legal hierarchy. But they entrenched regional particularism, and the resulting solidification of jurisdictional divisions bequeathed a map of a crazy quilt of laws, which changed little before the end of the ancien régime.

This book approaches the history of customary law from juristic, political, and constitutional perspectives. The writing down of official customs coincided with the outburst of learning and creativity unleashed by the Renaissance, which created a rare and powerful confluence of political exigency and legal logic. The medieval legal pluralism was gradually supplanted by a distinct legal nationalism, and the notion of "French law" arose.[3] The royal campaigns continued in full gear during the Wars of Religion (1562–1598) when confessional conflicts were tearing France apart.[4] A series of legislative reforms took place in the 1560s in tandem

[1] Homologation means granting approval or recognition by the highest authority in the realm, the king or the emperor.

[2] The classic study by Klimrath divided the major redactions of the customs into three periods: the first to 1504; the second from 1505 to 1554; and the third from 1555 to about 1600. Henri Klimrath, "Études sur les coutumes" [1837], in *Travaux sur l'histoire du droit français* (Paris: Joubert, 1843), vol. 2, 135–70.

[3] The term "droit français" came into use in the 1560s. Jean-Louis Thireau, "Le comparatisme et la naissance du droit français," *Revue d'histoire des facultés de droit et de la science juridique* 10–11 (1990), 154.

[4] The best study of the reformation of customs is René Filhol, *Le premier président Christofle de Thou et la réformation des coutumes* (Paris: Recueil Sirey, 1937).

with the customary law redactions. Together they manifested the belief that the preservation of the monarchical edifice was predicated on the restoration of the core ideals of law and justice. Customary law campaigns held out the king as the protector of the interest of the subjects, pledging effective delivery of justice during the seemingly desolate years. This understanding adds a new dimension to the conventional view that the royal government in the late sixteenth century was completely powerless in the midst of civil war.

In old France, the king was foremost the distributor of justice. Law was understood primarily as the means for the king to ensure justice for his subjects. But the customary law redaction, through royal commissioners, was not merely clarifying certain points of law at the request of particular individuals or groups. Instead, it was an occasion in which the king declared that he had the power to regulate old liberties and rights by royal civil service. He promised to respect customs and privileges agreed upon in the popular assemblies, but made it clear that he was the ultimate arbiter of them.[5] In the sixteenth century, constitutional thinkers subjected under royal dominium the vast realms of law that had previously remained in autonomy, putting forward a new conceptualization of sovereign power. The redaction of *coutumes* was the expression of a sovereignty which was indivisible in the juridical sense yet could be discharged, exercised, and administered in a consultative mode. Sovereignty was vested in the king alone, but he allowed the people to declare customs that governed their private affairs in local communities. Jean Bodin (1530–1596) captured the idea in the following words: the king who "is subject to neither his laws nor the laws of his predecessors" ensures, in his "just and reasonable conventions," the observation of laws in which the people hold interest "en général, ou en particulier."[6] *Roi justicier* became *roi législateur.*

Many customs needed to be modified and abrogated as much as defended and preserved; not all deserved the same level of respect in law. The notion that the king could change common law when deemed necessary for the benefit of common good (*bien commun* or *intérêt commun*) facilitated royal administrative measures, which diverged from common law but were justified for the purpose of governing the kingdom. Customary law campaigns demonstrated the crown's commitment to law. As he ordered the seigneurs, and everyone else, to abide by the customs issued in his name, the king affirmed he would do the same, putting himself under the positive law. One can discern the idea of the rule of law, in

[5] Throughout the ancien régime, "one could almost say that all French people were privileged." Bernard Barbiche, *Les institutions de la monarchie française à l'époque moderne: XVIe–XVIIIe siècle* (Paris: Presses universitaires de France, 1999), 4.

[6] Jean Bodin, *Les six livres de la république* (Paris: Jacques du Puys, 1576), book 1, ch. 9, 133–34. There are several different versions of *République*, including the 1577 unauthorized Genevan edition. The first Latin edition appeared in 1586. Page numbers in this book come from the original French publication of 1576.

police as well as in private law of property.[7] This rule of law (*État de droit*; *Rechtsstaat*) was grounded on the new conception of the political will.[8] Michel de L'Hôpital (*c.*1505–1573), the Chancellor of France under Francis II (r. 1559–1560) and Charles IX (r. 1560–1574), articulated the political agenda to achieve a good administration of justice in conformity with the law under unchallenged royal will.

This book argues that the sixteenth century under the Valois witnessed the rise of a full recognition of royal prerogatives, the kind normally associated with the Bourbons in the seventeenth and eighteenth centuries. The symbolic meaning of the assertion that only those customs promulgated in the name of the king had the force of law deserves attention. For contemporary writers, the term "absolute" meant the king legislated of his own accord. It seemed clear during the religious wars that the king ought to be absolute because only he could preserve the realm. The idea of unity around the crown converged with the idea of unity in the law. The robust conception of exclusive legislative power saw its expression in the redaction of the customs.

The following chapters present a synthetic view of French law and the state, focusing on the period between 1300 and 1600 but also reflecting on the years leading to the creation of the Civil Code in 1804.

1. State of the Question

Legal history concerns both history of law and law in history. One can identify two distinct methods. The first, an approach of *histoire juridique*, focuses on the origins and evolution of the sources of law, mostly positive law currently in force, and the role of doctrine in conceptualizing them. The second, an approach of *histoire littéraire*, notes positive law was often removed from the reality of life and thus centers its attention instead on the practice of law within cultural and social frameworks.[9] This book attempts to find a middle ground, discussing law as a

[7] The legal science of public governance in the Middle Ages marked the origins of the concept of the rule of law. Alain Wijffels, "Une très brève histoire du droit dans la civilisation occidentale (1000–2000)," *Annales de droit de Louvain* 77 (2017), 397–411. As Wijffels notes, the term "rule of law" comes from a later period and it can mean many different things in different political contexts but the ideal of public affairs in compliance with law was prevalent in the Middle Ages and the sixteenth century. Olivier Descamps and Alain Wijffels, "Approches historiques de la notion de *ius commune* en Europe occidentale," in Mireille Delmas-Marty, Kathia Martin-Chenut, and Camila Perruso (eds.), *Sur les chemins d'un jus commune universalisable* (Paris: Mare & Martin, 2021), 53–73.

[8] The oft-quoted schema of the transition of France from a judicial monarchy to a legislative monarchy, then to an administrative monarchy has ample utility in legal history. Michel Antoine, "La monarchie absolue," in Keith M. Baker (ed.), *The Political Culture of the Old Regime*, vol. 1 of *The French Revolution and the Creation of Modern Political Culture* (Oxford: Pergamon Press, 1987), 18.

[9] The terms *histoire juridique* and *histoire littéraire* come from Robert Descimon, "Declareuil (1913) contre Hauser (1912): Les rendez-vous manqués de l'histoire et de l'histoire du droit," *Annales: Histoire, sciences sociales* 57 (2002), 1615–36.

system of rules of government and also as evolving phenomena toward the goal of the freedom of the individual. It is premised on the belief that an examination of the sources of law and juristic writings as *historical* evidence is necessary before either a theorization of legal principles or a recounting of interactions between law and society can be envisaged. But first, what is custom?

Concept of Custom

A basic distinction can be drawn between custom as socially constructed norms of conduct on the one hand and custom as norms manifested by court decisions on the other hand. One can call the former "sociologists' customary law" and the latter "lawyers' customary law." Legal anthropologists and sociologists internalize the axiom that no society is without law—*ubi societas ibi jus* (where there is society, there is law)—and subscribe to the view that all sorts of social control, including habits and usages, are law. By contrast, legal historians define law as rules and standards recognized by actors with formal authority. A generally accepted definition of custom in legal history is "the ensemble of usages or rules of a social group that acquired binding force through the repetition of public and peaceful acts for a long period of time."[10] Binding force here is more than community pressure; informal rules imposed by means of social disapproval do not have the attributes of law because they lack enforcement power. This book adheres to the view that custom is something that is not only followed as a matter of practice but also recognized and enforced by courts as a matter of law.

Distinguishing custom as law from other elements of society reflects the distinctive jurisprudential approach that forms a key aspect of the Western legal tradition.[11] Customs were privileges but not all privileges became private law. In Europe law was primarily a system of civil law rules ascertained through adjudication.[12] The "legal" concept of law *tout court* has critics, but it captures vital strands of historical evidence that can be subsumed only with difficulty under a

[10] John Gilissen, "Loi et coutume: quelques aspects de l'interpénétration des sources du droit dans l'ancien droit belge," *Tijdschrift voor Rechtsgeschiedenis* 21 (1953), 263–64.

[11] David J. Bederman, *Custom as a Source of Law* (Cambridge: Cambridge University Press, 2010), 16. The concept of custom as law was absent in East Asia, for instance. For comparison of European and Asian legal traditions, see Marie Seong-Hak Kim, *Law and Custom in Korea: Comparative Legal History* (Cambridge: Cambridge University Press, 2012); Marie Seong-Hak Kim, "Custom as a Source of Law in European and East Asian Legal History," in Olivier Moréteau, Aniceto Masferrer, and Kjell Å Modéer (eds.), *Comparative Legal History* (Cheltenham: Edward Elgar Publishing, 2019), 186–211.

[12] Civil law (*jus civile*) means citizens' law. In the *Institutes*, law was distinguished between the civil law of Rome and the law of all nations, namely, natural law. *Institutes* 1.2.1. Civil law comprised the law of all peoples (*jus gentium*) and the law of a particular polity (state law). State law was in turn divided into written law (*jus scriptum*) and unwritten law (*jus non scriptum*): the former was identified in a broad sense with statute (*lex*), the latter with custom (*consuetudo*). See *The Institutes of Justinian*, trans. J. B. Moyle, 5th ed. (Oxford: Clarendon Press, 1913).

purely cultural or social paradigm. In a project concerned with looking at early modern France from a legal perspective, overly inclusive concepts of law and custom would needlessly obscure the matter.

As in many European languages, the French language has two different words for law, *droit* and *loi*, derived from the Latin terms *jus* and *lex* (*Recht* and *Gesetz* in German). *Droit* connotes a legal right, broadly defined, whereas *loi* has a narrower positivist meaning of law, relating to what was enacted by a legislative body. *Droit* and *Recht*, meaning "straight," carry a certain moral load, as illustrated in the concept of custom (*le droit coutumier*) which requires the popular belief that the rule or practice has obligatory force. In premodern history, however, the difference between *droit* and *loi* was tenuous at best. *Loi* often entered customary texts and *droit coutumier* legislative texts. The *lois* were sometimes merely confirmations of the existing *coutumes*, and bad customs (*mauvaises coutumes*) were subject to abrogation.[13] A general custom referred to provincial and municipal custom that took the name of a province or a city; a local custom, mostly in the form of *loi municipale*, could depart from it on specific points. It has been aptly noted that "law is only a successful custom."[14] The important distinction lay, then, not so much between *droit* and *loi* as between custom as fact and custom as law.[15]

Custom in medieval France covered a broad spectrum of what we call private law in modern times. Public law and private law are two different realms of governmental activity.[16] In general, public law refers to measures in the form of legislation, relating to crime and police as well as judicial administration of evidence and procedure; private law refers to an ensemble of rules ascertained by legal scholars and applied by a judge to disputes between individuals according to established procedures. Matters of property, succession, gifts, status of persons, and matrimonial regime were all governed by custom. Many were *usages*—privileges—of a feudal origin when the seigneurs exercised jurisdiction over their lands and people, though feudal law was the subject of learned laws.

When applicable custom and legislation were absent, judges appealed to *jus commune*. *Jus commune* referred to Roman law and church law adopted by

[13] Gilissen, "Loi et coutume," 296.

[14] Yves Jeanclos, "Si la loi était une coutume qui a réussi?" in Antoine Astaing and François Lormant (eds.), *Le juriste et la coutume du Moyen Âge au Code civil: Actes du colloque international organisé à Nancy, les 1er et 2 juillet 2010* (Nancy: PUN, Éditions universitaires de Lorraine, 2014), 259. See also Yves Jeanclos, "Coutume et loi, une approche logistique du droit," in Marc Puech (ed.), *De code en code: Mélanges en l'honneur du doyen Georges Wiederkehr* (Paris: Dalloz, 2009), 429–42.

[15] In modern law, "custom in fact," lacking recognition that confers legal force on it, is regarded as a mere usage which supplements the intent of the parties in a juristic act.

[16] The division between public law and private law comes from the Roman jurist Ulpian who set forth in the *Digest*: "Public law is that which respects the establishment of the Roman commonwealth, private that which respects individuals' interests." *Digest*, 1.1.1. *The Digest of Justinian*, vol. 1, ed. Alan Watson, Theodor Mommsen, and Paul Krueger (Philadelphia: University of Pennsylvania Press, 1985), 1.

medieval scholars from the *Corpus juris civilis* and the *Corpus juris canonici*.[17] The *Corpus juris civilis* is a collection of Roman statutes and writings of jurists, compiled in the sixth century on the order of Emperor Justinian (r. 527–565) of the East Roman Empire. Roman law entered France in the twelfth century and maintained its dominant presence in doctrine and jurisprudence. Custom normally did not deal with obligations, such as contract or liability law, which were governed by Roman law principles from *Digest* in the *Corpus juris civilis*.[18] Issues of marriage and parentage were reserved to canon law.

European jurisconsults had long accepted the idea that all particular legal norms, whatever their sources, should be considered the implementation of a set of rules from the compilations of Justinian, which had, in theory, universal application to all litigants.[19] While the notion of *jus commune* allowed a remarkable doctrinal unity in continental Europe, the place of Roman law in the legal hierarchy varied in different countries. In the Holy Roman Empire, Maximilian I (r. 1493–1519) established in 1495 the Reichskammergericht, the imperial supreme court, and decreed the comprehensive reception of Roman law. Roman law was the *droit supplétoire* (or *droit supplétif*), to resort to as the general custom when particular custom failed, but local law or custom was to apply insofar as it was consonant with the relevant precepts of Roman law.[20] The Holy Roman Empire was the only entity in medieval Europe that granted Roman law the status of the common law, and the sweeping nature of its recognition rendered the use of the formulas like *jus commune* or *gemeines Recht* quite malleable.[21] France, which never recognized Roman law as its *droit commun*, was a different story.

A long-standing debate in French legal historiography revolves around the question of *droit commun* in the Middle Ages. Historians disagree over whether there existed in the thirteenth century general legal principles, customary in

[17] *Jus commune* was not a single set of rules but commonly observed materials—methods, standards, or approaches to law—that medieval doctors delineated since the reemergence of Roman law in the late eleventh century. It interwove various sources of *jura propria* (particular laws). *Jus commune* was a positive law in Italy.

[18] The *Corpus juris civilis* consists of four parts, *Codex*, *Digest*, *Institutes*, and *Novel*. The term *Corpus juris canonici* was used from the thirteenth century to denote the body of church law.

[19] Marie-France Renoux-Zagamé, "La méthode du droit commun: Réflexion sur la logique des droits non codifiés," *Revue d'histoire des facultés de droit et de la science juridique* 10–11 (1990), 134–35.

[20] John Gilissen, *La coutume. Typologie des sources du Moyen Âge occidental* 41 (Turnhout: Brepols, 1982), 58. Both the Reichskammergericht and the Reichshofrat judged in accordance with common law, although many cases in the law courts of the princely territories were still decided by older collections of custom. See Olivia F. Robinson, T. David Fergus, and William M. Gordon, *European Legal History* (London: Butterworths, 2000), Chapter 11.3.

[21] Robert Jacob, "Philippe de Beaumanoir et les clercs. Pour sortir de la controverse du *Ius commune*," *Droits: Revue française de théorie, de philosophie et de culture juridiques* 50 (2011), 169. "The importance of custom as a source of law in the earlier history of the civil law tradition" became in modern civil law jurisdictions "a source of national pride and scholarly interest as France became self-consciously a nation-state." John Henry Merryman, *The Civil Law Tradition: An Introduction to the Legal Systems of Western Europe and Latin America* (Stanford: Stanford University Press, 1969), 23 and 12.

nature with nothing particularly Roman, that formed the matrix of French law. Some have argued that customs were written down in *coutumiers* well before the penetration of Roman law into France and that French private law took shape largely free from the influence of the learned law. Others, by contrast, have highlighted the pervasiveness of changes ushered in by the introduction of the *Corpus juris civilis*; for them, the notion of *droit commun* appeared in France as a result of the intellectual breakthrough caused by Roman law. The latter group claimed that the continued uncritical acceptance of the notion of popular consent in historiography perpetuated a "myth of custom," hindering the accurate understanding of the French legal development.[22] It is not surprising that this interpretive contention centers on the particular time period when French kings achieved an impressive increase in royal domain and political unity.

The debate over medieval *droit commun* has keen implications for the Renaissance period. Jurists in France, a country of *mos gallicus*, attempted to historicize Roman law in departure from the teaching of Italian doctors.[23] Legal humanism regenerated the study of Roman law but it also spurred scholarly interest in ancient customs as the foundation of French law. Charles Dumoulin (1500–1566) famously declared that customs, not Roman law, were the common law in France: "*Ergo consuetudines nostrae sunt ius commune.*"[24] Legal humanists' reassessment of the place of *jus commune* in France was a historical exercise that took place against the backdrop of the codification of custom.[25] Reforming

[22] See, among others, Jean-Louis Halpérin, "La détermination du champ juridique à la lumière de travaux récents d'histoire du droit," *Droit et société* 81 (2012), 403–23.

[23] Renoux-Zagamé, "La méthode du droit commun," 135. For legal humanism, see Donald R. Kelley, *Foundations of Modern Historical Scholarship: Language, Law and History in the French Renaissance* (New York: Columbia University Press, 1970); Donald R. Kelley, "Jurisprudence in the French Manner," in *The Human Measure: Social Thought in the Western Legal Tradition* (Cambridge, MA: Harvard University Press, 1990), 187–208.

[24] Charles Dumoulin, *Prima pars Commentariorum in consuetudines Parisienses*, "De Fiefs," # 109, in *Caroli Molinaei, Omnia quae extant opera*, ed. François Pinsson, 5 vols. (Paris, 1681), vol. 1, 23.

[25] Scholars disagree over whether the sixteenth-century *rédactions* can be properly called codifications. Some caution against using "codification" (both in French and in English), a term they argue should be reserved for lawmaking activities of modern nation-states, undertaken with the clear aim of social reform. Raoul C. Van Caenegem defined "a true codification" as "an original work" which, in contrast to a compilation, "must be intended as a general, exhaustive regulation of a particular area of law," and which "involves a coherent programme and a consistent logical structure." *An Historical Introduction to Private Law* (Cambridge: Cambridge University Press, 1992), 12. Caenegem separates two types of code: "a codification with the sole aim of (re)formulation and systemization of the law in force, which avoids all substantial reform and all revolutionary innovation, and which faithfully reflect the past, limiting itself to recording and ordering the existing law," on the one hand, and "a codification . . . as an instrument of social reform aimed at the future," on the other hand. Others underscore a reforming nature. According to Gazzaniga, codification requires three essentials: "a political will, a social rupture, and a technique." For him, the redaction of customs, taking place in the background of the civil war, squarely satisfied them all, as it aimed "to facilitate knowledge and simplify the application of the rules and to reduce lawsuits and fix the law as much as possible." Jean-Louis Gazzaniga, "Rédaction des coutumes et codification," *Droit: Revue française de théorie, de philosophie et de culture juridique* 26 (1997), 79–80. Some others went so far as to say that "these redactions were the first preparatory work for the writing of the Civil Code of 1804." René Filhol, "La rédaction des coutumes en France aux XVe et XVIe siècles," in John Gilissen (ed.), *La rédaction des*

customs was basically an effort to deal with gaps and deficiencies in French law to preserve it without being overrun by Roman law. In the Holy Roman Empire, professional jurists employed by the territorial princes and municipalities also collected customs, but the impact was nominal because customary and political jurisdictions were largely coterminous and the supremacy of Roman law remained undisturbed.[26] In France, the diversity of customs was perceived as far more problematic, prompting legal humanists to try to extract general principles from the customs of different provinces that could serve as a *droit commun coutumier* throughout the kingdom.

The redaction and reformation of custom brought greater coherence and clarity in a broad swath of legal relations. In the sixteenth century, acquisition of landed property became more common, and the fragmentation of lands due to partible inheritance also raised concerns. Marriage contracts typically served as a means to deviate from otherwise inflexible customary rules, yet a more universal treatment in law became necessary. The rights and autonomy of individuals were given a central place in private law. "When *la coutume* speaks of power, *l'usage* speaks of duty."[27] As the laws determined the scope of individuals' power to manage their private affairs, careful planning became all the more important, augmenting the value of skilled legal work. The vectors of customary law were no longer the communities but local courts. Lawyers eagerly channeled customary norms in legal fields, in conditions, validity, evidence, and so on. All sorts of provisos in contracts were possible. There is much truth in the observation that the campaigns to record customs not only saved French customary law as a category but also saved its practitioners as a profession.[28] The growing professionalization of the legal process was effectively seized and fostered by the state.

In the *pays de droit écrit*, Roman law was regarded as one of the general customs approved by the king. In the *pays de droit coutumier*, the *coutumes*

coutumes dans le passé et dans le présent: Colloque organisé les 16 et 17 mai 1960 par le Centre d'histoire et d'ethnologie juridique (Brussels: Institut de Sociologie de l'Université libre de Bruxelles, 1962), 78. This book adopts the generally accepted definition of codification as "enunciation, more or less complete and methodical, of the whole of the rules of law," made by "the competent legal and administrative authority," a definition that seems applicable to the redaction of customs without too much irony or anachronism. John Gilissen, "Les phases de la codification et de l'homologation des coutumes dans les XVII Provinces des Pays-Bas" (Part 1), *Tijdschrift voor Rechtsgeschiedenis* 18 (1950), 44, citing his communication, "Le ressort des coutumes codifiées aux XVIe et XVIIe siècles dans les XVII Provinces des Pays-Bas, essai de géographie coutumière," *Revue du Nord* 31 (1949), 234. For extended discussions on the meaning of codification, see Puech (ed.), *De code en code*; Bernard Beignier (ed.), *La codification: Actes du colloque organisé les 27 et 28 octobre 1995 à Toulouse* (Paris: Dalloz, 1996).

[26] For example, the collection of the laws of Freiburg-im-Breisgau by Ulrich Zasius (1461–1535).

[27] Jérôme-Luther Viret, "Droit, usages et coutume sous l'Ancien Régime: L'exemple de la prévôté de Paris au milieu du XVIIe siècle," *Revue historique de droit français et étranger* 77 (1999), 505–506. Customs carried heavy "moral load." Iain Stewart, "'Customs in Common': The Old Emperor's Clothes," *Macquarie Law Journal* 6 (2009), 145.

[28] Charles Donahue, "Comparative Law before the Code Napoleon," in Mathias Reimann and Reinhard Zimmermann (eds.), *The Oxford Handbook of Comparative Law* (Oxford: Oxford University Press, 2006), 20.

homologated by the king became the law in defined territorial areas, coinciding more or less with the administrative boundaries. Each *coutume* was declared sovereign within its jurisdictional unit, binding on all its inhabitants—clergy, nobles, and commoners. In the king's name, the provisions of the *coutumes* applied in principle to all persons, property, and acts of civil life.[29] The official texts of custom achieved the kind of stability and immutability of learned law and royal edicts.

By the end of the sixteenth century, the long tension among the different sources of law had been resolved in favor of *la loi du roi*.[30] The base of the authoritative legitimacy of custom was transferred from immemorial practice to the royal will. Multiple other sources were still routinely cited in judicial briefs, but doctrinal jurists did not question the supremacy of legislation. Exclusive legislative power was an essential element of the conception of royal sovereignty that undergirded the "absolute" monarchy.

Royal Sovereignty and Law

The long-held idea of royal absolutism has taken much fire from historians of late. The conventional view of absolutist monarchy highlighted how the Bourbon kings tamed and disciplined the ruling elite class; recent scholarship has instead stressed that the royal government coopted and collaborated with it. Rejecting the "myth of absolutism," revisionist historians argue the Bourbon monarchs were obliged to seek the cooperation of local powers and the autonomy of provincial notables and their social networks in the seventeenth and eighteenth centuries were far more extensive than previously acknowledged.[31] One may discern some

[29] The redaction of custom brought customary law under the royal prerogative and "it all but clinched the identification of custom and ordinance." William Farr Church, *Constitutional Thought in Sixteenth-Century France: A Study in the Evolution of Ideas* (New York: Octagon Books, 1969 [1940]), 118. This echoes the opinion of Adhémar Esmein who noted: "It is often said that before the Revolution a large part of France—*les pays coutumiers*—lived under the empire of custom. This is false; the officially redacted customs, decreed in the name of the king, registered by the Parlement, had taken almost all the characteristics of the written law (*la loi écrite*)." Adhémar Esmein, "L'originalité du Code civil," in Jean-Louis Halpérin (ed.), *Le Code civil 1804–1904: Livre du Centenaire* (Paris: Dalloz, 2004), 16–17.

[30] The "loi du roi" was defined as "any measure emanating from the king, inspired by the good of the kingdom or the public interest and presenting a degree of generality and permanence, that is, applying to an indefinite series of people or cases." François Olivier-Martin, *Les lois du roi* (Paris: Librairie de droit et de jurisprudence, 1997), 11.

[31] The term "myth of absolutism" was coined by François-Xavier Emmanuelli in *Un mythe de l'absolutisme bourbonien: l'intendance du milieu du XVIIe siècle à la fin du XVIIIe siècle (France, Espagne, Amérique)* (Aix-en-Provence: Publications Université de Provence, 1981). An extensive literature has appeared since, ranging from Fanny Cosandey and Robert Descimon, *L'absolutisme en France: Histoire et historiographie* (Paris: Seuil, 2002) to Arlette Jouanna, *Le pouvoir absolu: Naissance de l'imaginaire politique de la royauté* (Paris: Gallimard, 2015). Absolute monarchy (and the ancien régime) is conventionally defined as the reigns of Louis XIV (r. 1643–1715) and his successors, although some historians have dated its emergence to an earlier era, finding the contemporary meaning of the term during the reign of Francis I. See Jean Jacquart, *François Ier* (Paris: Fayard, 1981); Robert J. Knecht, *Francis I*

theoretical affinity between the portrayal of a king in this collaborative partnership with the local forces and the traditional characterization of the absolute monarchy as a late form of feudalism. Marxist historiography defined absolutism as "*a redeployed and recharged apparatus of feudal domination*, designed to clamp the peasant masses back into their traditional social position—despite and against the gains they had won by the widespread commutation of dues."[32] According to this interpretation, the Bourbon kings, while allied with the feudal aristocracy, also attempted to neutralize the seigneurial class by enlisting the bourgeois who purchased hereditary offices, but the result was a *féodalisation* of the bourgeoisie, not the *embourgeoisement* of the monarchy.[33] In this view, the overall political process was a sort of conspiracy between the crown and the feudal elites, with the absolute monarchy serving as a device for perpetuating the latter's domination.

Compared with the Marxist approach, recent mainstream revisionist historiography has provided a far more subtle and balanced understanding of the monarchy. Its main thesis is that no rulers before the late eighteenth century could afford a purely professional bureaucracy in the localities and the kings in the seventeenth century had to make compromises. They were dependent on local elites, either judges in the parlements who performed administrative and judicial tasks or old-guard notables in the provincial estates who delivered the consent of the community to royal policies.[34] Privileges were extended in exchange for cooperation.

By stressing that there was a gap between the crown's claims of absolute power and political and social reality, the recent scholarship discounted the

(Cambridge: Cambridge University Press, 1984). As will be clear in the following pages, this book refers to the absolute monarchy (also ancien régime) broadly, as equivalent to the early modern period. A number of studies attacking the myth of absolutism are listed in Nicholas Henshall, *The Myth of Absolutism: Change and Continuity in Early Modern European History* (London: Longman, 1992). For appraisal, see Richard Bonney, "Absolutism: What's in a Name?" *French History* 1 (1987), 93–117; James B. Collins, *The State in Early Modern France*, 2nd ed. (Cambridge: Cambridge University Press, 2009 [1995]), xiv–xxv; Cesare Cuttica, "A Thing or Two about Absolutism and Its Historiography," *History of European Ideas* 39 (2013), 287–300.

32 Perry Anderson, *Lineages of the Absolutist State* (London: Verso, 2013 [1974]), 18 (emphasis original).

33 This was the subject of the famous debate between Boris Porshnev and Roland Mousnier. See the review article, John H. M. Salmon, "Venality of Office and Popular Sedition in Seventeenth-Century France," *Past & Present* 37 (1967), 21–43. Braudel labeled "la trahison de la bourgeoisie" the inclination of the bourgeoisie to plunge its wealth into ennobling offices rather than to advance its interests and identity through the cause of commercial capitalism. Fernand Braudel, *La méditerranée et le monde méditerranéen à l'époque de Philippe II*, 2nd ed. (Paris: A. Colin, 1966 [1949]), vol. 2, 68.

34 The older view of the provincial estates as rivals to royal power has largely been abandoned. As the *pays d'état* competed to win reductions from new special taxes, provincial elites received an increasing share of royal taxes that the crown redistributed to them, while they transferred the tax burden onto the peasantry. William Beik, *Absolutism and Society in Seventeenth-Century France: State Power and Provincial Aristocracy in Languedoc* (Cambridge: Cambridge University Press, 1985). The weakness of the crown's fiscal base has been thoroughly studied in James B. Collins, *Fiscal Limits of Absolutism: Direct Taxation in Early Seventeenth-Century France* (Berkeley: University of California Press, 1988); James B. Collins, *Classes, Estates, and Order in Early Modern Brittany* (Cambridge: Cambridge University Press, 1994).

constitutional discussion of absolutist sovereignty, a topic many earlier works had favored. Yet it has been faulted, in turn, for dwelling on semantics while tending to depict the idea of absolutism as a caricature. According to Richard Bonney, the term "absolutism" was a neologism dating from the French Revolution but the term "absolute power" was widely used in the Middle Ages and early modern period.[35] Medieval lawyers discussed at length the Roman legal maxim *princeps legibus solutus est*—the prince is freed (absolved) from the laws. Fourteenth-century Nominalist theologians put forward the notion of *potentia absoluta* of God.[36] John Locke (1632–1704) may have been in part responsible for the "English mythology or demonology of absolutism" by confusing "absolute" government with "arbitrary" government.[37] Nineteenth-century historians uncritically identified the absolute monarch as an autocrat or despot, enemy of popular consent and commoners' rights and liberties.

The revisionist argument that no French king, including Louis XIV (r. 1643–1715), thought of attacking the liberties of the nobles, the clergy, towns, and so on has considerable force, but mainly against the definition of absolute monarchy as an activist entity of attacking privileges. Could the idea of absolute power of the monarchy be deduced, rather, from its legal attributes shaped by long institutional development? According to *The Oxford English Dictionary*, "absolute" means, of ownership or authority, "free from all external restraint or interference; unrestricted, unlimited, independent." French legists from early on disseminated the idea that the will of the sovereign made law in the kingdom, as attested in the oft-quoted phrase *quod principi placuit legis habet vigorem* (what has pleased the prince has the force of *lex*).[38] One can argue that the homologation of *coutumes* in the late fifteenth and sixteenth centuries was a reassertion and extension of the medieval "absolutist" current. Many studies have focused on the crown's legislative authority in political theory, yet little attention has been paid to the king's control of the sources of law that directly concerned the privileges of the members of provincial estates and parlements.

[35] Bonney, "Absolutism: What's in a Name?" 94. See also Richard Bonney, *L'absolutisme* (Paris: Presses universitaires de France, 1989).

[36] Heiko A. Oberman, *The Harvest of Medieval Theology: Gabriel Biel and Late Medieval Nominalism* (Cambridge, MA: Harvard University Press, 1963). The word "absolute" in *pouvoir absolu* comes from *absolvere*, to absolve. Bonney, "Absolutism: What's in a Name?" 93–94; Daniel Lee, *Popular Sovereignty in Early Modern Constitutional Thought* (Oxford: Oxford University Press, 2016), 190–91. The formula *legibus solutus* is from Ulpian, in *Digest*, 1.3.31.

[37] In J. H. Burns' counting, the phrase "absolute, arbitrary Power" occurred seven times in Locke's *Two Treatises of Government* (1689). Cited from Richard Bonney, "Review of Nicholas Henshall, *The Myth of Absolutism: Change and Continuity in Early Modern European Monarchy* (London: Longman, 1992)," *English Historical Review* 110 (1995), 1254.

[38] Ambitious lawmaking activities took place under Philip IV the Fair (r. 1285–1314). See Sophie Petit-Renaud, "Le roi, les légistes et le parlement de Paris aux XIVe et XVe siècles: Contradictions dans la perception du pouvoir de 'faire loy'?" *Cahiers de recherches médiévales (XIIIe–XVe siècles)* 7 (2000), 143–58. http://journals.openedition.org/crm/889.

David Parker is one of the few historians who considered the absolute monarchy in terms of private law. In his study of the property regime under Louis XIV, Parker downplayed the crown's legal reforms. The king attempted "a series of legal compromises" but became "the feudal *rentier* par excellence" and "rarely used his sovereign powers to make significant alterations to the laws governing property rights."[39] Parker's work centers on the seventeenth century and touches on the customary law reforms only in passing. Yet a breezy statement like "anxiety about the integrity of fiefs led to the revision of the Paris custom of 1580" seems to obscure rather than clarify the historical nature of the customary law campaign.[40] As will be argued throughout this book, the reform programs of customs closely reflected contemporary doctrinal and jurisprudential progress. There is little evidence that the redaction of the *coutume* of Paris was ordered by the king to protect seigneurial rights and to benefit feudal interests of either new or old elites. On the contrary, numerous modifications that were inserted in the revised *coutume* had aims and consequences antithetical to the preservation of the feudal order.[41] If one is compelled to make an across-the-board generalization concerning the redaction and reformation of customs, it was an occasion of "gigantesques autodafés de droits féodaux et seigneuriaux."[42] The revised customs articulated the sentiments that certain feudal dues, which the seigneurs claimed to have been "founded in immemorial possession," would not be automatically recognized when in reality they were "more usurpation than possession," and that they must not be allowed to "prejudice the third estate."[43] The codification campaign may not have been a social war against the feudal hierarchy but it was not a reactionary conspiracy, either.

An important corollary is the venality of offices, the quintessentially French institution of private ownership of public offices. Neither the sale of offices nor absolute monarchy is exactly unexplored turf, but existing studies have rarely concerned customary law. The reformation of customs was carried out by the king with the support of legal professionals who entered the royal bureaucracy by purchasing offices. The political and social effects of the sale of offices have been

[39] David Parker, "Absolutism, Feudalism and Property Rights in the France of Louis XIV," *Past & Present* 179 (2003), 75, 89, 73.

[40] David Parker, "Sovereignty, Absolutism and the Function of the Law in Seventeenth-Century France," *Past & Present* 122 (1989), 65–66.

[41] See François Olivier-Martin, *Histoire de la coutume de la prévôté et vicomté de Paris*, 3 vols. (Paris: E. Leroux, 1922–1930).

[42] Robert Descimon, "Quelques réflexions à propos des commissaires du roi dans la rédaction et la réformation des coutumes au XVIe siècle," *Les cahiers du Centre de recherches historiques* 26 (2001), 93–106, # 5 (online paragraph number). http://journals.openedition.org/ccrh/1393.

[43] These are the words from the *procès-verbal* of the reformed *Coutume de Touraine* of 1559, in Charles A. Bourdot de Richebourg et al., *Nouveau coutumier général, ou Corps des coutumes générales et particulières de France, et des provinces: connues sous le nom des Gaules; exactement vérifiées sur les originaux conservez au greffe du Parlement de Paris & des autres cours du royaume*, 4 vols. (Paris: Brunet, 1724) [hereafter *Nouveau coutumier général*], vol. 4, 692.

regarded as questions more germane to the seventeenth century when the system had fully matured, but it was in the sixteenth century, in the backgrounds of the Wars of Italy (1494–1559) and the Wars of Religion, that the monarchy sold offices in earnest. The royal commissioners, whom the king personally appointed to preside over the assemblies of customary law redaction, came from the legal elites created by venality, normally prominent judges of the parlements. Christophe de Thou (1508–1582), *président* of the Parlement of Paris and *premier président* from 1562, who played by far the most important role in the reformation of *coutumes*, illustrates how the knowledge and skills of the professional *parlementaire* corps were tapped into by the state.[44]

Parker's thesis is that the venality of offices alienated public power into private hands in such a way that was the essence of the traditional fief or seigneurie holdings. There is little dispute about the fact that local elites, new and old, benefited from the early modern system of the state-based surplus extraction. Yet the question remains whether officeholding of the *robe* could be subsumed under the same type of land-based exaction.[45] More broadly framed, the issue would be whether the law was entirely reducible to socioeconomic interests. As revisionist scholarship has shown, even the Sun King could not push the provincial elites around as he wished. The rising costs of warfare prevented him from doing so, forcing him to depend on the sale of offices more than ever. One may ask then whether the relationship between the king and venal judges was more than a mere subterfuge aimed to keep the bargain that had been struck for a class conspiracy of domination.[46] A more focused attention to the nature and operation of the venality system, and the laws behind it, would help in understanding the meaning of the absolute monarchy beyond the stereotype of a despotic and centralizing kingship.[47]

Revisiting the Absolute Monarchy

One of the main criticisms leveled against the revisionist scholarship is that it overlooked how effectively the government of Louis XIV controlled magistrates by maneuvering their financial interests.[48] To purchase an office was to lend

[44] Marie Seong-Hak Kim, "Christophe de Thou et la réformation des coutumes: L'esprit de réforme juridique au XVIe siècle," *Tijdschrift voor Rechtsgeschiedenis* 72 (2004), 91–102.

[45] Parker notes that since the Middle Ages "the nexus between the possession of land and judicial property rights was never broken." "Absolutism, Feudalism and Property Rights," 76.

[46] Parker suggested that Roman legal concepts had long been assimilated to feudal culture. Ibid., 72 and 84. It is an important question that requires a separate discussion.

[47] "Centralization" is best avoided by the historian of early modern France, since it was first coined in 1794 during the Terror. Bonney, "Absolutism: What's in a Name?" 94.

[48] See John J. Hurt, *Louis XIV and the Parlements: The Assertion of Royal Authority* (Manchester: Manchester University Press, 2002).

money to the king, for which the king paid interest in the form of *gages*, or salary. Early on French kings mastered the technique of squeezing royal officeholders. They incessantly pressured judges for additional loans by resorting to various measures of the mixture of persuasion and intimidation, for example threatening to revoke offices or to create new ones, which would depress the value of their investment, and the *officiers* invariably caved in. Most of these features and expedients used by the government had already been in place in the sixteenth century.[49] Richelieu under Louis XIII (r. 1610–1643) and Colbert under Louis XIV of the Bourbon dynasty merely continued the old practice of extracting wealth from the magistrates, improving the rules of the game that had been devised by their predecessors under the Valois.[50]

In his seminal article on venality, David D. Bien described the system as the "commercialization of privileges."[51] The most important privilege brought by public offices, apart from prestige and power, was exemption from the taxes. This was a privilege the king actually created, unlike those entitlements claimed to have origins in time immemorial. The king declared during the redaction of custom that he would respect old customs, but not all of them, because some obscure ones, lost in time, no longer held justification. Only those which the king deemed to be in the interest of the public would henceforth have legal force, registered and published by the royal courts. Just like these revalidated customs, the perks that accompanied the offices were formal concessions of kings, registered in royal courts. Their value depended on the state's ability to protect them. The purchaser of the office needed assurance that "there were courts and police with the power to prevent poaching."[52] The king's enunciation of civil law principles through customary law redaction was sine qua non of the creation of state credit through venality. To be sure, custom, mainly concerned with the fief and the family, did not govern the sale of offices, which was conducted in contract. But customary law regulated important rights such as the disposal of property by sale or by will. When venality is viewed as a royal commercial venture—like tax farming in a later period—the significance of extending the king's dominion to private law becomes evident.

The sale of offices was a transaction between the king and the individual purchaser. Bodin wrote that an office was "comme une chose empruntée" (like a

[49] Office in the sixteenth century was part of "maintenance" of the administration; abuses, "already familiar," could be tolerated by "kings and advisors bedazzled by the potential revenues that might be expected to come from the sale of offices." Christopher Stocker, "Office as Maintenance in Renaissance France," *Canadian Journal of History* 6 (1971), 42.

[50] See Anne Rousselet-Pimont, *Le chancelier et la loi au XVIe siècle: d'après l'œuvre d'Antoine Duprat, de Guillaume Poyet et de Michel de l'Hospital* (Paris: De Boccard, 2005).

[51] David D. Bien, "Offices, Corps, and a System of State Credit: The Uses of Privilege under the Ancien Régime," in Baker (ed.), *The Political Culture of the Old Regime*, 92.

[52] Ibid.

thing borrowed).[53] He did not question that offices belonged to the king alone and *officiers* enjoyed the dignities of royal office only during their lifetimes. Bodin explained the system in terms of obligations. The office, once assigned, possessed a legally defined bundle of rights which the king, the legal owner, was obligated to respect.[54] Could one draw from this insight and frame the transaction between the king and the *officier*, that is, between the one who sold the office and the one who bought it, in reverse relations? When viewed in light of state credit, the *officier* held a portion of the public debt.[55] In public law, the king was the owner and the official the borrower; in private law, the king was the borrower (debtor) and the official the lender (creditor). The office, akin to an object of contractual lease, served as security for the money the king had borrowed against. Once the king issued an office in a *lettre de provision*, he could not demand it back arbitrarily outside the agreed terms, before he reimbursed the money that had been paid into the royal treasury.

The king entered the credit market as the interested party. An officeholder, in exchange for capital investment, enjoyed a usufruct of the office, retaining the right to designate his successor. The king had to be careful about how he treated his creditors, lest he jeopardize his credit rating, making it more expensive for the state to borrow. He thus made sure that he operated within the legal boundaries, without breaching public faith. As seen earlier, the king and his ministers did not neglect to realize capital gains from the increased market value of the offices. In brief, the system of borrowing on offices was the bedrock for running the "state as enterprise" by the monarchy.[56] The privileges conferred by venality made the legal elites loyal supporters of the absolute king.

The homologation of *coutumes* amounted to the king's declaration that he was free (absolved) from immemorial privileges, liberties, and all human laws. To claim absolute power, the king first had to redefine seigneurial privileges as well as local entitlements and immunities, while promising to respect his subjects' property rights in custom. The king relied on the popular assemblies to record customs. The perceived function of the assemblies was finding the law, not making it, so there was no inherent conflict with the idea that lawmaking authority belonged to the king alone. This seemed to conform to the nature of consent highlighted by Renaissance thinkers, in which *consensus principis* saw its limits by *consensus populi* in law. By the end of the sixteenth century, however, the idea of custom as fundamental law in its traditional meaning in medieval

[53] Bodin, *Les six livres de la république*, book 3, ch. 2, 310. See Daniel Lee, "'Office Is a Thing Borrowed': Jean Bodin on Offices and Seigneurial Government," *Political Theory* 41 (2013), 409–40; Lee, *Popular Sovereignty in Early Modern Constitutional Thought*.

[54] Lee, "'Office Is a Thing Borrowed,'" 421.

[55] Bien, "Offices, Corps, and a System of State Credit," 94.

[56] Robert Descimon, "Power Elites and the Prince: The State as Enterprise," in Wolfgang Reinhard (ed.), *Power Elites and State Building* (Oxford: Clarendon Press, 1996), 101–21. This seems to be a real dimension of the dependence of the nobles on royal favor in the seventeenth century.

constitutionalism had been replaced by the concept of sovereign authority of the king. It is important to recall that in the sixteenth century fundamental law did not mean natural rights or divine law; it simply referred to custom or privileges. Only during the religious wars did *loi fondamentale* come to acquire modern constitutional and confessional attributes.[57] In theory, custom could exist *secundum legem*, *praeter legem*, or even *contra legem*, but whatever authority it had now came from the king.[58] It lost its potency as a bridle on his lawmaking prerogative, and the king was released from "the limitations imposed upon him by the established constitution" or, simply, the constraints from "the past."[59]

Homologation, much the same as modern codification, was a mechanism by which the plenipotentiary state attempted to limit the arbitrariness of its laws and thereby augment its legitimacy and power. Popular agreement ceded its place as the crux of civil society to a lawful government in which the sovereign ruled through established law.

The king was absolute in the public and political affairs of the kingdom, but he did not meddle in private legal relations of his subjects, a point that scholars often miss. This may have been in part why the French monarch possessed relatively feeble economic resources, compared with his political powers.[60] Property matters were closely linked to state interests and could not be disregarded in the sphere of high politics, but the king did not, and could not, intervene arbitrarily in the private settlement of succession or marital regime.[61] It is then difficult to argue that the king actively changed the contents of custom for his benefit or that of his supporters. Instead, the codified *coutumes* became the cornerstone of the supreme power of the *lex loquens*, a king who spoke the law for the public good. Even at the height of royal power, "there was a sense of what a ruler could and could not do in law."[62] It is not surprising that contemporary thinkers saw the king's absolute power less as a threat to legal rights than as a force to guarantee them.

[57] Protestants, fighting for survival, claimed there were limits on the power of the king; radical Protestantism gave rise to a particular concept of fundamental law as the right to practice one's religion. Martyn P. Thompson, "The History of Fundamental Law in Political Thought from the French Wars of Religion to the American Revolution," *American Historical Review* 91 (1986), 1103–28.

[58] "According to the law," "outside of the law," and "against the law."

[59] Church, *Constitutional Thought*, 335. Jurists were compelled "to consider custom in relation to the royal authority," 282–83.

[60] Roland É. Mousnier, *The Institutions of France under the Absolute Monarchy, 1598–1789*, trans. Brian Pearce and Arthur Goldhammer, 2 vols. (Chicago: University of Chicago Press, 1979 and 1984), vol. I, 665, 740.

[61] This should be distinguished from the cases during the Middle Ages of expanding royal demesne through inheritance and achieving the territorial integration of France. The crown's feudal rights, forfeitures for treason, and claims to estates with no owner (known as *bona vacantia*, vacant successions) are also separate matters.

[62] Nicholas Henshall, "Early Modern Absolutism 1550–1700: Political Reality or Propaganda?" in Ronald G. Asch and Heinz Duchhardt (eds.), *Der Absolutismus-Ein Mythos? Strukturwandel monarchischer Herrschaft in West- und Mitteleuropa (ca. 1550–1700)* (Cologne: Böhlau Verlag, 1996), 30.

The crown would hear no nonsense of sharing sovereignty but would accommodate the interests of the elites in the manner by which that sovereignty was exercised. The Bourbon kings were not shy about issuing privileges and exemptions, but they would not break legal obligations lest it should undermine their own power. An insight from the modern theory of sovereignty is on point: the sovereign is he who determines a situation of exception.[63] The fact that the early modern king compromised with and made exceptions for local elites seems to affirm, rather than negate, the claim that he was indeed an absolute monarch.

In short, the redaction of customs and the consolidation of the venality system as the superstructure of the monarchy both advanced legalism. This book argues that the homologation of customary law in the fifteenth and sixteenth centuries marked the nexus between legal absolutism (*absolutisme juridique*), postulated by legists in the thirteenth and fourteenth centuries, and the absolute monarchy (*monarchie absolue*), advocated by theorists of the seventeenth and eighteenth centuries.[64] The absolute power of the king came from the absoluteness of his laws, including the customs, *and* his commitment to observe them. Royal promise to safeguard contractual relations in the venality of offices derived from the late medieval idea that the crown was endowed with a reserve of power. The king's authority was grounded on the residual power of the monarchy, to which all power ultimately reverted. This, in turn, is an idea based on the aforementioned Nominalist theology distinguishing between *potentia absoluta* and *potentia ordinata*: God has created the world in this way although he could have created it differently. As He freely limits His power, so does the king.

According to James B. Collins, the important transformation of the early modern French monarchy was "not the creation of an 'absolutism,' but the shift from a monarchical commonwealth to a monarchical state."[65] A commonwealth, a *république*, is an Aristotelian polity of collective group of citizens the main purpose of which is the public good; it transitioned, notes Collins, as a result of changes in the 1620s and 1630s to a new framework of government in which the notion of public good became the good of the king and of the state. One can link these changes to legal reforms in the late sixteenth century, which crystallized royal commitments straddling the representative and the absolute facets of the monarchy. As Collins points out, the commonwealth model in the sixteenth century had been inspired by humanist republicanism. One finds in Chancellor L'Hôpital, for instance, the civic humanism of Leonardo Bruni (*c.*1370–1444) invoking

[63] Carl Schmitt, *Political Theology: Four Chapters on the Concept of Sovereignty*, trans. George Schwab (Chicago: University of Chicago Press, 2005 [1922]), 5.

[64] See Jacques Krynen, *L'empire du roi. Idées et croyances politiques en France XIIIe–XVe siècle* (Paris: Gallimard, 1993), part 3 ("L'absolutisme").

[65] Collins, *The State in Early Modern France*, xxiii.

Ciceronianism.[66] Now the monarchy came to have a larger presence in daily life, and that was foremost through the medium of law. L'Hôpital did not question that the laws of the king must be absolutely obeyed.

The limits of absolute monarchy in its dealings with local powers reaffirmed the relationship between the king and local customs. The absolute king did not need to set himself against local privileges or *consensus populi*; he just needed to govern them. The use of the term *monarchie absolue* in its judicial attributes, predicated on legal rationalization, seems to represent adequately an institutional reality that is not seriously affected by the deficiencies of the concept of absolutism described as the king's power to impose his will on all.

Absolute government was not a distinct type of polity demarcating feudal monarchy from modern administrative bureaucracy. The venality system showed that the legal and social system of maintaining privileges, often called "feudal," was "essential for the credit and solvency of the developing, modern state."[67] Likewise, the progressive or rational nature of the monarchy should not be overemphasized; it is never desirable to make early modern France too modern. How the monarchy availed itself of the attributes of the law for a more effective governing of the state is the main topic of inquiry in this book.

2. French Legal History and Historiography

There exists an immense output of literature in French language on "la France coutumière." In comparison, custom has triggered only limited interest among Anglophone historians. There are as yet few discussions in English of custom and its codification, other than in broad outline.[68] Arguably this is due to the differ-

[66] Denis Crouzet, *La sagesse et le malheur: Michel de L'Hospital, chancelier de France* (Seyssel: Champ Vallon, 1998), 319. See Denis Crouzet, Élisabeth Crouzet-Pavan, Loris Petris, and Clémence Revest (eds.), *L'humanisme au pouvoir? Figures de chanceliers dans l'Europe de la Renaissance* (Paris: Classiques Garnier, 2020).

[67] Bien, "Offices, Corps, and a System of State Credit," 108.

[68] The range of scholarly works on the subject can be glimpsed in the conference proceedings, Florent Garnier and Jacqueline Vendrand-Voyer (eds.), *La coutume dans tous ses états: Actes du colloque international des 15 au 17 juin 2010 à l'occasion de la célébration du 500e anniversaire de la rédaction de la coutume d'Auvergne Clermont-Ferrand-Riom* (Paris: Éditions La Mémoire du Droit, 2013). Studies of the redaction of customs available in English include John P. Dawson, "The Codification of the French Customs," *Michigan Law Review* 38 (1940), 765–800; Kathleen A. Parrow, "Provincial Estates and the Revision of Customary Law in Medieval and Early Modern France: Evidence from the *Procès-verbal* Narratives," *Parliaments, Estates & Representation* 21 (2001), 57–71; Donald R. Kelley, "'Second Nature': The Idea of Custom in European Law, Society, and Culture," in Anthony Grafton and Ann Blair (eds.), *Transmission of Culture in Early Modern Europe* (Philadelphia: University of Pennsylvania Press, 1990), 131–72; Marie Seong-Hak Kim, "Custom, Community, and the Crown: Lawyers and the Reordering of French Customary Law," in Charles Parker and Jerry Bentley (eds.), *Between the Middle Ages and Modernity: Individual and Community in the Early Modern World* (Lanham: Rowman & Littlefield, 2007), 169–86. See also René Filhol, "The Codification of Customary Law in France in the Fifteenth and Sixteenth Centuries," in Henry J. Cohn (ed.), *Government in Reformation Europe, 1520–1560* (London: Macmillan, 1971), 265–83, translation of "La rédaction des

ence between English common law and the continental European traditions. The collection of customs had no role in the development of English law, hence the subject likely had little attraction for American or British scholars. But the lack of interest in the topic can also be ascribed to a trend in historiography. During the last four decades or so, the scholarly field of early modern France in the United States has taken a definite social and cultural turn. Historians have shied away from the so-called traditional political, institutional, and intellectual history, faulting its top-down, center-focused approach. Scholars have gradually expanded the notion of law to include aspects of social norms, symbols, and literary culture. Pluralism and regional variations have been seen as the dominant characteristics of the ancien régime law. The most notable shift has been the rise of cultural studies in law—the so-called constitutive approach—from the 1980s.

In the constitutive approach, law is part of the cultural context unfolding in society. Law shapes culture, individuals' minds, practices, and social relations: "legal thought is constructive of social realities rather than merely reflective of them."[69] Cultural studies has steered scholarly debates on law in a new direction and onto a different horizon. One may see a connection with the *Volksgeist* theory of Friedrich Carl von Savigny (1779–1861), who posited that law, properly understood, was "custom," or the "spirit of the people." Yet the Constitutive School differs from the German Historical School in important aspects. In the latter, law is a product of a nation's culture, embedded in social practices; in the former, law participates in the constitution of that culture. The nineteenth-century school assumed a transition from the law of the people to the law of the state; the twentieth-century school postulated "a transition from the law of the state to culture and daily social interactions."[70]

Broadly speaking, the cultural or constitutive approach is framed in the general idea that law is an instrument of dominance: the ruling social groups create law and legal institutions to exert influence over others. Law, according to this view, internalizes the preservation of the hierarchies in society of class, gender, race, and ethnicity. A postmodern shift toward law as a cultural expression—a system of "meaning"—has criticized the older positivist conception of law for its

coutumes en France aux XVe et XVIe siècles," in Gilissen (ed.), *La rédaction des coutumes dans le passé et dans le présent*. For literature in Japanese language, see, among others, Ōkawa Shirō, "16 seiki Furansu kanshūhō kōshiki hensan ron: Sharuru Deyu Mūran (1500–1566) no 'Furansu kanshūhō tōitsu ron' o sozai ni shite" [The Theory of the Official Compilation of French Customary Law in the Sixteenth Century: Charles Dumoulin's 'Theory of the Concord of French Custom'], *Hōkyō ronshū* (Aichi Daigaku Hōgakubu) 175 (2007), 1–55; Fujita Takahiro, "Furansu kanshū hōgaku to Rōmahō: Furansu kyōtsūhō to wa nanika (I)" [French Customary Law and Roman Law: What is French Common Law], *Dokkyō hōgaku* 78 (2009), 163–218; Fujita Takahiro, "Deyu Mūran to Kokiyū no kanshūhō ron" [Customary Law Theories of Dumoulin and Coquille], *Dokkyō hōgaku* 78 (2009), 303–17.

[69] Clifford Geertz, "Local Knowledge: Fact and Law in Comparative Perspective," in *Local Knowledge* (London: Fontana Press, 1983), 232. Geertz suggests that law is something that "makes" social life, in the sense of being "constructive," "constitutive," and "formational" of it.

[70] Menachem Mautner, "Three Approaches to Law and Culture," *Cornell Law Review* 96 (2011), 850.

overbearing statism.[71] The ensuing controversies pitted the cultural-sociological school of law against the formalist juristic school of law, as alluded to at the beginning of this chapter.

The majority of the works by historians of early modern France in the United States since the 1980s are heavily invested in social and cultural aspects of law, focusing on gender, daily life, and the family. In these works, litigation is presented as a dynamic site of social interactions between individuals, communities, and the state. Insightful research has shed important light on kinship structures, inheritance practices, as well as lineage strategies, and has shown that ordinary men and women from working-class families in the seventeenth century actively used legal processes to manage their household relationships and economies.[72] But scholarly predilection for social and cultural history, with the presumed belief that legal history would be amiss without references to extratextual realities, has had the effect of playing down the significance of the sources of law and the value of juristic and jurisprudential activities.[73]

Recent scholarship has stressed the early modern courts' discretion in legal interpretation and the motivation to reach equitable solutions by dint of negotiation and informal mechanisms of dispute settlement. It also has highlighted the powerful patronage system, predominant in the provinces, and underlined the autonomy of judges, supposedly beyond scrutiny from the capital.[74] The idea of

[71] Thomas Duve, "Legal Traditions: A Dialogue between Comparative Law and Comparative Legal History," *Comparative Legal History* 6 (2018), 18. For a glimpse of contention between the culturalistic and the positivistic approaches, see Pierre Legrand, "Jameses at Play: A Tractation on the Comparison of Laws," *American Journal of Comparative Law* 65 (2017), 1–132, and accompanying commentaries.

[72] See, among others, Suzanne Desan and Jeffrey Merrick (eds.), *Family, Gender, and Law in Early Modern France* (University Park: Pennsylvania State University Press, 2009); Julie Hardwick, *Family Business: Litigation and the Political Economies of Daily Life in Early Modern France* (Oxford: Oxford University Press, 2009); Julie Hardwick, *The Practice of Patriarchy: Gender and the Politics of Household Authority in Early Modern France* (University Park: Pennsylvania State University Press, 1998). The scholarly trend focusing on the relationship between law and social practice had been set off some three decades ago by Sarah Hanley, who argued that early modern French legal culture was dominated by magisterial elites who shaped law to protect their own interests, especially their lineal interests centered on venal offices. Sarah Hanley, "Endangering the State: Family Formation and State Building in Early Modern France," *French Historical Studies* 16 (1989), 4–27; Sarah Hanley, "'The Jurisprudence of the Arrêts': Marital Union, Civil Society, and State Formation in France, 1550–1650," *Law and History Review* 21 (2003), 1–40. Hanley's influence on feminist historians of early modern France is broadly acknowledged, though the latter have faulted her reliance on a few instances of royal legislation and case law at the expense of social and legal practices among the lower classes. See the review article, Matthew Gerber, "Family, the State, and Law in Early Modern and Revolutionary France," *History Compass* 7 (2009), 474–99.

[73] As one historian aptly put it: "It is difficult enough to establish what the law allowed, far more so to relate this to what men actually did, or how far their intentions were sustained by the courts." J. P. Cooper, "Patterns of Inheritance and Settlement by Great Landowners from the Fifteenth to the Eighteenth Centuries," in Jack Goody, Joan Thirsk, and E. P. Thompson (eds.), *Family and Inheritance: Rural Society in Western Europe, 1200–1800* (Cambridge: Cambridge University Press, 1976), 198.

[74] See, among others, Zoë A. Schneider, *The King's Bench: Bailiwick Magistrates and Local Governance in Normandy, 1670–1749* (Rochester: University of Rochester Press, 2008); Michael P. Breen, *Law, City, and King: Legal Culture, Municipal Politics and State Formation in Early Modern Dijon* (Rochester: University of Rochester Press, 2007). For a comprehensive listing of works

sensible and expedient resolution of conflicts has a definite appeal. But it seems worth noting that performing judicial duty was different from disposing of disputes through a commonsensical approach to facts. Most social and cultural studies of early modern law focus on the courts of first and second instances, which may explain in part their tendency to overstate equity and judicial discretion outside of royal oversight.[75] But magistrates in lower courts could not veer far from the jurisprudence of the sovereign courts. Further, the meaning of equity in early modern France had a clear public meaning; the *parlementaires* were never willing to let lower court judges share in their privilege to judge in *équité*.[76]

The views that ordinary people were not merely subjected to the law and legal institutions created by the elites and that they were actually involved in shaping and formulating legal standards and practices and therefore contributed to early modern state-building have greatly expanded the scope of legal history. At the same time, legal history makes the reasonable assumption, barring evidence to the contrary, that judicial administration functioned by virtue of the legal system and positive law, including codified customs. Judges may surely have been sensitive to local concerns, which could be used by litigants to their advantage. But the resourceful parties or creative counselors still had to argue their cases by citing applicable rules and authorities, and judges could not jettison the system they were very much part of. In the overtly legalistic and litigious society that was

in the "historical" approach to early modern French law, see the review article by Michael P. Breen, "Law, Society, and the State in Early Modern France," *Journal of Modern History* 83 (2011), 346–86. Many works in social and cultural studies of law, only partially listed in these pages, concern periods later than the sixteenth century, and this book's engagement with them is admittedly quite limited.

[75] It has been accurately stated: "it was the cumulative judicial precedents of the sovereign courts, not those of subaltern jurisdictions, that served not only to reshape French jurisprudence over the course of the early modern era, but also to disseminate." Matthew Gerber, *Bastards: Politics, Family, and Law in Early Modern France* (Oxford: Oxford University Press, 2012), 15.

[76] One notes a tendency among historians to emphasize "negotiation," "compromise," "arbitration," "collaboration," "consensus," "subtlety," "flexibility," "fluidity," "plurality," "contingency," "ambiguity," "complexity," or "multiplicity" to the point of obscuring what was really happening. A social historian of law has written that "[l]aw under the Old Regime did not provide clear-cut rules and principles; rather it provided a variety of concepts, languages, and procedures 'by which culture and community [were] established, maintained, and transformed'" and that "jurists routinely employed multiple, often conflicting, sources as their needs dictated" (footnote omitted). Michael P. Breen, "Patronage, Politics, and the 'Rule of Law' in Early Modern France," *Proceedings of the Western Society for French History* 33 (2005), 104, 102. But these characterizations of the ancien régime law, heavily skewed toward the virtue of social practices, could hold ground only if one is ready to disregard most law texts and doctrinal writings. Similarly, a history of emotion in law would broaden the scope of research only to the extent that it does not discount the nature of law as a work of *raison*. See Daniel Lord Smail, *The Consumption of Justice: Emotions, Publicity, and Legal Culture in Marseille, 1264–1423* (Ithaca: Cornell University Press, 2003). Risks of overemphasizing legal pluralism have been pointed out in Brian Z. Tamanaha, "Understanding Legal Pluralism: Past to Present, Local to Global," *Sydney Law Review* 30 (2008), 375–411; Brian Z. Tamanaha, "A Non-Essentialist Version of Legal Pluralism," *Journal of Law and Society* 27 (2000), 296–321. Breen's assessment that recent works of social history and law "can sometimes come perilously close to removing the law and those who administered it from the equation altogether" is all too apt and reasonable. Michael P. Breen, "Law and Social History in Early Modern France," in Barbara B. Diefendorf (ed.), *Social Relations, Politics, and Power in Early Modern France: Robert Descimon and the Historian's Craft* (Kirksville: Truman State University Press, 2016), 44.

France, legal texts and arguments were more than inconvenient obstacles that could be overcome through contextualized and nuanced analysis. The extent to which judicial business in lower courts was left unregulated is difficult to know precisely, but the judges in the parlements were not such a forgiving group as far as errant applications of law were concerned. For that matter, ascribing changes in the judge's interpretation of the law solely to political pressure would be less than helpful in making sense of early modern legal history.

Robert Descimon has pointed out a common problem in studying early modern legal history. Scholars tend to adhere to naïve syllogism: only the order of royal law—*la loi*—was legitimate; the existence of other concurrent legal orders reduced the effectiveness of royal legislation; therefore, royal ministers tried to suppress them and unify French law by absorbing them into *la loi*.[77] He cautions against viewing early modern France narrowly in terms of the centralizing state's relentless march toward legislative monopoly. Descimon's warning can be redirected, if counterintuitively, against the tendency, prevalent more in the United States than in France, to privilege culture and society to such an extent as to relegate the state law and learned arguments to a secondary status.[78] History has amply demonstrated that state law is not always the best instrument for protecting people. But safeguarding rights requires a legal system, or institution, with formal laws and procedures. It is still important to explain how the state law

[77] Robert Descimon, "Review of Anne Rousselet-Pimont, *Le chancelier et la loi au XVIe siècle, d'après l'œuvre d'Antoine Duprat, de Guillaume Poyet, et de Michel de L'Hospital* (Paris: De Boccard, 2005)," *Annales. Histoire, Sciences Sociales* 62 (2007), 1204.

[78] It has been argued that the disciplinary "barriers between *histoire* and *histoire du droit*" are "much more distinct (and often antagonistic) . . . in France than they are in the anglophone world." Breen, "Law and Social History," 47. The distance between historians and legal historians in France and that in the United States (and in other common law countries to a lesser extent) may be of a qualitatively different nature, however. In France, the reason for the lack of serious dialogues between historians and legal scholars studying history is, at least in part, ideological. Robert Descimon has lamented the lack of dialogues between them, which can be traced to the Dreyfus Affair in the Third Republic and subsequently put into relief by the emergence of the Annales School. Descimon, "Declareuil (1913) contre Hauser (1912)." The highly charged political tradition of French historiography is legendary. In the United States, by contrast, what separates history from history of law may be something more mundane, namely, the law school system. The unique institutional divide separates the academic fields of law and history and stands in the way of serious interaction between historians and jurists. Research from a historical perspective—works by history professors—highlights the centrality of law and legal institutions in the public sphere, often glossing over private law in favor of cultural and social impact of law. Research from a legal perspective—works by law professors—on the other hand focuses mostly on the doctrinal development of private law, including Roman law principles, feudal contract, common law decision-making, and custom in international law, with little attention to historical and social backgrounds. This observation is admittedly overbroad, but it seems true that, partly in consequence, legal history of customary law has been left in a chasm between the two approaches, as historians and jurists stay apart from each other. In France the law faculty stands on its territory as well, but arguably not to the same extent of seclusion as in US academia. In the United States, law school and history professors regularly go to different conferences and publish in different journals, and this seemingly near-total disregard of each other's activities explains the absence of controversies—yet—similar to the *Declareuil vs. Hauser*. The well-established, formidable presence of the legal history discipline in France contrasts with the United States where continental legal history, not to mention comparative legal history, is still in the fledging stage as an independent field of study.

evolved from other sources, to scrutinize the reasons behind the legislative act, and to verify the accuracy of the arguments used to justify the new law.[79]

There are several insights in legal historiography in Europe that this book considers helpful in studying early modern France. First, French legal historians have called for more attention to substantive private law, apart from institutional and political history. Emphasis on legal rules and concepts can facilitate more comparative, transnational discussions of law, free from the nationalist paradigm.[80] Second, in relation to the previous point, there is a growing argument among scholars in support of the integration of legal history and comparative law.[81] One of the key objectives of comparative legal history is to inquire into how people in the past made choices among the bodies of legal solutions to reach a better decision. Naturally, rational, external criteria were needed to justify choice among them, and delineating them was the job of jurists.[82] Law relies on legal constructs, contract and succession for example, and requires conceptualization. The survival of general norms and axiomatic doctrines depends on their persuasive authority, and it is necessary to describe how specific ideas, arguments, and formulations became more predominant than others at a given historical juncture. The centrality of legal texts is obvious because they are authoritative materials from which meanings of the rules can be extracted by commonly accepted means.[83]

One notable approach using the comparative-legal method is looking at legal history as the study of legal tradition. The notion of legal tradition has been in

[79] Gilissen, "Loi et coutume," 279.

[80] See Sophie Petit-Renaud and Anne Rousselet-Pimont, "Histoire des normes: l'émergence de la loi moderne," in Jacques Krynen and Bernard d'Alteroche (eds.), *L'histoire du droit en France: Nouvelle tendances, nouveaux territoires* (Paris: Classiques Garnier, 2014), 223–35; Jean-Louis Halpérin, "Histoire comparée du droit," in Krynen and d'Alteroche (eds.), *L'histoire du droit en France*, 183–203. See, in general, Jean-Louis Halpérin, *Profils des mondialisations du droit* (Paris: Dalloz, 2009).

[81] Mathias Reimann and Alain Levasseur, "Comparative Law and Legal History in the United States," *American Journal of Comparative Law* 46 (Supplement) (1998), 1–15; Thomas Duve, "Legal History and Comparative Law: A Dialogue in Times of the Transnationalization of Law and Legal Scholarship," *American Journal of Comparative Law* 66 (2018), 727–31, and accompanying articles in the symposium of that journal issue, in particular, Heikki Pihlajamäki, "Merging Comparative Law and Legal History: Towards an Integrated Discipline," *American Journal of Comparative Law* 66 (2018), 733–50. "Legal" approach in English to the legal history of Europe, including France, can be illustrated in the chapters in Reimann and Zimmermann (eds.), *The Oxford Handbook of Comparative Law*; Markus D. Dubber and Christopher Tomlins (eds.), *The Oxford Handbook of Legal History* (Oxford: Oxford University Press, 2018); Heikki Pihlajamäki, Mark Godfrey, and Markus Dubber (eds.), *The Oxford Handbook of European Legal History* (Oxford: Oxford University Press, 2018); Moréteau et al. (eds.), *Comparative Legal History*. For customary law, see, in addition to what have already been mentioned in the preceding notes, Amanda Perreau-Saussine and James Bernard Murphy (eds.), *The Nature of Customary Law: Legal, Historical and Philosophical Perspectives* (Cambridge: Cambridge University Press, 2007).

[82] "It is, above all, lawyers thinking about law, not societal conditions, that determines the shape of legal change in developed legal systems." Alan Watson, "The Evolution of Law: Continued." *Law and History Review* 5 (1987), 537; see also Alan Watson, *The Evolution of Law* (Baltimore: Johns Hopkins University Press, 1989).

[83] Martin Krygier, "Law as Tradition," *Law and Philosophy* 5 (1986), 250.

circulation for some time among legal philosophers and comparative law scholars, but the publication in 2000 of H. Patrick Glenn's *Legal Traditions of the World* prompted extensive discussion.[84] Glenn proposed that legal tradition be defined as a body of normative information, which is distinguished from "conduct." It permits us to "separate the information that precedes us from what we actually do in life and the decisions we actually make" and, as such, allows us to engage and judge conduct against that which "precedes the decision (in what we call the 'present')."[85] Since legal traditions are continually being reproduced, predicated on the choices we make in the present, the authority we ascribe to those norms is from today, not from the past. Yet legal tradition imposes important constraints on these choices: whereas the legal past is reinterpreted on the basis of the choices we make in the present, legal tradition as useful information of long standing prevents us from letting our cultural perspectives, preferences, options, emotions, sensibilities, and so on dictate those choices. Approaching legal history in terms of normative knowledge thus affirms the idea that history has a purpose of its own and is not simply a handmaid of the present.

Legal history ideally discusses ways in which local populations perceived the laws and explores how they reacted to legal changes. But assumed superiority of knowledge coming from lived experience and inferiority of learned arguments may not be as obvious as it appears.[86] Law is a discursive system, and a study relying exclusively on legal texts and juristic writings would be a pallid one, and so would a study narrowly focusing on practice, perception, and sentiment supposedly in the background of elusive social life. When the field of early modern French history has become a bit lopsided for the social and cultural models, notably in scholarship in English, there seems to be justification for a legal history based on the legal model. The following chapters aim to offer an even-handed look at France's complex legal past, with the hope to bridge the divides among *l'histoire*, *l'histoire du droit*, and *le droit*.

[84] H. Patrick Glenn, *Legal Traditions of the World: Sustainable Diversity in Law*, 5th ed. (Oxford: Oxford University Press, 2014 [2000]). As many as fourteen specialists participated in an unusual format of collective review of *Legal Traditions of the World*, each focusing on the particular chapter of his or her expertise. Nicholas H. D. Foster, William Twining, Andrew Halpin, and Gordon Woodman, "A Fresh Start for Comparative Legal Studies? A Collective Review of Patrick Glenn's Legal Traditions of the World, 2nd Edition," *Journal of Comparative Law* 1 (2006), 100–76.

[85] Mireille Hildebrandt, "The Precision of Vagueness, Interview with H. Patrick Glenn," *Rechtsfilosofie & Rechtstheorie* [Netherlands Journal of Legal Philosophy] 35 (2006), 354. See also H. Patrick Glenn, "Comparative Legal Families and Comparative Legal Traditions," in Reimann and Zimmermann (eds.), *The Oxford Handbook of Comparative Law*, 421–39.

[86] "The relationship between ideas and the ordering of society is one of the most complex historical problems." Bonney, "Absolutism: What's in a Name?" 95.

3. Structure of the Book

Chapter 2 offers a theoretical discussion and historiographic review of the nature of custom. It surveys the sources of law in medieval France, highlighting major legal and historical debates concerning custom as common law. The second section of the book, Chapters 3 through 5, explores the process by which customary law was recorded and reformed. Chapter 3 describes the launching of the official compilation of customs in the late fifteenth century as part of the attempt to systematize the laws of the kingdom. The royal codification campaigns in the sixteenth century, examined in Chapter 4, reaffirmed the legislative authority of the king. There was a close link between the yearning for national unity during the religious wars and the rise of the notion of French law. Chapter 5 examines the content of the *coutumes*, focusing on the custom of Paris of 1580, and major royal laws that aimed to facilitate their implementation.

The final section of the book explores the short- and long-term consequences of the redaction of customs for the development of the monarchy. Chapter 6 looks at how doctrinal and jurisprudential developments systematized and consolidated the legal hierarchy of the state. Legal humanist rhetoric challenged the conception of Roman law as *jus commune* and postulated custom as the common law of France. Chapter 7 investigates the changing relationship between judges and the crown over constitutional issues and discusses the venality of offices and its implications for the theory of state sovereignty. Chapter 8 reflects on the role of individuals in promoting the ideals of law and justice, seen against the backdrop of civil war, before proceeding to a short survey of the state of law in the seventeenth and eighteenth centuries. A conclusion follows.

A brief explanation on the sources is in order. Dumoulin's magisterial compendium of the customs, *Le grand coutumier général*, was published in Paris in 1567 and remained the most authoritative source since.[87] It was reissued in 1681. In 1699, two *avocats* at the Parlement of Paris, Claude Berroyer and Eusèbe de Laurière, conceived the idea of creating a new and comprehensive compilation of customs, commentaries, statutes, charters, and procedures that were in force in the kingdom. As a preface to this collection, they provided a list of the fifteen different editions of the *coutumiers généraux* published since 1517 and an alphabetical list of the texts and commentaries of the *coutumes*, from Abbeville to Vitry-en-Perthois, with short historical observations.[88] Their project, unfinished during their lifetimes, saw its completion in 1724 when Charles Bourdot de Richebourg put together in four volumes all the official customs that were

[87] Charles Dumoulin, *Le grand coustumier general: Contenant toutes les coustumes generalles & particulieres du Royaume de France & des Gaulles* . . ., 2 vols. (Paris: Jacques du Puys, 1567).

[88] Claude Berroyer, Eusèbe de Laurière, and Charles Du Moulin, *Bibliothèque des coutumes contenant la préface d'un nouveau coutumier général* . . . (Paris: Gosselin, 1669).

redacted and reformed after the royal ordinance of 1454.[89] These volumes remain the most commonly referenced sources for studying the customs of old France. A comprehensive modern bibliographic reference manual was compiled by André Gouron and Odile Terrin in 1975, including the collections of customs of the Midi not included in the volumes of Bourdot de Richebourg.[90] The present book relies on Bourdot de Richebourg's volumes and other printed sources rather than manuscript evidence. It brings together literature on custom, which is now large enough that the literature itself is a proper subject of research.

At the Estates General held in Orléans in 1560, Chancellor L'Hôpital declared: "Different languages do not cause the division of the kingdom, but different religions and laws do, splitting one kingdom into two. Hence the old proverb, *une foy, une loy, un roy*."[91] This statement, one of the many memorable utterances by the humanist chancellor during the religious wars, captured the predicament that befell France: disunity in religion and law endangered the survival of the state. In the sixteenth century *pietas* and *justitia* were one and the same thing.[92] Reform of justice meant the reform of morals. But here L'Hôpital was referring to a more fundamental and also pragmatic vision: "we have turned the laws, created to come to the aid of the mortals, to dreadful and fatal ruins of good people"; it was his contemporaries' duty to restore the laws to their original ideals and achieve justice and "concordia."[93] The paradox of early modern French history is unmistakable: the crisis of civil war became an unwitting fertile ground for the efforts to make law more reasonable and equitable and to create a more unified state grounded on royal sovereignty. The campaign of customary law and legislative

[89] *Nouveau coutumier général*, see note 43 in this chapter.

[90] André Gouron and Odile Terrin, *Bibliographie des coutumes de France, éditions antérieures à la Révolution* (Geneva: Droz, 1975). It provides a list of customary literature, including customary texts and commentaries, and cross-reference page numbers to Bourdot de Richebourg's volumes. George Washington University Jacob Burns Law Library houses a rare collection of the original editions of the *coutumes* published in the fifteenth and sixteenth centuries, including *Coustumes de la Prevosté et Vicomté de Paris, mises et redigees par escrit, en presence des gens des trois Estats de ladite Prevosté & Vicomté* (Paris: Jaques du Puis, 1580) (see Figure 4.2). The Library of Congress in Washington, DC, maintains a large number of French *coutumes*, as listed in Jean Caswell and Ivan Sipkov, *The Coutumes of France in the Library of Congress: An Annotated Bibliography* (Washington, DC: Library of Congress, 1977).

[91] Discourse at the Estates General at Orléans, December 13, 1560, in *Michel de L'Hospital et ses discours (1559–1562): La plume et la tribune*, ed. Loris Petris (Geneva: Droz, 2002), 400; also in *Discours pour la majorité de Charles IX et trois autres discours*, ed. Robert Descimon (Paris: Imprimerie nationale, 1993), 84. See Marie Seong-Hak Kim, *Michel de L'Hôpital: The Vision of a Reformist Chancellor during the French Religious Wars* (Kirksville: Sixteenth Century Journal Publishers, 1997), 64.

[92] Michel Reulos, "La notion de 'justice' et l'activité administrative du roi en France (XVe–XVIIe siècles)," in Werner Paravicini and Karl Ferdinand Werner (eds.), *Histoire comparée de l'administration (IVe–XVIIIe siècles): Actes du XIVe colloque historique franco-allemand, Tours, 27 mars–1er avril 1977, Beihefte Der Francia* 9 (Munich: Artemis Verlag, 1980), 33.

[93] *Carmina: Livre II. Michel de L'Hospital*, ed. and trans. David Amherdt, Laure Chappus Sandoz, Perrine Galand, and Loris Petris (Geneva: Droz, 2017), 112–15. The politics for L'Hôpital was an art of his faith. Crouzet, *La sagesse et le malheur*, 505.

reform in the sixteenth century were conscious responses of the state to society clamoring for general and stable laws and effective administration of the law.

Aspiration for a civil law—civil law presupposes unity—was arguably one of the most distinctive and enduring themes of France's legal tradition. It highlights the ideal to bring legal unity commensurate with the country's political unity. The Civil Code of 1804 did not happen in a vacuum; it came with the Revolutionary *rupture* but it was not a thunderbolt from nowhere. The historical forces behind *the* French law, long in the making, call for a fresh look.

2
Custom in Late Medieval France

Custom as the expression of popular will received plenty of learned discussion in European history. In the classical age, Roman jurists argued the authority of custom came from the consent of the people (*consensus totius populi*). In the medieval period, the canonists grounded custom's legal force on belief (*opinio juris et necessitatis*) and reason. From the Late Middle Ages through the end of the eighteenth century, legists maintained custom could exist only with the tolerance of the king (*patientia principis*).[1] By the era of national codification, custom had become an old taboo, an abandoned heritage.[2] It was under the influence of German legal historiography in the nineteenth century that custom was given new vigor. Savigny brought it to the center stage of legal-historical scholarship, postulating custom and its expression in law as the spirit of the people (*Volksgeist*), a symbol of national consciousness.[3]

Since Savigny, legal historians engaged in explaining the passage of custom from the realm of usage, representing the behavior of people (*sein*), to the realm of law, regulating the behavior of people (*sollen*). Savigny's vision of custom presupposed a European legal culture based on Roman law, which transcended national particularism but at the same time became firmly ingrained in German history. French historians at the time, many of whom had grown wary of the discourse of the so-called exegetical school, were inclined to see the ancien régime by reason of their nationalist agenda, elaborating on how custom had served at the specific junctures of the development of the monarchy. The classic tripartite periodization of French history—feudal monarchy, limited monarchy, and absolute monarchy—was first proposed by Adhémar Esmein (1848–1913) during this time, to remain in place ever since.[4] Across Europe in the late nineteenth

[1] Paul Ourliac, "Réflexions sur l'origine de la coutume," *Études d'histoire du droit médiéval en souvenir de Josette Metman, Mémoires de la Société pour l'histoire du droit des anciens pays bourguignons, comtois et romand* 45 (1988), 342.

[2] "Custom constitutes an old taboo for two centuries for jurists who are seemingly subjected to the Code Napoléon." André Gouron, "La coutume en France au Moyen Âge," in Jacques Vanderlinden (ed.), *La coutume=Custom*, vol. 2, *Europe occidentale médiévale et moderne/Medieval and Modern Western Europe*, Recueils de la Société Jean Bodin, vol. 52 (Brussels: De Boeck-Wesmael, 1990), 195.

[3] Reinhard Zimmermann, "Savigny's Legacy: Legal History, Comparative Law and the Emergence of a European Legal Science," *Law Quarterly Review* 112 (1996), 576–605.

[4] *La monarchie féodale* covers the period from the reign of Hugues Capet to Philip the Fair; *la monarchie tempérée* from the Philip the Fair to Henry IV; and *la monarchie absolue* through the end of the ancien régime. Esmein's *Cours élémentaire d'histoire du droit français à l'usage des étudiants de première année* first appeared in 1892. Jacques Poumarède, "Penser l'absolutisme. Approche

Custom, Law, and Monarchy: A Legal History of Early Modern France. Marie Seong-Hak Kim, Oxford University Press.
 DOI: 10.1093/oso/9780192845498.003.0002

century, legal history was propelled by a national paradigm.[5] As a discipline, it was fused with the field of constitutional law.[6]

In the early twentieth century, scholarly opinions diverged as to the nature of *droit commun* in medieval France. It reflected in part the division between the legal sociological school and the legal historical school: the former highlighted the distinctiveness of national cultures embedded in custom and saw law as an emanation of the collective sensitivity of a cultural group; the latter found such a relationship between law and society tenuous at best and instead stressed the importance of the constructive jurisprudence of law. The specific question in contention was whether the notion of *droit commun* emerged autonomously in France or only after custom was written down on the model of Roman law.[7] The disagreement revolved around the nature and scope of the influence of the reception of *jus civile*. Differences in opinion widened and intensified in the postwar years when research on *jus commune* became an intrinsic part of European legal historiography. The idea of the inherent unity of Europe's legal traditions extending back to ancient Rome held sway, along with the movement in favor of the construction of a supranational community of Europe.

The theme of common law in Europe received renewed attention in the closing decades of the twentieth century. There was an explosion of scholarly works on Roman law in the 1990s, coinciding with the surge of the ideal of European integration after the fall of the Soviet Union.[8] It has rekindled in the twenty-first century historiographical debates on *droit commun*. Examination of the recent polemic among French scholars presents several interconnected questions. For

historiographie des ouvrages pédagogiques en histoire des institutions françaises," in Jean-Pierre Allinne (ed.), *Itinéraire(s) d'un historien du droit: Jacques Poumarède, regards croisés sur la naissance de nos institutions* (Toulouse: CNRS—Université de Toulouse-Le Mirail, 2011), 633–34. See Jean-Louis Halpérin, "Adhémar Esmein et les ambitions de l'histoire du droit," *Revue historique de droit français et étranger* 75 (1997), 415–33.

[5] A succinct exposition of the historiography at the end of the nineteenth and the first half of the twentieth centuries can be found in Poumarède, "Penser l'absolutisme." For a critique of "classical handbooks of French legal history," by historians such as Esmein, Joseph Declareuil, Émile Chénon, and François Olivier-Martin, allegedly drenched in national pride, see Jean-Louis Halpérin, "Est-il temps de déconstruire les mythes de l'histoire du droit français?" *Clio@Themis: revue électronique d'histoire du droit* 5 (2012), http://www.cliothemis.com/Est-il-temps-de-deconstruire-les. For the European context, see Joachim Rückert, "The Invention of National Legal History," in Pihlajamäki, Dubber, and Godfrey (eds.), *The Oxford Handbook of European Legal History*, 22–83.

[6] Legal positivists tended to "harbor mistrust" toward the idea of a law that could supposedly undermine the constitutional order and national sovereignty. Ourliac, "Réflexions sur l'origine de la coutume," 342.

[7] Hippolyte Pissard, *Essai sur la connaissance et la preuve des coutumes* (Paris: Rousseau, 1910). For a summary of the early twentieth-century debate, see Eugen Ehrlich, *Fundamental Principles of the Sociology of Law*, trans. Walter Lewis Moll (Cambridge, MA: Harvard University Press, 1936), 442–61; Fredric Cheyette, "La justice et le pouvoir royal à la fin du Moyen Âge français," *Revue historique de droit français et étranger* 3 (1962), 373–94.

[8] "The representation of a Europe *sub lege romana* persists in the ideal actualized on a supra national European law." Laurent Mayali, "*Ius civile* et *ius commune* dans la tradition juridique médiévale," in Jacques Krynen (ed.), *Droit romain, jus civile et droit français* (Toulouse: Presses de l'Université des sciences sociales de Toulouse, 1999), 201.

one, it is symptomatic of national resistance against the "empire" of a European common law of Roman inspiration.[9] It is also connotative of the role of political power, that is, intervention of the king and his courts in custom. During the Late Middle Ages, judges of royal courts confirmed the regularity of local-specific practices, formalizing their binding force as customary law. Doctors of Roman law and canon law authenticated it as a legal source, capable of coexisting with the Justinian compilations. Disagreement over the precise political role in this process has pitted scholars against each other as to the autonomy of custom in relation to the expansion of royal justice.

This chapter examines the development of custom from the thirteenth century to the eve of Charles VII's decision in 1454 to launch the campaign to record customs.

1. Sources of Law

In Roman times, the term *consuetudo* was used quasi-synonymously with *mos* (will, inclination, or mores) and *usus* (usage or habit), to refer to norms of ordinary behavior. These were outside the formal law of the city of Rome. Since the third century, jurists recognized custom as something more than mere manners or usages.[10] According to Ulpian, judicial decisions in disputed cases affirmed the existence of custom: "When it appears that somebody is relying upon a custom either of a *civitas* or of a province, the very first issue which ought to be explored, according to my opinion, is whether the custom has ever been upheld in contentious proceedings."[11] Others went further to argue that custom had the power to void preexisting law. A section in the *Digest* attributed to Julian stated that statutes "may be repealed not only by vote of the legislature but also by the silent agreement of everyone expressed through desuetude," that is, by falling out of use by common consent.[12] It followed that *consuetudo* based on consent prevailed over a contrary *lex*. "Ancient customs, when approved by consent of those who follow them, are like statute." Such agreement needed not be explicit; tacit consent of the people could suffice.[13]

After antiquity, Roman jurists' distinction between custom as usage and custom as law became blurred. The meaning of *consuetudo* in the Middle Ages before the twelfth century is seldom disputed. It referred to fiscal exactions, taxes, fines,

[9] Descamps and Wijffels, "Approches historiques," 64. Exaltation of *droit commun* in France may be based on an ill-conceived national sentiment vis-à-vis Italy and Germany: Italy was "the cradle of the rediscovery of Roman law," Germany was the "*laboratoire* and *conservatoire* of its reception." Ibid.

[10] Robert Jacob, "La coutume, les mœurs et le rite. Regards croisés sur les catégories occidentales de la norme non écrite," in Jérôme Bourgon (ed.), *La coutume et la norme en Chine et au Japon* (Saint-Denis: Presses universitaires de Vincennes, 2001), 146; Kelley, "'Second Nature,'" 133.

[11] *Digest* 1.3.34.

[12] *Digest* 1.3.32.

[13] *Institutes* 1.2.9, 1.2.11.

or duties, imposed by feudal lords on the people in their estates. The river and road tolls, *corvées*, various kinds of license or rental fees (*redevances*) and payments in kind (*prestations*), and the rights of justice were all called custom.[14] Customs, oral rules prescribing profits or monopoly of the seigneurs, were considered by the population arbitrary, undue, or bad.[15] From the twelfth century, villagers and townspeople began to wrest various concessions from feudal lords, which were called *franchises* or *libertés*, or simply *coutumes*.[16] The term that had designated in the eleventh century the rights and privileges of the seigneurs thus came to signify exemptions from the same. A waiver of or immunity from legal obligation in civil law, that is, a general requirement of the law, meant privilege (*privilegium*), which created a relationship under a particular law (*privatae leges*; *lois privées*; private law).[17] Liberty and privilege were understood as synonymous.[18] The movement to draw up documents to reshape the relationship between the lords and inhabitants progressed, and the charters obtained by the townspeople declared the abolition of onerous customs. This is how the word *consuetudines* (plural of *consuetudo*) took a positive connotation to indicate exemptions which the rural or urban populations collectively extracted from their lords.

By the thirteenth century, custom had come to refer to the laws in force at the local level. It was a product of feudal decentralization. The fragmentation of the fiefs brought a multitude of seigneurial courts, in particular in regions in the west where the saying was "fief and justice are wholly one."[19] In theory all justice emanated from the king (*toute justice émane du roi*), but in reality the crown did not have the monopoly of justice. Seigneurial courts exercised jurisdiction, called *juridiction subalterne*, over criminal prosecutions as well as lawsuits involving feudal rights and dues. When law as authoritative statements of norms was absent, the alternative was the proof of custom. In a mosaic of jurisdictions, the party appearing before the court was required to establish by what custom he should be tried and what that custom was.

[14] Gilissen, "Loi et coutume," 264–65. The usage of the term survives in the modern word "customs," fees paid when passing borders.

[15] Henri Beaune, *Introduction à l'étude historique du droit coutumier français jusqu'à la rédaction officielle des coutumes* (Lyon: Briday, 1880), 329–30; see Olivier Guillot, Yves Sassier, and Albert Rigaudière, *Pouvoirs et institutions dans la France médiévale*, vol. 1, *Des origines à l'époque féodale* (Paris: Armand Colin, 1994).

[16] Jean-Marie Carbasse, "Contribution à l'étude du processus coutumier: La coutume de droit privé jusqu'à la révolution," *Droits: Revue française de théorie juridique* 3 (1986), 27. The word "franchise" came from "*l'affranchissement*" (freeing) of the serfs.

[17] *Digest* 1.3.16.

[18] Daniel Lee, "Roman Law, German Liberties and the Constitution of the Holy Roman Empire," in Quentin Skinner and Martin Van Gelderen (eds.), *Freedom and the Constitution of Europe*, vol. 1: *Religious and Constitutional Liberties* (Cambridge: Cambridge University Press, 2013), 262.

[19] Howell A. Lloyd, *The State, France, and the Sixteenth Century* (London: G. Allen & Unwin, 1983), 53.

In both England and France, the emergence of custom as enforceable law was not so much a process of natural growth of rules that had already been there in popular practices as a conscious innovation. The rise of royal courts coincided with the disintegration and reconstitution of feudal principalities. With the recovery of royal power, the king's courts encroached on private justice, which had meant in practice freedom from justice, or "the definition of liberty itself."[20] Custom, once proved in royal court, could become a legal norm, separated from simple facts of feudal usage or privilege.[21] In England, from the twelfth century royal courts progressively applied general custom of the realm for the whole kingdom, which came to be known as the "common law."[22] In France, the delay in reclaiming royal power prevented such a development from taking place. It was not until the end of the fifteenth century that the Capetians succeeded in bringing the last of the fiefs under royal control. The French courts relied on a set of choice-of-law rules for determining which custom to apply to the specific cases brought before them.[23] There is little dispute that the development of customary law took place in the wake of the intellectual breakthrough paved by the renaissance of Roman law.

The Growth of Royal Courts

By the late eleventh century, the restoration of the *Corpus juris civilis* had been completed by Irnerius (*c.*1050–*c.*1130), who had started the famed Bologna school of Roman law. Medieval scholars at the newly established universities in Italy began churning out vast glosses and commentaries and tried to reconcile the seemingly contradictory views in the *Corpus juris* on the legal force of custom.[24]

[20] Ernest Désiré Glasson, *Histoire du droit et des institutions de la France* (Paris: F. Pichon, 1887), vol. 8, 494.

[21] René Filhol, "La preuve de la coutume dans l'ancien droit français," in *Recueils de la société Jean Bodin*, vol. 17 (Brussels: Édition de la librairie encyclopédique, 1965), 357, reproduced in *Aux alentours du droit coutumier, articles et conférences du doyen René Filhol* (Poitiers: Université de Poitiers Faculté des sciences sociales, 1988).

[22] In England, royal courts authorized *stare decisis*, and the governing reasoning (*ratio decidendi*) was written down to be cited to support new decisions. Substantive customs of the whole kingdom were generalized by means of the decisions of judges dispatched from London. See Paul Brand, "Law and Custom in the English Thirteenth Century Common Law," in Per Andersen and Mia Münster-Swendsen (eds.), *Custom: The Development and Use of a Legal Concept in the Middle Ages* (Copenhagen: DJØF Publishing, 2009), 17–32.

[23] See Fredric L. Cheyette, "Choice of Law in Medieval France," in Morris D. Forkosch (ed.), *Essays in Legal History in Honor of Justice Felix Frankfurter* (Indianapolis: Bobbs-Merrill, 1966), 481–96.

[24] Debates among medieval scholars were reflective of the political world of the time. Those who advocated the importance of custom were often the ones who were employed by the municipal assemblies in burgeoning Italian cities and had reason to highlight the authority of urban statutes as legal custom contrary to imperial laws. Irnerius, on the other hand, writing at a time when the emperor mounted serious attempts to restore the Holy Roman Empire, chose to place imperial will over popular will: a gloss attributed to him was unequivocal in placing *lex* above *consuetudo*, and this interpretation became the dominant opinion. Irnerius' argument was based on the historical background of

Roman law entered southern France from about 1160 via public notaries who accompanied merchants traveling to Languedoc; from there it spread to the north and the west.[25]

An ordinance issued by Louis IX (r. 1226–1270) in 1251 separated the zone of the *consuetudo gallicana* from that of *jus scriptum*, thereby giving rise to the division of France into *pays de droit coutumier* in the north and *pays de droit écrit* in the south.[26] The partition had to do with feudal developments involving ecclesiastical possessions.[27] In the *pays de droit écrit*, Roman law was applied as the common law in matters of private interest, although the nature of *droit écrit* was not always clear. Some scholars have argued that *droit écrit* in these provinces, known as the Midi, was not exactly *droit romain* and was instead a mélange of Visigothic Roman law and more recent elaborations of the *Corpus juris civilis* developed by scholars in Italy and southern France.[28] The *droit écrit*, where it was the source of the law, was received as custom. In 1312, Philip IV (r. 1285–1314) declared that Roman law was followed in France as customary law, not written law, and this by the permission of him and his ancestors.[29] When French legists wrote "the French king is the emperor in his own kingdom" (*Rex Franciae in regno suo princeps est*), they were affirming the French crown's rejection of the Holy Roman emperor's claim of universal dominion as well as the authority of *jus commune*.[30] Since Roman law derived its validity from the royal will and was allowed in France only as one of the customs, other customs in the kingdom could derogate from it.

different texts collected in Roman law. David Ibbetson, "Custom in Medieval Law," in Perreau-Saussine and Murphy (eds.), *The Nature of Customary Law*, 157. See also Emanuele Conte, "Roman Law vs Custom in a Changing Society: Italy in the Twelfth and Thirteenth Centuries," in Andersen and Münster-Swendsen (eds.), *Custom*, 33–50.

[25] Jean Hilaire, "La France méridionale avait-elle une frontière sous l'Ancien Régime?" *Bulletin Académie des sciences et lettres de Montpellier* (February 2008), 45–54.

[26] Ordinance of Vincennes in April 1251, art. 4. The text is in Eusèbe de Laurière, Louis George Oudard-Feudrix de Bréquigny et al. (eds.), *Ordonnances des roys de France de la troisième race recueillies par ordre chronologique (1051–1514)* (Paris: Imprimerie royale, 1723), vol. 1, 63. The line of demarcation extended roughly from Geneva to La Rochelle, separating about two-thirds of the kingdom to the north and center from the south. But the borders long remained malleable, and it was only in the sixteenth century that it became more solidly drawn, as a result of the renaissance of Roman law and the publication of customs. Jean Hilaire, *La vie du droit: Coutumes et droit écrit* (Paris: Presses universitaires de France, 1994), 101–103; Carbasse, "Contribution à l'étude du processus coutumier," 33–34.

[27] Hilaire, *La vie du droit*, 161–67.

[28] Pierre Tisset, "Mythes et réalités du droit écrit," in *Études d'histoire du droit privé offertes à Pierre Petot* (Paris: Libraire générale de droit et de jurisprudence, 1959), 553–60.

[29] The famous edict read: "On all contentious issues that do not touch the spiritual order, the faith and the sacraments, our kingdom is mainly governed by custom and usage, not by the written law. If, in some parts of this kingdom, our subjects, by permission of our ancestors and ours, follow the written law on several points, they are bound by them not as written laws but as custom, in conformity with the written law introduced into usage [*juxta scripti juris exemplar moribus introducta*]." *Ordonnances des roys de France de la troisième race*, vol. 1, 501–502. See Émile Chénon, *Histoire générale du droit français public et privé des origines à 1815*, 2 vols. (Paris: Sirey, 1926), vol. 1, 508–10; Ōkubo Yasuo, "Furansu chūsei ōken to Rōma hō" [Royal Power in Medieval France and Roman Law], *Hōsei shi kenkyū* 23 (1973), 29–71.

[30] André Bossuat, "La formule 'Le roi est empereur en son royaume': Son emploi au XVe siècle devant le Parlement de Paris," *Revue historique de droit français et étranger*, 4th ser., 39 (1961), 371–81.

North of the Massif Central, the influence of Roman law was modest and the provinces featured a great diversity of customs.[31] General customs, covering duchies, counties, and municipalities, were interspersed with a multitude of local customs, controlling more limited areas such as particular seigneurial territories or parishes. In these small enclaves, the contrary customs of the surrounding *pays* had no authority at all.[32]

There is a common misconception that Roman law was unknown in the *pays de coutumes* or conversely there was no local custom in the *pays de droit écrit*. In reality, custom and written law coexisted in many regions and were enforced concurrently. The provinces in the Midi did not have regional customs, but there were a number of local customs that continued to exist all the way to the Revolution.[33] In Languedoc, Dauphiné, and Provence, local customs, called "droit étroit," often departed from Roman law.[34] They were not case law created by the courts of appeals but private agreements between a lord and his subjects who decided to forgo a legal framework for their acts.[35] Urban customs were collected and they received commentaries: the custom of Montpellier was written down in 1204 and that of Toulouse between 1283 and 1286.[36] Often these were former municipal statutes that had integrated Roman law then in force into the laws of the city and surrounding territories. Political disputes between consuls and ecclesiastical lords were frequent. Roman law had relatively limited influence among the Toulousains, which historians ascribe in part to their distrust or even hostility toward Rome during the time of the Albigensian crusade.[37]

In the *pays coutumiers*, general customs were often waived by particular usages.[38] The jurisdiction of the Parlement of Paris, which covered about one third of the kingdom, included areas with an array of different customs, some fifty municipal or provincial customs in the sixteenth century, not to mention areas governed by written law. Burgundy, Berry, Brittany, Poitou, Normandy, and Champagne each had a well-established regional *coutume*. In general, the south enjoyed greater unity of law than in the center and the north.

[31] Carbasse, "Contribution à l'étude du processus coutumier," 30–31.

[32] Jacques d'Ableiges, *Le grand coutumier de France*, ed. Edouard Laboulaye and Rodolphe Dareste (Paris: Auguste Durand et Pedone-Lauriel, 1868), book 4, ch. 1, 599.

[33] These customs persisted, despite "marked hostility of the parlements." Pierre-Clément Timbal, "La succession testamentaire dans la coutume de Toulouse," *Extrait des Annales de la faculté de droit d'Aix-en-Provence*, Nouvelle série no. 43 (1950) (Aix-en-Provence: Imprimerie d'Éditions provençales, 1950), 5–6.

[34] Beaune, *Introduction à l'étude historique*, 453.

[35] Anne Zink, "Les éditions de coutumes à France à l'époque moderne," *Ivs Fvgit* 15 (2007/8), 471.

[36] For the texts of medieval charters and coutumes, including those of Montpellier, Carcassonne, and Burgundy, see Charles-Joseph-Barthélemy Giraud, *Essai sur l'histoire du droit français au Moyen Âge*, 2 vols. (Paris: Videcoq, 1846).

[37] Jacques Poumarède, "Droit commun *versus* coutume de Toulouse, XIIIe–XVIIIe siècle," in Allinne (ed.), *Itinéraire(s) d'un historien du droit*, 143.

[38] Beaune, *Introduction à l'étude historique*, 449.

The boundaries between the *pays de droit écrit* and the *pays de droit coutumier* were far from clear-cut. Auvergne was where *droit écrit* and *coutumes* existed side by side. The question of the sources of law in Auvergne, or a specific region within Auvergne, has long been the subject of debate. The city of Clermont, with its powerful bishop, was governed by written law, but not surrounding *bailliages*. There were constant contests regarding the applicable laws, bringing numerous cases to the Parlement of Paris over inheritance disputes or business relations that went wrong.[39] Charles VII confirmed in 1455 the attachment of Auvergne to the region of *droit coutumier*, but it continued to contain numerous tiny pockets of Roman law which often cut villages into separate jurisdictions.[40]

During this time, royal civil service continued to expand. A brief overview of judicial and administrative organizations follows.

Justice and Administration

The central administration of the kingdom of France consisted of four organs: king, ministries, sovereign courts, and royal councils. The ministers were headed by the chancellor, who was the first magistrate of the kingdom and the holder of the royal seal. As the monarch's personal representative, the chancellor supervised the certification and dispatch of royal decisions and directives and, as the head of the king's council, was the spokesperson of the king to the sovereign courts, the Estates General, and the assemblies of notables. In the early modern period, the *secrétaires d'État* specialized from 1547 in different domains of war, foreign affairs, Paris-royal household-marine, and Huguenot affairs. The sovereign courts included the Parlement of Paris, the Chambre des comptes, and the Grand conseil. Royal councils included Conseil étroit, Conseil d'État privé, and Conseil d'État du roi et des finances.[41]

There were three kinds of administrative units in the provinces: *gouvernement*, *généralité*, and *intendance*. The provinces, subdivided into *pays*, did not always correspond to administrative districts. A *gouvernement* was under the authority of a *gouverneur* who served as the representative of the person of the king and retained military functions. Royal letters of provision for the governors stated their functions as "whatever may need to be done for the good of ourselves, our affairs and the utility of the public weal."[42] A *généralité* was a financial district administered from 1577 by *trésoriers généraux* of France. An *intendance* was

[39] André Castaldo, "Droit coutumier et droit écrit: Encore l'Auvergne (Parlement, 22 décembre 1386)," *Revue historique de droit français et étranger* 90 (2012), 171–72.

[40] Hilaire, *La vie du droit*, 57; Martine Grinberg, *Écrire les coutumes: Les droits seigneuriaux en France, XVIe–XVIIIe siècle* (Paris: Presses universitaires de France, 2006), 75.

[41] *Le contrôleur general des finances* was created in 1665 in the ministry; several *Conseils* were added in the course of the seventeenth and eighteenth centuries. The best source of succinct information on royal administration is Barbiche, *Les institutions de la monarchie française*. In English, see Collins, *The State in Early Modern France*, 10–20.

[42] Lloyd, *The State, France, and the Sixteenth Century*, 61.

served by an *intendant*, a *commissaire*. There were two separate bureaucratic hierarchies: *officiers* and *commissaires. Officiers* obtained the position for a capital sum paid into the royal treasury. The late fifteenth and sixteenth centuries witnessed the rapid increase in venal officials. The commissioners were agents whom the king directly charged with temporary missions which, unlike offices, he could revoke at will.[43]

The parlements were the highest courts in the kingdom. Under the Parlement of Paris and provincial parlements stood various lower courts (see Map 2.1). The royal jurisdiction of first instance was *prévôté*, which originated from the eleventh century.[44] The *prévôtés* heard appeals from seigneurial courts, and their decisions in turn could be appealed to *bailliages* and *sénéchaussées*, which appeared at the end of the twelfth century. Royal justice spread because the parties could appeal their cases to these courts. The *bailliage* and *sénéchaussée* were not just judicial units but administrative, military, and fiscal units. A *bailli* or a *sénéchal* was a *noble d'épée*, often a great seigneur who did not reside in his jurisdiction, while his judicial attributions were exercised in his name by magistrates of *robe longue*.[45] In March 1552, Henry II created a new level of jurisdiction, the *présidiaux*, to serve as the courts of final appeal for certain cases.

The Parlement of Paris evolved from a section in the Curia regis specializing in judicial affairs. It came to form a distinct structure and procedure from 1307, with a fully organized bench and bar having emerged by the mid-fourteenth century.[46] The first continuous records of the Parlement of Paris, *Les Olim*, or the

[43] Gustave Dupont-Ferrier, "Le rôle des commissaires royaux dans le gouvernement de la France spécialement du XIVe au XVIe siècle," in Gabriel Le Bras (ed.), *Mélanges Paul Fournier. De la Bibliothèque d'histoire du droit, publiée sous les auspices de la Société d'histoire du droit* (Paris: Recueil Sirey, 1929), 171–84.

[44] In some provinces, different names—*châtellenie* (Normandy) and *vicomté* (Île-de-France)—were used. Throughout this book, commonly known English spellings are used for geographical names, whenever possible, some without diacritics.

[45] The term *bailliage* was used normally in the north, and the term *sénéchaussée* in the south, but not necessarily. Dupont-Ferrier identified eighty-six of them at the beginning of the sixteenth century. See the list in Gustave Dupont-Ferrier, *Les officiers royaux des bailliages et sénéchaussées et les institutions monarchiques locales en France à la fin du Moyen Âge* (Paris: E. Bouillon, 1902), 875–916; also Société de l'histoire de France, "Liste: Des bailliages et sénéchaussées de France, distribués par provinces et par pays, conformément à un ancien tableau de la superficie du royaume," *Annuaire historique pour l'année* 14 (1850), 27–52, https://www.jstor.org/stable/23399394. There were over four hundred by 1789, each with a growing number of judges and lawyers. Barbiche, *Les institutions de la monarchie française*, 349; Martine Grinberg, Simone Geoffroy-Poisson, and Alexandra Laclau. "Rédaction des coutumes et territoires au XVIe siècle: Paris et Montfort-l'Amaury," *Revue d'histoire moderne et contemporaine* 59 (2012), 8.

[46] John P. Dawson, *The Oracles of the Law* (Ann Arbor: University of Michigan Law School, 1968), 273–78. See Félix Aubert, "Recherches sur l'organisation du Parlement de Paris au XVIe siècle (1515–1589)," in *Extrait de Nouvelle revue historique du droit français et étranger* (Paris: Sirey, 1912); Félix Aubert, *Histoire du Parlement de Paris de l'origine à François I, 1250–1515*, 2 vols. (Paris: A. Picard et fils, 1894); Joseph H. Shennan, *The Parlement of Paris* (Ithaca: Cornell University Press, 1968).

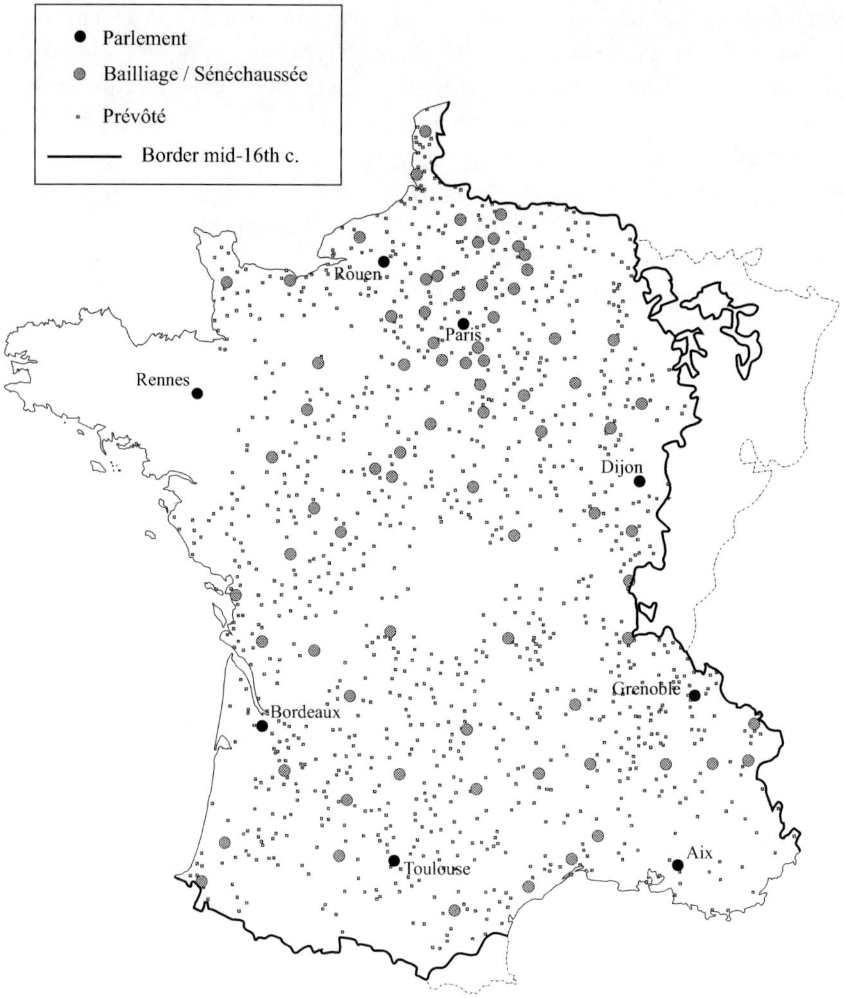

Map 2.1 Judicial organization, *circa* 1500

Adapted from the map in Gustave Dupont-Ferrier, *Les officiers royaux des bailliages et sénéchaussées* (1902).

registers of *arrêts*, dated from as early as 1254.[47] Unlike in Italy where the legal profession was governed and regulated by the guild, lawyers in France were attached to the state.[48] When French kings attempted to build royal

[47] *Les Olim* (meaning *autrefois*, in the old days) is a collection of reports of the Parlement of Paris from 1254 to 1318. The reports were edited into four volumes. *Les Olim ou registre des arrêts rendus par la cour du roi sous les règnes de saint Louis, de Philippe le Hardi, de Philippe le Bel, de Louis le Hutin et de Philippe le Long, publiés par le Comte Beugnot membre de l'Institut* (Paris: Imprimerie royale, 1839–1848).

[48] The Florentine guild of lawyers and notaries, known as *Arte dei Giudici e Notai*, dates from the early thirteenth century. For lawyers in France, see Roland Delachenal, *Histoire des avocats au*

administration, the nobles were largely excluded from judicial or financial posts; indeed they were seldom found in the law schools leading to them.[49] Those who were recruited to the royal bureaucracy were the rising merchant class. Their common education and training at the law faculties, all taught in *jus commune*, made legal professionals an unusually coherent group, forming a tight-knit community.[50] As agents of the king, they shared largely the same professional ideals and reasoning process, speaking the same language, literally and figuratively.[51] The Parlement routinely overturned the decisions of lower courts on appeal, and in this way a certain standardization of customs could be achieved.[52]

The provincial parlements were created in the newly annexed territories on the model of the Parlement of Paris. The Parlement of Toulouse (Languedoc) and the Parlement of Grenoble (Dauphiné) were established in 1443 and 1453 respectively, followed by Bordeaux (Guyenne) in 1462, Dijon (Burgundy) in 1477, Rouen (Normandy) in 1499, Aix (Provence) in 1502, and Rennes (Brittany) in 1553 (see Map 2.2).[53]

Parlement de Paris 1300–1600 (Paris: E. Plon Nourrit et cie, 1885); Jean-Louis Thireau, "Lumières et ombres de la profession d'avocat au tournant des XVIe et XVIIe siècles d'après le dialogue des avocats au Parlement de Paris," *Revue internationale d'histoire de la profession d'avocat* 5 (1993), 51–67; Bernard Quilliet, "La situation sociale des avocats au Parlement de Paris à l'époque de la Renaissance (1480–1560)," in José Luis Alonso Hernández (ed.), *Espace, idéologie et société au XVIe siècle* (Grenoble: Presses universitaires de Grenoble, 1975), 121–52; Jean-Louis Gazzaniga, "Avocats, littérateurs et érudits au XVIe siècle," in Bernard Durand and Laurent Mayali (eds.), *Excerptiones iuris: Studies in Honor of Andre Gouron* (Berkeley: Robbins Collection 2000), 261–81; Jean-Louis Gazzaniga, "Quand les avocats formaient les jurists et la doctrine," *Droits* 20 (1994), 31–41, https://books.openedition.org/putc/12979; William Forsyth, *The History of Lawyers, Ancient and Modern* (New York: James Cockcroft, 1875); Wilfrid R. Prest (ed.), *Lawyers in Early Modern Europe and America* (New York: Holmes & Meier Publishers, 1981); Richard L. Kagan, *Lawsuits and Litigants in Castile, 1500–1700* (Chapel Hill: University of North Carolina Press, 1981); David Avrom Bell, *Lawyers and Citizens: The Making of a Political Elite in Old Regime France* (Oxford: Oxford University Press, 1994); Christopher W. Brooks, *Lawyers, Litigation and English Society since 1450* (London: Hambledon, 1998).

[49] Albert Cremer, "La genèse de la notion de noblesse de robe," *Revue d'histoire moderne et contemporaine* 46 (1999), 24. Mostly sons of the urban elites were drawn to the study of law and were trained to undertake law business.

[50] Jonathan Dewald, "Social Groups and Cultural Practices," in Mack P. Holt (ed.), *Renaissance and Reformation France* (Oxford: Oxford University Press, 2002), 48. All royal judges needed at least a *licence* in law, and typically this represented seven years of university study. Jonathan Dewald, "The Perfect Magistrate: Parlementaires and Crime in Sixteenth-Century Rouen," *Archiv für Reformationsgeschichte* 67 (1976), 288. *Avocats* at the parlements were also graduates in both civil and canon law. From early on, notaries were considered to form a profession separate from lawyers. Even in the Italian guild comprising both judge-lawyers and notaries, the two groups were clearly distinguished. Drawing up contracts, deeds, marriage agreements, and wills was for the most part the province of notaries. Marie Seong-Hak Kim, "Lawyers," in *Europe, 1450 to 1789: Encyclopedia of the Early Modern World* (New York: Charles Scribner's Sons, 2004), vol. 3, 459–64; Dawson, *The Oracles*, 278–90.

[51] There were fourteen universities in sixteenth-century France, with six of them established in the years 1432–1464 alone, reflecting the needs for trained officials at the time of national recovery. Dewald, "Social Groups and Cultural Practices," 49.

[52] The term *arrêts*, meaning judicial decrees, implies finality.

[53] The Parlement of the principality of Dombes was created in 1523 in Lyon (later transferred to Trévoux) and remained independent from the crown between 1560 and 1762, to be suppressed in 1771. Four parlements, in Pau, Metz, Besançon, and Douai, were created in the seventeenth century. Nancy was added in the eighteenth century. Map 2.2 does not include the Parlement of Turin

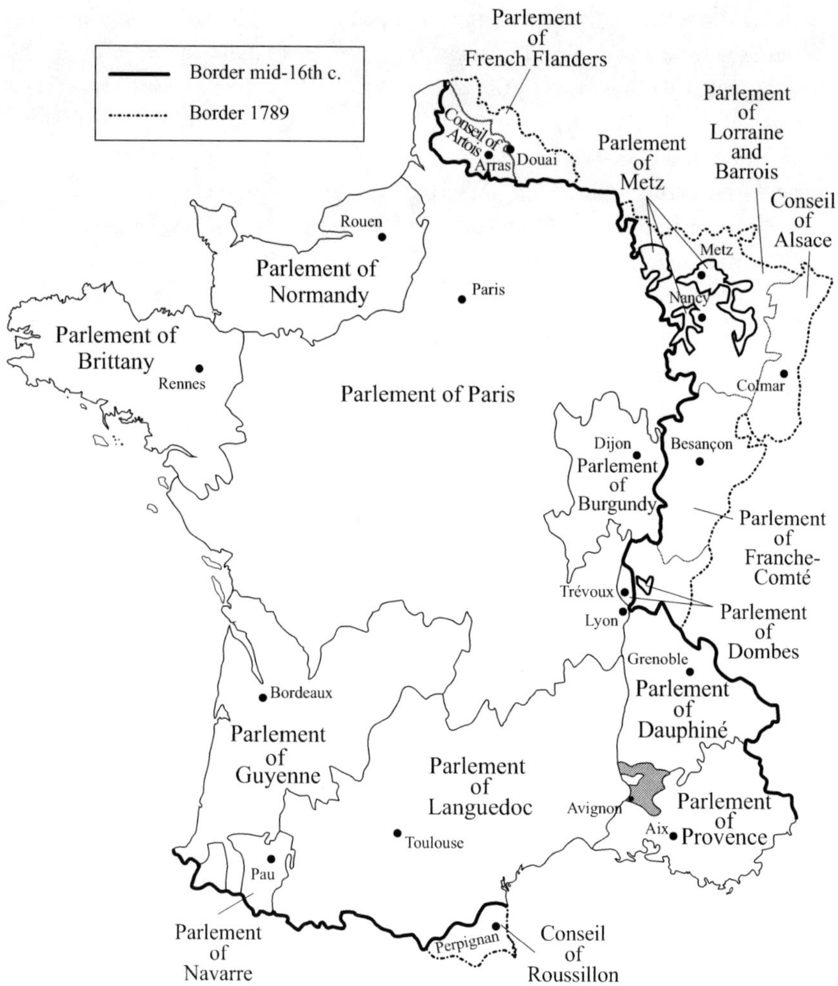

Map 2.2 Parlements and Conseils souverains/supérieurs

Proof of Custom

When royal courts first emerged, they were just another seigneurial jurisdiction, vying for legal business with all others.[54] Soon feudal courts could not compete with the king's courts, which offered more rational methods and techniques of proof informed by the Romano-Canonical inquest. Traditional procedures relying on judicial duel and ordeal were transformed in the royal courts into accusatory procedures, where the parties were required to substantiate their claims by

(Piedmont) (1537–1559), Conseil of Pignerol (1643–1696), and Conseil of Bastia (Corsica) (created in 1768). See the complete list in Barbiche, *Les institutions de la monarchie*, 341.

[54] Cheyette, "Choice of Law in Medieval France," 488.

means of evidence (*preuve*). As the courts became more professional, judicial practice constituted a forensic custom, *usus fori*. Each court had its own practice, and the Parlement of Paris in the thirteenth century already insisted that its own procedural "style" (*stilus curiae*) be observed.[55] A series of decisions by the Parlement in the procedural matter could create a new custom, capable of modifying the law.[56] Unlike *coutumes privées* ("customs of the litigants"), the court custom needed no proof. Through the judicial process and procedural rules, royal courts more or less controlled which custom could be invoked in litigation.

Legal professionals at the royal courts did not like bizarre methods of evidence. They loathed the irrational modes of proof such as swearing on the tomb of a saint to rebut the accusation of homicide, or the right of private vengeance.[57] An ordinance of 1270 by Louis IX formalized the procedure of inquest, known as *enquêtes par turbe*. It consisted of proof based on written evidence and witness examination. If the custom was neither disputed nor contested, it formed *coutumes notoires*, and the judge could apply it *sua sponte*, taking notice of it on his own authority; for others, proof by *turbe* was needed.[58] The local inquest involved calling on a group of respectable citizens, typically not fewer than ten, to give a unanimous statement as to the existence of the custom at issue.[59] The replies of the *turbiers* were put into writing and sealed.[60] After the inquiry was made, the judge evaluated the custom's obligatory character, taking into consideration relevant Roman law or written charters, and decided whether to adopt or reject it on a case-by-case basis. The establishment of the custom determined the rights. Some examples from the court record are instructive.

In 1290, the Parlement of Paris heard a dispute between a Jacques Coquin and his brother and brother-in-law, Isambert Coquin and Theobald Mathieu. Jacques claimed the portion belonging to him in the family fiefs by reason of his right of primogeniture, whereas his opponents contended that Jacques must be content, under the custom of the city of Paris, with what his father and mother had given him as an advance at the time of his marriage and that the balance must be divided equally between his brothers and sister. The court wrote: "an inquest

[55] Ibbetson, "Custom in Medieval Law," 160; Peter Stein, *Roman Law in European History* (Cambridge: Cambridge University Press, 1999), 92–93.

[56] Georges Boyer, "La notion d'équité et son rôle dans la jurisprudence des Parlements," in *Mélanges offerts à Jacques Maury*, vol. 2: *Droit comparé: Théorie générale du droit et droit privé* (Paris: Dalloz & Sirey, 1960), 258, reproduced in Georges Boyer, *Mélanges d'histoire du droit occidental* (Paris: Sirey, 1962), vol. 1, 210–35.

[57] Delachenal, *Histoire des avocats au Parlement de Paris*, 249.

[58] Filhol, "La preuve de la coutume"; Pissard, *Essai sur la connaissance et la preuve des coutumes*, 65–74. *Turbe*, from Latin *turba*, means mob or crowd.

[59] Laurent Waelkens, "L'origine de l'enquête par turbe," *Tijdschrift voor Rechtsgeschiedenis* 53 (1985), 337–39. "There is every reason to think that this form of jury derived from the same antecedents as the English jury." Dawson, *The Oracles*, 269.

[60] A specimen of *turbe* deposition from 1397 is provided in Jean Bart, "Transcrire, rédiger, réformer les coutumes," in Laurence Giavarini (ed.), *L'écriture des juristes: XVIe–XVIIIe siècle* (Paris: Classiques Garnier, 2010), 49.

having been made concerning the usage aforesaid and the arguments of the parties understood, it was pronounced by the judgment of our court that in the said fiefs situated outside the limits of the city of Paris the said Jacques shall have his part or portion by reason of his right of primogeniture, according to the custom of the places where the said fiefs are situated."[61]

In a case in 1318, seventeen witnesses of a Salvin Lombard took an oath before the two auditors delegated by the Parlement. The auditors handed them the text of the alleged custom. The witnesses then withdrew and deliberated among them. They returned and told the auditors that they were completely in accord about the custom. Upon unanimous consent, they chose a person to speak on behalf of all the witnesses. The elected reporter answered to the interrogation of the auditors that the custom was notorious and truthful, and that they knew it and had seen it observed several times at the Châtelet of Paris. Then, each person was interviewed separately about his knowledge, and replied *quilibet pro se* (each one for himself) that, for more than twenty years, in several different cases involving several different parties, he had seen the said custom observed notoriously and judged consistently at the Châtelet of Paris. Subsequently, the fourteen witnesses of Jean de Senlis, the other party, were interrogated. They declared themselves to be in discord, not in agreement: only six believed in the veracity of the custom invoked by Jean de Senlis. Finally, the court gave a verdict in favor of Salvin Lombard, writing "the said custom in Lombard to be fully and adequately commendable."[62]

As medieval society grew more complex, it was necessary to identify objective norms dealing with the relations among the people and raise them to the level of stable law.[63] Initially, the proof of custom was distinguished from fact-finding. The king prohibited using *enquêtes par turbe* to prove facts in litigation, which instead was to be established by deposing each witness separately. The proof of custom was undertaken as a group whereas the proof of facts was undertaken individually.[64] But the *turbiers* as witnesses to a custom soon became indistinguishable from witnesses to a fact.[65] Here one sees that custom approximated a popular verdict delivered by the jury. It was the judge, not the fact-finder, who

[61] *Les Olim*, vol. II, 1290 (# 10), 302. The translation is from John P. Dawson, *Comparative Law* (Ann Arbor: University of Michigan, 1937), 64.

[62] *Les Olim*, vol. II, 1318 (# 4), 678–81. This case is reported in Filhol, "La prevue de la coutume."

[63] Peter Stein, "The Civil Law Doctrine of Custom and the Growth of Case Law," in *Scintillae Iuris: Studi in memoria di Gino Gorla* (Milan: Giuffrè, 1994), vol. 1, 371.

[64] Filhol, "La preuve de la coutume," 361. An *arrêt* in *Les Olim* indicates that the proof of custom in the *pays coutumier* required that the votes of the *turbe* be taken as a group, and not individually (vol. III [Part 2], 1317 [# 60], 1147–48); by contrast, an earlier *arrêt* states: "inquiry shall be made by individual witnesses, since the district of Agen is governed by the written law" (vol. II, 1287 [# 6], 268). In the latter case, the finding of the *turbe* concerned the facts, not the law, hence the likely difference. In the *pays coutumier*, the proof of an alleged custom called for two *turbes* in agreement, as required in Roman law and canon law. Bart, "Transcrire, rédiger, réformer les coutumes," 36. *Enquête par turbe* was abolished in 1667.

[65] Fredric L. Cheyette, "Custom, Case Law, and Medieval 'Constitutionalism': A Re-Examination," *Political Science Quarterly* 78 (1963), 384.

determined "what substantive rules would settle the claim on the basis of the facts."[66] The articulation of the evidence was crucial for substantive rules of law to rise, capable of creating and enforcing the rights.[67] The "accumulation of jurisprudential facts" turned private law into a "jurisprudential matter."[68] Civil law vocabularies, categories, and modes of reasoning stimulated the transformation of traditional habits of feudal society into rights and obligations created by state law. These legal vocabularies "would become part of the idea of the modern sovereign state."[69] Customary law declared in the form of written court decisions became an instrument to regulate society.

The writing down of customs began in the late twelfth century in the Mediterranean regions, spreading to northern Europe in the following century. Starting with Normandy, the customs of Vermandois, Orléans, Touraine, Anjou, Poitou, Berry, and Beauvaisis were put into writing. These collections were known as *coutumiers*. The *Grand coutumier de Normandie* (*Summa de legibus*), originally composed in Latin between 1200 and 1245, was translated between 1270 and 1280 by an anonymous author.[70] The appearance of the *coutumiers* coincided with the expansion of royal justice, with the creation of a large number of the offices of *bailli* and *sénéchal*.[71] For practicing lawyers, the proof of custom by *enquête par turbe* was a sorely inadequate and deeply frustrating method. When a claim was disputed and there was no valid written charter supporting the claim, an obvious way to move was to ask whether it had been recognized before.[72] And the obvious way to know whether it had been recognized before was, as Ulpian said, to see whether the court had previously upheld the claim. This is why royal officials and lawyers began compiling court cases and procedures, in order to reduce the burden of local inquests. The *coutume* of Clermont in Beauvaisis was composed by Philippe de Beaumanoir (1247–1296), a royal *bailli*, in 1283.[73] The *coutumiers* were not legal texts but rather manuals lawyers prepared for use in litigation, as a reference material for their own practice.[74]

[66] Cheyette, "Choice of Law in Medieval France," 493.

[67] Robert Jacob, "Beaumanoir versus Révigny: The Two Faces of Customary Law in Philip the Bold's France," in Sarah-Grace Heller and Michelle Reichert (eds.), *Essays on the Poetic and Legal Writings of Philippe de Remy and His Son Philippe de Beaumanoir of Thirteenth-Century France* (Lewiston: Edwin Mellen Press, 2001), 265–67; Jacques Krynen, "Entre science juridique et dirigisme: Le glas médiéval de la coutume," *Cahiers de recherches médiévales* 7 (2000), 174, http://journals.openedition.org/crm/892.

[68] Gouron, "La coutume en France au Moyen Âge," 211.

[69] Cheyette, "Choice of Law in Medieval France," 496.

[70] Ernest-Joseph Tardif (ed.), *Coutumiers de Normandie*, 3 vols. (Rouen, 1881–1903).

[71] Gilissen, *La coutume, Typologie des sources*, 25.

[72] Cheyette, "Choice of Law in Medieval France," 491.

[73] Philippe de Beaumanoir, *Les coutumes de Beauvaisis*, ed. Amédée Salmon, 2 vols. (Paris: A. Picard et fils, 1899–1900); English translation in *The Coutumes de Beauvaisis of Philippe de Beaumanoir*, trans. Frank R. P. Akehurst (Philadelphia: University of Pennsylvania Press, 1992).

[74] Esther Cohen, *The Crossroads of Justice: Law and Culture in Late Medieval France* (Leiden: Brill, 1993), 31.

Some *coutumiers* obtained a quasi-official nature as general or local custom, rendering the *turbe* proceedings superfluous or exceptional. The *Grand coutumier de Normandie* and the *Très ancienne coutume de Bretagne*, written between 1312 and 1325, were such examples.[75] Others, like the *Coutumes de Beaumanoir*, were private works with no official binding force. All these *coutumiers* closely reflected social and intellectual developments of the time.

Medieval Doctrine of Custom

Medieval doctors of law set out on the task of reconciling customs, of Germanic and feudal origins, with Roman law. They were preoccupied with devising the doctrine of legal custom, separate from popular usage. For this purpose, they used analytical tools and concepts of learned law. André Gouron wrote: "If no revival of law at the universities, no customary law."[76] The fact that medieval scholars at the universities attempted to array custom into a system that could measure up to the civil law framework does not mean they were motivated by a desire to resist the advance of Roman law. The traditional belief that customs in France emerged in the twelfth and thirteenth centuries as a popular defense against Roman law no longer holds ground. Far from a hostile reaction, the process was an embracement of the written law, taking place in imitation of its form and in partial reception of its content.[77]

According to the canonists, there were two defining elements required for custom to obtain the force of law: first, repetition by people of the similar act, anchored in time immemorial; and second, *opinio necessitatis*, or popular belief of its binding force. The first criterion of long and repeated usage concerned legitimacy granted by tradition and antiquity. The Roman texts simply talked of a *longa consuetudo*, but medieval doctors, unsatisfied with this imprecision, tried to impose a specific length of time, referring to the rules of prescription. From the end of the twelfth century, the learned doctrine abandoned the notion of time

[75] Both continued to be applied until the official redactions in Brittany (1580) and in Normandy (1583). See M. Planiol (ed.), *Très-ancienne coutume de Bretagne* (Rennes, 1896); Jean-Philippe Lévy, "Les preuves dans la *Très ancienne coutume de Bretagne*," *Annales de Bretagne et des pays de l'Ouest* 59 (1952) 39–59.

[76] "Sans renaissance des droits 'universitaires', point de coutume." Gouron, "La coutume en France au Moyen Âge," 205. See also André Gouron, "Aux origines de l'émergence du droit: Glossateurs et coutumes méridionales (XIIe siècle–milieu du XIIIe siècle)," in Étienne Bravasa, Claude Emeri, and Jean-Louis Seurin (eds.), *Religion, société et politique: Mélanges en hommage à Jacques Ellul* (Paris: Presses universitaires de France, 1983), 255–70.

[77] The writing-down of customs from the thirteenth century served to demonstrate local specificities different from Roman law, but at the same time it was no doubt propelled by a rush to imitate it. Louis Assier-Andrieu, "De l'idéologie à la culture: les géographies coutumières," *Clio@Themis: revue électronique d'histoire du droit* 9 (2015), # 18, note 32. http://www.cliothemis.com/De-l-ideologie-a-la-culture-les.

beyond memory in favor of *diuturnitas*, the passing of a defined period of time, usually ten to forty years.[78]

Early on it was acknowledged that neither repetition nor long use was sufficient to engender a law. Jacques de Révigny (1230–1296) distinguished between *usus* and *consuetudo*.[79] *Usus* was the material element of custom, but it could not create law by itself; to this must be added the moral element of consent, which existed explicitly in a law or statute but only implicitly in custom. What needed to be proved by *turbe* was not the practice itself but *opinio juris*, the belief of the population of a particular locality that it was a binding rule. In their desire to reconfigure custom in imitation of Roman law, medieval professors, known as the Orléans School, borrowed the concept of the consent of the community (*consensus populi*).[80] They devised a theory that the obligatory force of custom came from the tacit consent of social group whose activities it regulated. The central place reserved to *consensus* led the doctrine to focus on substantiating unanimity, or at least acceptance by a majority of the people. The result was an intellectual makeover of custom, transformed from popular usages into imperative norms. Custom was transported from the realm of representing human and social behaviors into the realm of regulating them.[81]

Doctors and Practitioners

By the end of the thirteenth century, the theorization of customary law had been completed. Doctors of law successfully turned custom into a law and a science. The problem was that they were largely indifferent to showing how *opinio necessitatis*, the general conviction of law held by a community, could be ascertained. It was relatively easy to prove the existence of a usage; far more difficult was to prove the obligatory element of popular consent. The notion of consent, or approbation given by the people who observed custom, was postulated as the gist of custom. But what exactly was popular belief and when and how could the tacit consent of the people be known?

According to Robert Jacob, the theory of *opinio necessitatis* is at best circular: medieval authors posed popular consent as an element essential to the birth of a rule, but then presumed that the consent had been acquired as soon as the rule

[78] Jacob, "Beaumanoir versus Révigny," 258; Halpérin, *Profils des mondialisations*, 87.

[79] See Kees Bezemer, "Jacques de Révigny (d. 1296): Roman Law as a Means to Shape French Law," *Clio@Themis, Revue électronique d'histoire du droit* 10 (2016), http://www.cliothemis.com/Jacques-de-Revigny-d-1296-Roman.

[80] André Gouron, "Sur les origines de l'expression 'droit coutumier,'" in *Droit et coutume en France aux XIIe et XIIIe siècles* (Aldershot: Variorum, 1993), 254.

[81] "In privileging the consensual character born out of a prudent and rational behavior, this view approximated custom to a judicial institution of contract, the existence of which was grounded on the expression of will." Laurent Mayali, "La coutume dans la doctrine romaniste au Moyen Âge," in Vanderlinden (ed.), *La coutume/Custom*, vol. 2: *Europe occidentale médiévale et moderne*, 20.

was attested as such.[82] In Jacob's opinion, the validity of *opinio necessitatis* depended in reality less on the assent of the community than on judicial validation and acclamation; otherwise, it would be altogether too vague to have any conceptual value. Jacob argued that Beaumanoir, the author of the authoritative *Coutumes de Beauvaisis*, was unequivocal that court decision in a contested case was the only sure way of proving custom.[83]

> Beaumanoir wrote:
>
> Custom is proved by one of two methods, and the first of these methods is when the custom is generally observed throughout the county, and has been observed for as long as man can remember, without challenge: for example, when a commoner acknowledges a debt, he is commanded to pay it within seven days and seven nights, and the gentleman is given fifteen days; this custom is so clear that I have never seen it challenged. And the other way a custom can be acknowledged and held as a custom is if there has been a dispute and one of the parties cites a custom in his argument, and it is approved in the judgment, as has happened many times in distributions among heirs and in other disputes. And a custom can be adopted [*prouver*] by these two methods, and the count is obliged to uphold this custom and leave it upheld by his vassals so that no one abolishes it. And if the count himself wanted to abolish it or permit it to be abolished, the king should not allow it, for he is supposed to observe and to cause to be observed the customs of his kingdom.[84]

Beaumanoir distinguished between usage and custom in the following terms: "The difference between *coutume* and *usage* is that customs must be observed, but there are certain privileges which would be invalid if someone wanted to bring a suit to challenge them and obtain a judgment on the matter."[85] When the court settled a legal point in contention, its decision, as *res judicata*, was a form of proof, a "new, convenient if contingent, foundation" of custom, which was "another name for *stare decisis*."[86] The test for an approved or notorious custom was

[82] Robert Jacob, "Les coutumiers du XIIIe siècle ont-ils connu la coutume?" in Mireille Mousnier and Jacques Poumarède (eds.), *La coutume au village dans l'Europe médiévale et moderne* (Toulouse: Presses universitaires du Mirail, 2001), 105.

[83] Jacob, "Beaumanoir versus Révigny," 256. See also Jean-Marie Carbasse, "Philippe de Beaumanoir, Coutumes de Beauvaisis," *Revue d'histoire des Facultés de droit et la science juridique* 22 (2002), 135–54.

[84] *Les coutumes de Beauvaisis*, ed. Salmon, ch. 24, no. 683, vol. 1, 346–47. The English translation is from *The Coutumes de Beauvaisis*, trans. Akehurst, 249.

[85] *Les coutumes de Beauvaisis*, ed. Salmon, ch. 24, no. 684, vol. 1, 347. The word "usages" at this time corresponded to "privileges" in modern English.

[86] Jacob, "Beaumanoir versus Révigny," 259. *Stare decisis* is a legal principle that rules laid down in previous judicial decisions must be followed unless they are against the ordinary principles of justice.

whether it had been upheld in prior court decisions.[87] A single judgment could create custom, but repeated judgments in the positive in similar matters reinforced the validity of the customary rule invoked by the party.[88] Along the same line, if the judge decided in a repeated manner that the proof of custom was not satisfactorily presented, the rule would have difficulty surviving.[89] A specific practice might continue its existence in society, but it could no longer be invoked in litigation. As seen earlier, judicial decision was a form of law, for which no evidence was required. For Beaumanoir, memory only mattered when one was to attest to an absence in everyone's recollection of a given point in order to challenge it in an adversarial lawsuit.[90] A past judgment, not the perception of *consensus populi*, proved that there was tacit consent, and the judge was required to follow it.

Here, one notes the distance between the theory of custom articulated by doctors at the universities and the opinion of custom held by legal practitioners. The *coutumiers* in the thirteenth century were mostly written by lawyers and royal officials, not by professors of law. Those authors wrote down contemporary practices, rather than formulating legal principles or recording the rules handed down from the past. But the prestige of the medieval doctors was seemingly invincible. Révigny stated: "I affirm that an act of judgment is not necessary. In fact, it is the tacit consent of the people that creates a custom."[91] Eventually the views of the "school men" prevailed over those of the practitioners. Yet they left a thick layer of uncertainty surrounding the notion of custom.[92]

Custom and Reason

Custom in conformity with the law (*consuetudo secundum legem* or *praeter legem*) was widely accepted, but custom contrary to the law (*contra legem*) was a major stumbling block for doctrinal authors. A partial solution was found when the canonists began to require that custom conform to reason (*ratio*).[93] The conflation of reason and custom has a long history in Europe's past. Church law introduced

[87] In 1310, the Parlement of Paris decreed that "concerning notorious customs, and those proposed as notorious, the said Prévôt [of Paris] shall inform himself, and they shall have what effect they can and should; and let other customs similarly proposed henceforward [shall] be received for proof so far as they are reasonable." *Les Olim*, vol. III (Part 2), 1310 (# 42), 547. Translation is from Dawson, *Comparative Law*, 66.

[88] Jacob, "Beaumanoir versus Révigny," 259.

[89] Régine Beauthier and Pierre-Olivier de Broux, "Un regard historien: Sources du droit, sources du pouvoir?" in Isabelle Hachez et al. (eds.), *Les sources du droit revisitées*, vol. 4: *Théorie des sources du droit* (Brussels: Facultés universitaires St. Louis, 2012), 724.

[90] The memory of a rule having never been challenged is pertinent only when there is a point in controversy. Jacob, "Beaumanoir versus Révigny," 258–59.

[91] Laurent Waelkens, *La théorie de la coutume chez Jacques de Révigny: Édition et analyse de sa répétition sur loi De quibus (D. 1, 3, 32)* (Leiden: Brill, 1984), 488.

[92] Jacob, "Beaumanoir versus Révigny," 269.

[93] Krynen, "Entre science juridique et dirigisme," 176–77; Gilissen, *La coutume*, Typologie des sources, 30–31; Ibbetson, "Custom in Medieval Law," 158.

into custom a naturalist vision of the reasonableness and necessity of the usage.[94] Both Roman law and canon law required that custom be not contrary to reason. While the civilians did not contend that custom's inconformity to reason would lead to its invalidation, the canonists subjected the authority of customary law to strict ethical criteria, in addition to the consent of the relevant community. Long usage and acceptance by the people were no longer sufficient to presume custom's normative value. Canon law scholars argued that custom must not contradict the Truth—the Holy Scripture—and reason. It was equated with *usus rationabilis*.[95] Custom was against reason when it contradicted religious teaching, church law, civil law, good morals, and so on. Customary and natural laws were thus blended into a peculiar concoction.

The theory of custom must be understood in the context of the hierarchical structure of ecclesiastical society, in particular the growing affirmation of pontifical sovereignty. The canonists insisted on the necessity of *permissio*, express or tacit, by the pope for any norm to be valid. The doctrinal tendency to perceive the normativity of custom only when it was supported by superior values opened the door to the intervention of the *princeps*, who was supposedly the ultimate guardian of those values. The king's right to abolish bad custom (*malae consuetudines*) had been recognized without challenge from as early as the eleventh century.[96] Custom's subordination to sovereign commandment meant it came under political control.[97] As judges took up the task of classifying customary rules as odious or favorable and rejected local customs that did not fit their ideals of justice, a distinct realm of judicial latitude was created.[98] The authority of *jus commune* was precisely that it was just. The principles of Roman law legitimated political power and prevented its degeneration into tyranny. Judges were justified in refusing to apply customs deemed contrary to *ratio* or equity.[99] A custom judged contrary to the truth, reason, law, legislation, or also public utility or natural equity could be declared *mala consuetudo* and abrogated.[100] Having set out from the Roman law notion of consent, church law doctors came to affirm the crown's authority over custom.

[94] Bederman, *Custom as a Source of Law*, 173.

[95] Krynen, "Entre science juridique et dirigisme," 176. In the *Summa Theologica*, Thomas Aquinas stated that a *lex* against *ratio* was properly not law but "a perversion of law," an expression of a tyrannical will; ergo custom that was not reasonable was not valid. Cited from ibid., 178.

[96] François Olivier-Martin, "Le roi de France et les mauvaises coutumes au Moyen Âge," *Zeitschrift der Savigny-Stiftung für Rechtsgeschichte. Germanistische Abtheilung* 58 (1938), 108–37; Stephen D. White, "Bad Custom (*malae consuetudines*) in Eleventh-Century France," in Andersen and Münster-Swendsen (eds.), *Custom*, 51–66.

[97] Krynen, "Entre science juridique et dirigisme," 179–80; Albert Rigaudière, "Loi et État dans la France du bas Moyen Âge," in Noël Coulet and Jean-Philippe Genet (eds.), *L'État moderne: Le droit, l'espace et les formes de l'État, actes du colloque tenu à la Baume, 11–12 octobre 1984* (Paris: Éditions du CNRS, 1990), 38.

[98] Jacob, "La coutume, les mœurs et le rite," 151.

[99] Watson, "The Evolution of Law: Continued." 556.

[100] Krynen, "Entre science juridique et dirigisme," 180.

The medieval doctrine maintained its authority, continuing all the way into the nineteenth-century positivism that highlighted the authority of the sovereign to make law. Around this time, a new concept of popular consent in custom emerged in Germany, in the form of the work of Savigny. The historiography of Savigny and the Historical School exhibited a certain romanticization of custom as an autonomous mode of social regulation, but it above all stressed a literary heritage of Roman law. To Savigny, legal history meant "updating this cultural tradition" of the reception of Roman law.[101] His model was the humanist Hugues Doneau (Donellus) (1527–1591), who sought to return Roman law to its original form. Both regarded Roman law as a supranational law.

2. Theories and Debates

Savigny's famous pamphlet *Vom Beruf unserer Zeit für Gesetzgebung und Rechtswissenschaft* was published in 1814, followed by his introductory essay to the inaugural volume of the *Zeitschrift für geschichtliche Rechtswissenschaft* in 1815.[102] In them, he powerfully attacked the formalist conception of law and judicial practice that had dominated legal science in his time. He objected to the proposal made by Anton F. J. Thibaut (1772–1840) to create a common civil code for all German states on the model of the French code. If the creation of a code had to be done, argued Savigny, it would need to be based not on natural law—with its "infinite arrogance"—but on *jus commune*, that is, Roman law deeply rooted in popular customs in Germany.[103] He strived to free Roman law from the rigid legislative rationalism embedded in natural law and the Enlightenment.

The debate between the Germanists and the Romanists pit the historical school of law against the positivist school headed by John Austin (1790–1859). The positivists argued that law drew its legal force from approval by the legislator and was thus equated with the commands of the sovereign.[104] In this theory, the sources of

[101] Werner Gephart, *Law, Culture, and Society: Max Weber's Comparative Cultural Sociology of Law*, Recht als Kultur 7 (Frankfurt am Main: Vittorio Klostermann, 2015), 33.

[102] Friedrich Carl von Savigny, *Of the Vocation of Our Age for Legislation and Jurisprudence*, trans. Abraham Hayward (London: Littlewood and Co., 1831). See Andreas Rahmatian, "Friedrich Carl von Savigny's *Beruf* and *Volksgeistlehre*," *Journal of Legal History* 28 (2007), 1–29.

[103] For a juxtaposition of the French *civilisation* and the German *Kultur*, see Helge Dedek, "When Law Became Cultivated: 'European Legal Culture' between *Kultur* and Civilization," in Geneviève Helleringer (ed.), *Towards a European Legal Culture* (Munich: Beck, 2014), 351–74.

[104] John Austin, *The Province of Jurisprudence Determined* (London: Murray, 1832). Positivist scholars refused to recognize a source of law other than legislation; custom had legal force only when it was explicitly allowed in the law. This theory, known as the "recognition theory" (*Gestattungstheorie*), linked custom to the authority of the state. The German legal science revolted against the recognition theory, proposing a theory known as the "conviction theory" (*Überzeugungstheorie*). This latter view emphasizes the nature of customary law as an explicit and spontaneous expression of the spirit of the people and argued the *opinio juris* of custom existed prior to recognition or implementation by any institutions. Alf Ross, *On Law and Justice* (London: Stevens, 1958), 106; Alf Ross, *Theorie der*

law other than the codes—custom, scholarship, case law, or even natural law—were given only secondary importance.[105] Savigny and his disciples maintained, on the contrary, that law inhered in the consciousness of the populace (*Volksbewusstsein*) and that custom was the expression of this popular persuasion.[106] Rejecting legal positivism, they popularized the idea of custom as the epitome of immutable justice, self-sufficient in theory and practice. Savigny's students Georg Friedrich Puchta and Georg Beseler each expounded on custom and jurists' role in developing it.[107] The tenets of the Historical School, a mix of romantic, democratic, and nationalist agenda and its understanding of medieval customary law had a complex influence on French national historiography.

Henri Klimrath (1807–1837) was an early French convert to the Historical School. He was among those historians who cherished the liberal and democratic elements of customary law, objecting to the dogmatic legal formalism and the purely grammatical mode of the exegetical school.[108] He embraced the notion of the mythical origin of custom; the view of custom as something that grew from within society, emanating from the agreement of the people, conferred innate superiority on it. A general aversion to the law imposed from above, not to mention from outside, was pervasive. Klimrath viewed the feudal period, from 888 to 1461, as the origin of the matrix of French law, *la coutume*. In 1837, he created the first cartography of *la France coutumière*, which classified and demarcated the boundaries of general customs. This map remains an excellent representation of the mosaic of jurisdictional divisions in old France.[109]

From the last quarter of the nineteenth century, French jurists advocated a shift in legal philosophy away from a speculative and mechanical approach toward rational and functional jurisprudence. François Gény (1861–1959) was one of the most forceful advocates of customary law against literal interpretation of the Civil

Rechtsquellen: Ein Beitrag zur Theorie des positiven Rechts auf Grundlage dogmenhistorischer Untersuchungen. Akademische Abhandlung (Leipzig: Linz, 1929), 430–37.

[105] Stein, *Roman Law in European History*, 116–23.

[106] Friedrich Carl von Savigny, *System des heutigen römischen Rechts* (Berlin: Veit, 1840–1849).

[107] Georg Friedrich Puchta, *Das Gewohnheitsrecht: erster und zweiter Teil* (Erlangen, 1828–1837); Georg Beseler, *Volksrecht und Juristenrecht* (Leipzig: Weldmann, 1843). See Hans-Peter Haferkamp, "The Science of Private Law and the State in Nineteenth Century Germany," *American Journal of Comparative Law* 56 (2008), 667–89.

[108] See Jacques Poumarède, "Défense et illustration de la coutume au temps de l'exégèse: Les débuts de l'école française du droit historique," in Claude Journès (ed.), *La coutume et la loi: Études d'un conflit* (Lyon: Presses universitaires de Lyon, 1986), 95–112; Philippe Rémy, "Le rôle de l'exégèse dans l'enseignement du droit au XIXe siècle," *Annales d'histoire des facultés de droit* 2 (1985), 92–105.

[109] See Klimrath's essay, "Études sur les coutumes," in *Travaux sur l'histoire*, vol. 2, 133–338, and the accompanying map. Jean Hilaire has pointed out that Klimrath's map does not accurately reflect the variations in notarial practices which Hilaire believes would be a better indicator of the delimitations of customs. Hilaire, *La vie du droit*, 159. See also Jean Hilaire, "Coutumes et droit écrit: Recherche d'une limite," *Mémoires de la Société pour l'histoire du droit et des institutions des anciens pays bourguignons, comtois et romands* 40 (1983), 153–75. See the map of the geographical groups of succession practices in the north of France in Jean Yver, *Égalité entre héritiers et exclusion des enfants dotés: Essai de géographie coutumière* (Paris: Sirey, 1966).

Code.[110] According to Gény, the need to coordinate competing interests in society and maintain legal stability made it essential to recognize sources of law other than statutes. The inevitable lacunae and obsolescence of statutes over time justified the function of custom as a key source of law. He argued that custom, endowed with the material psychological element of *opinio necessitatis seu juris*—the conviction in the minds of those who observed it because it was obligatory—was fully on the same foothold as the law. To become an imperative norm, a usage must amount to the exercise of a right by those who practiced it and, for that purpose, not just an element of will but *opinio juris*, "truly specific" of genuine custom, was required.[111] But Gény's doctrine was also accompanied by the recognition of legislation, justice, and law, those instruments that made authority possible and effective. Customary law did not have a universal character because it originated in a distinct legal community.[112] Gény adopted the idea of Édouard Lambert (1866–1947), who said that the only way *opinio necessitatis* could be recognized was through jurisprudence.[113] Gény thus argued in favor of granting jurisprudence the force of customary law, which should be viewed as a formal source of law, capable of filling the gaps in legislation.[114]

According to Gény, the Historical School's supposition of a romantic and mysterious *opinio juris* was as much a fiction as the exegetical school's hypothesis of tacit approval of custom by the legislator. In his opinion, the Historical School attempted a purely subjective conception of customary law for no specific gains; such an abstract and idealistic concept not only lacked utility but also risked "denaturizing" the custom's "objective reality."[115] Raymond Saleilles (1855–1912)

[110] François Gény, *Méthode d'interprétation et sources en droit privé positif: Essai critique* (Paris: Librairie générale de droit et de jurisprudence, 1932 [1899]).

[111] Ibid., vol. 1, ch. 110, 320. For Gény's view of custom from a comparative perspective, see Marie Seong-Hak Kim, "La coutume et la raison comme sources de droit dans la première moitié de l'ère Meiji," in Beatrice Jaluzot (ed.), *Droit japonais, droit français, Quel dialogue?* (Geneva: Schulthess, 2014), 57–77.

[112] Gény, *Méthode d'interprétation*, vol. 1, ch. 110, 323.

[113] Édouard Lambert, *La fonction du droit civil comparé* (Paris: V. Girard & E. Brière, 1903); Ourliac, "Réflexions sur l'origine de la coutume," 342; Jacob, "Les coutumiers du XIIIe siècle," 104.

[114] Gény, *Méthode d'interprétation*, vol. 2, ch. 183, 222. "Jurisprudence is, in our modern times, the only truly fertile, and in any case the most frequent, occasion to form legal custom, especially general custom. In fact, once established, on a certain point, jurisprudence, with its uncontestable authority, at least in fact, and also because of the continuity and consistency of our extrajudicial practice, frequently determines the practices in harmony with its tendencies. . . . When the practices suggested [by jurisprudence] have taken roots through long usages, we have all the elements of a true legal custom . . . of which the jurisprudence represents the point of departure and the essential determinant." Ibid., vol. 1, ch. 116, 347. But he cautioned: "it is important to note that jurisprudence does not here constitute a source of independent law, nor even a custom *sui generis*. In these hypotheses, it functions only as a force of propulsion of the custom, but a propeller which is so indispensable, and of such inevitable effects in our social and political condition, that a transposition of ideas and even a simplification of the formula would suffice to bring to it all the credit for the creation of which it is in effect the capital instrument." Ibid., vol. 2, ch. 149, 51. For Gény's view of jurisprudence, see Mitchel de S.-O.-L'E. Lasser, *Judicial Deliberations: A Comparative Analysis of Judicial Transparency and Legitimacy* (Oxford: Oxford University Press, 2009), 170–74.

[115] Gény, *Méthode d'interprétation*, vol. 1, ch. 116, 347.

argued that jurists, following Savigny, were inclined to rid judicial opinions of any appearance that they even remotely relied on the universal concepts of reason, equity, and justice. In interpreting law, however, one must consider utility; justice and social utility dictate that a judge use all legitimate resources when he decides, and the judge must be free to search for a rule on which to base his decision.[116] For Max Weber (1864–1920), the weakness of the Savigny School came from the fact that it placed too much, not too little, emphasis on formal reason.[117] Weber said that the Historical School's belief in Roman law as a timeless and universal logic impeded its practical adaptation to the present. In his opinion, the Roman law *Pandect* school opposed rationalism and natural law but ended up reaffirming them, conditioned within its own Romanist framework.

Be that as it may, Gény and his colleagues helped restore custom on the central stage of law.[118] Gény's theory prompted the reexamination of the history of custom in France. Not all his contemporaries were convinced, to be sure. Adhémar Esmein argued that recognizing custom as law would be like turning the clock backward, only to create uncertainty and instability in law, not to mention violating the principle of the separation of powers.[119] For him, the formation of custom had practically ceased by the end of the sixteenth century, and custom since then became tightly merged into the state law hierarchy. Esmein cautioned about the tendency among historians to "confuse an opinion that inspires the law with the authority that enacts it."[120]

Droit Commun de France

The twentieth-century debate over custom was centered on *droit commun* in France. In the prologue of his *Coutumes de Beauvaisis*, Beaumanoir mentioned "droit commun" several times.[121] Historians were puzzled about what this term meant. They wondered what Beaumanoir's sources were, because it seemed

[116] Raymond Saleilles, "École historique et droit naturel d'après quelques ouvrages récents," *Revue trimestrielle de droit civil* 1 (1902), 80–112.

[117] Savigny's search for a pure historical Roman law was susceptible to becoming an ahistorical dogmatic study. For Savigny's influence on Max Weber, see Gephart, *Law, Culture, and Society*, 132–35.

[118] "Although custom seems to have only a narrow role in our social organization," Gény stated, "it still retains its indispensable productive force and, supported by authorities or tradition, which are only its rudimentary elements, it still reserves an important place in our civilization." Gény, *Méthode d'interprétation*, vol. 2, ch. 183, 222.

[119] Adhémar Esmein, "La coutume doit-elle être reconnue comme source du droit civil français?" *Extrait du Bulletin de la Société d'études législatives* (Paris: Arthur Rousseau, 1905).

[120] Adhémar Esmein, *Eléments de droit constitutionnel français et comparé*, 6th ed. (Paris: Recueil Sirey, 1914), 44.

[121] Beaumanoir, *Les coutumes de Beauvaisis*, ed. Salmon, vol. 1, 4 (no. 6): "le droit qui est communs à tous ou roiaume de France" (the law which is common to all the kingdom of France). It goes without saying that the meaning of the term "common law" here is not the same as the one in American law, the judge-made law.

impossible to prove any direct textual borrowing either from a Roman or canonical compilation or the doctrine of the commentators.[122] P. Van Wetter believed that the *droit commun* in Beaumanoir indicated Roman law that had been incorporated into custom or royal ordinances.[123] Others asserted, on the contrary, that it meant general rules of French customs.[124] In 1960, Pierre Petot argued that compilers of French *coutumiers*, including Beaumanoir, conceived the idea of the existence of a *droit commun*, rules common in the various customary regions of France, as opposed to the universalist pretention of the university scholars adhering to Roman law.[125] According to Petot, Beaumanoir referred to general rules upheld by the law courts, apart from mere privileges. He thus rekindled the old debate, popularizing the belief that there existed a common core of substantive principles—constituting a unity—in seemingly disparate local customs in France, which were distinct from Roman law as *jus commune*. The debate continued unabated, and the first decade of the twenty-first century witnessed a full-blown scholarly discussion, touching on almost all key aspects of medieval French law, including the role of the state in private law. It deserves analysis in detail.

In an article published in 2007 and 2008, André Castaldo disputed the views of Gérard Giordanengo and Jacques Krynen that Roman law, not custom, was the *droit commun* in the thirteenth century.[126] In their respective works, Giordanengo and Krynen asserted that custom as a body of authoritative legal principles was created by jurists who borrowed Roman law principles and terminologies. The jurists of the time considered the law of the Compilations of Justinian "la raison écrite et le droit commun de la France," stated Giordanengo, "while denying, understandably, that its use could mean submission to the Empire."[127] Krynen

[122] Jacob, "Philippe de Beaumanoir et les clercs," 165.

[123] P. van Wetter, "Le droit romain et Beaumanoir," in Walther Hörmann (ed.), *Mélanges Fitting* (Aalen: Scientia, 1969 [1907]), vol. 2, 534–82. Salmon's Note 1 in *Les coutumes de Beauvaisis*, 4, indicates that the debate dated from the seventeenth century with Thomas de la Thaumassière (1631–1702).

[124] For a brief reference to various opinions, see "Introduction" in *The Coutumes de Beauvaisis*, trans. Akehurst, xxiii.

[125] Pierre Petot, "Le droit commun en France selon les coutumiers," *Revue historique de droit français et étranger* 37 (1960), 412–29.

[126] André Castaldo, "Pouvoir royal, droit savant et droit commun coutumier dans la France du Moyen Âge: Le roi est-il le maître du droit privé, via le droit romain? À propos de vues nouvelles I," *Droits* 46 (2007), 117–58; André Castaldo, "Pouvoir royal, droit savant et droit commun coutumier dans la France du Moyen Âge: Le droit romain est-il le droit commun? À propos de vues nouvelles II," *Droits* 47 (2008), 173–48. See Giordanengo's rebuttal, "Roma nobilis, orbis et domina. Réponse à un contradicteur," *Revue historique de droit français et étranger* 88 (2010), 91–150. Krynen did not respond directly. His case was represented in part in Jacob, "Philippe de Beaumanoir et les clercs." The debate is discussed in Nicola Warembourg, "La notion de 'droit commun' dans l'Ancienne France coutumière: Point d'étape," *GLOSSAE. European Journal of Legal History* 13 (2016), 670–84. The debate is briefly referenced in Ada-Maria Kuskowski, "The Development of Written Custom in England and in France: A Comparative Perspective," in Richard W Kaeuper, Paul Dingman, and Peter Sposato (eds.), *Law, Governance, and Justice: New Views on Medieval Constitutionalism* (Leiden: Brill, 2013), 109–10.

[127] Gérard Giordanengo, "*Jus commune* et 'droit commun' en France du XIIIe au XVe siècle," in Jacques Krynen (ed.), *Droit romain, jus civile, et droit français* (Toulouse: Presses de l'Université des

argued Roman law was the veritable source of positive law in the Middle Ages: all laws of local origin were read against Roman law and, in the absence of particular applicable provisions in custom, Roman law applied directly in its quality as *droit commun*.[128] For Krynen, the medieval doctrine of *jus commune* brought a legal Romanization of the kingdom in the northern provinces.[129] He stressed that customary law did not emerge spontaneously but only as a result of judicial precedents backed up by royal authority.[130] In Castaldo's opinion, on the other hand, the influence of Roman law on medieval practitioners was unduly exaggerated by admirers of learned law when, in reality, thirteenth-century authors fully recognized the presence of general custom.

One central issue of contention was the role of the crown and the courts in the emergence of customary law. Krynen brought into relief the nexus between *droit privé* and the construction of the medieval and early modern monarchies: the king had the duty and power to abolish *mauvaises coutumes* and the "abolition of bad customs, concession of customs, and legislation of private law, all these demonstrate that the monarchy was very much mindful of the politics of law."[131] Castaldo demurred. For him, those "bad customs" modified by the king and his judges dealt merely with the "'*privilegia, libertates et consuetudines*' of the churches, corps, and cities," and therefore they did not conclusively prove that the king controlled *droit privé*.[132] The gist of the differences between the two historians seems to lie in the question as to whether the king, in organizing a state, needed to intervene in private law. Put differently, was the crown's recognition of custom an integral part of the affairs of politics and royal sovereignty? Broadly speaking, those who argue that written private law was a key instrument of the Capetian state seem to embrace the general tenets of positivism.

Castaldo was more skeptical than Krynen about the power of the Parlement of Paris in controlling custom. It is commonly assumed that the Parlement kept a

sciences sociales de Toulouse, 1999), 233; Gérard Giordanengo, "Le pouvoir législatif du roi de France (XIe–XIIIe siècle): Travaux récents et hypothèses de recherche," *Bibliothèque de l'École des chartes* 147 (1989), 283–310.

[128] Jacques Krynen, "Le droit romain 'droit commun de la France,'" *Droits: Revue française de théorie, de philosophie et de cultures juridiques* 38 (2003), 21–35.

[129] Ibid., 23. "No custom of any *pays coutumier* escapes the influence of the learned law." Krynen, "Entre science juridique et dirigisme," 186.

[130] Jacques Krynen, "Voluntas domini regis in suo regno facit ius: Le roi de France et la coutume," in Aquilino Iglesia Ferreirós (ed.), *El dret comú I Catalunya* (Barcelona: Fundació Noguera, 1998), 59–89; translated into English as "The Absolute Monarchy and the French Unification of Private Rights," in Julius Kirshner and Laurent Mayali (eds.), *Privileges and Rights of Citizenship: Law and the Juridical Construction of Civil Society* (Berkeley: Robbins Collection, 2002), 27–55.

[131] Krynen, "Voluntas domini regis," 70. In a similar opinion, Rigaudière argued that royal judges' power to declare the law in contentious private cases came from the king's power to make law. Albert Rigaudière, "Législation royale et construction de l'État dans la France du XIIIe siècle," in André Gouron and Albert Rigaudière (eds.), *Renaissance du pouvoir législatif et genèse de l'État* (Montpellier: Société d'histoire du droit et des institutions des anciens pays de droit écrit, 1988), 205.

[132] Castaldo, "Pouvoir royal [I]," 137.

tight grip on the contents of custom through appeals, as it could exercise censure on the lower court judges.[133] Krynen stated: "At a time when judicial action was not always categorically distinguished from legislative action, the *parlementaires* could legitimately consider that they legislated by means of jurisprudence. And it is significant that they themselves raised to the level of law the authority of the *chose jugée* in customary matters."[134] According to Castaldo, however, the judge simply "states its existence"; it was "for the judge to say if custom exists; but the judgment does not create a custom."[135] He continued: "it is not the Parlement that declares such and such custom 'unreasonable,' *proprio motu*, but the party (ordinarily the defendant) who demands that the judge see to it; if one party demonstrates custom, the court only refuses the opponent the right to bring up again the proof of the existence of that custom."[136] In other words, the judge "*reconnaît*," not "*fait*," *la coutume*; the judge is its "*révélateur*," not its "*auteur*."[137] Besides, Castaldo pointed out, the Parlement's role in unifying jurisprudence by means of appeals was mostly restricted to procedural, not substantive, matters.[138]

Krynen argued that between the thirteenth and fifteenth centuries "ample matters regulating the relations among private individuals fell under the control of legislation."[139] His broad conception of the political acts of the crown led him to downplay the opinion that the kings of France abstained from the domain of private law. He thus declared: "the non-intervention of the central power in the sphere of *droit privé* is a myth."[140] Castaldo disagreed. The king and his judges

[133] "Through the game of appeal, in effect, the Parlement really has customary law in its palm"; its control shapes in two stages, first "the determination of the applicable custom," and next "the application of custom thus determined." Jean Hilaire, "La procédure civile et l'influence de l'État autour de l'appel," in Jacques Krynen and Albert Rigaudière (eds.), *Droits savants et pratiques françaises du pouvoir (XIe–XVe siècle)* (Bordeaux: Presses universitaires de Bordeaux, 1992), 152. See also Jean Hilaire, "Le roi et nous. Procédure et genèse de l'État aux XIIIème et XIVème siècles," *Histoire de la justice* 5 (1992), 3–18.

[134] Krynen, "Voluntas domini regis," 74–75.

[135] Castaldo, "Pouvoir royal [I]," 153, citing Paul Ourliac and Henri Gilles, *La période post-classique (1378–1500)*, vol. 1: *La problématique de l'époque, les sources* (vol. 13 of *Histoire du droit et des institutions de l'Église en Occident*) (Paris: Éditions Cujas, 1971), 78.

[136] Castaldo, "Pouvoir royal [I]," 156. "*Proprio motu*" means "by one's own motion," to wit, an official act taken without a formal request from another party. It is the same concept as *sua sponte*.

[137] Ibid., 154–55. Castaldo cited John Gilissen who stated that, because custom is sanctioned mostly by judicial authority, "one has often affirmed that custom is not definitely established until from the moment where the judges note it and apply it. But this jurisprudential confirmation is not required for the group to feel and accept the manner of behavior as obligatory, that is, as the rule of law." Gilissen, *La coutume*, Typologie des sources, 25.

[138] Castaldo, "Pouvoir royal [I]," 153. Castaldo claimed there was no evidence in the records of the Parlement of Paris that the term *jus commune* referred to Roman law.

[139] Krynen, "Voluntas domini regis," 69. The king "est tenus à garder et a fere garder les coustumes de son roiaume" (is supposed to observe and to cause to be observed the customs of his kingdom), from Beaumanoir, *Coutumes du Beauvaisis*, ch. 24 (no. 683). For Krynen, Beaumanoir likely meant by "garder" protection as well as guidance (*la tutelle*). Krynen, "Voluntas domini regis," 66. For Castaldo, by contrast, "garder" in this chapter meant "conserver" and "sauvegarder," different from "la tutelle." Castaldo, "Pouvoir royal [I]," 134, note 5.

[140] Krynen, "Voluntas domini regis," 63.

were mainly preoccupied with questions of public power, and their incursions in private law were "very circumscribed" and were "of low magnitude."[141] Castaldo admitted "controlling the procedure is truly an act of sovereignty, which attests to the royal concerns about organizing the Parlement and improving its procedure," but stressed "penal procedure has nothing to do with private law." Castaldo faulted Krynen for "abusing the perimeter of private law" by including procedure, methods of proof, penal matters, and all these things, in the realm of private law.[142]

Disagreement between these two scholars thus revolved around the difference between substantive (determining rights and duties through fact and law) and procedural (enforcing substantive rules) law, and more broadly the difference between public and private law. Of course, where the precise divide lies between procedural and substantive rules is never an easy question, even more so in the medieval times with no taxonomy of legal categories. It suffices to recall that since classical times the spread of law from the center proceeded by the means of separating between procedural and substantive rules and effecting a sort of compromise between the two.[143] The medieval monarchies negotiated with local powers, as the royal government agreed to honor their customary rights but required that the proof of custom take place following the procedures laid down by the center.

Private Law and Political Power

According to Krynen, the belief that *voluntas populi* alone was sufficient for creating law is overly simplistic, because it disregards the element of power or the will of the sovereign. Robert Jacob shares a similar opinion. For Jacob, the idea that every society has law in the form of spontaneous, autonomous custom has unfairly diminished the influence of Roman law in doctrine and also placed inadequate emphasis on the role of the king and his judges in the development of

[141] Castaldo, "Pouvoir royal [I]," 140. Castaldo cites Gouron that, when the formula "nonobstant toute coutume contraire" made its appearance in the fourteenth century, it "only rarely concerns civil law of customary elaboration."

[142] Castaldo, "Pouvoir royal [I]," 140–42.

[143] James Q. Whitman, "Western Legal Imperialism: Thinking about the Deep Historical Roots," *Theoretical Inquiries in Law* 10 (2009), 328. A similar method, which Whitman called "the grand bargain," was used during the time of European expansion to the Hispanic New World from the sixteenth century and also colonial imperialism in the nineteenth and twentieth centuries. The native litigants who flocked to the pluralistic colonial courts were, unbeknownst to them, part of a process for creating a hierarchical order of legal pluralism. See Lauren A. Benton, *Law and Colonial Cultures: Legal Regimes in World History 1400–1900* (Cambridge: Cambridge University Press, 2002). For comparison of colonial customary law policies, see Kim, *Law and Custom in Korea*, 235–49; Marie Seong-Hak Kim, "Can There Be Good Colonial Law?: Korean Law and Jurisprudence under Japanese Rule Revisited," in Marie Seong-Hak Kim (ed.), *The Spirit of Korean Law: Korean Legal History in Context* (Leiden: Brill Nijhoff, 2016), 129–54 (comparing the Dutch and the Japanese colonial law policies).

custom.[144] Jacob argues that, in reality, the notion of *consensus populi* was a fiction put forth by jurists who used Roman terms to show that the kings of France or England ruled with the agreement of their people and that their laws conformed to the customs of the people. The French king had reason to want to avoid the perception that he ignored or changed custom at will.[145] As the "guardian of custom," the crown acknowledged that its power was founded on popular agreement.[146] Historians' reluctance to acknowledge these political implications and their obsessive focus instead on autonomous custom perpetuated the "enigma of popular adhesion."[147] It has caused legal historiography to evade the real question of how custom became a legal norm, concluded Jacob.

Judges had broad power over custom. They could authorize the parties to prove custom, or they could decide that no proof was necessary; they could declare that the demonstration of the proof was insufficient and refuse to apply the custom. With the techniques of proof at its disposal, the court could reject ancient usages under the cover of respecting procedural rules.[148] Krynen thus stressed "the absolute liberty of maneuver" of judges, who were free from "the norms whatever they are."[149] For Castaldo, however, the affirmation or rejection of custom by judges on specific issues always had limitations. He reminded readers that, even where the "written law" was the source of the law, it was received only as a custom.[150] The demarcation between the *pays coutumier* and *pays de droit écrit* in the thirteenth and fourteenth centuries was far from clear. When a case arose in a border area like Auvergne, the situation could be quite complicated. The sources of law in *pays de droit écrit* were not evident ipso facto and were far from identical among them, according to Castaldo, so the content of *droit écrit*, as a *coutume générale* specific to the *pays*, had to be verified in individual cases. The Parlement of Paris always wanted to be certain about the way in which written law had been "digested" in the form of custom. Thus judges, whether in the customary law or in the written law regions, encountered the common questions of the choice of law problem. Answering this "truly prejudicial (*préjudicielle*) question" put a limit on judicial discretion, argued Castaldo.[151]

[144] Jacob, "Les coutumiers du XIIIe siècle," 103–105; Giordanengo, "Jus commune et droit commun," 229–30.

[145] It has been argued that Roman constitutional law was far more favorable to local privileges and immunities than the common law of England. Henshall, "Early Modern Absolutism," 51.

[146] Hilaire, "La France méridionale."

[147] Jacob, "Les coutumiers du XIIIe siècle," 104–105.

[148] Cheyette, "Choice of Law in Medieval France," 488.

[149] Krynen, "Voluntas domini regis," 74.

[150] Castaldo, "Pouvoir royal [II]," 217–19.

[151] Castaldo, "Droit coutumier et droit écrit," 172. There was always a question as to "the hierarchy between *le droit écrit* as *coutume générale* of the *pays* and la *coutume locale*" (citing Jean Hilaire). The lawsuit from Auvergne analyzed by Castaldo concerned the legal force of a *transaction*, which was made orally without being put in writing although the parties had agreed they would be bound by written instruments only. Should the party be allowed to bring the proof of custom by witnesses that conventions in such cases could still be validated? The Parlement in the case at hand decided in the positive. Roman law recognized the validity of oral *transactio*. Castaldo, "Droit coutumier et droit écrit," 177.

How can one appraise these different opinions? It would be helpful to keep in mind that judicial texts from this time period are seldom amenable to concrete conclusions; the parties only vaguely invoked the jurisprudence of the court before which the action was brought. During the time of Beaumanoir, actual usage may have been transformed into binding custom extrajudicially, without having been affirmed by judicial decrees. Still, repeated judicial decisions most often served as a point of affirmation, or crystallization, of the accepted conduct of the people. The *coutumiers* like Beaumanoir's were the work of jurists who had been invariably imbued with learned law. The Roman elements could provide an aura of intellectual legitimacy, making their *coutumiers* look more respectable.[152] It is possible, then, that *coutumiers* diverged from actual practices because their authors instinctively tended to describe customs in terms of the principles borrowed from Roman law or canon law. The adoption of Romano-Canonical procedures in royal courts expanded judicial discretion. "It was up to the judges to decide," for example, how the issues of "exceptions or counterpleas affected the question that the jury would ultimately be asked"; only after these procedural matters were squared away could substantive legal rules be considered in judicial process.[153] Where there were no consistent procedural rules governing the court, it would have been infeasible to expect "customary rules of substantive law" to emerge.

What was the role of the crown in all this? The thirteenth century was a time when the European monarchs, the nobility, and the papacy vied for political power. The Roman law doctrine of sovereignty eclipsed the importance of the suzerain–vassal relationship characteristic of feudal monarchy. In the sovereign–subject relationship, the kings freed themselves from the constraints of consulting vassals, exercising power instead through a royal council that they controlled. They issued statutes (*établissements*) and ordinances from early on.[154] Jurists stressed the dignity and legitimacy of the law (*la loi*) as a privilege of the power of the prince.[155] Royal intervention in custom was part of the king's duty to "*faire*

[152] "Whether relevant or not, they studded their work with numerous quotations from Justinian." Cohen, *The Crossroads of Justice*, 36. For the writing of customs and the professionalization of legal practice, see Hannah Skoda, "Legal Performances in Late Medieval France," in Paul Dresch and Hannah Skoda (eds.), *Legalism: Anthropology and History* (Oxford: Oxford University Press, 2012), 279–306.

[153] Cheyette, "Custom, Case Law," 374–75.

[154] See F. R. P. Akehurst, *The Etablissements de Saint Louis: Thirteenth-Century Law Texts from Tours, Orléans, and Paris* (Philadelphia: University of Pennsylvania Press, 1996). Long believed a work of official legislation, promulgated before the departure of Louis IX for Africa in 1270, its royal origin has been questioned. From the nineteenth century, historians are in agreement that it was the work of a jurist rather than a general ordinance. Beaune, *Introduction à l'étude historique*, 270–27.

[155] Petit-Renaud, in "Le roi, les légistes," # 2, cites Jehan Boutillier, author of *Somme rural ou le grand coustumier general de practique civil et canon*, written about 1393, who used the formula that the king "can make law and edict at his will."

justice."[156] The revival of the notion of public justice, as opposed to private justice, upheld the crown's superior authority to control and redress the defects and errors of custom for the benefit of common good (*bonum commune*; *commun profit*). There is little dispute that the normalization of custom took place in virtue of the jurisprudential activities of new elites who were educated in the law faculty at the medieval universities and recruited to serve the emerging state. Theorists, on their part, continuously expanded the notion of "royal case" (*cas royal*), reserving to royal judges those cases deemed imperative for public order.

After his barbed critique of Krynen, Castaldo proposed a broad perspective encompassing their divergent opinions on the issue.[157] The meaning of *droit commun* concerns "not a (pre)sentiment of unity but a discovery of the existence of features common to various customs." He admitted that the content of the customary common law in the second half of the thirteenth century was incomplete and that the concept "did not designate more than a few rules presented in the work of Beaumanoir." Yet, he added, their emergence followed the "crystallization of territorial customs" at the end of the twelfth and thirteenth centuries, and the authors came to discern what they called a customary common law, which was "very different from the *jus commune* of the Italian, Spanish, or German authors." He concluded: "the spirit of the time is not for the prospect of a unification of private law; the authors only notice that more and more rules are calling on this notion of *droit commun coutumier*. We do not go further than this observation."[158]

Could it be that these contending opinions have to do less with differences from contradicting historical evidence than with ideological—politically tinged—disagreement? Few scholars would deny that French customary law was informed by Roman law and construed by judicial practice; even fewer would argue that French customs were disregarded by the king and his courts in their preference for Roman law. It has been suggested that the history of *droit commun* is part of the history of representations, or beliefs.[159] The *jus commune* was "more the expression of a legal culture than the manifestation of a positive law."[160] In its turn, custom from the Middle Ages to the present has been dominated by a "spell," under which its concept "turned into a foundation of knowledge" everyone attempts to propagate.[161] Considered this way, then, there is no reason that

[156] Michel Reulos, "Vers la présentation coordonnée et logique du droit français," in André Stegmann (ed.), *Pouvoir et institutions en Europe au XVIe siècle, vingt-septième colloque internationale d'études humanistes, Tours* (Paris: J. Vrin, 1987), 277.

[157] See Castaldo, "Pouvoir royal [II]," 241–43.

[158] Castaldo cited Ourliac: "it probably took a few years to realize that there were customs, and the writing of the *coutumiers* had to be a result of this realization." Paul Ourliac, "Législation, coutumes et coutumiers au temps de Philippe Auguste," in Robert Henri Bautier (ed.), *La France de Philippe Auguste, le temps des mutations* (Paris: Centre nationale de la recherche scientifique, 1982), 478.

[159] Renoux-Zagamé, "La méthode du droit commun," 138.

[160] Mayali, "*Ius civile* et *ius commune*," 216.

[161] Jacob, "Les coutumiers du XIIIe siècle ont-ils connu la coutume?" 105.

Roman law as a tradition should not be seen as a source of common law along with French custom. Custom as *droit commun* does not dismiss the influence of *jus commune*, or vice versa. Yet, the tension between French law and Roman law was real.

Krynen has observed that the view of French custom as *droit commun*, privileging its consensual nature, confirms many historians are partisans of the "supremacy of the community."[162] For Castaldo, on the contrary, the "infatuation of historians of law with the *jus commune*" and their "immoderate love" for "state law and . . . *professeurs*" are "destined to ruin what has been the unique genius of the French Middle Ages, that is, precisely the shaping of the *droit coutumier*."[163] The idea of the dynamic movement of law—diffusion of legal institutions, rules, and culture—is deeply embedded in European history since antiquity. All the while, a potent spirit of local law has sustained national history, forming an equally integral part of Europe's legal tradition and resistant to being effaced by the force of unity. Conventional wisdom has it that the definition and classification of the sources of law are laden with ideology. Discussion of French custom amply affirms the point.

What about the "myth" of custom? The proliferation of myths in recent historiography can be baffling, but it certainly serves to highlight the issues.[164] Modern legal theorists like H. L. A. Hart have argued that rules are laws when they are accompanied by certain defining elements, namely, recognition, change, and adjudication.[165] Legal historians would agree in principle that these were what separated law in European history from other prescriptive rules or practices, such as religion, morals, or political systems. This formulation can apply to medieval custom: when custom was recognized as law and treated as such, there was customary law. It is different from arguing that internalized custom is simply law and law is simply internalized custom, which would be as unsatisfactory as the medieval concept of *opinio juris*.[166] The rule of change then becomes pertinent: a law

[162] Jacques Krynen, "'De Nostre certaine science . . .': Remarques sur l'absolutisme législative de la monarchie médiéval française," in André Gouron and Albert Rigaudière (eds.), *Renaissance du pouvoir législative et genèse de l'État* (Montpellier: Société d'histoire du droit et des institutions des anciens pays de droit écrit, 1988), 132.

[163] Castaldo, "Pouvoir royal [I]," 121, 118. The "admirers of *jus commune*" put forward an "apology for an intellectual power, in the name of 'science'" (122); historians' "excessive love" for *jus civile* amounts to "a remarkable naiveté" (123).

[164] See Douglas J. Osler, "The Myth of European Legal History," *Rechtshistorisches Journal* 16 (1997), 393–410.

[165] Hart (1907–1992) distinguished between primary rules (prescriptive rules) and secondary rules (accompanied by rules of recognition, change, and adjudication). The rule of recognition requires legislative authority to impose rules to be obeyed; the rule of change provides a foreseen mechanism for change of the rules, that is, who can amend the rules and which process should be followed; and the rule of adjudication gives the power to judges to decide over disputes rising over the primary rules. Herbert Lionel Adolphus Hart, *The Concept of Law* (Oxford: Clarendon Press, 2012 [1961]), 92–94.

[166] In the medieval theory, a custom is law because it has *opinio juris*, and the presence of *opinio juris* is proven because that custom is law. See Larry May, "Custom, Opinio Juris, and Consent," in

exists when it can be created or changed or, put differently, when a new one can abrogate the old one.[167] In this perspective, one can conclude that popular practices which did not require judicial recognition and remained outside the mechanism for change are customs but not customary law. The courts played an important role in controlling custom, although the extent to which they were able to manage its content remains far from clear.

3. Courts and Litigants

On the eve of the launching of the official recording of customs in the mid-fifteenth century, there were three different ways of proving custom. The first was the collections of customs (*coutumiers*), private treaties in which the authors made their observations of legal practices and the rules used at the courts, written or unwritten, and mixed them with the elements of Roman law. Second, the registers of law clerks and the *procès-vervaux* (proceedings) of the *enquêtes par turbes* were used as means of establishing the existence of customs. Finally, special charters, privileges, or immunities granted to residents of localities by the lords or by the king in his domains and the treaties concluded between the bourgeois and their seigneurs also served as law. In the *pays* located outside his domains, the king recognized written customs and executed them as "the new laws for the common interest of his kingdom."[168] These customary law sources coexisted with royal edicts and ordinances, Roman law, and church law.

The fourteenth century had seen the appearance of a large number of collections of court decisions and procedures.[169] *Stylus curiae parlamenti by* Guillaume du Brueil,[170] the *Coutumes notoires du Châtelet de Paris*,[171] *Le grand coutumier de*

Larry May and Jeff Brown (eds.), *Philosophy of Law: Classic and Contemporary Readings* (Malden: Wiley-Blackwell, 2010), 54–69.

[167] The Roman concept of determining the existence of law through its change was a step toward "the invention of legal technology." Jean-Louis Halpérin, "The Concept of Law: A Western Transplant?" *Theoretical Inquiries in Law* 10 (2009), 337.

[168] Beaune, *Introduction à l'étude historique*, 438–48. See Ada-Maria Kuskowski, "Inventing Legal Space: From Regional Custom to Common Law in the *Coutumiers* of Medieval France," in Meredith Cohen and Fanny Madeline (eds.), *Space in the Medieval West: Places, Territories, and Imagined Geographies* (Farnham: Ashgate, 2014), 133–58 (arguing the authors of the *coutumiers* created a juridical space that contributed to legal harmonization).

[169] For jurisprudence on custom in the fourteenth century, see H.-L. Bordier, "Commentaires sur un document relative à quelques points de la coutume de Paris et de la jurisprudence du Parlement au quatorzième siècle," *Bibliothèque de l'École des chartes* 1 (1844), 396–435.

[170] Written around 1330, it was printed in 1515. De Brueil was an *avocat* at the Parlement of Paris.

[171] A collection of 186 decisions rendered from 1300 and 1384, the *Coutumes notoire* included the records of *enquêtes par turbe* at the Châtelet de Paris; it was published by Julien Brodeau in vol. 2 of *Commentaire sur la coutume de la prévosté de Paris* (Paris: P. Rocolet, 1658–1669).

France by Jacques d'Ableiges,[172] the *Décisions* by Jean des Mares,[173] and the *Somme rural* by Jehan Boutillier[174] were all compiled by royal officials to help with legal practice. Each of these volumes attested to the rise of the *gens de robe* since the reign of Philip IV. Jacques d'Ableiges stated: "Custom is an unwritten but reasonable law, necessary and beneficial for any human needs and for the common interest, imposed in the regions by the prince and observed and approved notoriously by the court for forty years."[175] Note he did not mention popular consent. It seems clear from this that linking the rule of custom with an expression of popular will was the work of the doctors of Roman law, not the authors of *coutumiers*. In *Somme rural*, written around 1383, Boutillier examined usages and excluded what the men of law would consider a bad law (*un droit haineur*) and contrary to the written law.[176] The *coutumiers* were largely truncated transcriptions of court decisions, written by authors to use as handbooks or manuals for laymen.[177] Whether custom was an expression of consent was rarely their concern.

The *coutumiers*, written down by private authors, lacked general official force, and the parties in litigation still needed to prove what the applicable custom was. Judges had varying degrees of latitude in dealing with immemorial practices as sources of law. Judicial norms used at royal courts may or may not have had a direct bearing on the content of a learned law, yet it is beyond dispute that they were enforced through fastidious adherence to procedural propriety on the model of *jus commune*. The theory of "notorious" custom helped place judicial doctrine among the sources of law.

It would be an understatement to say that the Late Middle Ages marked one long battle against the proliferation of diverse solutions to legal problems. Apart from the proof of custom, litigants were quite resourceful in manipulating the bewildering jurisdictional boundaries for their interests. The parties in all venues engaged in a modern version of forum shopping. In parishes located on the borders of several provinces, they diligently tried to figure out which district's custom was most advantageous and which tribunal would be most favorable for their

[172] Ableiges was the secretary of Jean, duke of Berry (1340–1416), and subsequently examiner at the Châtelet. *Le grand coutumier*, written between 1385 and 1402, was a collection of court decisions and procedures of the Parlement of Paris and Châtelet de Paris, and was widely used in Paris and surrounding areas throughout the fifteenth century. See Olivier-Martin, *Histoire de la coutume de la prévôté et vicomté de Paris*, vol. 1, 90–101; Félix Aubert, "Les sources de la procédure au Parlement de Philippe le Bel à Charles VII," *Bibliothèque de l'École des chartes* 51 (1890), 505–10.

[173] Jean des Mares was *avocat général* of the Parlement de Paris and he collected sentences and procedures at the Châtelet de Paris.

[174] *Somme rural ou le grand coustumier general de practique civil et canon* was written about 1393. Boutillier was a *bailli*. See Félix Aubert, "Les sources de la procédure au Parlement au XIVe siècle," *Bibliothèque de l'École des chartes* 80 (1919), 122–44.

[175] Ableiges, *Le grand coutumier de France*, book 2, ch. 3, 192–93.

[176] Beaune, *Introduction à l'étude historique*, 441.

[177] Gilissen, "Les phases de la codification" (Part 1), 44.

cases.[178] Sometimes they proffered one locality's custom for one issue and a different locality's for another, all in the same case. The villagers often claimed that they were governed under the custom of nearby cities that included particular privileges. All this caused much difficulty for the judge, who had to make endless inquiries into the immemorial usages invoked by the parties.[179] Proving custom using the usual mode of *enquête par turbe* had become complicated and cumbersome, creating an "evidentiary crisis of custom."[180]

The parties increasingly preferred enlisting the service of legal professionals like *avocats* or *procureurs*.[181] They struggled to find more effective means of proving custom, and one solution was to use lawyers as local witnesses to custom. As time went on, the *enquêtes par turbes* lost their character as the jury consisting of peers and instead became the assemblies of legal practitioners.[182] It did not solve the problems of *turbes*, however.[183] Uncertainty of custom continued to bring the proliferation of lawsuits, incurring exorbitant expenses and impeding faster justice. The inquest process did not go well with the dominant legal culture: the irritation of the judges at the Parlement at having to deal with the *enquête des turbes* seemed obvious.[184]

The French kingdom in the Late Middle Ages was marked by the agglomeration of customs, governmental traditions, and fiscal obligations. Swelling litigiousness in society prompted the king to declare in 1454 the official recording of customs. It was part of ongoing royal efforts to demonstrate that the crown could offer a better brand of justice. The next chapter examines the unfolding campaign to write down and systematize custom, fueled by the burgeoning legal humanist scholarship.

[178] The famous "Marches séparantes" exemplified the tentativeness of legal boundaries. As a vestige of the relationship between the conflicts between the dukes of Brittany and the French king, several parishes surrounded by the Duchies of Anjou and Brittany and the County of Poitou enjoyed a special status of being governed by the laws of Anjou, Brittany, and Poitou concurrently. See Émile Chénon, " Les Marches séparantes d'Anjou, Bretagne, et Poitou," *Nouvelle revue historique de droit français et étranger* 16 (1892), 18–62, 165–211.

[179] Hilaire, "La France méridionale."

[180] James Q. Whitman, "Why Did the Revolutionary Lawyers Confuse Custom and Reason?" *University of Chicago Law Review* 58 (1991), 1332.

[181] See Claire Dolan, "Entre les familles et l'État: Les procureurs et la procédure au XVIe siècle," *Journal of the Canadian Historical Association/Revue de la Société historique du Canada* 10 (1999), 19–36. Although the distinctions between *avocats* and *procureurs* were not as clear as in the modern English legal profession (barrister and solicitor), each group held an exclusive right on a specific activity. Only the *advocatus*, not *procurator*, had the right to plead before the court. The saying went that the *procureur* had the pen (*plume*) and the *avocat* the pleading (*plaidoirie*). *Procureurs*, performing a public function, needed to purchase a venal office; *avocats* did not. Kim, "Lawyers."

[182] Olivier-Martin, *Histoire de la coutume de la prévôté et vicomté de Paris*, vol. 1, 84–86. By the fifteenth century, the members of *enquête par turbe* were usually professional lawyers.

[183] Filhol, "La preuve de la coutume," 364.

[184] Cohen, *The Crossroads of Justice*, 28.

3
The Redaction of Customs

Nearly a half century ago, Emmanuel Le Roy Ladurie proposed a "system of customary law." In a much celebrated article in *Annales ESC*, he explained how regional customs in sixteenth-century France conferred on a particular locality its cultural identity.[1] He suggested that the ethnographer-historian "select a number of pertinent criteria whose presence, absence, or diverse manifestations are associated with an entire family of cultural traits, which themselves give each customary region its specific configuration."[2] This approach to custom as cultural traits was expected to help subsume peculiar characteristics of local communities and discern the collective consciousness of their inhabitants under a structural system.

Since then, scholars, mostly legal historians, have taken a more reserved stance. Some argued that a cultural approach, or an overdetermined socio-historical structuralism, to custom would not fully reflect the categories that were used to formalize social practices to grant them the force of law. Others questioned whether custom in the form of the *coutumiers* could serve as an accurate indicator of a geographical community's identity. Bernard Derouet, writing in the same journal as Le Roy Ladurie some two decades later, asserted that regional divergence in private law in France from the fifteenth through nineteenth century rarely corresponded to the variety of family habitudes. The recorded customs were not social but judicial practices to use in the court of a territorial jurisdiction.[3] Jean Hilaire has shown that authors of commentaries written on the customs in the west of France often had to digress from actual patterns of the institution of the family in order to conform to jurisprudence. He thus warned that failure to recognize the gap between the *coutumiers* and notarial practices "au champ" would result in a skewed picture of the reality in localities.[4] Louis

[1] Emmanuel Le Roy Ladurie, "Système de la coutume: Structures familiales et coutume d'héritage en France au XVIe siècle," *Annales. Économies, Sociétés, Civilisations* 27 (1972), 825–46; reprinted in *La Territoire de l'historien* (Paris: Gallimard, 1973), 222–51; translated as "A System of Customary Law: Family Structures and Inheritance Customs in Sixteenth-Century France," in Robert Forster and Orest Ranum (eds.), *Family and Society: Selection from the Annales: Économies, Sociétés, Civilization* (Baltimore: Johns Hopkins University Press, 1976), 75–103; also in Goody et al. (eds.), *Family and Inheritance*, 37–70.

[2] Le Roy Ladurie, "Système de la coutume," 826.

[3] Bernard Derouet, "Les pratiques familiales, le droit et la construction des différences (15e–19e siècles)," *Annales. Histoire, Sciences Sociales* 52 (1997), 371.

[4] Jean Hilaire, "Coutumes rédigées et 'gens des champs' (Angoumois, Aunis, Saintonge)," *Revue historique de droit français et étranger* 65 (1987), 545–73 (reprinted in ch. 2, "La vie 'aux champs' après la rédaction des coutumes (Angoumois, Aunis, Saintonge)," in Hilaire, *La vie du droit*, 125–56).

Custom, Law, and Monarchy: A Legal History of Early Modern France. Marie Seong-Hak Kim, Oxford University Press.
 DOI: 10.1093/oso/9780192845498.003.0003

Assier-Andrieu pointed out that "praxis" studied by sociologists and ethnologists was not the same as the "acts of practice" of jurists which concerned a particular phase of normative activity.[5] Finally, Alan Watson cautioned about the "danger of misconstruing similarity of customary law with societal similarity"; for him, the classification of customary law resulted more from the choice of legal approaches than from the autonomous manifestation of popular practices.[6] These opinions show that *géographie coutumière* is to a large degree hinged on judicial construction and classification.

This chapter examines the royal campaign to record customs in the late fifteenth and early sixteenth centuries. The king launched the operation with the goal of reducing lawsuits, so the main concern was to extract rules from customary practices to use in court. Much technical work was devoted in various regions to the drafting of the *coutumes* in order to give them a logical order and structure, a process that was aptly called "écrire les coutumes."[7] The development of law in Western Europe was "above all a phenomenon of writing, of *literacy*."[8] Custom truly became law when it was captured in writing.

[5] Assier-Andrieu, "De l'idéologie à la culture," # 20 (online paragraph number); Louis Assier-Andrieu, "Penser le temps culturel du droit. Le destin anthropologique du concept de coutume," *L'homme. Revue française d'anthropologie* 160 (2001), 81–82. See also Anne Zink, *L'héritier de la maison: Géographie coutumière du Sud-Ouest de la France sous l'Ancien Régime* (Paris: Éditions de l'École des hautes études en sciences sociales, 1993).

[6] Alan Watson, "An Approach to Customary Law," *University of Illinois Law Review* 3 (1984), 575, note 49. Custom matters only "for those who believe that there is a very close correlation between the law of a society and the life of the society," and, in his view, there is none. Watson, "The Evolution of Law: Continued," 550. "Legal rules are not peculiarly devised for the particular society in which they now operate," Alan Watson, *Legal Transplants: An Approach to Comparative Law* (Athens: University of Georgia Press, 1993), 97. This opinion seemed to contradict not only the time honored observation of Montesquieu (1689–1755) that geographical and sociological factors influenced legal changes but also Savigny's *Volksgeist* theory that law was properly "custom," the "spirit of the people." But Watson's thesis had more to it. His point was that, once law-creative process began, it was largely up to the legal elite, not society, and that this was the case for custom as well. For him, most societies persist in the myth that customary law emerges from past popular behavior because the belief that a judge is just making up a rule would seemingly deprive the system of customary law of its authority, but, in reality, the development of private law was primarily the work of jurists. "The Evolution of Law: Continued," 549. Watson's other works include *The Evolution of Law* (Baltimore: Johns Hopkins University Press, 1989); *The Evolution of Western Private Law* (Baltimore: Johns Hopkins University Press, 2001). On Watson's theories of legal evolution, see Michael H. Hoeflich, "Law, Society and Reception: The Vision of Alan Watson," *Michigan Law Review* 85 (1987), 1083–94. Among the most controversial is Watson's claim that there is little correlation between society and legal change. He did not dispute that legal elites responded to societal needs but said those needs were what they believed society needed. His thesis stressing the autonomy of law met criticisms: see, among others, Otto Kahn-Freund, "On Uses and Misuses of Comparative Law," *Modern Law Review* 37 (1972), 1–27. For debate surrounding Watson's thesis, see William Ewald, "Comparative Jurisprudence (II): The Logic of Legal Transplants," *American Journal of Comparative Law* 43 (1995), 489–510.

[7] Grinberg, *Écrire les coutumes*; Martine Grinberg, "Écrire le droit: les coutumes, la langue et le 'bon usage,'" in Giavarini (ed.), *L'écriture des juristes*, 57–71.

[8] Assier-Andrieu, "De l'idéologie à la culture," # 19 (emphasis original). For the significance of law in writing, see Laurence Giavarini, "Autour de *L'écriture des juristes*. Sur la question de l'action de l'écriture et du droit," *Clio@Themis, Revue électronique d'histoire du droit* 7 (March 2014), http://www.cliothemis.com/Autour-de-L-ecriture-des-juristes.

The redaction began when Roman law was the juristic standard and conceptual tool for all laws. The royal undertaking needs to be discussed against the backdrop of the intellectual movement of legal humanism that set out to redefine the relationship between Roman law and French custom. The development of customary law was the result of long and careful doctrinal and jurisprudential work to systematize the sources of law, supported by the state's initiative to streamline judicial administration. The royal campaign marked the convergence of the crown's judicial and legislative agenda, with a keen eye on what can be called in modern times judicial economy.

1. Ordinance of Montils-lès-Tours (1454)

In April 1454, Charles VII issued an ordinance in Montils-lès-Tours. It was part of the effort for territorial and institutional restructuring in the aftermath of the Hundred Years War.[9] Legal reform was a natural extension of tax and military reforms. When territories were added to France, the crown gave express consent that the inhabitants would be allowed to practice their traditional laws and enjoy privileges. Each provincial parlement was the bulwark of customs. The result was a fragmentation of royal jurisdictions on top of the maze of feudal districts.

Royal political consolidation required tackling the tangled mass of the sources of law and overhauling judicial administration. In Article 125 of the Ordinance of Montils-lès-Tours, the king declared the launching of the official recording of customs.[10] He commanded that *coutumes*, *usages*, and *stiles* of all customary law regions be "drawn up and put into writing" in accord with the *coutumiers* and *gens de bien*. The key section of this famous article, the last article of the ordinance, deserves to be quoted at length:

> Thus the parties in judgment, both in our Court of Parlement and before other judges of our kingdom, both ours and others, propose and allege several usages, procedures, styles, and customs, which are various due to the diversity of the *pays* of our kingdom, and then they prove them, and in consequence lawsuits are often very long and the parties are subject to large fees and expenses; if customs, usages, and styles of the *pays* of our kingdom were written down, trials would be much shorter, and the parties would be spared the expenses and

[9] Grinberg, *Écrire les coutumes*, 74.

[10] Louis George Oudard Feudrix de Bréquigny (ed.), *Ordonnances des rois de France de la troisième race, recueillies par ordre chronologique* (Paris: Imprimerie royale, 1790), vol. 14, 312–14; François A. Isambert, Nicolas Decrusy, and Alphonse Honoré Taillandier (eds.), *Recueil général des anciennes lois françaises, depuis l'an 420 jusqu'à la révolution de 1789* (Paris: Belin-Leprieur, 1825) [hereafter *Recueil général*], vol. 9, 252–54. "Usages" meant privileges. "Stiles" referred to the manner and the means by which a right was to be enforced, distinguished from the substance of that right; in modern vocabulary it is equivalent to "procedures."

> outlays, and also judges could adjudicate cases better and with greater certainty (because often it happens that the parties claim contrary customs in the same *pays*, and often customs mutate and vary to their liking, from where great damages and inconveniences occur to our subjects).
>
> We, wishing to abbreviate lawsuits and disputes between our subjects, to relieve them from the outlays and expenses, to bring certainty to judgments as much as possible, and to remove all manners of variations and contradictions, order, decree, declare, and state that customs, usages, and styles of all the *pays* of our kingdom be drawn up and put into writing, accorded to by the *coutumiers*, practitioners, and people of each of the so-called *pays* of our kingdom, and that customs, usages, and styles so accorded to be laid down and written in books, which will then be brought to us, so as to be seen and visited by the members of our Grand Conseil or our Court of Parlement, and for us to decree and confirm them; and these usages, customs, and styles thus decreed and confirmed will be observed and maintained in the *pays* where they exist and also in our Court of Parlement which has jurisdiction over proceedings from those *pays*; and judges in our kingdom of our Court of Parlement as well as our *baillis*, *sénéchaux*, and other judges will judge in accordance with those usages, customs, and procedures, without allowing any proof other than what will be written in the said book; and we want those customs, styles, and usages thus written, granted, and confirmed, as has been said, to be maintained and observed in judgment and outside the courtroom. But we do not intend any change in the procedures at our Court of Parlement. And we prohibit and forbid all lawyers of our kingdom from alleging or proposing customs, usages, and styles other than those which will be written, accorded to, and decreed as it has been said; and we enjoin the said judges to punish and correct those who do the opposite, and not to hear or receive any person alleging, proposing, or saying otherwise.[11]

There are four main points in this article. First, the king, having observed the inconveniences of the *enquêtes*, was convinced that customs, if officially written down, would shorten lawsuits and save money and that judgments would become more certain. Second, in order to achieve these results, practitioners of custom of each *pays* needed to reach an agreement about what their customs were and codify them in the form of a book. Third, the customary usages and procedures accorded to must be reviewed by the members of the royal council and "decreed and confirmed" by the king. Finally, no proof of custom other than the written texts thus promulgated would be allowed; no one could argue that the custom changed or was abolished by a new custom.[12] Together, this ambitious

[11] Ibid. [12] Chénon, *Histoire générale du droit français*, vol. 2, 292.

royal project justified the state's intervention in private legal matters on account of procedural irregularities and inefficiency in judicial administration.

Royal letters repeatedly cited the problem of enormous expenses of lawsuits, incurred mainly because custom had to be proved each time. The ordinance of 1454 mentioned "grands fraiz et despens." At the Estates General at Tours in 1484, the *cahiers* demanded that not only customs and "stilles du royaume" but also the records of their registration in different jurisdictions be made available to the public so that anyone could consult the law texts, without having to pay fees.[13] In 1506, Louis XII deplored "de merveilleux fraiz, à cause des preuves," declaring his desire to provide relief to the "poor subjects who were and are gravely molested and exhausted due to innumerable lawsuits, questions, and differences."[14] Francis I acknowledged the problems of "uncertainty, variety, contrariety, or repugnance" of customs.[15] In 1609, Henry IV referred to the multiplicity of customs which incurred "frois extraordinaires."[16] Throughout the early modern period, to curtail litigation remained the greatest motivation for systematizing the law and custom.

During the first phase of the campaign following the 1454 ordinance, the results were modest. The custom of Burgundy (duchy and county) was published in 1459 under the authority of the duke of Burgundy, not the king.[17] The custom of Touraine was recorded in 1462 and that of Anjou the following year, though they were not homologated, that is, not officially promulgated.[18] The *coutumes* of Mehun-sur-Yèvre and Troyes were redacted in 1481.[19] A personal letter from Louis XI indicated he planned to conduct a systematic comparison of French customs with those of Italy.[20] Philippe de Commines attested that the king wanted to

[13] Georges Picot, *Histoire des États généraux, considérés au point de vue de leur influence sur le gouvernement de la France de 1355 à 1614* (Paris: Hachette & cie, 1872), vol. 1, 462.

[14] *Lettres patentes*, Touraine, 1507, *Nouveau coutumier général*, vol. 3, 600. The king again mentioned "innumérables frais," ordinance of June 1510 issued in Lyon, in *Ordonnances des rois de France*, vol. 21, 420–36, and *Recueil général*, vol. 11, 579.

[15] *Lettres patentes* of Francis I, included in the *Coutume de Nivernais* (1534), *Nouveau coutumier général*, vol. 3, 1166. See Dawson, "French Customs," 775; Filhol, *Le premier président Christofle de Thou*, 77. The king vowed to modify customs that were "inequitable and unreasonable," with the help of "raison écrite" and "équité naturelle." *Lettres patentes* of Francis I, included in the *Coutume de Berry* (1539), *Nouveau coutumier général*, vol. 3, 989. See Joseph van Kan, *Les efforts de codification en France: Étude historique et psychologique* (Paris: Rousseau & cie, 1929), 23.

[16] *Lettres patentes* of Henry IV, October 5, 1609, included in the *procès-verbal* of the *Coutume de Chaulny*, *Nouveau coutumier général*, vol. 2, 691.

[17] Émile Champeaux, "Coutumes de Bourgogne et coutumes du duché de Bourgogne," *Mémoires de la Société pour l'histoire du droit et des institutions des anciens pays bourguignons, comtois et romands* 2 (1935), 49–76.

[18] For customs redacted during this period, see Klimrath, "Études sur les coutumes," 135–43.

[19] The *procès-verbaux* of Mehun-sur-Yèvre (August 1481) and of Troyes (September 1481) are in *Nouveau coutumier général*, vol. 3, 269 and 926, respectively.

[20] Louis XI's letter of August 5, 1481, shows that the king commanded his counselor D. Bouchaige to bring a Florentine who could inform him of the customs of Florence and Venice, as he planned to "give order to customs in the matter of justice and police of the kingdom." In *Lettres de Louis XI, Roi*

see in his kingdom "one custom, one weight, one measure system" and to have "all the customs be redacted in French, in one beautiful book."[21] Apparently the king held a desire that went far beyond his predecessor's. Why did he hold such a strong opinion about the necessity of "one custom" in the kingdom? His main motivation, according to Commines, was "to avoid the guile and pillage by lawyers (which is so serious in this kingdom that nothing is like it and the noble people in this kingdom must know it well)." Louis XI's sentiment about law courts was not a secret: he "wished with all his heart to bring order to his kingdom and in particular to tackle lengthy lawsuits. In doing this, he tried to bridle the courts of parlements; he did not want to reduce their number or authority, but there were several things about them that made him hate the courts, albeit reluctantly."[22]

2. Launching the Royal Campaigns

On January 28, 1494, Charles VIII issued *lettres patents* indicating his intent to push forward afresh the campaign to record customs. In a series of orders that followed, the king revised some key methods of the operation to make it more expedient.[23] In January 1496, he created a standing commission and appointed Thibault Baillet (*c.*1445–1525), *président à mortier* of the Parlement of Paris, to preside over the examination of the drafts of the recorded customs.[24] In September 1497, the king instructed that the commissioners proceed to solemn publication of the redacted custom once it was examined by the magistrates of the local parlements.[25] Note that all these developments took place when Charles VIII was in the midst of his campaign to conquer Naples, launching the Wars of Italy.

de France, ed. Joseph Vaesen and Étienne Charavay, vol. 9 (Paris: Librairie Renouard, 1905), 59–60; Dawson, "French Customs," 771, note 15.

[21] Philippe de Commines, *Les mémoires de messire Philippe de Commines, chevalier, seigneur d'Argenton sur les principaux faits et gestes de Louis XI, et Charles VIII son fils, rois de France* (Rouen: Jean Berthelin, 1634), book 6, ch. 6, 515–16. See René Grandilhon, "L'unification des coutumes sous Louis XI," *Revue historique* 194 (1944), 317–23.

[22] *Les mémoires de messire Philippe de Commines*, vol. 2, book 6, ch. 6, 515–16.

[23] *Lettres patentes* of January 28, 1494, in *Ordonnances des rois de France*, vol. 20, 431–35; *lettres patentes* of January 19, 1496, issued in Lyon, *Nouveau coutumier général*, vol. 4, 639.

[24] Jean Yver, "Le président Thibault Baillet et la rédaction des coutumes," *Revue historique de droit français et étranger* 64 (1986), 19–42.

[25] The royal letter issued in Moulins, September 2, 1497, in *Ordonnances des rois de France*, vol. 21, 6–8. See Filhol, *Le premier président Christofle de Thou*, 61–62; François Olivier-Martin, "Un document inédit sur les travaux préparatoires de l'ancienne coutume de Paris," *Nouvelle revue historique de droit français et étranger* 42 (1918), 202–203.

Enlisting the Estates

An important change came less than a month before the king's death on April 7, 1498. Charles VIII issued a royal letter on March 15 in Amboise and significantly modified the existing procedures that appeared to arouse resistance from the population to the campaign. In this edict, the king expressly prescribed the holding of an assembly of the estates (*les gens d'Église, nobles, noz officiers, practiciens & autres gens de bien*) in *bailliages, sénéchaussées*, and other jurisdictions under the supervision of royal commissioners.[26] Under this new scheme, the drafts of customs prepared by local practitioners would be discussed in the presence of the three estates. Those customs agreed upon (*accordées*) through "common accord and consent of the estates" would be published by the commissioners in the name of the king; only articles that had not been agreed upon (*discordés*) would be sent to the Parlement. The king stipulated:

> If any difference and disagreement arise, as to which the said estates cannot agree, the said difficulties, differences, and disagreements shall be drawn up and put into writing together with the causes of those differences and be brought to us, so that they can be ordered and taken care of by us, and the remainder of the said customs shall be entirely published. . . . And, nevertheless, if on making the said publication certain difficulties arise concerning some articles of the said customs, we . . . have given and give you . . . power and authority to determine them with the consent in all cases of the said three estates in each *bailliage, sénéchaussée* and jurisdiction, or of the larger and wiser part thereof.[27]

The new procedure thus provided for the direct participation of the constituent members in the process, allowing the three estates to have their opinions heard and reflected in the redactions. The first *coutume* published under the new procedures was the *coutume* of Bourbonnais in 1500.[28]

The holding of an assembly of the three estates, as prescribed in the Edict of Amboise, distinguished the French operation in a crucial way from similar operations elsewhere in Europe. A brief comparison with the Holy Roman Empire would prove the point. Emperor Charles V (r. 1519–1556) ordered in 1531 the codification of customs in Burgundian-Habsburg Netherlands, an imperial

[26] *Lettres patentes*, March 15, 1498, issued in Amboise, *Ordonnances des rois de France*, vol. 21, 18–20, also preserved in the *procés-verbaux* of the *Coutume de Melun* (1506), *Nouveau coutumier général*, vol. 3, 427–28, the *Coutume de Sens* (1506), vol. 3, 483–84, and the *Coutume de Touraine* (1507), vol. 4, 639–41.

[27] "The larger and wiser part thereof" (*la plus grande & saine partie d'iceux*) was a canonist formula, central in the church's theory of collective action. But the discretion of fixing the text by vote following this formula was rarely exercised and in the earlier redactions many articles were withheld from publication entirely. Dawson, "French Customs," 776, notes 34 and 35.

[28] *Nouveau coutumier général*, vol. 3, 1207.

command equivalent to the French ordinance of 1454.[29] As in France, the redaction in the Seventeen Provinces was part of the attempts by the central government to control and harmonize at least some of legal sources by conferring on them the official status of law. Generally speaking, the Habsburg imperial operation, which would be drawn out over the next two centuries, proved far less effective. The emperor in his decree of 1531 did not call for the gathering of a local assembly of the estates. There was no specific requirement that customs be discussed in the assemblies of the local population; the imperial edict simply enjoined local authorities to produce the drafts of customs and send them to the central government.[30] With the strong tradition of provincial autonomy in the Low Countries, there was already sizable resistance to orders from the center, and the lack of mechanism for local input seriously marred the customary redaction process in the Empire.

The participation of the local estates made the French enterprise a singular historical phenomenon. One must note that Charles VIII, while allowing the participation of the popular assemblies, also increased their control by royal commissioners. The commissioners were ordered to advise the three estates on the customs that needed to be "corrected, adjusted, abridged, or interpreted" due to their "hard, iniquitous, and unreasonable" nature. This indicated that the task of the commissioners was no longer restricted to recording and registering customs as hitherto observed but extended to bringing reason into them (*y pourveoir ainsi que de raison*).[31] The language invoking reason, methodically repeated in the *lettres patentes* appointing royal commissioners, revealed the true nature of the operation: it was not just drafting customs but improving them. The king's traditional power to abolish bad custom would now be exercised more systematically, in direct contact with the three estates through his commissioners.[32]

Royal commissioners, who were judges from the sovereign courts of parlements, were authorized to verify the redacted customs and order the *baillis* and *sénéchaux* to enter them at once into public registers. It greatly simplified the process. In the Seventeen Provinces, by contrast, there was a clear division between "codification" by the local authority and "homologation" by the central authority; a good number of customs, having been drawn up by local governments, did not receive official consecration by the imperial government, especially before the Perpetual Edict of 1611.[33] Political and religious unrest stood

[29] Gilissen, "Les phases de la codification" (Part 1), 41. This imperial edict was renewed in 1540, 1546, 1551, 1569, and 1611. There were at least 700 *coutumes* in the Seventeen Provinces.

[30] Ibid., 47–48.

[31] *Lettres patentes*, March 15, 1498, issued at Amboise, *Nouveau coutumier général*, vol. 4, 639.

[32] Olivier-Martin, "Un document inédit," 203, note 1; Olivier-Martin, "Le roi de France et les mauvaises coutumes," 111.

[33] John Gilissen, "Les phases de la codification et de l'homologation des coutumes dans les XVII Provinces des Pays-Bas" (Part 2), *Tijdschrift voor Rechtsgeschiedenis* 18 (1950), 288. Holland and

in the way in both France and the Low Countries, but in France the redaction operation was more or less tightly supervised by the king, from the issuance of *lettres patentes* to the publication, registration, and diffusion of the written *coutumes*.

The role of the three estates in the redaction of customs was far more substantive and concrete than the symbolic legislative role of the Estates General or provincial estates. The representative institution, a notion unknown to antiquity, was born to vote on the king's demand for supplementary resources.[34] But the idea that royal revenues had to be approved by the estates did not last for long, and by the sixteenth century the Estates General had lost its right to consent to royal taxation. It instead became a main forum for the subjects in which they voiced their grievances and communicated them to the king in the *cahiers de doléances*. If the king determined that they had valid grounds, he had them studied by the royal council and followed up with legislative and regulatory measures, although he was never obliged to do so.[35]

The provincial estates were the miniatures of the Estates General. The great ancient fiefs in Burgundy, Dauphiné, Provence, Languedoc, Guyenne, Brittany, and Normandy each had the *états provinciaux* (see Map 3.1). The centers of some provinces also had one, as in Maine, Anjou, Touraine, Orléans, and Auvergne.[36] The estates theoretically deliberated in the gathering of the three orders—the clergy, the nobility, and the third estate—but, by the seventeenth century, they were in most cases aristocratic councils or the assemblies of notables, which negotiated financial concessions from the king and would off-load the tax burden onto others.[37] Like the Estates General, the provincial estates mainly played the role of presenting complaints from the *pays* to the king in the *cahiers* after each session.

The Estates General repeatedly demanded the simplification and clarification of the laws. It met eight times after the Middle Ages, in 1484 (Tours), 1560–1561

Zeeland did not see the homologation of customs, and a Roman-Dutch law prevailed there in the seventeenth century.

[34] Philip IV summoned in 1302 the gathering of the three estates of the realm to obtain the subjects' consent to a novel principle of taxation.

[35] Barbiche, *Les institutions de la monarchie française*, 92–93.

[36] Ibid., 313–18. The provinces were subdivided into *pays*: the *pays* with the estates were called *pays d'états*, those without *pays d'élection*. The king submitted his demands for taxes, a fixed amount or desired contribution, to the provincial estates through his *commissaires*, such as the *governeur* or *intendant*. The expression *don gratuit* (free gift) was used in several provinces. The distinction between *pays d'états* and *pays d'élection* became insignificant by the beginning of the sixteenth century, at a time when *élections*, the primary tax boards, covered most of the kingdom. In several provinces, Normandy before 1655 for example, the two regimes, *états* and *élections*, coexisted. The provincial estates borrowed money at the king's behalf.

[37] J. Russell Major, *From Renaissance Monarchy to Absolute Monarchy: French Kings, Nobles, & Estates* (Baltimore: Johns Hopkins University Press, 1994), 22; Julian Swann, *Provincial Power and Absolute Monarchy: The Estates General of Burgundy, 1661–1790* (Cambridge: Cambridge University Press, 2003); Beik, *Absolutism and Society in Seventeenth-Century France*.

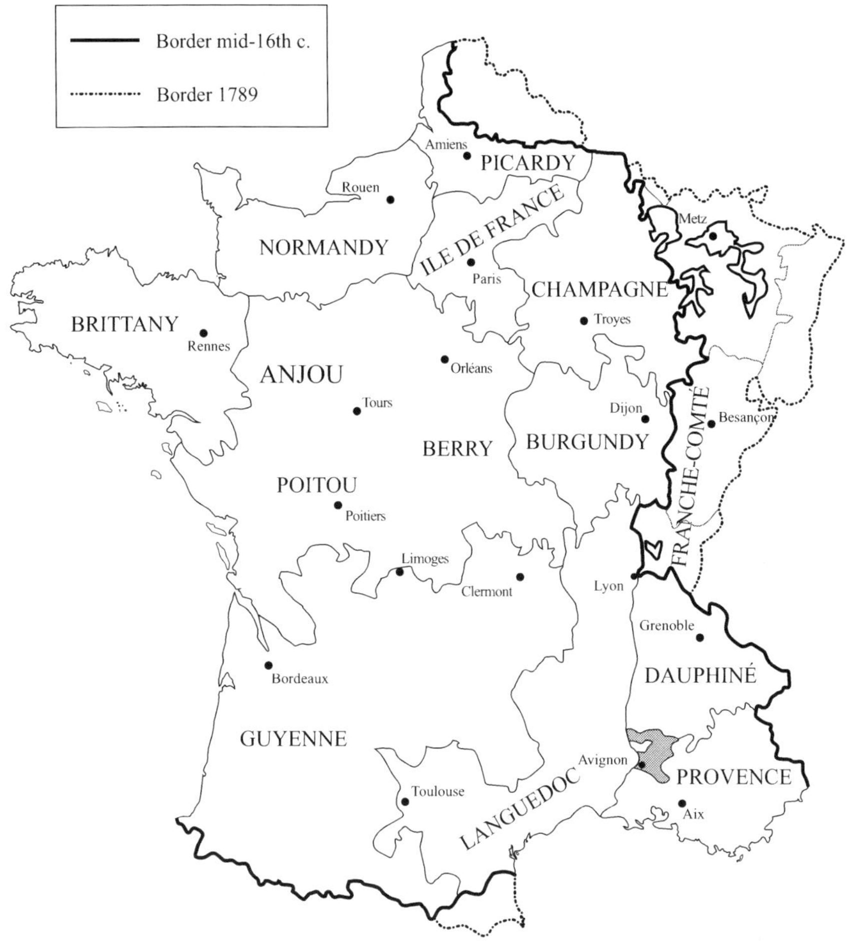

Map 3.1 Administrative divisions in the sixteenth century

(Orléans), 1561 (Pontoise), 1576–1577 (Blois), 1588–1589 (Blois), 1593 (Paris), 1614–1615 (Paris), and 1789 (Versailles).[38] The Estates General which gathered in Tours in 1484 petitioned the king to rebuild the law courts, reduce uncertainty in

[38] For the first and the second estates, the principal electoral assembly took place at the seat of the *bailliage* or *sénéchaussée*. For the third estate, elections took place on different levels: first in the villages and towns, next intermediate cities, and finally the seats of the *bailliages* or *sénéchaussées*. Barbiche, *Les institutions de la monarchie française*, 92. The elections at the *bailliage* and *sénéchaussée* levels were held under the supervision of the courts. The majority of the delegates were judges in lower courts and lawyers. At the Estates General at Blois in 1576, only a small fraction of the delegates of the third estate was someone other than *gens de justice*. See Mark Greengrass, "A Day in the Life of the Third Estate: Blois, 26th December 1576," in Adrianna E. Bakos (ed.), *Politics, Ideology, and the Law in Early Modern Europe: Essays in Honor of J. H. M. Salmon* (Rochester: University of Rochester Press, 1994), 77.

law, and suppress complex processes in judicial administration.[39] From Tours to Orléans to Blois, deputies were in one voice clamoring for reliable sources of law.[40] Both the general public and legal practitioners were overwhelmed with the ever-growing piles of royal ordinances and, above all, the appalling diversity of customs. The ideal of a faster, cheaper, and more equal justice for all was one of the most important themes in early modern French society.

The recurring problems of the proof of custom and lengthy judicial process, with the spiraling cost of lawsuits, had to be dealt with at the local level. Custom, unlike general ordinances, was applicable to a defined region and the assembly was the gathering of the estates of that locality alone.[41] The members of the three estates participated individually, not as elected deputies.[42] The redaction assembly was a mechanism by which the king substantiated his commitment to allow local populations to decide on their customs. The rights and responsibilities of the inhabitants of each locality were taken seriously. Once promulgated, the customs were mandated to be "absolutely [*inviolablement*] guarded and observed without infringement, as *loy perpetuelle*." This language was regularly inserted into the royal letters.

Royal Campaigns in the Early Sixteenth Century

Louis XII further improved the procedure. In March 1505, he decided that three or four commissioners would be appointed for the redaction of each *coutume*, instead of maintaining a large standing central commission.[43] The standard procedures were as follows. The king sent out royal letters to the *baillis* and *sénéchaux*, ordering the process to start within two months. Provisional *cahiers* were prepared by local experts. Subsequently, the assembly of the three estates of the *bailliage* was convoked, presided over by royal commissioners. Individual articles had to be adopted by a majority vote within each of the three orders and then unanimously by the three orders. If problems remained unresolved, the commissioners sent inquiries to the Grand Conseil. When a *coutume* received official approval by the king, its text was printed and distributed by a local publisher designated by the commissioners. The *coutume* was decreed and registered by the court clerk, just like legislation. These procedural formalities were observed with little change throughout the ancien régime.

[39] See Jacques Krynen, "Réflexion sur les idées politiques aux États généraux de Tours de 1484," *Revue historique de droit français et étranger* 62 (1984), 183–204.

[40] Major, *From Renaissance Monarchy to Absolute Monarchy*, 22.

[41] Filhol, *Le premier président Christofle de Thou*, 73.

[42] Chénon, *Histoire générale du droit français*, vol. 2, 295.

[43] *Lettres patentes* of March 4, 1505, in *Ordonnances des rois de France*, vol. 21, 332–34; *Nouveau coutumier général*, vol. 4, 638–41.

Under Louis XII almost all the customs in the center and the north of France were recorded. Several in the west and in the Midi were also written down. The customs that had been put into writing without meeting the new procedural requirements were republished. The homologation of the Comté du Perche took place in 1505, followed by Bar, Melun, and Sens in 1506; Auxerre, Touraine, Péronne, and Amiens in 1507; Anjou, Maine, Chartres, and Dreux in 1508; and Troyes, Orléans, Artois, Vitry-en-Perthois, Chaumont, and Meaux in 1509.[44]

In March 1510, the official redaction of the custom of Paris took place under the presidency of Thibault Baillet.[45] The customs of the capital had long been elaborated by the lawyers at the Châtelet. Created in the thirteenth century, the Châtelet de Paris was the royal *bailliage* court in Paris, the seat of its jurisdiction comprising the city and the Île-de-France, officially called the Prévôté et Vicomté de Paris. The Châtelet exercised appellate jurisdiction for inferior royal tribunals and also for seigneurial and ecclesiastical courts in Paris and the surrounding areas. Its competence extended across the kingdom for cases involving the acts passed under the royal seal.[46] The codification of the *coutume* of Paris came relatively late, because the authoritative *La grande coutumier de France*, compiled by Jacques d'Ableiges at the end of the fourteenth century, had been widely in use in the Paris area.

From the end of the fifteenth century, practitioners at the Châtelet set out to put together a collection of customs, culled from the practices of the tribunals of the Prévôté et Vicomté.[47] The redaction in 1510 resulted in a collection of 199 articles, to be known as the *ancienne coutume de Paris*. It served as the main source of doctrinal and jurisprudential developments in the kingdom before it was reformed in 1580. After Paris, the reign of Louis XII saw the redaction of the customs of Auvergne in 1510, and Angoumois, Poitou, Dax, Bayonne, and La Rochelle in 1514.[48] The momentum continued under Francis I. The ordinance of

[44] The edict of September 18, 1509, reaffirmed that "people of the three estates of each *bailliage* and *sénéchaussée* of our kingdom are to be assembled in good and great number." The text is included in the *procès-verbal* of the *Coutume de Meaux*, *Nouveau coutumier général*, vol. 3, 410–11.

[45] Olivier-Martin, *Histoire de la coutume de la prévôté et vicomté de Paris*, vol. 1, 104–109; François Olivier-Martin, "Un coutumier du Châtelet de la fin du XVe siècle," *Travaux juridique et économiques de l'université de Rennes* 1 (1907), 411–32; François Olivier-Martin, "Un document inédit," 206–27, includes the *procès-verbal* of the preparatory assembly held in July 1507.

[46] Barbiche, *Les institutions de la monarchie française*, 351.

[47] The king commanded that the modification and approbation of customs take place with caution, making sure all objections were heard. *Lettres patentes*, *Nouveau coutumier général*, vol. 3, 26–27. This letter was dated January 21, 1511, in Bourdot de Richebourg's collection, but Jean-Marie Pardessus, the editor of the *Ordonnances des rois de France*, pointed out that the letter, appointing commissioners for the codification of the *Coutume de Paris*, could not have been issued in January 1511 because the redaction had already taken place in March 1510. He believes instead this letter was issued on September 18, 1509. Pardessus produces a royal letter from Blois, issued on January 21, 1511, that concerned the publication of the *Coutume de Paris*. *Ordonnances des rois de France*, vol. 21, 442–43.

[48] See Hilaire, "Coutumes rédigées et 'gens des champs'"; René Filhol (ed.), *Vieux coustumier de Poictou* (Bourges: Édition Tardy, 1956). The custom of Auvergne was co-presided over by Antoine Duprat, *premier président* of the Parlement of Paris, who had originated from the region. This shows

1521 professed the need to correct the "diversity of opinions in interpretation to ensure the observance of customs among practitioners."[49] During Francis' reign, the *coutumes* of Loudunois (1518), Bordeaux (1521), Nivernais (1534), Senlis (1539), Brittany (1539), and Berry (1539) were published.

The size of the areas covered by *coutume* greatly varied. Four parlements had only one *coutume générale* within their entire jurisdictional districts: the Parlement of Rouen was governed by the *coutume* of Normandy; the Parlement of Rennes the *coutume* of Brittany; the Parlement of Dijon the *coutume* of Burgundy; and the Parlement of Besançon the *coutume* of Franche-Comté.[50] The provinces of Guyenne, Gascony, Languedoc, Provence, and Dauphiné did not have *coutume générale* of their own, although the territories of the parlements in these provinces (the Parlements of Bordeaux, Toulouse, Aix, and Grenoble) included *coutumes locales*.

The jurisdiction of the Parlement of Paris, by far the largest, included an array of customs. Émile Chénon divided the districts of custom within its territory into eleven groups, each of which included multiple customs: (1) *groupe parisien*: the custom of Paris and four small customs of Étampes, Dourdan, Montfort-l'Amaury, and Mantes; (2) *groupe beauvaisien*: three general customs of Senlis, Clermont-en-Beauvaisis, and Crespy-en-Valois; (3) *groupe picard*: five general customs of Péronne, Amiens, Ponthieu, Boulenois, and Calais; (4) *groupe vermandois*: customs of Saint-Quentin, Ribémont, Coucy, Noyon, Laon, Reims, and Châlons-sur-Marne; (5) *groupe Champagne et Brie*: two customs of Melun and Meaux in Brie and four customs of Vitry, Troyes, Sens, and Chaumont-en-Bassigny in Champagne; (6) *groupe orléanais*: three principal customs of Montargis, Orléans, and Blois and five small customs of Chartres, Dreux, Châteauneuf-en-Thimerais, Grand Perche, and Perche-Gouët; (7) *groupe angevin*: two customs of Maine and Anjou; (8) *groupe tourangeau*: the principal custom of Tours, the jurisdiction of which included Touraine and a part of Berry, and secondary customs of Loudunois and Mirebeau; (9) *groupe poitevin*: the principal custom of Poitou and secondary customs of La Rochelle, Saint-Jean d'Angély, and Angoumois, in addition to the Marches séparantes; (10) *groupe central*: four important customs of Berry, Marche, Auvergne, and Bourbonnais; and, finally, (11) *groupe nivernais*: three customs of Nivernais, Saint-Pierre-le-Moutier, and Auxerre.[51]

that the king wanted to cater to the local sentiments. See Christophe Vellet, "Portraits individuels, portrait de groupe: Antoine Duprat et quelques acteurs de la rédaction de la coutume d'Auvergne," in Garnier and Vendrand-Voyer (eds.), *La coutume dans tous ses états*, 61–78.

[49] *Lettres patentes* of Francis I, March 13, 1521, included in the *Coutume de Bourbonnais*, *Nouveau coutumier général*, vol. 3, 1302.

[50] See Chénon, *Histoire générale du droit français*, vol. 2, 321–25. The parlements created after the sixteenth century, of Nancy, Metz, and Douai (except Besançon), and the Conseil souverain of Artois each had multiple and fragmented *coutumes* within their jurisdictions.

[51] Ibid., 323–25. For *Marches séparantes*, see supra Chapter 2, note 178.

Charles Dumoulin wrote stupendous commentaries on many of these *coutumes*.[52] While he exposed the diversity of individual customary rules, Dumoulin assured legal scholars and practitioners that it was possible to extract certain common underlying principles from what seemed like a heap of disarrayed dispositions. Under his influence, jurists began to explore a sort of compatibility between the sources of law, studying how the application of customs to specific situations would compare with the application of Roman law rules. This development took place in the atmosphere of the historically oriented intellectual movement known as legal humanism. Before discussing Dumoulin's work, it is first necessary to examine the humanist school of law.

3. Humanist School of Law

The French humanist school was a historical school of Roman law. The teaching of Roman law at medieval universities had long been dominated by the methods of the Italian jurist Bartolus of Sassoferrato (1313–1357). Preoccupied with the practical application of Roman law to the problems of their own time, jurists, known as the Commentators, wrote exhaustive commentaries on all parts of the *Corpus juris civilis*. They popularized the methods of interpreting the contemporary local statutes of the Italian city states in virtue of those established by the *jus commune*. In the fifteenth century, however, the newly emerging learning of the Renaissance laid the ground for critical evaluation of the methods of Bartolus and his successors. Lorenzo Valla (1405–1457) rejected medieval commentaries on the *Corpus juris civilis*, and Angelo Poliziano (1454–1494) studied the Florentine manuscript of the *Digest* in order to correct errors in the printed edition.[53] These Italian humanists deeply influenced the Frenchman Guillaume Budé (1467–1550).[54]

Budé applied the humanist methods to the study of classical Roman law to explain its historical development from the origin to the compilation of Justinian.[55] Historical consciousness was the hallmark of humanism. Through a distinct philological analysis, which had been introduced to France by Andrea Alciato (1492–1550), humanists showed the law that had guided the Roman people was not the same as the law taught by Bartolists. The more the jurists resorted to the *jus commune* to find solutions to contemporary problems, argued humanists, the further they drifted away from the *Corpus juris civilis*.[56] Armed with the

[52] Dumoulin, *Le grand coustumier general*.
[53] See Caenegem, *Historical Introduction to Private Law*, ch. 3.
[54] Douglas Osler, "Budaeus and Roman Law," *Ius commune* 13 (1986), 195–212.
[55] Michel Reulos, "L'importance des praticiens dans humanisme juridique," in Centre d'études supérieures de la Renaissance (ed.), *Pédagogues et juristes; Congrès du Centre d'études supérieures de la Renaissance de Tours, été 1960* (Paris: Librairie philosophique J. Vrin, 1963), 124.
[56] Stein, *Roman Law in European History*, 75–77.

knowledge of antiquity, humanist scholars tried to illumine the original meanings of the texts of Justinian. They challenged the civil law's claim to universal validity and questioned whether it was justified to apply Roman law to contemporary France.

French legal humanism was far from a monolithic, stagnant phenomenon; it underwent constant changeover. Three distinct phases in its evolution can be identified.[57] First, early humanists in the 1530s and 1540s tried to reconcile their new methods, known as the *mos gallicus*, or "French manner," with the old *mos italicus*, the method of Roman law studies in Italy. Barthélemy de Chasseneuz (1480–1541), Pierre Rebuffi (1487–1557), André Tiraqueau (1488–1558), and Dumoulin belonged to this group.[58] Second, in the mid-century, humanism focused on searching for authentic Roman law. Historicist humanism in the school of Jacques Cujas (1520–1590) attempted to return to the original form of Roman law. In a similar spirit, systematic humanism tried to regroup the texts of the *Corpus juris civilis* into a coherent and logical body. Éguiner-François Baron (*c.*1495–1550), François Connan (1508–1551), François Duaren (1509–1559), François Baudouin (1520–1573), and Hugues Doneau (1527–1591) were part of this movement.[59] Finally, the third current of humanism, the humanism of legal practitioners, emerged in the later decades of the century. Guy Coquille (1523–1603), Étienne Pasquier (1529–1615), Antoine Loisel (1536–1617), René Choppin (1537–1601), and Louis Charondas Le Caron (1534–1613) displayed a pragmatic propensity, concerned more with actual practice and contemporary preoccupations and less with the textual analysis of Roman law.

Legal Humanism

The historical insight questioning the immediate applicability of the code of Justinian in France prompted humanists to turn their attention to custom. Early commentators of customs were scholars of learned law who attempted to come to grips with the customary legal systems in the north of France.[60] The influence of the Bartolist approach on the supposed novelty of humanist method has been well recognized. The sources used by the early generation of French jurists revealed close continuity with the commentators or postglossators.[61] Chasseneuz

[57] Jean-Louis Thireau, "Humaniste (Jurisprudence)," in Denis Alland and Stéphane Rials (eds.), *Dictionnaire de la culture juridique* (Paris: Presses universitaires de France, 2003), 795–800.

[58] Donald R. Kelley, "Civil Science in the Renaissance: Jurisprudence in the French Manner," in *History, Law and the Human Sciences: Medieval and Renaissance Perspectives* (London: Variorum Reprints, 1984), 269.

[59] Kelley, *Foundations of Modern Historical Scholarship*, 100–15.

[60] Donahue, "Comparative Law before the Code Napoleon," 12.

[61] Patrick Arabeyre, "Aspects du 'nationalisme culturel' dans le domaine du droit au début du XVIe siècle: Les grands juristes français selon Barthélemy de Chasseneuz," *Annales de Bourgogne* 74 (2002),

and Tiraqueau wrote on the customs of Burgundy and Poitou respectively. Tiraqueau, famous for his commentaries on marriage law and *retrait lignager* (power of redemption) in 1546, frequently cited Franciscus Accursius (*c.*1182–*c.*1260) and Bartolus, while seldom referring to humanist authors.[62] They can be called the last Bartolists in the sense that they rejected the purely scholarly preoccupation and underscored the importance of the law to meet current practical needs.[63] Nicolas Bohier (1469–1539) published in 1508 the first commentary on the *coutume* of Berry of 1481, and Jean Sainson authored in 1516 a treatise on the *coutume* of Touraine which had been written down in 1507.[64] Their commentaries aimed mainly to interpret specific customs and explain their rationality in light of Roman law and canon law. For them, the only common law was Roman law.[65]

The dominant scholarly movement in the mid-sixteenth century was driven by the desire to restore the original virtue and purity of Roman law. The humanists noted that the recovery of authentic Roman law was complicated by the obscure form in which the books of the *Corpus juris* were arranged. Neither the *Digest* nor the *Codex* had a rational ordering, and each contained repetitions and contradictions. Humanists shared a strong predilection for order.[66] Central to legal humanism was the belief that law existed as the whole of general principles, which must give satisfaction to different situations. From the mid-century, the humanist quest evolved to an effort to organize the provisions in the *Corpus juris* and establish unity in their interpretation. The *Commentaria juris civilis* by Connan, a *maître des requêtes*, became the manifesto for this new Romanist direction. A student of Alciato, Connan condensed the materials of the *Digest* and the *Codex* and arranged them in a systematic order. After his premature death at the age of 43, his unfinished commentaries were collected and published in 1553 by Barthélemy

161–88; Patrick Arabeyre. "Culture juridique et littérature européennes chez les derniers bartolistes français (première moitié du XVIe siècle)," *Clio@Themis: Revue électronique d'histoire du droit* 2 (2009), https://www.cliothemis.com/Culture-juridique-et-litterature. See also J.-Henri Pignot, *Un jurisconsulte au seizième siècle: Barthélemy de Chasseneuz, premier commentateur de la coutume de Bourgogne et président du Parlement de Provence, sa vie et ses œuvres* (Geneva: Slatkine Reprints, 1970); Christian Dugas de La Boissonny, "Barthélémy de Chasseneuz (1480–1541)," in Antoine Astaing and François Lormant (eds.), *Le juriste et la coutume du Moyen Âge au Code civil: Actes du colloque international organisé à Nancy, les 1er et 2 juillet 2010* (Nancy: PUN-Éditions universitaires de Lorraine, 2014), 91–100.

[62] Accursius was an Italian jurist, famous for his collection of glosses, annotations on the compilation of Roman law. In 1543, L'Hôpital penned congratulatory verses on the publication of Tiraqueau's commentaries on marriage law. Émile Dupré Lasale, *Michel de L'Hospital avant son élévation au poste de chancelier de France* (Paris: Thorin et fils, 1875), 95 and 317.

[63] Arabeyre, "Culture juridique et littérature européennes," # 17, # 24.

[64] See Jasmin Hepburn, "A Lawyer and His Sources: Nicolas Bohier and Legal Practice in Sixteenth-Century France," in Paul J. du Plessis and John W. Cairns (eds.), *Reassessing Legal Humanism and Its Claims: Petere Fontes?* (Edinburgh: Edinburgh University Press, 2016), 244–81.

[65] Arabeyre, "Culture juridique et littérature européennes," # 33–34.

[66] Fred H. Blume et al., *The Codex of Justinian: A New Annotated Translation, with Parallel Latin and Greek Text Based on a Translation by Justice Fred H. Blume* (Cambridge: Cambridge University Press, 2016).

Faye (?–1581), a judge at the Parlement of Paris.[67] Doneau and Louis Le Caron also undertook the project of laying out the Roman law texts according to classical ideals.

Cujas and Doneau and their followers were little interested in legal practice; they turned away from contemporary problems by choice.[68] They were almost purely academic in their disposition as well as outlook. Engrossed in textual analyses of Roman law during the time of classical jurists, they approached Roman law as a study of the past, not rules and principles useful to practitioners. The result was that their methods and ideas had little impact on activities of legal professionals.[69] Roman law was not treated in France as legislation, unlike Germany and Italy, and customary law was free to depart from it, so Roman law could be studied objectively as an intellectual pursuit, without adapting to current practical needs. But it meant it had become a strictly scholarly venture. There is a certain truth in the idea that Roman law as legal science in France was a victim of its own success. Law schools, having enjoyed great success in the sixteenth century, began to decay after 1600, in part because of their limited relevance to legal practice.[70] The humanist contempt for the alleged barbarism of glossators clashed with the approaches of the rising cohort of practitioners.[71]

Intellectual gratification or cultivated pleasure in rediscovering an intelligent system of the past was of limited interest for practicing jurists, who found it difficult to reconcile the innovation and achievements of humanism with their work. While legal scholars tried to understand and recover the purity and precision of

[67] *Francisci Connani commentaria Juris civilis* (Paris, 1553). Following Connan's wish, Faye dedicated the volume to Michel de L'Hôpital, then chancellor to the duchess of Berry. In the preface, Faye affirmed that L'Hôpital, when he was a judge at the Parlement of Paris, had been preparing a synthesis of Roman law like Connan's work. In his testament, L'Hôpital referred to the books of civil law he had started writing but left unfinished. Jacques-Auguste de Thou stated that L'Hôpital's work, which "still has not seen the light," should "be published some day for the good of the kingdom because it truly deserves immortality." Jacques-Auguste de Thou, *Histoire universelle depuis 1543 jusqu'en 1607* (Basel: Jean Louis Brand Müller, 1742), vol. 4, 824. See Marie Seong-Hak Kim, "Civil Law and Civil War: Michel de L'Hôpital and the Ideals of Legal Unification in Sixteenth-Century France," *Law and History Review* 28 (2010), 799. L'Hôpital and Faye both obtained a doctorate from the University of Padua.

[68] Jean-Louis Thireau, "Hugues Doneau et les fondements de la codification modern," *Droits: Revue française de théorie, de philosophie et de culture juridiques* 26 (1997), 83. A recent study has argued that Cujas was far from an anti-Bartolist. Xavier Prévost, *Jacques Cujas (1522–1590): Jurisconsulte humaniste* (Geneva: Librairie Droz, 2015); Xavier Prévost, "Reassessing the Influence of Medieval Jurisprudence on Jacques Cujas' (1522–1590) Method," in du Plessis and Cairns (eds.), *Reassessing Legal Humanism and Its Claims*, 88–107.

[69] Stein's observation is worth quoting in length: "One reason for the obvious distaste that many practitioners felt for the academic humanists was their rudeness and acrimony to each other. . . . Since a lawyer may be taking one position today and a different position next week, he must avoid being personal. The humanists accepted none of these conventions and they hurled as much abuse on each other as they did on Tribonian or Bartolus. This feature of their writing led to an underlying feeling that, however good their scholarship, they were not true jurists: their writings had an alien tone." Peter Stein, "Legal Humanism and Legal Science," *Tidschrift voor Rechtsgchiedenis* 54 (1986), 305. Petty (and thus more vicious) rivalry in the academic world has a long history.

[70] Dawson, *The Oracles*, 340–42.

[71] Stein, *Roman Law in European History*, 75; Thireau, "Le comparatisme et la naissance du droit français," 158. Glossators used marginal annotations (*glossae*) in studying Roman legal texts.

the law of the ancient times, judges and lawyers mostly cared about finding reliable rules and principles they could apply to concrete situations. When the applicable law was absent, a hard-pressed judge needed authoritative statements with persuasive weight, more likely found in the commentaries of Bartolus and his successors than the humanist writings: "the scholar could be a humanist but the practitioner had to be a Bartolist."[72] Even Connan was criticized for writing as a philosopher rather than a jurist, with insufficient attention to the practical consequences of his work.[73]

Jus Commune and *Jus Proprium*

Skepticism of the supposed universal force of Roman law and disenchantment with the theoretical basis of *jus commune* rekindled humanist interest in ancient customs and the constitutions of France. The idea that laws were relative to each society had a powerful appeal. The approach of humanist practitioners to custom was not very different from their approach to Roman law. It must not be forgotten that most of them, although deeply imbued with Gallican sentiment, were convinced Romanists.[74] The utility of Roman law was obvious: it offered general principles and rules of construction as well as rational and equitable solutions for common legal problems.[75] When they interpreted royal decrees or customs, lawyers referred to the common concepts, principles, logic, and terminology of civil law and canon law they had learned at the universities. Jurists throughout Europe argued the legal norms from the *jus commune* and rarely from the *jus proprium*.[76] Confronted with lacunae and obscurities in legal question, they instinctively turned to the *Corpus juris*.

The campaign of compiling the customs, then in full force in the second half of the sixteenth century, was closely interwoven with these developments. It was critical for jurists to forge logical relationship between Roman law and custom. They were overall confident that the principles of Roman law could be utilized without overwhelming French custom.[77] They searched for a common spirit

[72] Stein, "Legal Humanism and Legal Science," 304.

[73] Thireau, "Hugues Doneau," 83; see also Jean-Louis Thireau, "L'enseignement du droit méthodes au XVIe siècle. Continuité ou rupture?" *Annales d'histoire des facultés de droit et de la science juridique* 2 (1985), 27–36.

[74] Reulos, "L'importance des praticiens," 126.

[75] François Oliver-Martin, *La coutume de Paris: Trait d'union entre le droit romain et les législations modernes* (Paris: Recueil Sirey, 1925), 16.

[76] Jurists cited passages from the learned laws and listed precedents. Manlio Bellomo, *The Common Legal Past of Europe, 1000–1800*, trans. Lydia G. Cochrane (Washington, DC: Catholic University of America Press, 1995), 81–83, 91, 211.

[77] Reulos, "L'importance des praticiens," 121.

among the customs that could serve as the basis of a customary common law (*le droit commun coutumier*).

The one individual who single-handedly carried out a synthesis of the Bartolist scientific methods of Roman law, the feudists' interest in the Frankish origin of feudal law and customs, and the humanist doctrinal ideals, all at once, was Dumoulin. Contemporary jurisprudence unabashedly followed his opinions and arguments. Dumoulin's imprint on modern French law is widely acknowledged.[78]

4. Dumoulin and the Oracles of Law

Dumoulin practiced law as an *avocat* at the Châtelet de Paris and then the Parlement of Paris (see Figure 3.1).[79] As a practitioner, his main emphasis was on customary law, yet he also wrote on Roman law and canon law. His treatises on contracts, usury, and *rentes* were seamlessly weaved with custom.[80] Fiercely independent and nonconformist, he moved effortlessly between technical legal analysis critiquing feudal customs and political exposition upholding the imperium of the king.[81] Dumoulin's aggressive and often abusive style gave an extraordinary

[78] See, for instance, Jean-Louis Thireau, "Aux origines des articles 1217 à 1225 du Code civil: *L'extricatio labyrinthi dividui et individui* de Charles Du Moulin," *Tijdschrift voor Rechtsgeschiedenis* 51 (1983), 51–109 (discussing Dumoulin's theory of divisible and indivisible obligations).

[79] The 1581 edition of Dumoulin's *Omnia quae extant opera* included Julien Brodeau's "La vie de Maistre Charles du Molin," which remains the major source for Dumoulin's biographical information. Born in Paris in 1500, Dumoulin studied law in Orléans and Poitiers, earning a doctorate from the University of Orléans in 1522. See Jean-Louis Thireau, *Charles du Moulin, 1500–1566: Étude sur les sources, la méthode, les idées politiques et économiques d'un juriste de la Renaissance* (Geneva: Droz, 1980). See also Géraldine Cazals, "Molinaeus Noster Charles du Moulin (1500–1566), oracle du droit, praticien engagé et fondateur de l'école juridique française, un modèle de jurisconsulte dans la France au XIXe siècle," in Anne Dibigny-Reverso, Xavier Prévost, and Nicolas Warembourg (eds.), *Liber amicorum, Mélanges réunis en homage au professeur Jean-Louis Thireau* (Paris: Mare & Martin, 2019), 57–100; Wim Decock, "Charles Dumoulin (1500–1566)," in Olivier Descamps and Rafael Domingo (eds.), *Great Christian Jurists in French History* (Cambridge: Cambridge University Press, 2919), 97–116; René Filhol, "Dumoulin," in R. Naz (ed.), *Dictionnaire de droit canonique* (Paris: Letouzey, 1953), vol. 5, 41–67; Henri Aubépin, *De l'influence de Dumoulin sur la législation française. Extrait de la Revue critique de législation et de jurisprudence* (Paris: Cotillon, 1855); Donald R. Kelley, "*Fides istoriae*: Charles Dumoulin and the Gallican View of History," *Traditio* 22 (1966), 347–402; Kelley, *Foundations of Modern Historical Scholarship*, 151–82; John H. M. Salmon, *Society in Crisis: France in the Sixteenth Century* (New York: St. Martin's Press, 1975), 27–58.

[80] *Rentes* were perpetual annuities, a common form of public lending. Royal *rentes* were set up on the Hôtel de ville de Paris. Dumoulin developed the theory of *rentes* as an instrument of capital funding, separate from usury prohibited by the church. He justified charging interest at a moderate rate, defined as one-twelfth, or eight and one-third (8 1/3) percent, of the principal. See Thireau, *Charles Du Moulin*, Chapter 6.

[81] Dumoulin's impatient spirit was a sign of his genius, which also came with certain insecurity. He published polemics against Counter-Reformation Catholicism and later against Calvinism. His antipapal writings compelled him to flee to Basel and Geneva, and from 1553 he lectured in Tübingen and Montbéliard, before returning to France in 1557. A staunch supporter of the Gallican church during the early years of the Wars of Religion, Dumoulin authored in 1564 a radical treatise opposing the reception of the decrees of the Council of Trent to France. This work, *Conseil sur le fait du concile de Trent*, earned him brief imprisonment in Paris. Filhol aptly captured his character: Dumoulin was of a

Figure 3.1 Charles Dumoulin (1500–1560)
Source: Creativecommons.org

edge to his work. Almost every juristic theory he proposed was adopted not only by the Parlement of Paris in interpreting the Parisian custom but also by the provincial parlements in construing their customs. His legal theories became a new orthodoxy in his own lifetime.

Commentaries on the Custom of Paris

In 1539 Dumoulin published his commentary on the *Coutume de Paris* of 1510. Titled *Commentarii in Parisienses consuetudines*, it dealt with the first chapter of the *coutume*, *Des fiefs*.[82] This was followed by the commentary on the second

genial personality, but also had a genuinely mean streak, "angry at everything and everyone, perpetually persecuted but inviting himself to be persecuted." Filhol, *Le premier président Christofle de Thou*, 37–38.

[82] *Prima pars Commentariorum in consuetudines Parisienses, authore D. Carolo Molendineo* (Paris: P. Le Preux, 1539). Different editions are listed in Marie Seong-Hak Kim, "Charles Dumoulin's *Commentarii in consuetudines Parisienses*," in Serge Dauchy, Georges Martyn, Anthony Musson, Heikki Pihlajamäki, and Alain Wijffels (eds.), *The Formation and Transmission of Western Legal Culture: 150 Books that Made the Law in the Age of Printing* (Heidelberg: Springer, 2016), 82–85. *Prima pars Commentariorum* was studied in 1773 by Pierre-Paul-Nicolas Henrion de Pansey, in *Traité des fiefs de Dumoulin, analysé et conféré avec les autres feudistes* (Paris: Valade, 1773).

chapter, *Des censives*, in 1558.[83] He left only fragmentary notes for other chapters. Fiefs were lands held on condition of feudal service. *Censives* were holdings by commoners subject in perpetuity to *cens*, annual dues owed to the landlord. With the decline of feudalism, the tenant paid a fixed amount, called quitrent, in commutation of various obligations. Dumoulin was the bluntest critic of the *coutume*. He ascribed its defects to the excessive influence of the nobility and the commissioners' passive attitudes. He claimed that the assembly of the estates in Paris played into the hands of feudal nobles who were adamantly opposed to any change affecting their rights.[84] He criticized the commissioners for failing to warn the estates sufficiently about inequitable customs or to push them hard enough to come up with better solutions. As a result, the assembly moved too fast, without enough opportunities for discussion. The *coutumes* of other *pays* too, finalized without the adequate input of the professionals, proved susceptible to various interpretations and litigation. A general problem with the first waves of the campaign was that the *coutumes*, once written down, did not receive serious discussion by "the Senate," he argued.[85]

Dumoulin wrote in Latin. All other authors in the first half of the sixteenth century wrote their commentaries of *coutumes* in Latin. It may sound ironic that the vernacular texts of customs received Latin commentaries, which then became the authoritative reference materials of French customary law, but it shows that the readers of these early commentaries were practicing lawyers and judges of the parlements.[86]

Dumoulin analyzed the text of the *coutume* line by line, and often word by word, using copious glosses. Each gloss was divided into numbered paragraphs that were apostilled with a concise notice. But his commentaries were more than textual exegesis; they were veritable historical criticism. He combined a humanist exposition of history, philology, and law on the one hand and the Bartolist project of addressing contemporary legal problems on the other. Accompanied by exhaustive references to court decisions, his remarks amounted to an authoritative appraisal of each provision of the *coutume*, either granting approval or registering disapproval.

Dumoulin's commentaries revealed his deep hostility to various feudal dues. He argued that feudal services and seigneurial exaction were little more than base servitudes.[87] While rejecting seigneurial justice and personal subjection, he upheld contractual obligations and property rights in fiefs and *censives* in the

[83] *Secunda pars Commentariorum analyticorum in consuetudines Parisienses* (Paris: P. Le Preux, 1558). The two commentaries were included as *Commentarii in duos priores titulos consuetudinis parisiensis* in vol. 1 of *Omnia quae extant opera* (5 vols.).

[84] Aubépin, *De l'influence de Dumoulin*, ch. 2, 17–19.

[85] The "Senate" referred to the Parlement of Paris. Thireau, *Charles Dumoulin*, 257–58.

[86] Reulos, "Ver la présentation coordonnée et logique du droit français," 279.

[87] Church, *Constitutional Thought*, 107.

Parisian custom. His reasoning underpinning feudal property relations was that custom should be interpreted in accordance with equitable principles.

Dumoulin developed a theory of sovereignty grounded in what he saw as the essence of feudal contract.[88] Feudalism stood on the principle of heredity, but the king acceded to the throne not by virtue of heredity but by virtue of his legal rights. The king was the supreme seigneur of the lands in his kingdom, and to the monarchy belonged all the attributes of sovereignty, laws, privileges, and justice. But the king would not negate his obligations to the royal domain, nor would he arbitrarily take away the seigneurs' rights to fiefs, all the while repudiating their political presumptions and pretensions.[89] This was because the king was the source of all laws and yet derived his authority from them. The king could not dispose of the law, no more than any of his subjects could. His "eminent" interest came from the law. Dumoulin urged the abrogation of seigneurial jurisdictions because they stood in the way of national unity and strong royal power.[90] By separating fief from justice, he firmly established the idea that the king was the fount of all justice.

For Dumoulin, the crown needed to establish a general set of laws to govern the kingdom effectively, and this could be achieved by ascertaining the common elements of local customs. Dumoulin declared in his commentaries on the *coutume* of Paris that French custom was different from *jus commune* and that the French people had their own "Frankish and Gallic common law" in the form of "general and common customs."[91] Particular customs were only expressions of one original custom, unique and universal, that existed in the kingdom of the Franks. "The custom of Paris is at the center of the customs across the French kingdom, Belgium, and all the Gaul."[92] Thus, "Roman law of *jus commune*, compiled under the great Justinian, must be examined so long as it conforms to reason, that is, so long as it does not conflict with the customs of the people who approved them."[93]

Confident that only local custom deserved to become the basis of legitimate law, he faulted contemporary intellectuals for what he saw as their blind adherence to the *Corpus juris civilis*. Dumoulin had a vision to create a "brief, clear, and

[88] Kathleen Davis, "Sovereign Subjects, Feudal Law, and the Writing of History," *Journal of Medieval and Early Modern Studies* 36 (2006), 240.

[89] According to Davis, the suggestion that Dumoulin's arguments amounted to "a systematic attack on the feudal vision of French society" misses the constitutive force of feudal historiography. Ibid., 239.

[90] It has been said that any account of the process that brought about an absolute monarchy must start with Dumoulin's work. Quentin Skinner, *The Foundations of Modern Political Thought* (Cambridge: Cambridge University Press, 1978), vol. 2, 264.

[91] "Consuetudines generals & communes erant jus peculiare & commune Francorum & Gallorum." Dumoulin, *Prima pars Commentariorum in consuetudines Parisienses*, "De Fiefs," # 107 (*Omnia*, vol. 1, 22).

[92] "Consuetudo Parisiensium est caput omnium hujus regni, & totius etiam Belgicae consuetudinum." Ibid., # 2 (*Omnia*, vol. 1, 3).

[93] Ibid., # 111 (*Omnia*, vol. 1, 23).

equitable compilation" of a general custom. He enunciated this ideal of *consonantia* in his *Oratio de concordia et unione consuetudinum Franciae* (Oration on the Union and Concord of the Customs of France).[94] Written in 1545, *Oratio* was a blueprint for turning the reform of customs then in progress at the local level into the agreement of law at the national level.[95] This short treatise was a de facto manifesto of the unity of French law, French people, and the French Republic. Written in Latin, it has not been readily accessible, so relatively extensive quotes would be justified.

Union and Concord of the Customs of France

Dumoulin began by emphasizing the importance of clear laws:

> Nothing is more necessary or beneficial in the Republic than clear and equitable order of good laws; nothing is more dangerous or pernicious than their confusion and uncertainty, where the good and peace-loving citizens cannot have their personal safety or their property protected, any more inside the City itself than outside among outlaws and brigands. . . . Because of the confusion and uncertainty of the laws, the judge in truth cannot protect these good subjects, no more than they can restrain the bad people.[96]

He lamented that countless customs scattered all over the kingdom were contradictory to the point of being completely meaningless. The pitiful state of *enquêtes par turbe*, the usual method of proving custom, raised his ire in particular. The *enquêtes* were marred by corruption, subjectivity, and unreliableness. There was no way to prove custom in legal proceedings other than using confused testimonies, which could turn out a million different things:

> Depending on whether the parties were diligent or negligent, were corrupt, or were members of a league or weak, this proof was sometimes white, sometimes black, sometimes of a changing color, often in the same *bailliage*.[97] Sometimes it even happened that, if both parties were equally powerful and members of a league, they each proved customs in a diametrically opposite way, contrary to and incompatible with each other. From that, witnesses of bad faith

[94] *Oratio de concordia et unione consuetudinum Franciae*, in *Caroli Molinaei, Omnia quae extant opera*, vol. 2, 690–92. This short treatise has been translated into French: Philippe Gonzalez de Gaspard, "Le discours sur la concorde et l'union des coutumes de France de Charles Du Moulin (Présentation et traduction)" (DEA de philosophie du droit, Université Panthéon-Assas Paris II, 2000). Discussion in this section benefited from Gonzalez de Gaspard's translation.

[95] *Oratio* was not dated. It has commonly been believed to have been written in 1546, but others argue that it was written between 1544 and 1545. Gonzalez de Gaspard, "Le discours sur la concorde et l'union des coutumes de France," 7.

[96] *Oratio*, in *Omnia quae extant opera*, vol. 2, 690.

[97] "*Modo alba, modo nigra, modo versicolor.*"

> multiplied, and men became accustomed to perjury, bribery, and quarrels. Evil grew day by day.[98]

Judicial administration in France was held up as hostage in a muddled coexistence of learned law and custom:

> France had almost no light, no real science of civil law, and students did not learn it seriously, since it was practically of no use. Why should anyone learn *les Lois* through long and hard work, and at no small expense, when a person about to speak of it is immediately shut down by a contrary or opposite custom, presented through *preuve* with no explanation?[99]

Having painted these bleak pictures, Dumoulin proceeded to show how to improve the situation. He argued that obscurities and contradictions abounding in local and provincial laws could be corrected by a compilation of laws common to the kingdom of France. "Nothing would be more praiseworthy in the entire Republic, more useful or desirable," than bringing the customs to consonance (*consonantia*).[100] He presented the *coutume* of Paris, superior to any other *coutumes*, as the model for a common law. Besides, the jurisdiction of the Parlement of Paris covered most *pays coutumiers*. Dumoulin effectively envisaged a *jus commune* based on the custom of Paris that could stand up to the Roman *jus civile*.[101]

A number of advantages would result from having a uniform law, claimed Dumoulin. First, a great number of unjust customs that had slowly crept into law, by mistake or through ignorance, would be reformed and brought to justice and equity. Second, through reconciling *coutumes* with one another, one could look for one *coutume* that is consistent with the laws from a general point of view or create something that is more just and useful than the others. Third, conflicting and contradictory customs on a given subject would be reduced to one single custom, the shortest and best. Fourth, many impervious, ambiguous, and convoluted customs would be made clear and easy. Fifth, one could discard absurd and superfluous customs. Sixth, incomplete customs would be made complete; many obscurities in customs which have long and frequently consumed the highest courts and which are reproduced in the contradictory court decisions would succumb to one sure law, in a most evident and absolute manner. Finally, seventh, one could shut down the road leading to litigation not only for private merchants but also for the cabal of more powerful men who, swayed by favors, depravity, or ambition, have objected to unifying customs of a particular place.[102]

98 *Oratio*, in *Omnia quae extant opera*, vol. 2, 690. 99 Ibid. 100 Ibid.

101 Davis, "Sovereign Subjects, Feudal Law," 237; Paul Ourliac and Jean-Louis Gazzaniga, *Histoire du droit privé français de l'an mil au Code civil* (Paris: Éditions Albin Michel, 1985), 161.

102 *Oratio*, in *Omnia quae extant opera*, vol. 2, 690.

The last point, prevention of rampant lawsuits, was of particular concern. Several customs, "very disparate, contradictory, sometimes obscure, iniquitous, stupid, and truncated," were prone to create disputes and multiply them, augmenting the gains and subtleties of legal practitioners of bad faith. Dumoulin complained that uncertain and confusing customs had emboldened dishonorable *avocats* who exploited them to commit frauds:

> Eager to pervert existing customs or to invent new ones, they made sure, once they obtained a particular judgment for the parties whom they had fraudulently suborned, that it be passed and established as *res judicata*. By repeating this technique for years, they could feign the existence of a custom as they wanted it and, through this artifice, could seek some wealthy inheritance or other iniquitous gains.[103]

This ignoble situation would be put to an end with the concord of customs:

> One can have a small collection, which would be very short, clear, accessible and indisputable and be in perfect harmony with the *jus commune* and natural equity, suitable for the public interest as well as for the interest of each individual.[104]

It would "cut off and tame this infinite multitude of the epidemic of lawsuits which shake and crush France so miserably and bring it grave dishonor before other nations." Only lawyers with no conscience, driven by their insatiable desire for more lawsuits, would want to keep the laws as obscure and haphazard as they currently were.

Dumoulin was not oblivious to the challenges his program entailed. How would the customs, each having enjoyed autonomous authority for so long, cope with the prospect of being subsumed into one general law; how could the provinces, jealous of their franchises and independence, be brought to accept the custom of Paris? The diversity of people caused the diversity of laws; could different peoples be brought under the same civil law when they had particular situations in each lawsuit? His response was forthright: the French are one people. From early on they lived under a unified rule, observing the same laws; beneath the particularism of the *coutumes* lay the common spirit that inspired them. He elaborated:

> I affirm, first of all, that the people of Gaul are one people. They once lived within one province, even though it was a very vast land, as attested to in Book I of the commentaries by Julius Caesar. Secondly, I say that one should not refer to

[103] Ibid. [104] Ibid., 691.

> the Gallic people as a whole but should consider only those who may claim themselves without distinction to be part of a region of customary law, those who speak the same or nearly the same language.
>
> Thirdly, because these peoples have always had recourse to the same form–is it not–of customary law, if any difference in law exists within each *bailliage* and among many *bailliages*, this variety consists only in the peculiarities of each *bailliage*. On all other things and kinds considered one by one, we can easily assume that all the customs I am speaking of were at the beginning the one and the same custom, although by the passage of time they became varied in each *bailliage* on certain specific points. And this diversity, in all accounts, lacks all rationality and usefulness and is only conducive to deception and to engendering trials.
>
> I am not opposed that some places, for valid reasons, need to withdraw from certain points of a general custom, as it is also necessary to retain a local custom, to the extent that it excludes all objection and all fabrication of lawsuits and does not prevent the consonance and certainty of customary law as a whole.[105]

Now that several customs had already been discussed, drawn up, and recorded, it was easier to reduce them to a single body. Dumoulin emphasized that the redaction was carried out in the assembly of the estates. Many points have been wisely resolved: "according to what is equitable and good, provisions have been not only added or removed but changed, this with the consent of not just a majority but the entire people, and with the consent of all citizens; better yet, not just with unanimous consent but at the urgent demand of all citizens." This overwhelming desire and approbation on the part of the people for the reformation of customs showed that they were unified for the sake of equity and "for the greater interest of the kingdom as a whole."

Dumoulin offered to prepare the first draft of a unified custom, which could then be taken up by a group of experienced men to be assigned. This compilation, before it is approved by the authority of the king and the Senate, "should be sent to all the *bailliages* of the *pays de droit coutumier*. The inhabitants of the localities would be ordered to decide, within six months or any other appropriate period of time, whether they accept the customs as written or, if not, they examine them diligently and promptly to identify any points that need to be modified or replaced and make their reasons known."[106] In all cases, the result of this "ευνομια" (*eunomie*, good legislation), a systematic body of national customary law, must be approved by royal authority. Finally, Dumoulin did not neglect to add: "The government of the state would make sure that this transformation is completed on the condition that

[105] Ibid. [106] Ibid., 692.

the modified articles apply only to future agreements, ensuring that it would not have perverse results for the agreements already concluded and those in the making, or for those who conclude a marriage contract by specific, tacit or express, covenants."[107] In other words, the new unified custom would not be applied ex post facto. His deep concerns about protecting freedom of contract and preserving existing legal relations were clearly on display.

The historian Jacques-Auguste de Thou (1553–1617), the son of Christophe de Thou, attested that Dumoulin's commentaries on the custom of Paris and other works, "full of erudition," were "seen among us as the *oracles de droit*."[108] De Thou regretted Dumoulin's immense merits went unrewarded and he was instead subject to injustice and ingratitude. Dumoulin's vision of a unified law seemed distant from reality in the 1540s, but he powerfully propelled a new round of customary law campaign in the 1550s. His call that abusive customs that had crept into the codified texts must be excised struck a chord with legal practitioners, who began demanding the reformation of customs.

5. *Vers la réformation*

In the 1550s and 1560s, the king was deluged with requests from local officials and lawyers to dispatch royal commissioners and authorize them to summon the three estates so that they could undertake the reformation of custom. Sometimes the provincial parlements made the request, as the Parlement of Brittany did in 1565.[109] The official justification for revisiting the customs that had already been published was that their *procès-verbal* was lost. The *procès-verbal* was the record of the debates among the three estates, composed by the presiding royal commissioners. Equivalent to the minutes of the assembly, it documented all the discussions, objections raised to each article, modifications suggested, and final decisions taken by the assembly.[110] Without it, local inhabitants would be compelled again to resort to *turbes des témoins* to prove a contested custom.[111] Often initial steps for calling the assembly were taken by local lawyers. The custom of Sens had been compiled in 1495 and published in 1506, but its minutes were not preserved.[112] A local *avocat* Jean Penon wrote a commentary on each article in 1552, but as a private work it could not substitute for the authority of the official

[107] Ibid., 691. This would be an example of ευνομια.

[108] Jacques-Auguste de Thou, *Histoire universelle depuis 1543 jusqu'en 1607* (London, 1734), vol. 5, book 38, 123.

[109] Filhol, *Le premier président Christofle de Thou*, 40–53, 77.

[110] Grinberg, *Écrire les coutumes*, 72.

[111] The *lettres patentes* of Henry II of August 17, 1555, issued for the *Coutume de Sens*, specifically mentioned this problem. *Nouveau coutumier général*, vol. 3, 530.

[112] Anette Smedley-Weill and Simone Geoffroy-Poisson, "Les assemblées d'états et la mise en forme du droit," *Les cahiers du Centre de recherches historiques* 26 (2001), 35.

procès-verbal. Penon, along with the city officials, petitioned the king to allow the reformation of their custom, arguing that due to the absence of the proceedings the articles had to be proved by local inquest, giving rise to much abuse and inconvenience.[113] The custom of Auxerre had been officially compiled in 1507, but its people demanded reformation on the grounds that the *procès-verbal* was lost.[114] The *procès-verbal* of the *Coutume de Paris* in 1580 noted that many *coutumes* within the jurisdiction of the Parlement of Paris were missing their proceedings or that they were interpolated, giving rise to contradictory interpretations of their provisions by the Parlement.[115]

Leaving aside the question of the presence or absence of the *procès-verbal*, the principal reason for calling for the estates was to modify existing customary rules. Proponents for change claimed that "doubts and obscurities" surrounding them brought endless lawsuits.[116] To those who wondered why custom needed to be modified so often, the local *avocat* Jean Brèche at the *présidial* of Tours responded that custom must be "accommodated and revised following the morals of the times," to be in line with the development of jurisprudence.[117] The changing morals translated into the changing economic conditions of the sixteenth century.

In 1555, the king responded to the supplications from his subjects by appointing royal commissioners to convoke the local assemblies. The new phase of the campaign, known as the reformation of customs, began.

[113] These developments were described by Jean Penon in the first edition of the reformed *Coutume de Sens*. After the *coutume* was approved, de Thou put Penon in charge of supervising the printing of the text. Filhol, *Le premier président Christofle de Thou*, 41. The importance of the invention of the printing press in the dissemination of the custom as law cannot be overstated. Zink, "Les éditions de coutumes," 468.

[114] The document was most likely not lost because it was included in Bourdot de Richebourg's compilation, *Nouveau coutumier général*, vol. 3, 584–91, but the people of Auxerre claimed its disappearance anyway. Filhol, *Le premier président Christofle de Thou*, 48. Twice the date was set for the reunion of the estates but each time it was postponed because the commissioners could not come. In June 1561, Elie le Briois, *lieutenant particulier*, appeared before the queen mother and pleaded with her not to disappoint his people. *Avocat* Guillaume Dubrocq came to Paris to consult with the commissioners and started the preparatory works by drawing the tax role of the estates.

[115] "Les procès-verbaux d'icelles estoient perdus & aditez, ou bien chargez de plusieurs renvois faits en notredite Cour." *Nouveau coutumier général*, vol. 3, 56.

[116] See Jean-Louis Thireau, "Les trois rédactions de la coutume de Touraine," in Garnier and Vendrand-Voyer (eds.), *La coutume dans tous ses états*, 111–34.

[117] Filhol, *Le premier président Christofle de Thou*, 47.

4
The Reformation of Customs

On August 17, 1555, Henry II commissioned *président* of the Parlement of Paris Christophe de Thou, *conseiller* Barthélemy Faye, and *avocat du roi* Gille Bourdin to proceed with a new publication of the custom of Sens.[1] The estates were convoked and in November the *Coutume de Sens* was published. It was deposited with the clerk the following March, replacing the text from fifty years earlier. This marked the beginning of the new phase of the royal campaign, mostly revisiting and revising the customs that had been published in the earlier round.[2] For the next twenty-five years, de Thou crisscrossed the nation presiding over the redaction assemblies. Under his watch, ten customs were reformed within the jurisdiction of the Parlement of Paris: Sens (1555; originally recorded in 1506); Vermandois-Laon (1556; 1507); Le Grand Perche (1558; 1505); Touraine (1559; 1507); Poitou (1559; 1514); Melun (1560; 1506); Auxerre (1561; 1507); Péronne (1567; 1507); Amiens (1567; 1507); and Paris (1580; 1510). Four customs, in Montfort, Mantes, Étampes, and Dourdan, were officially compiled for the first time in 1556.[3]

Some comparison between France and the Holy Roman Empire would be illuminating. First, whereas in France the customs underwent a reformation phase, this process was missing in the Empire.[4] The French monarchy's decision to revise the published *coutumes* attested to the achievements of legal humanism, which made it necessary to bring the customs in conformity with the doctrinal and jurisprudential progress. In Germany, the absence of a comprehensive appellate jurisdiction prevented lawyers from undertaking selective adaptation of customs to Roman law to serve their practical needs. The imperial Kammergericht was not the same as the Parlement of Paris. As a result, Germany

[1] The *Lettres patentes* of Henry II, August 17, 1555, *Nouveau coutumier général*, vol. 3, 530. Christophe de Harlay replaced Bourdin in the assembly.

[2] For the reformation phase, see Filhol, *Le premier président Christofle de Thou*; Filhol, "La rédaction des coutumes"; Filhol, "The Codification of Customary Law"; Dawson, "French Customs"; Descimon, "Quelques réflexions à propos des commissaires du roi"; Parrow, "Provincial Estates and the Revision of Customary Law"; Kim, "Christophe de Thou et la réformation des coutumes; Kim, "Custom, Community, and the Crown."

[3] In 1580 de Thou undertook the redaction of the custom of Eu overriding the contest from the Parlement of Rouen that it was under its jurisdiction.

[4] Gilissen, "Les phases de la codification" (Part 1), 62.

Custom, Law, and Monarchy: A Legal History of Early Modern France. Marie Seong-Hak Kim, Oxford University Press.
 DOI: 10.1093/oso/9780192845498.003.0004

saw a much more sweeping displacement of customs, amid some intense resistance of local liberties.[5]

Second, the fact that the reform of customs in France took place in the popular assemblies of the three estates was of major significance. By the reformation phase, the consultative procedures of recording customs at the local assemblies had been well established. The smooth operation of the assemblies under supervision by royal commissioners projected a clear measure of popular consent, while the commissioners and legal experts increasingly controlled the actual process and set conditions for the validity of legal norms. What had been claimed and acknowledged on the "customary" basis could now be rejected because it lacked "legal" basis. In the Habsburg Netherlands, codification attempts, seemingly forced down from the center, tended to be met with local defiance or at best indifference. In France, the king maintained the position that he would not dictate the contents of customs governing private relations of his subjects; he only authenticated the customs agreed upon by them. Laws were made on the petition of the subjects, and only after their consultation.[6] A powerful narrative it was.

The reformation of customs took place through the worst of the religious wars. De Thou regularly sent the king reports about the religious situations of the places he visited to preside over the assemblies.[7] The outbreak of the wars in 1562 temporarily interrupted the campaign, and again from 1567 to 1579. The operation resumed in 1580, when Henry III commissioned de Thou to reform the ancient custom of Paris. The resulting *Nouvelle Coutume de Paris* replaced the *Ancienne Coutume de Paris*. The political implications were profound. At a time when royal authority seemingly reached the lowest point during civil war, redrawing customs in the popular assembly was "an excellent way of reminding the provinces of royal authority which they had a tendency to forget."[8] The redaction assembly was a symbolic rendezvous between the king and his subjects. The formality of convention, a transaction between the three estates, was to a large degree a legislative contrivance. Popular participation in declaring custom to be law provided an opportunity for the king to offset the centrifugal forces without compromising either his authority or his commitment to custom. The message was clear: the ultimate authority to say what the laws were resided with the crown.

This chapter examines the reformation phase of the customary law campaign through the end of the sixteenth century.

[5] See Gerald Strauss, *Law, Resistance and the State: The Opposition to Roman Law in Reformation Germany* (Princeton: Princeton University Press, 1986).

[6] Beauthier and de Broux, "Un regard historien," 726.

[7] Filhol, *Le premier président Christofle de Thou*, 52.

[8] Ibid., 49.

1. De Thou's Tour de Force

According to Étienne Pasquier, the campaign to reform customs took off thanks to the *Édit du semestre* issued in 1554.[9] The semester system required that each office at the parlements have two incumbents on active duty for six-month terms.[10] A device implemented to increase the number of offices for sale, it freed up presidents and magistrates at the parlement for half of the year, during which time they could be commissioned by the king into various other functions.[11] De Thou started his work of reforming customs using his time off from the court.[12] He was assisted by two judges of the Parlement, most often Barthélemy Faye and Jacques Viole (1517–1584). These three judges were repeatedly appointed to various commissions.[13] They were from elite families in Paris, tightly connected through marriage. Teamed up for customary law redaction, these three *parlementaires* were literally inseparable.[14]

[9] Pasquier, *Lettres*, in book 7, letter 10 (to M. de la Bite, *juge général* of Mayenne), *Les œuvres d'Estienne Pasquier, contenant ses recherches de la France* (Amsterdam, 1723), vol. 2, cols. 184–85.

[10] Etienne Girard and Jacques Joly, *Trois livres des offices de France* (Paris, 1658), vol. 1, 19–20; *Recueil général*, vol. 13, 373. The edict was registered at the Parlement of Paris on April 28 after numerous remonstrances, under the title *Édit du semestre et règlement nouveau des épices et jugemens des procès par commissaires*. The short-lived semester system, scrapped in 1558, was one of the worst rounds of abuse the Parlement of Paris suffered at the hands of the king, before the abolition of the law court by Chancellor Maupeau in 1771. Descimon (ed.), *Discours pour la majorité de Charles IX*, "Introduction," 16; Frederic J. Baumgartner, *Henry II, King of France 1547–1559* (Durham: Duke University Press, 1988), 88–89; Kim, *Michel de L'Hôpital*, 37–39.

[11] The Parlement of Paris consisted of several permanent chambers. The Grand-Chambre was the most important one, exercising leadership over and supervising other chambers. In the sixteenth century the Chambre des enquêtes became the main body receiving inquests and rendering judgments. The Chambres des requêtes was a chamber that decided on petitions for royal grace. It came to have original jurisdiction over litigation involving special parties, the high nobles for example, who were exempted from suit in the ordinary courts. Most cases heard at the Parlement were civil in nature, and from 1515 serious criminal cases were assigned to the separate Chambre criminelle, called the Tournelle, staffed by judges from the Grand-Chambre. Around 1500, there were between eighty and ninety magistrates at the Parlement of Paris, headed by the first president and several presidents. The five presidents of the Grand-Chambre were *présidents à mortier*, wearing a black velvet hat with two golden braided ribbons called a *mortier*. Below them were presidents of other chambers. See Félix Aubert, *Le Parlement de Paris au XVIe siècle. Extrait* de *Nouvelle revue historique de droit français et étranger* (Paris: Sirey, 1906); Aubert, *Histoire du Parlement de Paris*, vol. 1, 34–37; Dawson, *The Oracles*, 274–75; Frederic J. Baumgartner, *France in the Sixteenth Century* (New York: St. Martin's Press, 1995), 88.

[12] Filhol, *Le premier président Christofle de Thou*, 18, note 4.

[13] Their collaborations were not limited to reforming customs: the king entrusted them with the trials of the *vidame* of Chartres and the prince of Condé in 1560 after the so-called conspiracy of Amboise. *Mémoires de Condé, pour servir à l'histoire de France, & d'éclaircissement à celle de M. De Thou* (The Hague, 1743), vol. 2, 375. See Jules de Petigny, "Testament de François de Vendôme, vidame de Chartres, 1560," *Bibliothèque de l'École des chartes* 11 (1850), 327–42.

[14] Descimon, "Quelques réflexions à propos des commissaires du roi." The early generations of the de Thous served at the municipal government in Orléans in the fifteenth century. Jacques de Thou moved to Paris to occupy the post of *avocat du roi* at the Cour des aides, an office he acquired from his mother's family, the Violes, a respected judicial family in the capital. Jacques de Thou's son, Augustin de Thou, who was Christophe's father, married into another distinguished *parlementaire* family, the Merles, and served as *conseiller clerc* in the Chambre des enquêtes in 1535 and *président à mortier* of the Parlement in 1544. Barthélemy Faye, originating from Lyon, was a cousin six degrees removed

De Thou came from a family that was an ultimate example of illustrious judicial dynasty built upon the judicious practice of the sale of offices (see Figure 4.1).[15] Before he purchased the presidency of the Parlement of Paris in 1554, he was an *avocat* at the Parlement.[16] His career advance could be seen as unusual in that he moved directly from the bar to the presidency at the Parlement, without having occupied the *conseiller* post.[17] In less than ten years, in December 1562, he would be elevated to the top post at the Parlement of Paris, the office he held for twenty years until his death. As the First President of the most important court in France, he was arguably the single greatest authority in jurisprudence. He was also active in the Paris municipal government.[18] His knowledge and clout in city

from the mother of Jacques Viole. He married in 1542 the sister of Jacques. See Descimon, "Quelques réflexions à propos des commissaires du roi," # 22, and the accompanying genealogical charts.

[15] Christophe was born in 1508 and studied law in Poitiers between 1530 and 1532. One of his brothers was Adrien de Thou, *conseiller clerc* and *chanoine* of Notre-Dame. Christophe married Jacqueline de Tuleu, dame de Cély, daughter of Jean de Tuleu and cousin of François Olivier. The latter was Chancellor of France between 1545 and 1560. They had at least five children: Jean became *conseiller* at the Parlement and *maître des requêtes*; Christophe-Auguste was the *grand maître des eaux et forets* and *bailli* in Melun; and Jacques-Auguste, the author of *Histoire universelle*, was *président à mortier* at the Parlement of Paris. A daughter, Catherine, married Achille de Harlay, who succeeded Christophe de Thou as the *premier président* at the Parlement de Paris in 1582, and another daughter, Anne, married Philippe Hurault de Cheverny, Chancellor of France from 1583. For de Thou's biographical information, see Filhol, *Le premier président Christofle de Thou*, 5–10; Descimon, "Quelques réflexions à propos des commissaires du roi," # 22; Philippe Hamon, "La chute de la maison de Thou: La fin d'une dynastie robine," *Revue d'histoire moderne et contemporaine* 46 (1999), 53–84; Étienne Pattou, "Généalogie de la Maison de Thou," 2004, http://racineshistoire.free.fr/LGN/PDF/de-Thou.pdf.

[16] According to Pasquier, Pierre Séguier, de Thou, Jacques Aubry, and Denis Riant were the four most famous lawyers of the century. Pasquier, *Les œuvres*, vol. 2, col. 184. Great seigneurs often retained renowned *avocats* as their counsels to whom they entrusted the administration of their property. De Thou's clients included powerful figures of the time, such as Diane de Poitiers, Connétable Montmorency, and Maréchal Saint-André. As a counsel for the House of Laval, de Thou had the *comté* of Laval seized and sold so that he could get reimbursed for the advances he had made, an incident which provoked a sizable scandal. Filhol, *Le premier président Christofle de Thou*, 11.

[17] De Thou's was one of the four president posts and thirty judgeships newly created that year. At the time of his appointment, Pierre Séguier, *avocat du roi*, was also appointed to a presidency, but as the fourth-tier president, below the third-tier presidency to which de Thou was placed. Séguier had been superior in rank to de Thou who was a mere *avocat*. The precedence in the Parlement's hierarchy was a serious matter. The *parquet* protested that the ranking of de Thou and Séguier should be reversed. Séguier demanded that de Thou's letter of appointment not be registered, in order to preserve "the dignity and recognition of the office of *avocat du roi*." Ultimately, Séguier withdrew his demand, choosing not to resist the royal wishes, even though the members of the *parquet* wanted to continue protest. Filhol, *Le premier président Christofle de Thou*, 17; Édouard Maugis, *Histoire du Parlement de Paris de l'avènement des rois Valois à la mort d'Henri IV* (Paris: A. Picard, 1913), vol. 1, 202–203. This incident captured the gist of the venality system: the king created the post for sale, de Thou could afford to purchase it, the king was satisfied with his candidacy, and that was that. Despite this awkward start, Séguier and de Thou cooperated closely to serve as mediators between the Parlement and royal power. They both represented the moderate voice in the Parlement. See Nancy Lyman Roelker, *One King, One Faith: The Parlement of Paris and the Religious Reformations of the Sixteenth Century* (Berkeley: University of California Press, 1996), 138–39.

[18] De Thou was a city councilor (*échevin*) of Paris in 1535, and *prévôt des marchands* in 1552, the year in which he also entered the college of royal notaries. As *échevin*, he led the city to adopt a series of police measures to assure peace which were strictly implemented during the Wars of Religion. He remained a *conseiller de ville* of Paris until 1576, when he resigned the seat for his son Jean. Filhol, *Le premier président Christofle de Thou*, 14. See also Barbara B. Diefendorf, *Paris City Councillors in the Sixteenth Century: The Politics of Patrimony* (Princeton: Princeton University Press, 1983).

Figure 4.1 Christophe de Thou (1508–1582)
Source: gallica.bnf.fr
Bibliothèque nationale de France

politics served him well as he dealt with the assemblies of the three estates in 1580 during the reformation of the *coutume* of Paris.

Assembly of the Estates and Royal Commissioners

The process of the reformation differed little from those of the original redaction, governed by specifically mandated legal formalities and rituals. It involved three distinct phases: preparatory works to draw up the draft text of the custom; the public assembly in the presence of royal commissioners where objections to the draft were heard and addressed; and the publication of the text agreed on by the three estates and approved by the king.

The process was set in motion when the royal commissioners, having received the royal letters of commission, sent a notice to officials of the *bailliage* to announce their coming and instructed them to call the assembly of the estates of the three orders. The *bailli* selected a committee, which prepared the draft for discussion in the general assembly or, if the *bailliage* already had a homologated *coutume*, reviewed it and suggested modifications. The preparatory committee was most often composed of local *avocats* and *procureurs*. Legal practitioners were presumed to be well versed in the customs of the district and their expertise was valued more than lay opinion. The text of custom drawn up by them technically substituted for local inquests.[19] In general, royal commissioners stayed out of these preliminary sessions. The exception was in Paris where the commissioners presided over the preparatory assemblies.[20]

The next phase was the solemn "assemblée des trois Estats." The *baillis* or *sénéchaux* called the general assembly to order in the presence of royal commissioners. The appearance *in loco* of the commissioners, personally selected by the king, and their ceremonious opening of the gathering of the three estates augmented an aura of import of the assembly. The *procès-verbal*, written in the narrative form by the presiding commissioners, was formulaic but it exuded a feel of intimacy and confidence. The *procès-verbal* of the reformed *coutume* of Touraine begins:

> The year one thousand five hundred fifty-nine, Sunday, the eighth day of the month of October. We, Christofle de Thou, Président, Barthélemy Faye, & Jacques Viole, Conseillers du Roy in his court of Parlement, arrived in the town of Tours, in order to proceed here with the redaction of the Coustumes du Duché and Bailliage de Touraine, in accordance with the lettres patentes from the said Seigneur addressed to us, & c.
>
> And the following day, the ninth day of the said month & year, we were transported to the Palais Royal of the said place, where appeared, for the Estate of the Church, Reverend pere en Dieu Messire Simon de Maillé, Archevesque, Seigneur Baron du Palais Archiepiscopal de Tours, Seigneur Chastellain des chastellenies d'Arthonne, de Vernon & de saint Martin de Candes.[21]

The list continued with the names of all the individuals present, by title and function, in the order of precedence of the estates: the clergy, the nobility, and the third estate.

In principle, every member of the district was required to be present in person or by proxy. The roll call noted down the absentees, who were declared in default. Most nobles and prelates were represented by *procureurs*, assisted by their domain stewards, and the *tiers état* from the towns and villages by *procureurs* and

[19] It was increasingly common that lawyers' testimonies served as proof in the *enquêtes par turbes*. See Smedley-Weill and Geoffroy-Poisson, "Les assemblées d'états et la mise en forme du droit."

[20] Olivier-Martin, *Histoire de la coutume de la prévôté et vicomté de Paris*, vol. 1, 110. The formalities described in this chapter applied only to *coutumes* dealing with matters of private law, not the codification of technical procedural *stiles*. The latter were often drafted in a commission that only involved officers, lawyers, and prosecutors of different jurisdictions in the *bailliage*. Chénon, *Histoire générale du droit français*, vol. 2, 297.

[21] *Nouveau coutumier général*, vol. 4, 675.

syndics.[22] Without the lawyers' services, no one felt confident in navigating through the thickets of customs. The *procès-verbaux* usually listed the names of the royal officers who were present under the category of the *quatrième état* (fourth estate).[23] Often the names of local lawyers were put down in this category as well. It was the time when *gens de robe* aspired to a status distinct from the third estate. Annotations (*apostilles*) were made during discussion to separate the statements by legal practitioners from others. Keeping procedural integrity was paramount: everyone swore an oath to advise and tell the truth on the custom of the *bailliage*. Then the commissioners designated a spokesperson for each estate, just like selecting an orator for each order in the Estates General.

Before debate on specific items of custom began, participants had the opportunity to challenge the validity of the convocation of the estates. This was arguably the most contentious phase of the assembly. The codification of the customs took place in a *bailliage*. Jurisdictional contests were ripe because the territorial and legal boundaries did not coincide with the historical borders of customs.[24] The constituency of the *bailliage* and *sénéchaussée* did not always overlap with that of the *pays*.

Jurisdictional challenge came from all directions. Townsfolk cited their charters and *coutumes locales*; the clerics—bishops, delegates from the cathedral chapters, abbots of monasteries, and parish priests—and the nobles—seigneurs holding the fiefs and especially those with the right of feudal justice—claimed personal privileges or local customs of their manors. In 1559, some clerics protested that they were improperly summoned because they were not under the jurisdiction of the *sénéchaussée* of Poitou; they were governed by the written law of the *pays de droit écrit*, not the customs of Poitou, they claimed.[25] It was during the reformation in the *prévôté* of Paris that the most strenuous contests took place. A significantly larger number of remonstrances were presented in 1580 than in 1510.[26] Many disputed the jurisdiction of the Châtelet. Objections from the clergy revolved around the privileges, immunities, and franchises of major religious houses holding lands and lordships. The king's lawyers, *procureurs généraux* and *avocats généraux*, countered that all the lands in question were

[22] Filhol, *Le premier président Christofle de Thou*, 87. Some lawyers represented more than one client at the assembly.

[23] Royal officials included *bailli*, *lieutenant général*, *lieutenant particulier du bailli*, and *procureurs du roi* and *avocats du roi* of each jurisdiction.

[24] At the assembly held in Senlis in 1539, the first called to speak, the Bishop Count of Beauvais, protested through his attorney that he was not under the jurisdiction of the *bailliage*. Grinberg et al., "Rédaction des coutumes et territoires," 9. On other occasions, the deputies argued that their presence did not constitute the waiver of jurisdictional challenge.

[25] Parrow, "Provincial Estates and the Revision of Customary Law," 64, note 30.

[26] Olivier-Martin, *Histoire de la coutume de la prévôté et vicomté de Paris*, vol. 1, appendix, 545–46; Grinberg et al., "Rédaction des coutumes et territoires," 42.

located within the *prévôté* and no one could challenge the rights of the king and the jurisdiction of his court, the Châtelet, over them.[27] The *procès-verbaux* of the reformed customs were full of heated exchanges between the royal agents and local seigneurs.

The royal commissioners stood firm. Their letters of commission stipulated that they reject any claim of privilege, even from the peers of France, although the latter were exempt from being present in the assembly.[28] The king declared that the kingdom's laws, including custom, were based on territorial jurisdiction, not personal jurisdiction. The *bailliage* was a legal space in which every inhabitant belonged, and its custom governed all territories including seigneurial fiefs, the estates were told.

Remonstrances were also filed by royal officials from neighboring *bailliages*, who supposedly feared administrative encroachment by the *prévôté* of Paris to the detriment of their own districts.[29] These jurisdictional disputes led to an unnecessary fragmentation of customs. For example, the *coutumes* of Montfort-l'Amaury, Dourdan, Étampes, and Mantes were all independently promulgated, even though they contained substantially the same contents as the others and could have easily been absorbed into the *coutume* of Paris to create a larger and more unified judicial district.[30]

Once jurisdictional challenges were addressed, the royal commissioners read the draft text composed by the preparatory committee and discussion followed, article by article. Articles agreed upon by majority within each order and by the unanimity of the three estates, and assented to by the *procureur du roi*, were admitted as accorded. When an article could not be "accordé par les trois ordres," it was declared "discordé," and one moved on to the next, although in later publications, at times, the vote of two of the three estates could prevail over the other.[31] Dissension tended to form along the lines of three estates. The ecclesiastical as well as lay seigneurs vigorously defended their feudal rights against the third estate.[32] Dumoulin criticized the clergy at the redaction of the custom of Montfort-l'Amaury (1556) for having failed to support the proposal of the third estate that a

[27] Collectively called *gens du roi* (the king's men), *avocats généraux* and *procureurs généraux* were specially appointed lawyers, safeguarding royal interests. The *procureur du roi* was the king's prosecutor; the *avocats du roi* presented the king's case before the judges. Aubert, *Histoire du Parlement de Paris*, vol. 1, 141–75; Delachenal, *Histoire des avocats au Parlement de Paris*, 163–70; Jean-Marie Carbasse (ed.), *Histoire du Parquet* (Paris: Presses universitaires de France, 2000). The *procureur du roi* could present a case only in writing whereas the *avocat du roi* could speak for the king, so the latter had precedence over the former in procession. Barbiche, *Les institutions de la monarchie française*, 337.

[28] Smedley-Weill and Geoffroy-Poisson, "Les assemblées d'états et la mise en forme du droit," # 23.

[29] Grinberg et al., "Rédaction des coutumes et territoires," 20–41.

[30] Filhol, *Le premier président Christofle de Thou*, 188–89; Grinberg et al., "Rédaction des coutumes et territoires," 15; Glasson, *Histoire du droit*, vol. 8, 50.

[31] "Selon l'intention de la plus grande partie de l'assemblée," *Procès-verbal* of des *Coutumes* of Auxerre (1561), *Nouveau coutumier général*, vol. 3, 629.

[32] Smedley-Weill and Geoffroy-Poisson, "Les assemblées d'états et la mise en forme du droit," # 34.

portion of the confiscated property be preserved for the children, thereby squandering a chance "for the two estates to form a majority and pass the law"; the clergy's "avarice was greater than *charité & utilité publique*."[33]

The redaction and reformation of customs provided the local population opportunities to revisit long-standing disputes and gripes both within the community and with its neighbors. Different parties used the occasion to bring up old issues, such as challenges to various kinds of rental fees, the river and road tolls, and so on, and try to settle them to their advantage. It was the royal commissioners' task to keep the bickering in check and get the process moving. They were understandably inclined to construe the customs along the lines of the jurisprudence of the parlement where they sat as judges.[34] Claims were made during the reformation phase that the earlier redaction did not follow proper procedures or accurately reflect the immemorial practices of the locale in question. The cases of Touraine and Poitou are instructive.

The custom of Touraine was recorded in 1461 soon after the ordinance of Montils-lès-Tours but was not registered with the clerk for failure to follow the required formula. The new redaction in 1507 offered an opportunity to modify a key provision. In 1461 the rule disallowing a widow to cumulate gifts (*don*) and dower rights (*douaire*) governed only commoners; in 1507 the rule was extended to the nobles.[35] The custom went through another revision in 1559 which, compared with the earlier ones, saw less antagonism among the estates; the commissioners' job of reconciling their competing interests proved less laborious.[36]

Article 145 of the custom of Poitou, reformed in 1559, replaced Article 126 in the 1514 text. The old provision had required that widows complete rendering homage to the lord and pay for *rachat* (feudal redemption) if they wished to retain the holdings of their deceased husbands. The new article in 1559 provided: "If a husband died after having done faith and homage and paid the duties for his wife, the widow could, if she wished, enter in faith and do homage to her feudal lord, and the latter would be bound to receive it without her paying for *rachat* or other seigneurial duties."[37] The *procureur de roi* supported the change because forcing the widow to pay for *rachat* would be a *chose dure, inique & déraisonnable*. But a seigneur de la Trimouille, Vicomté de Thouars, protested through his lawyer. He contended that the original article "had been from time immemorial received and inviolably kept and observed," and that changing these *droits anciens féodaux* which had been observed for such a long time with no questions asked would be

[33] *Nouveau coutumier général*, vol. 3, 153, note d. See Dawson, "French Customs," 780, note 49.

[34] Thireau, "Les trois rédactions de la coutume de Touraine," 124.

[35] *Procès-verbal* of *anciennes coutumes de Touraine*, *Nouveau coutumier général*, vol. 4, 628–41; Grinberg, *Écrire les coutumes*, 81.

[36] Thireau, "Les trois rédactions de la coutume de Touraine," 132–33.

[37] *Nouveau coutumier général*, vol. 4, 788.

"greatly prejudicial" to him.[38] In the end, the commissioners decided that the seigneurs would preserve their right to remonstrate and ordered that the reformed article take force for the future, without prejudice to the past.[39]

Once the three estates had the opportunities to express their opinions about specific provisions, the royal commissioners assumed a more direct control over the process. The fact that similar languages were used in discussion at the assemblies of different *coutumes* attested to the commissioners' influence, ready to resort to procedural technicalities if necessary to keep the assemblies in line.[40] In many cases, the seigneurs and cities had been instructed in the royal letters to write down specific rights and privileges they were claiming and send them in advance to the *bailli* or *sénéchal* so that they could be attached to the draft of the *coutume*. Many seigneurs failed to do so, with the result of having those customs declared "non avenues," meaning they forfeited their rights to assert them afterward.[41]

Various editing methods were used in finalizing the texts. Even where there was no disagreement about the content of customs, formulating them in writing was a whole different exercise. Words were added or deleted to give precision to the meaning of the articles; entire articles were deleted or added; the order of the chapters, titles, and articles was rearranged; or headings were modified.[42] Obviously these methods brought into relief the importance of written law. When the reformation of the *coutume* of Amiens was reformed in 1567, for example, the phrase "s'il est au pays" was changed to "s'il est au pays de Bourgogne sujet à la coutume," to clarify and remove potential doubts.[43] The *ancienne coutume* of Paris had provided: "As between the daughters who succeed either in the direct or collateral line, there is no right of primogeniture."[44] The *nouvelle coutume* restated it: "When there are only daughters coming to direct or collateral succession, the right of primogeniture does not take place and they take in equal portions."[45] Heightened attention to precise language in provisions not only prevented

[38] This language is from the *procès-verbal* which was part of the 1727 edition of the revised *coutume*. It includes some divergences, as cited in the study by Parrow, from the text in Bourdot de Richebourg's *Nouveau coutumier général*. Parrow, "Provincial Estates and the Revision of Customary Law," 62, note 21, and 66–68.

[39] "Pour avoir lieu à l'avenir, & sans préjudice du passé." *Nouveau coutumier général*, vol. 4, 827. The language in the 1727 text is more descriptive: "sans préjudice de leurs droits qu'ils peuvent avoir par conventions, titres particuliers, ou autrement," cited from Parrow, "Provincial Estates and the Revision of Customary Law," 68, note 49. The new language became the default rule, even though the parties could agree on a different arrangement.

[40] The commissioners often wrote comments in the margin of the preparatory texts prepared by local practitioners. For such notes made by the commissioners for the *Coutume* of Péronne, see Filhol, *Le premier président Christofle de Thou*, 143, notes 2 to 10.

[41] Chénon, *Histoire générale du droit français*, vol. 2, 295, 322.

[42] Grinberg, *Écrire les coutumes*, 79–80.

[43] Ibid., 80.

[44] Art. 26, *Nouveau coutumier général*, vol. 3, 32.

[45] Art. 19, ibid., vol. 3, 31.

confusion but fostered techniques in legal construction. Redactions of customs contributed to the development of textualism in French law.

Those who still objected to the articles reserved the right to appeal to the Parlement. The royal commissioners systematically forwarded the claims of dissenting feudal lords over to the court, which was to determine the issues in litigation on a specific controversy. In the meantime, the disputed articles were applied provisionally.[46] This meant those who contested them were compelled to wait until the case was brought to the Parlement for a judgment. It often took a long time, and the contesting parties were put at a disadvantage of having to challenge the law fully operative in the intervening years. The unspoken expectation was that those who had dissented would not have the will or energy to pursue the matter outside the assembly halls, and indeed that was what happened in most cases.[47] Understandably, feudal lords were not eager to present themselves before the Parlement. Once the *coutumes* were published, objections raised during the redaction more or less dissipated.

Custom Becomes Perpetual Law

Normally royal commissioners concluded their work in the assembly within several days. The prerogative of authenticating the final text belonged exclusively to the crown, in whose name the commissioners decreed the official custom. It was then sent to the Parlement for registration. Once the verification of the text was completed, its publication followed immediately. The formula used in most *coutumes* was as follows: "The said customs thus redacted, agreed upon, and moderated are published and registered at the *bailliages* and thenceforth preserved and observed as law and perpetual and irrevocable edict."[48] The official text became the only authentic proof of the custom, which now enjoyed the obligatory force as *loi perpetuelle*.

The reformation of customs in *bailliages* solidified the legal territorial divisions, cutting through historical, feudal, seigneurial, or parish borders.[49] The *bailliage* served as a jurisdictional unit from the thirteenth century, but its boundaries had constantly fluctuated, with its enclaves shifting depending on homages paid to the fiefs. Now it became a more secure building block of royal jurisdiction. Previously, territory had little relevance to custom, which revolved around personal relations

[46] Olivier-Martin, *Les lois du roi*, 92. The 1605 edition of the *coutume* of the Vitry en Perthois, after nearly one hundred years of its redaction, still ends Art. 16 with the phrase, "Not in agreement, remitted to the Court." Parrow, "Provincial "Estates and the Revision of Customary Law," 61.

[47] Dawson, "French Customs," 780; Descimon, "Quelques réflexions à propos des commissaires du roi," # 5.

[48] *Coutume du Grand Perche*, *Nouveau coutumier général*, vol. 3, 661. Any attempt to assert custom other than the published custom was explicitly prohibited.

[49] Grinberg et al., "Rédaction des coutumes et territoires," 52–53.

and the forms of the exercise of power. The conception of territory compelled the inhabitants in the district to think in spatial terms.[50]

Defining territorial boundaries of law was an important aspect of state-building. Inferior jurisdictions were reduced in number and competence. Royal justice infiltrated into the provinces, disrupting municipal and ecclesiastical justice.[51] The assemblies of the estates where jurisdictional contests took place represented an arena where the feudal past (history) and the administrative state (territory) jostled together. The partition of the provinces into *bailliages* with defined legal boundaries made it easier to control from the center with reinforced administrative apparatus.[52] *Procureurs du roi* became the agents of royal power pushing forward a bureaucratic and legal coherence and evenness.[53] To be sure, the entangled claims of authority and particularism inherent in feudal society persisted throughout the ancien régime. Nonetheless, the king found an opportunity to superimpose on old feudal relations a new vision of relationship with his subjects. The redaction assembly became a site in which the doctrine of royal sovereignty, vigorously articulated by political theorists at the time, saw its full application at the local *bailliage* level.[54] Claims of special rights and privileges withered before the notion of territorial sanctity, a foundation for sovereignty.

As the reform of local customs progressed in the mid-sixteenth century, there was growing anticipation for the overhaul of the most important custom in the kingdom, the *coutume* of Paris. Since Dumoulin dissected its articles in his massive commentaries in the 1530s, its revision seemed a matter of time. The *lettres patentes* issued on December 15, 1579, entrusted de Thou with the reformation of the custom of Paris, "the capital of our kingdom, on whose model all other cities govern and direct themselves."[55] The *conseillers* of the Parlement of Paris Claude Anjorrant, Mathieu Chartier, Jacques Viole, and Pierre de Longueil were appointed to assist de Thou.

2. *La Coutume de Paris* (1580)

The process of the reformation of the custom of Paris can be reconstructed thanks to the official *procès-verbal* and the manuscripts of *avocat* Simon Marion (1540–1615).[56] Elaborate preliminary work preceded the royal letter of January

[50] The custom essentially became territorial legislation. Glasson, *Histoire du droit*, vol. 8, 26.

[51] Lloyd, *The State, France, and the Sixteenth Century*, 75.

[52] Grinberg et al., "Rédaction des coutumes et territoires," 15, 53.

[53] Florent Roemier, "Avocat général et coutumes, " in Astaing and Lormant (eds.), *Le juriste et la coutume du Moyen Âge au Code civil*, 140–69.

[54] Filhol, *Le premier président Christofle de Thou*, 80.

[55] *Nouveau coutumier général*, vol. 3, 56.

[56] The *procès-verbal* in *Nouveau coutumier général*, vol. 3, 56–85. The manuscripts of Simon Marion, *avocat* at the Parlement of Paris and later *avocat général du roi*, provide complete

19, 1580, in which the king ordered the convocation of the estates of the Prévôté et Vicomté de Paris. The initial task of compiling a revised draft of the custom was undertaken by the lawyers at the Châtelet, the sanctuary of the custom of Paris.[57] The provisional text was circulated among judges at the Châtelet, whose comments were gathered to refine the draft. The text adopted by the Châtelet was then submitted to a new commission of *avocats* of the Parlement. The lawyers of the Parlement were not always of the same opinion as their counterparts at the Châtelet. Pleading cases on appeal from diverse localities within the vast jurisdiction of the Parlement of Paris, they were more attuned to its jurisprudential trend, in particular when matters were not explicitly regulated by particular local customs. Members of the Parlement were likely more favorably disposed toward the emerging notion of the common law of the customs, that is, the idea of a body of customary law delineated from the masses of different provincial customs.[58]

Étienne Pasquier was one of the ten *avocats* at the Parlement of Paris who were charged with preparing the draft *coutume*. He described in detail the commission's activities.[59] For eight days in January 1580, Pasquier joined his colleagues, after the mid-morning meal, at the house of Pierre Versoris who lived near the Palais de Justice. There, some of the most famous *avocats* of the time—Mathieu de Fontenay, Jehan Durant, Jacques la Faye, Jacques Canaye, Claude Mangot, Jean Vulco, François de Montholon, Pierre Versoris, René Choppin, and Pasquier—worked together, to bring forth "all we have observed in our memory about the decisions of the Parlement, not only in the prévosté and vicomté of Paris but in other provinces, concerning general questions not specific to particular local customs, and in this way we accommodated the articles."[60]

The redaction of the new *coutume* faithfully observed the formalities stipulated in ancient public law; it was the high point of regularity and solemnity. The draft was submitted to the assembly of the three estates that gathered at the Châtelet on February 18, 1580. The assembly discussed the text from February 22 through March 4.[61] One notes some differences from 1510. In 1580, it was more or less the

documentation of the progressive elaboration of the reformed text. Bibliothèque nationale, mss. fr. [manuscrits français] 5281 and 5282. They were published in François Olivier-Martin, "Les manuscrits de Simon Marion et la coutume de Paris au XVIe siècle," *Travaux juridiques et économiques de l'Université de Rennes* 8 (1923), 135–40.

[57] Pierre Séguier, *lieutenant civil* of the prévoté, presided over a commission of lawyers at the Châtelet. Olivier-Martin, *Histoire de la coutume de la prévoté et vicomté de Paris*, vol. 1, 122–26.

[58] Olivier-Martin, *La coutume de Paris: trait d'union*, 16.

[59] Pasquier, *Lettres*, in book 19, letter 15 (to Anne Robert), *Les œuvres*, vol. 2, cols. 575–82. Anne Robert (1559–1617) was a prominent *avocat* at the Parlement of Paris and a renowned author. On Robert, see Marie Houllemare, "Un avocat parisien entre art oratoire et promotion de soi (fin XVIe siècle)," *Revue historique* 630 (2004), 283–302.

[60] Pasquier, *Les œuvres*, vol. 2, col. 578.

[61] Simon Marion was designated by the order of nobility to serve as one of its spokespersons. Antoine Loisel appeared as the counsel for the queen mother Catherine de Médicis, who participated in the assembly in the capacity of the dame of Saint-Maur-des Fossés and of Mélun. Loisel was also a designated speaker of the clergy. Louis de Sainction spoke for the third estate. Olivier-Martin, "Les

work of legal practitioners who represented the delegates of the estates.[62] Not just in Paris but in other *bailliages* as well, the operation at the beginning of the century had been decentralized and the intervention of royal commissioners marginal, but in the second half of the century their presence became more conspicuous.[63] They were supposed to play the role of neutral arbitrators, but the *procès-verbaux* showed their considerable influence over the direction of the debates. The *procès-verbal* became shorter, which evidenced the commissioners' tighter control of the assemblies. The estates largely went along with the changes proposed to them, in deference to the professional judgment of the high magistracy.[64]

The publication of the new *Coutume de Paris* marked a critical juncture in the history of French law (see Figure 4.2). It was a learned product, informed by the jurisprudence of the Parlement of Paris. Pasquier stated "the *Coutume de Paris* is nothing other than a summary of the general spirit at the court of the Parlement."[65] It became a standard reference for French jurists in the ancien régime, against which all other customs were measured.[66] Considered the most faithful and complete expression of a common law of customs, the reformed *coutume* of Paris seemed one important step toward the unification of civil law in France, bearing out Dumoulin's vision. It took the political acumen and clout of de Thou to turn his one-time colleague's ideas into reality.

The successful overhaul of the custom of Paris was a key achievement for de Thou personally. In January the same year he had also completed the redaction of the custom of Eu at the request of the Duc de Guise, the count of Eu. The Parlement of Rouen unsuccessfully contested the Parlement of Paris' claim that this comté-pairie was within its jurisdiction.[67] After de Thou's death in 1582, the custom of Orléans, originally written in 1509, was reformed in 1583 by Achille de Harlay (1536–1616), de Thou's son-in-law and immediate successor as the

manuscrits de Simon Marion," 137; Olivier-Martin, *Histoire de la coutume de la prévôté et vicomté de Paris*, vol. 1, 113. Loisel took part in the discussion of Articles 12 and 82. See the *procès-verbal* in *Nouveau coutumier général*, vol. 3, 78.

[62] Olivier-Martin, *Histoire de la coutume de la prévôté et vicomté de Paris*, vol. 1, 109–13; Olivier-Martin, *La coutume de Paris: trait d'union*, 12.

[63] Descimon, "Quelques réflexions à propos des commissaires du roi," # 21.

[64] Thireau, "Les trois rédactions de la coutume de Touraine," 132–33.

[65] "La coutume de Paris n'estre autre chose qu'un abregé de l'air général des Arrêts de la Cour de Parlement." Pasquier, *Les œuvres*, vol. 2, col. 578.

[66] On *retrait lignager*, "we have made an express article in our new Coustume de Paris, which serves as a guide for all other [*coutumes*]." Étienne Pasquier, *L'interprétation des Institutes de Justinian: Avec la conférence de chasque paragraphe aux ordonnances royaux, arrestz de parlement et coustumes générales de la France*, ed. Étienne-Denis Pasquier and Charles Giraud (Paris: Videcoq ainé, 1847), book 2, ch. 37, 237. On land easements (*servitude foncières*) as well, "I am of the opinion that we can refer to that of Paris." Ibid., book 2, ch. 51, 267. For *retrait lignager*, see infra Chapter 5, note 61 and accompanying text.

[67] *Nouveau coutumier général*, vol. 4, 166; Filhol, *Le premier président Christofle de Thou*, 52.

COVSTVMES
DE LA PREVOSTE'
ET VICOMTE' DE PARIS,
MISES ET REDIGEES PAR
eſcrit, en preſence des gens des trois Eſtats de
ladite Preuoſté & Vicomté:
PAR
Nous Chreſtofle de Thou premier Preſident, Claude Anjorant,
Mathieu Chartier, Iaques Viole & Pierre de Longueil,
Conſeillers du Roy en ſa Cour de Parlement, &
Commiſſaires par luy ordonnez.

A PARIS,
Chez Iaques du Puis, Libraire Iuré à la Samaritaine.
1580.
AVEC PRIVILEGE DV ROY.

Figure 4.2 *Coutumes de Paris* (1580)
Source: Special Collections of the Jacob Burns Law Library, George Washington University

premier président of the Parlement of Paris.[68] These two customs, revised in the same spirit, formed the twin pillars within the court's jurisdiction.

The reformation of the customs outside the district of the Parlement of Paris took place under the initiatives of the provincial parlements. The revision of the customs of Burgundy (1575), Brittany (1580), and Normandy (1583) were overseen by the commissioners from their respective parlements.[69] A handful of customs were homologated in the seventeenth and eighteenth centuries but, other than them, the customs that had not gone through the redaction process in the sixteenth century remained unpublished until the end of the ancien régime (see Map 4.1).[70]

The *Coutume de Paris* was exported to French overseas colonies. In 1712 Louis XIV ordered its imposition in Louisiana.[71] A large part of it was retained in the Louisiana Civil Code of 1808. The custom of Paris served as the basis of the French Civil Code in 1804.

3. From Consultative to Absolute Monarchy

The redaction and reformation of customs engaged the populations from the cities and countryside alike. Under Louis XII, mostly delegates from towns gathered in the assemblies, but under Henry II and his successors rural parishes and inferior jurisdictions were urged to send in their mandates to the *bailliage* and have themselves represented by *procureurs*.[72] The rights of the third estate to participate in the process and consent to their laws were taken seriously.

[68] *Lettres patentes*, *Nouveau coutumier général*, vol. 3, 808–809. Achille de Harlay was assisted by Jacques Viole and Nicolas Perrot, *conseillers* at the Parlement of Paris. Achille's father was Christophe de Harlay, *président à mortier* at the Parlement of Paris, who had served as a commissioner along with Christophe de Thou.

[69] The local *coutumes* in Normandy, were appended to the general *coutume* and published as *Coustumes du pais de Normandie, anciens ressors et enclaves d'iceluy* (Paris, 1586). See Jean Yver, "La rédaction officielle de la coutume de Normandie (Rouen, 1583): Son esprit," *Annales de Normandie* 36 (1986), 3–36; Schneider, *The King's Bench*, 110–14.

[70] For a list of customs not homologated, see Jean Bouhier, "Observation sur la coutume de Bourgogne," ch. 1, no. 4, in *Les œuvres de jurisprudence*, ed. Joey de Bevy (Dijon: Louis-Nicolas Frantin, 1787), vol. 1, 353; Philippe-Antoine Merlin, "Coutume," in *Recueil alphabétique des questions de droit* (Paris: Garnery, 1827), vol. 2, 732. The last custom homologated before the Revolution was that of Hattonchâtel (November 1787). Jean Coudert, "La dernière rédaction de coutume avant la Révolution: La difficile réformation des usages de Hattonchâtel (1784–1788)," *Revue historique de droit français et étranger* 67 (1989), 237–72.

[71] H. Patrick Glenn, "Eason-Weinmann Lecture: The Common Laws of Europe and Louisiana," *Tulane Law Review* 79 (2005), 1041–63; Vernon Valentine Palmer, "Historical Notes on the First Codes and Institutions in French Louisiana," in Olivier Moréteau, Julio Romañach, and Alberto Luis Zuppi (eds.), *Essays in Honor of Saúl Litvinoff* (Baton Rouge: Claitor's Publishing, 2008), 231–54; Robert Pascal, "The Sources of Civil Order according to the Louisiana Civil Code," *Tulane Law Review* 54 (1980), 916–41; John A. Dickinson, "New France: Law, Courts, and the Coutume de Paris, 1608–1760," *Manitoba Law Journal* 23 (1995), 32–54.

[72] Albert Babeau, "La représentation du tiers état aux assemblées pour la rédaction des coutumes au XVIe siècle," *Revue historique* 21 (1883), 92.

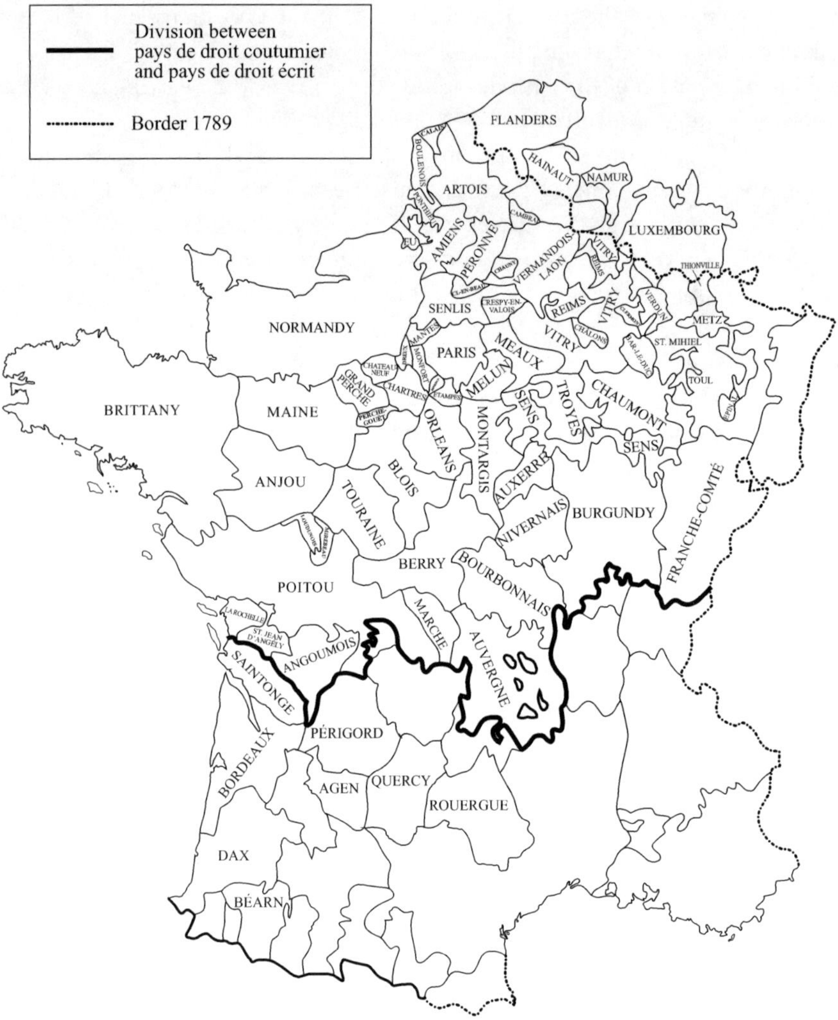

Map 4.1 *La France coutumière*
Adapted from the map in Henri Klimrath, *Travaux sur l'histoire du droit français* (1843).

At the national level, the Estates General continued to demand the systematization of laws.[73] The *cahiers* of the nobility in Orléans in 1560 petitioned that the laws be made clear "so that the parties can understand the merit of all causes and become themselves the first judge and that they reason with each other without litigation."[74] They insisted that the redaction of customs be completed in the *pays*

[73] Reulos, "Vers la présentation coordonnée et logique du droit français," 275.
[74] Picot, *Histoire des États généraux*, vol. 2, 192.

coutumier; as for the *pays de droit écrit*, "all the necessary laws" should be reduced to one corpus "in French language in clear and unambiguous terms."[75] The nobles called for a better organization of royal laws, asking the king to "confirm the ordinances that are necessary, with explicit commandment to have them observed and destroy the rest."[76] The third estate, in largely the same voice, demanded that all laws "that have been maintained and observed to date among the subjects be collected, discarding the unnecessary"; once assembled, the laws must be obeyed absolutely; in this way, one could "cut short all lengthy and costly lawsuits" and "curtail the malice of the parties and judicial officials."[77] It called for uniformity in legal procedures across the kingdom.[78] On behalf of the king, Chancellor L'Hôpital replied that "the king will review the edicts and ordinances issued by his predecessors and abolish those that are superfluous and unnecessary."[79]

The deputies at the Estates General of Blois in 1576 were again united in demanding that the king carry to completion the effort to streamline the laws.[80] They asked that Roman law and canon law sources be reduced to a coherent body of texts, written in clear French, in vocabularies easy to understand. They complained about the inconsistency in judicial interpretations of laws over the past century. The growing mass of obsolete royal ordinances needed particular attention. In theory, the registration of royal law at the parlements served the purpose of giving public notice of new laws, but it helped little for lay people: "many edicts are published by the sovereign courts, but they contain changes and modifications that reside only in the court registers, and as a result the people have no idea what they are."[81] The clergy proposed "all the edicts, ordinances, and customs be reviewed by certain scholars and persons with experience" and they "compile a volume and a *cahier* containing them with a view to avoid the confusion and heterogeneity of laws, preserve them so they would remain useful and essential in this kingdom, and abrogate all others."[82] The nobility declared that it would be desirable to update the customs in accordance with the courts' interpretations that had accumulated for over a century and also stressed that the "customs should not be changed or altered without the consent of the inhabitants."[83]

The king's responses to these demands were discreet: he reaffirmed that legal changes would have to be initiated with popular participation, but he preserved his power, for the sake of public utility, to override particular privileges that were not in the common interest. At the Estates General at Orléans in 1560, the

[75] Ibid. [76] Ibid., 193. [77] Ibid. [78] Ibid., 157.

[79] Rousselet-Pimont, *Le chancelier et la loi*, 333.

[80] Picot, *Histoire des États généraux*, vol. 2, 558. The Estates General was held to deal with the religious situation after the formation of the Catholic League; it met in Blois again in 1588–1589 for the same reasons, complicated by the dynastic question raised by the existence of a Protestant heir. Apart from these pressing political questions, the deputies each time demanded the reform of the sources of law.

[81] Ibid., 560. [82] Ibid. [83] Ibid., 558.

nobility demanded in its *cahiers de doléances* that their right to temporary or lifetime lease be changed to lease in perpetuity. The king replied he "cannot justly infringe on the conventions of people conforming to the law."[84] Another demand to change similar rules drew the king's reply that "it is left to the customs of the localities."[85] In February 1563, the Conseil du Roi received a petition, made "on behalf of the younger noble brothers in the regions of Anjou and of Maine," to relax the rule of primogeniture. After communicating with the king's lawyers and the Parlement, the royal council declared that "one cannot touch customs unless remonstrance has been made at the assembly of the estates of the said places."[86]

If the substances of customs were left to popular assemblies to discuss, the procedures of turning them into law were in the hands of the king through his commissioners. The control of legal procedures showed where the real locus of authority was.[87] The royal commissioners' work on behalf of the king was judicial in appearance but legislative in nature. Contemporary authors were not oblivious of the change. René Choppin stated: "the newly reformed customs we leaf through are more like the laws and orders of the commissioners, who carried out the reformation according to their own judgment, rather than the ancient *statuts* of *coustumes* of the provinces, because the jurisprudence and usage of the Palais modified many things."[88] Guy Coquille called the commissioners the "principal authors of the Coutume de Paris and other provinces."[89] In short, the estates' liberty to have a say on their custom was maintained, but "this small liberty accorded to the people obscured neither the sovereign authority of the king nor the dependence of his subjects."[90]

Gaining Hearts, Reining in Privileges

François Olivier-Martin (1879–1952) emphasized that the king recognized and respected the liberties, franchises, and privileges of the people of old France:

[84] Filhol, *Le premier président Christofle de Thou*, 71.

[85] Filhol, "La rédaction des coutumes," 68, notes 2 and 3. [86] Ibid., note 4.

[87] "The element of procedure is of the greatest importance, for it is through the unitary litigation process that variants of what is felt to be the desired substantive rule become isolated and barred from application." M. B. Hooker, *Legal Pluralism: An Introduction to Colonial and Neo-Colonial Laws* (Oxford: Clarendon Press, 1975), 186.

[88] *Commentaires sur la coustume d'Anjou*, "Avant-Propos," in *Les œuvres de René Choppin* (Paris: Jacques d'Allin, 1643), vol. 1, Part 3, Question 3 (De l'ancienne forme d'écrire les coustumes), 51.

[89] Guy Coquille, *Les coustumes du pays et comté de Nivernois*, in *Les œuvres de Maistre Guy Coquille, Sieur de Romenay, contenans plusieurs traitez touchant les libertez de l'église gallicane, l'histoire de France & le droict françois* (Bordeaux: Claude Labottière, 1703), vol. 2, 3. "The *coutumes* take their force of law by the authorization that the king grants by his commissioners," 313.

[90] Robert Descimon and Alain Guéry, "Un État des temps modernes?" in Jacques Le Goff (ed.), *L'État et les pouvoirs* (Paris: Seuil, 1989), 219. Just as the modern court judgment is entered by the judge as a matter of law, the custom became law not as an outcome of the consent of the representative assembly but in virtue of the authority of the king, who convoked the assembly and dismissed it after the work was done.

> The king, to the end, respected the right of the people of the three estates of towns and the *pays* to give themselves customs by agreeing among themselves. He only wanted to authorize these redactions, taking provisional measures while waiting for them to suppress bad customs and to settle irreducible disputes through his arbitration. The people of the estates, by respecting the forms, by obeying reason, and above all by reaching concord among them, are entirely the masters of deciding the law that governs them.[91]

The royal campaign was an undertaking to clarify customs—a sort of restatement—with the assent of the subjects. In some cases, the king allowed limited and temporary derogations for the sake of equity by abolishing unreasonable customs, but, argued Olivier-Martin, he did not aim to modify customs without the consent of the people and the redaction in no way changed that. This was not because the king lacked the power to do so but because he "normally respected the traditional domain of custom and intervened only in exceptional circumstances and for the reasons of common interest." "En gros," he affirmed, "the domain of ordinances is public law."[92]

Olivier-Martin's argument adds certain subtleties to the older view that the king relegated property and succession issues entirely to the autonomous domain of custom. Paul Viollet (1840–1914) stressed the "quasi impuissance" of royal power in private law and maintained that the "policy and administration" constituted "the real legislative domain of the king."[93] For Olivier-Martin, however, the monarchy, fully respecting the consultative nature of customary law, achieved the "*triomphe de la volonté royale*: from the contractual principle emerged legislative power."[94] More recently, Jean-Marie Carbasse set forth a similar view in the following terms: "If the monarchical state tolerated much diversity, it was not because of its lack of power [*impuissance*]; it was rather by principle. The king, in effect, was not just 'guardian of customs'; he also led in his traditional mission to respect and to have respected the '*droits et propriétés*' of his people . . . and thus their privileges and liberties."[95]

[91] Olivier-Martin, *Les lois du roi*, 96.

[92] Ibid., 119.

[93] Paul Viollet, *Histoire des institutions politiques et administratives de la France* (Paris: L. Larose et Forcel, 1898), vol. 2, 205.

[94] Olivier-Martin, *Les lois du roi*, 67. For Olivier-Martin's life and works, see the necrology by Gabriel Lepointe, "François Olivier-Martin (1879–1952)," *Revue historique de droit français et étranger* 30 (1953), 1–29; see also Svetlana Kochkina, "Listening to the Dead with Our Eyes: François Olivier-Martin's Library, a Mirror Image of a Legal Historian," *Library & Information History* 32 (2016), 203–18; Jacques Poumarède, "Olivier-Martin, François-Jean-Marie," in Patrick Arabeyre, Jean-Louis Halpérin, and Jacques Krynen (eds.), *Dictionnaire historique des juristes français (XIIe–XXe siècle)* (Paris: Presses universitaires de France, 2007).

[95] Jean-Marie Carbasse, "Unité et diversité de l'ancienne France," in Pierre Villard and Jean-Marie Carbasse (eds.), *L'unité des principaux États européens à la veille de la Révolution* (Paris: Université René Descartes, 1992), 4–5.

The idea of the monarchy's benevolent indifference has come under scrutiny of late. Jacques Krynen has suggested that Olivier-Martin's opinion be seen as a reflection of particular historiographical preferences and biases. According to him, the thesis of the king's enlightened abstention was a result of reaction against legal positivism that sprung from the French Revolution. Nineteenth-century European historiography emphasized the legal autonomy of the populace. When scholars rehabilitated custom as the spirit of the people and the original and pure expressions of law, they were voicing a historicist denunciation of the all-powerful state's expansive reach. They looked back to a primordial past, before the modern administrative state menacingly barged into private legal relations and activities. History writing at the turn of the twentieth century was infused with hostility to the public authorities' attempts to control minute aspects of private lives. French historians' distaste for, and wariness about, the modern state wielding law as an instrument of control disposed them to idealize custom as ancient French law protected by the benevolent king in the monarchical era and to explain the codification of customs in terms of the work of a moderate monarchy (*monarchie tempérée*). Put off by a legal *dirigisme* in postmonarchical France, argued Krynen, Olivier-Martin embraced the ideological framework of the nationalist—royalist—historiography, lauding the measured position of the crown toward customs, and thus proposed the theme of royal nonintervention.[96]

"C'est le peuple qui fait la loi"

Krynen points out that Olivier-Martin likely accepted the statements of sixteenth-century authors a little too faithfully. At issue was the timeless maxim of Coquille that the customs were based "on the consent of the people of three estates."[97] Coquille wrote "the people of each province have the right to establish law upon them, which is *coutumes* and unwritten law." He continued: "The commissioners, delegated by the king to preside over the assemblies of the estates, authorized them, inspiring the power of law in them. But in fact, it is the people who make the law."[98] These oft-repeated pronouncements have been regarded by historians including Olivier-Martin as capturing the fundamentally popular—contractual—nature of written custom in early modern France. Krynen and other scholars argue, however, that it is necessary to distinguish between the "intent" and the "effect" of the reforms of custom. One may argue that Charles VII had no intention to do anything other than what the deputies of the Estates General had asked

[96] Krynen, "The Absolute Monarchy," 29; Krynen, "Entre science juridique et dirigisme." French nationalism had both liberal and conservative variants.

[97] Olivier-Martin, *Les lois du roi*, 93.

[98] "Mais en effet, c'est le peuple qui fait la loi." Guy Coquille, *Questions, réponses et méditations sur les articles des coustumes* in *Les coustumes du pays et comté de Nivernois*, in *Les œuvres de Maistre Guy coquille*, vol. 2, 125.

for, to wit, making lawsuits shorter and less expensive by abolishing dreaded *enquêtes par turbes*.[99] This was the opinion of Coquille and other authors who stressed the contractual thesis of custom. But the effect of redacting customs far surpassed whatever aims the king had professed in the ordinance of 1454. In fact, it is not unreasonable to argue that, when Charles VIII and his successors authorized the commissioners to modify customs deemed inadequate or undesirable, their intent was not simply to confirm or verify existing customs but to create new rules.[100]

Coquille's emphasis on the consensual nature of written custom can be seen itself as a sort of protest, voiced by those in legal quarters against the authoritarian ways in which the redaction of customs proceeded, broadly dominated by Parisian royal commissioners.[101] Many in the provinces welcomed the king's initiatives, but the official campaign had the potential of turning into political intrusion from the center, and the movement to reform—change—the existing customs could pose a threat to local liberties, this for all the workings of local assemblies.[102] Faced with what they viewed as the increasing royal reach into the realm of local private law, local elites had reason to feel ambivalent. This is why Coquille emphasized "c'est le people qui fait la loi," while also stating that it was the king, through his commissioners, who "y inspir[e] la puissance de loi." He was reaffirming what he saw as the ground rule in the royal campaign, that is, the king granted legal force to the law that was made by the people. This way Coquille and his fellow authors highlighted the king's commitment to respect his laws, including custom. The king was mindful that any change to the law was likely to be disruptive to people who had arranged their affairs on the basis of the existing law. Historians in general agree that the redaction process was a ceremonial reenactment of the original social compact, concluded between the king represented by the commissioners on the one hand and the three orders of society on the other. Elaborate rituals of convoking the estates served to coax the reticent seigneurs to participate in the assemblies, as the solemnity of the homologation process affirmed local rights and privileges.[103] Popular consent did matter but it could also be a way of authorial flourish for Coquille and others.

One may ask whether there was enough incentive for the king to meddle in private legal relations in the first place. Could it be that the king stayed away less because he respected customs as an embodiment of popular will (although this

[99] Auguste Lebrun, *La coutume: Ses sources—son autorité en droit privé. Contribution à l'étude des sources du droit positif à l'époque moderne* (Paris: Librairie générale, 1932), 74.

[100] "The king was no longer content with authenticating the text and certifying its truthfulness. Now the king intervened in the making of the text and, in a sense, made it his own text." Lebrun, *La coutume*, 79–80. Officially published customs no longer contained simply the rules of the customary origin; they were veritable laws which emanated from the legislative power.

[101] Krynen, "The Absolute Monarchy," 47.

[102] Kelley, "'Second Nature,'" 141.

[103] Grinberg, *Écrire les coutumes*, 72; Martine Grinberg, "La rédaction des coutumes et les droits seigneuriaux: Nommer, classer, exclure," *Annales. Histoire, Sciences Sociales* 52 (1997), 1019–21; Donald R. Kelley, "Jurisprudence in the French Manner," in *The Human Measure*, 203.

was never denied) than because he had little to gain by doing so? The king was concerned to maintain the elite corporate households so that they could safeguard the sociopolitical order of the *res publica*. Beyond that, there was no stake for him in the outcome of marital settlements or succession arrangements of his subjects; it would have made little sense to get involved in private legal proceedings and compromise his commitment to honor and adhere to the impartial laws.

All in all, the official recording of customs reaffirmed the king as the master of the legal order in his kingdom. The hierarchy of *lex–consuetudo* marginalized old custom's normativity vis-à-vis the king's law in regulating social relationships. The people continued to develop new practices and consider them obligatory, but only those approved by the king could be invoked in justice; they could assert other customs only when there was no existing law, including the homologated customs, to cover the questions in dispute.[104] Henceforth, "custom has a boss who approves or disapproves it and a tribunal which decides and controls it."[105] Customary law lost an ability to evolve according to the wishes of the populace.[106] As customs were put into an official and definitive version, they were deprived of the possibility of adaptation. There was no more abrogation "par désuetude," as the change of custom now required prescribed legislative procedures; this was Hart's secondary rules of change of a legal system.[107] As Donald Kelley put it, "under conditions of that fearful oxymoron of written custom all interested parties were vulnerable."[108]

Olivier-Martin preferred depicting the redaction of customs in terms of the benevolent will of the otherwise powerful monarch. No wonder Coquille appealed to him. But historians are often known for being overly eager to accept the rhetorical nationalist utterances of legal humanists.

4. Enter the Lawyers

According to John Dawson, the extraordinary efficiency of the customary law reform was "due to the silent conquest by a professional class of the local popular assemblies" which, "under the skillful guidance of the commissioners, had become a passive but willing instrument in a program of moderate reform."[109]

[104] Beauthier and de Broux, "Un regard historien," 728.

[105] Champeaux, "Coutumes de Bourgogne et coutumes du duché de Bourgogne," 75. Custom was "no longer the expression of the self-regulation, changeable and adaptable, of a given social group." Jean Bart, *Histoire du droit privé: De la chute de l'Empire romain au XIXe siècle* (Paris: Montchrestien, 1998), 110.

[106] Krynen, "Entre science juridique et dirigisme," 174.

[107] See supra Chapter 2, note 165 and accompanying text.

[108] Donald R. Kelley, "Lord Deliver Us from Justice," *Yale Journal of Law & the Humanities* 5 (1993), 164.

[109] Dawson, "French Customs," 779, 790.

Official customs were the products of the dominant professional opinions which valued legal stability and certainty. The process was a "stroke of genius" on the part of the monarchy: the king moderated the harshness of customary solutions in private law and "gained the heart of his subjects."[110] By allowing the people to elaborate their customs, he turned his traditional obligations to political gains and confirmed the primacy of legislation in both public and private law.

Speaking of gains, it was the legal profession that arguably emerged with the most. Customary redaction revealed the increasing influence of the community of lawyers who were deeply imbued with the legal acculturation of the times.[111] Legal practitioners, who had been compelled in the past to argue their cases from the often obscure and indigestible *coutumiers*, now had official texts at their disposal. Customs were reduced to a written corpus, deposited in the archives of the parlements of each jurisdiction. The result was that custom, "enmeshed in all the complications of an elaborate legal technique," was soon withdrawn from the realm of practices and turned into a rational and learned law.[112]

Lawyers, broadly defined, were, as usual, "wholly conscious of the political realities of their own time."[113] When they began labelling legal customs, they were ready to carve out their sphere of influence and lay hold of the situation to their profit. The masses were increasingly alienated from the labyrinth of legal process; the procedures at the royal courts became more convoluted, distant from the lay people's reach. It may have seemed a way of reducing meritless lawsuits, yet lawyers would not of course be shy of using their professional monopoly to their advantage, for example, by inciting and prolonging lawsuits.

Most changes made in the reformation phase, with strong doses of Roman law, could not have come from spontaneous demand from local communities. The revisions, often technical, "were too numerous and too uniform to be explained in terms of deeply rooted popular conviction."[114] The next chapter examines the contents of the reformed customs, juxtaposing them with the ambitious legislative agenda of the king.

[110] Descimon and Guéry, "Un État des temps modernes?" 219.

[111] Kim, "Custom, Community, and the Crown," 176.

[112] Dawson, "French Customs," 794.

[113] Ibbetson, "Custom in Medieval Law," 157.

[114] Descimon, "Quelques réflexions à propos des commissaires du roi," # 19–24.

5
La Coutume and *la Législation*

The reformation of the *coutume* of Paris took place after many other *coutumes* had already gone through revisions, so in many respects it was a true synthesis. The *Coutume de Paris* of 1510 contained 199 articles; the *Coutume de Paris* of 1580 boasted 362 articles. The increase in the number of articles attested to the growing complexity in society, but the fundamental goals of perpetuating the family's landholding and ensuring the economic viability of the household remained solidly embedded in them. Deference to kinship ties was profound. The new custom of Paris clarified and reduced unreasonable and inequitable ancient privileges parading as custom, although many existing seigneurial rights were preserved without change. The very first article is a case in point. Article 1 of the *ancienne coutume* stated:

> By the custom of the city, Prévôté et Vicomté de Paris, the feudal lord, for want of person and by reason of rights and obligations not performed or paid, may seize the fief coming from him, exploit it as fully forfeited, and take the profits during the period of seizure.[1]

Article 1 of the *nouvelle coutume* read:

> The feudal lord, for want of person or by reason of rights and obligations not performed or paid, may seize the fief coming from him, exploit it as fully forfeited, and take the profits during the period of seizure, in charge of using them as a good father of the family.[2]

The redactors in 1580 simply deleted the opening phrase, deemed superfluous, and added at the end that the seigneur was to enjoy his feudal rights in a responsible manner. Touting the revised *coutume* as a corpus of rules embodying

[1] "Par la Coustume de la Ville, Prevosté & Vicomté de Paris, le seigneur féodal, par faute d'homme, droits & devoirs non faits & non payez, peut mettre en sa main le fief mouvant de luy, & iceluy fief exploicter en pure perte, & faire les fruicts siens pendant la main-mise." *Nouveau coutumier général*, vol. 3, 1.

[2] "Le seigneur féodal par faute d'homme, droits & devoirs non faits & non payez, peut mettre en sa main de fief mouvant de luy, & icelui fief exploiter en pure perte, & faire les fruits siens pendant la main-mise: à la charge d'en user par luy, comme un bon pere de famille." Ibid., vol. 3, 29.

Custom, Law, and Monarchy: A Legal History of Early Modern France. Marie Seong-Hak Kim, Oxford University Press.
 DOI: 10.1093/oso/9780192845498.003.0005

egalitarianism would be misleading, no less than dismissing it as a sixteenth-century apparition of feudalism.

In the early modern period, litigants before the sovereign courts were mostly landowners, comprising the nobles holding seigneurial property, merchants, or corporative groups like the clergy and the guilds. Those with substantial property were the ones who had greatest interest in the law and could afford professional legal services.[3] In theory royal courts were open to all subjects, and peasants and artisans brought disputes to courts of first instance in an increasing number, but those cases only rarely made their way to the parlements. Most legal needs at the individual level were met by notaries. Marriage contracts were primary instruments by which succession and property matters were arranged. Families resorted to them to circumvent rigid customary rules. Contracts could serve as defensive tools as long as they did not violate good morals and equity.[4]

Roman law distinguished between compulsory or mandatory law (*jus cogens*) and non-compulsory or default law (*jus dispositivum*). The former are laws the application of which cannot be evaded by means of a different expression of intention by the parties, whereas the latter are those whose application can be avoided by means of special expression of intent. The parties are free to enter, or to refrain from entering, into a legal relation governed by compulsory provisions, but once they have entered, they are bound by those provisions. Legal requirements for the validity of a marriage, the law of succession, and the law of real rights are examples of *jus cogens* in private law. *Jus dispositivum*, by contrast, takes effect either where no arrangement has been made by the parties in regard to a given legal relation or where, even if an arrangement has been made, that arrangement is incomplete or defective.

Reformed articles in the *Coutume de Paris* clarified requisite elements of juridical acts in the property regime. They reflected the changing perceptions of social appropriateness in legal relations. The parties wanting to assert their rights were now expected to declare their intent clearly and explicitly. With the presence of specific provisions in the codified *coutume*, what mattered was not so much the proof of law as the proof of intent of the independent individual. The absence of contrary intent in legal transactions was evidence that the parties wished to be governed by the customary law provisions. Understandably, a well-crafted private agreement was critical, and competent lawyers' services became ever more valuable. In general, customary law moved in the direction of the individualization of property rights and served to enliven the land market, in response to the

[3] "The justice for the poor and the orphan, as well as criminal justice, served as showcases for Europe's monarchies." Descimon, "Power Elites and the Prince," 114.

[4] The principle that the content of a juristic act should not be contrary to public order or good morals dated from Roman law and was stipulated later on in French and German law (*ordre public*; *öffentliche ordnung*). See, for example, Articles 6 and 1133 in the French Civil Code.

demographic expansion of the sixteenth century and giving a nod to changing economic situations.

This chapter examines major aspects of the content of the custom of Paris, with reference to other regional customs. Focus will be on the customs revised with the influence of Roman law. Strictly speaking, the *coutume* of Paris was only the custom of the people of Paris, but it carried broader authority, to which many commentators turned when the custom of a particular jurisdiction was absent or proved insufficient.

Reforms of custom improved law, yet there were plenty of problems left unaddressed. The royal government in the 1560s attempted to correct some of them through edicts and ordinances. Most legislative measures dealt with the administration of justice and police, but, as the government tried to ensure coherence in the legal system, an effective regulation of private law matters like succession and marital property also became necessary. Legislation initiated by Chancellor Michel de L'Hôpital, the top judicial official from 1560 through 1568, complemented the reformation campaign of custom led by First President de Thou. Both efforts aimed to ameliorate royal justice, precisely when the kingdom was plunged into the unprecedented crisis of political and social disintegration during the religious wars.

1. Contents of Customs

The *Coutume de Paris* of 1580 consisted of sixteen titles, covering a broad swath of matters including possession, acquisition, prescription, easements, mortgages, inheritance, monetary arrangements between spouses, marital authority, personal capacity, dower, gifts, testaments, intestate succession, the power of redemption, and custody and guardianship.[5] While the *coutume* did not cover the law of

[5] The organization of the *Coutume de Paris* (1580) is as follows: Title 1, "On fiefs" (*De fiefs*) (Arts. 1–72); Title 2, "On quitrents and seigneurial rights" (*Des censives & droits seigneuriaux*) (Arts. 73–87); Title 3, "Which goods are movable and which are immovable" (*Quels biens sont meubles, & quels immeubles*) (Arts. 88–95); Title 4, "On complaint in case of seizure, and new and simple seizure" (*De complainte en cas de saisine, & de nouvellete, & simple saisine*) (Arts. 96–98); Title 5, "On personal surety and hypothecary actions" (*Des actions personnelles & d'hypotheque*) (Arts. 99–112); Title 6, "On prescription" (*De prescription*) (Arts. 113–28); Title 7, "On redemption rights of heirs" (*De retrait lignager*) (Arts. 129–59); Title 8, "Judgments, executions, and seizures" (*Arrests, executions & gageries*) (Arts. 160–83); Title 9, "On servitudes and the reports of court masters" (*Des servitudes & rapports de jurez*) (Arts. 184–219); Title 10, "Community property" (*Communauté de biens*) (Arts. 220–46); Title 11, "On dower rights" (*Des douaires*) (Arts. 247–64); Title 12, "On guardianship of nobles and bourgeois" (*De garde noble, & bourgeoise*) (Arts. 265–71); Title 13, "On gifts and mutual gifts" (*Des donations & don mutual*) (Arts. 272–88); Title 14, "On wills and their execution" (*Des testamens, & executions d'iceux*) (Arts. 289–98); Title 15, "On succession in direct and collateral lines" (*De succession en ligne directe, & collaterale*) (Arts. 299–344); Title 16, "On public proclamations" (*De criées*) (Arts. 345–62). For a summary of each title, see Jerah Johnson, "La Coutume de Paris: Louisiana's First Law," *Louisiana History: The Journal of the Louisiana Historical Association* 30 (1989), 151–53.

obligations, which was governed by the principles of Roman law, it included enforcement measures such as the seizure of property for debt recovery.[6] Marriage formation was under the purview of canon law, and written customs had little to say about it. First, examination of some general characteristics of inheritance and settlement rules in custom, old and new, is in order.

Inheritance and Settlement

An individual could dispose of his or her assets *inter vivos* or *post mortem*, through gift, sale, and will. Inheritance took place through either testamentary bequest or intestate succession. The division between the *pays de droit coutumier* and the *pays de droit écrit* indicated differing conceptions of, and approaches to, these juridical acts. In the *pays de droit écrit* in the Midi, where the influence of Roman law was strong, a person enjoyed considerable liberty in disposing of property by gifts and wills. Roman law allowed a broad freedom of patrimonial bequest; the testator was only subject to specific limitations of providing a guaranteed share for children (*légitime*). Under the principle of the unity of patrimony, all property—movable, immovable, lineage, and individual—formed a single mass and was treated in the same manner, regardless of its nature or origin. When the deceased did not have children, the property devolved on the ascendants and the nearest collaterals, without any distinction made as to the type of property.[7] The designation of the heir (*institution d'héritier*) served as a remedy for the fragmentation of noble patrimony.

Regulation of property was more stringent in the *pays coutumiers* in the northern and central regions. Constraints on destabilizing the existing pattern in landholding were strong. Custom did not favor testamentary bequest.[8] In Île-de-France, the use of the last wills and testaments was uncommon other than for persons with substantial fortunes. An individual who chose to make a will was subject to numerous restrictions aimed to discourage bypassing the customary rules of succession.[9] The prevailing idea was that the custom, not the deceased (*de*

[6] Janwillem Oosterhuis, *Specific Performance in German, French and Dutch Law in the Nineteenth Century: Remedies in an Age of Fundamental Rights and Industrialization* (Leiden: Brill, 2011), 38.

[7] Jean Brissaud, *A History of French Private Law*, trans. Rapelje Howell (Boston: Little, Brown, 1912), 642.

[8] Olivier-Martin, *Histoire de la coutume de la prévôté et vicomté de Paris*, vol. 2, 448–505.

[9] In western France, advantaging one child over the others was virtually impossible under customary rules. Xavier Martin, *Le principe d'égalité dans les successions roturiers en Anjou et dans le Maine* (Paris: Presses universitaires de France, 1972). Well-to-do commoners were eager to find means to avoid the requirements of equal distribution in order to maintain and build family fortunes. Ralph E. Giesey, "Rules of Inheritance and Strategies of Mobility in Prerevolutionary France," *American Historical Review* 82 (1977), 272–78.

cujus), designated the heirs.[10] The continuity of property ownership was ensured through the operation of law; succession *ab intestat* was the most dominant mode of devolution. The custom of Paris preserved the principle "le mort saisit le vif" (the dead seizes the living), resulting in the automatic and immediate succession of the property by the nearest kin.[11] There could be no gap in the ownership of the freehold estate, and the legal title vested instantly. A testament was valid without the heir ("Institution d'hoirie n'a point de lieu").[12]

Scholars in the early sixteenth century distinguished, drawing on Bartolus, two kinds of customary law status: *statut réel* and *statut personnel*.[13] In the *coutume* of Paris, and in most other *coutumes* in the *pays de droit coutumier*, rules of succession differed depending on the condition, status, and capacity of persons and the nature, origin, and quality of the property involved. Whether succession took place in direct or collateral lines mattered; in the case of direct succession, whether it was to devolve on a descendant or an ascendant had different rules.[14] Property to transmit through intestate succession was distinguished between real property (*immeubles*) and movable property (*meubles*). Subject to its origin, the real property of *de cujus* was divided into *propres* and *acquêts*, also called *conquêts*. *Propres* was family patrimony, or the inherited land, and *acquêts* was the land acquired through means other than inheritance. The underlying idea was that an individual who had no part in the acquisition of the *propres* should not be allowed to dispose of it at will; for *acquêts* or *conquêts*, property acquired through one's own effort and labor, no such restrictions were necessary.[15] Finally, depending on its quality, real property was divided into noble estates (*biens nobles*) and commoner estates (*biens roturiers*).[16] The former consisted of fiefs, the latter *censives*. In the Paris region in general, it was the status of the property, not the status of the deceased, that determined under which rule the estate would fall. The principle of equal division governed all movable property, *censives*, and fictitious real property like annuities, known as *rentes*.[17]

[10] *De cujus* means the deceased author of succession. For intestate succession in customary law regions, see Brissaud, *A History of French Private Law*, 621–23.

[11] "Le mort saisit le vif, son hoir plus proche & habile à lui succeder." *Nouvelle coutume de Paris* [hereinafter N. C. de Paris], Art. 318, *Nouveau coutumier général*, vol. 3, 52. In *ancienne coutume de Paris* [hereinafter A. C. de Paris], Art. 132 states: "En la Prevoste & Vicomte de Paris, le mort saisit le vif son hoir." *Nouveau coutumier général*, vol. 3, 10. See Olivier-Martin, *Histoire de la coutume de la prévôté et vicomté de Paris*, vol. 2, 75.

[12] N. C. de Paris, Art. 299, *Nouveau coutumier général*, vol. 3, 51; A. C. de Paris, Art. 120, ibid., vol. 3, 10.

[13] Chénon, *Histoire générale du droit français*, vol. 2, 326–29.

[14] Beaune, *Introduction à l'étude historique du droit coutumier français*, 520.

[15] Brissaud, *A History of French Private Law*, 273–74. Various restrictions on the freedom to alienate *propres*, and in some cases *acquêts* too, existed in the form of *réserve coutumière*, as will be seen below.

[16] See Yves F. Zoltvany, "Esquisse de la coutume de Paris," *Revue d'histoire de l'Amérique française* 25 (1971), 365–84.

[17] *Rentes* were interest-paying investment securities. See supra Chapter 3, note 80.

Most notable among the rules governing the *biens nobles* was the *droit d'aînesse*. The essence of feudal succession, primogeniture persisted through the waning of feudalism because of the need to protect estates from fragmentation. Under feudal law, fiefs were either the fiefs of dignity (duchies or baronies) or common lordships. The former were passed on in their entirety to the eldest son of the deceased, provided he indemnified his younger siblings; the latter were transmitted in accordance with a moderate form of primogeniture. Properties were inherited by male heirs to the exclusion of female heirs of the same degree. Thus, brothers inherited before sisters, and nephews before nieces.[18] When there were only daughters, the fief was shared equally among them or went to the closest in the collateral line. The feudal right of primogeniture survived widely in custom. Again, different *coutumes* had different rules, depending on stronger or weaker feudal remnants. In areas extending from the mouth of the Seine to the Pas-de-Calais, a designated share of the property, called *préciput*, was set aside for the eldest of the nobility before the estate's partition among the heirs.[19]

Lengthy negotiations took place during the redaction and reformation of the customs over how to determine the scope of the *droit d'aînesse*. Under the new *coutume* of Paris, the eldest son obtained the court and manor and two-thirds of the property, if there was a single younger sibling, and one-half of the property, if there were two or more younger siblings; the rest was shared equally.[20] Customs in the north and the east (Amiens, Péronne, part of Vermandois) were more favorable to the eldest, leaving only a small part of patrimony to the younger sons and often in usufruct only. Some customs in the west (Maine and Anjou) gave a part of succession share to the youngest, normally a third, *en bienfait* (in kindness).[21]

Most contemporary authors, even those critical of antiquated feudal rules, defended primogeniture for the sake of the preservation of the social order. André Tiraqueau called it "droits favorables," far from "droits odieux," because "the honor and dignity of families are preserved by the eldest males."[22] He separated the *droit d'aînesse* from other feudal laws and justified it in terms of preventing

[18] Didier Veillon, "Quelques observations sur le droit commun coutumier français (XVIe–XVIIIe s.)," *Slovenian Law Review* 4 (2007), 219–20; Beaune, *Introduction à l'étude historique*, 310.

[19] Brissaud, *A History of French Private Law*, 634–38.

[20] N. C. de Paris, Arts. 15 and 16, *Nouveau coutumier général*, vol. 3, 31.

[21] See *Coutume de Maine*, 1508, Art. 239, *Nouveau coutumier général*, vol. 4, 486; *Coutume d'Anjou*, 1508, Art. 222, *Nouveau coutumier général*, vol. 4, 550–51. René Filhol, "Protestantisme et droit d'aînesse au XVIe siècle," *Recueil de mémoires et travaux de la Société d'histoire du droit écrit* 7 (1970), 197.

[22] Tiraqueau, *De Nobilitate et de jure primogeniorum*. See Jacques Bréjon, *Un jurisconsulte de la Renaissance: André Tiraqueau (1488–1558)* (Paris: Recueil Sirey, 1937), 184. Antoine Loisel stated in *Institutes coustumières* that it would be reasonable that the eldest "takes the double of each of the other children" (*le double de chacun des autres enfans*). *Institutes coustumières ou Manuel de plusieurs et diverses reigles, sentences et proverbes tant anciens que modernes du droict coustumier et plus ordinaire de la France* (Paris: Abel L'Angelier, 1611; ed. Michel Reulos, Paris: Recueil Sirey, 1935), book 4, title 3, LXII, 58. Other jurists of the time, including Le Caron, Coquille, and de L'Hommeau, all shared the opinion that primogeniture was a desirable law. Across Western Europe, there was a growing

the partition of noble patrimony.[23] Dumoulin was also an ardent advocate of primogeniture. "The law of allowing only lifetime interest to the younger children seems iniquitous to many," but in fact, according to him, it had a desirable effect because it would motivate them to seek careers in more productive work; they would be better off to obtain a post in the army or in an institution commensurate with their noble status. Dumoulin said that primogeniture was especially "useful in regions near the frontier so that there are people powerful enough to defend the territory."[24] The fragmentation of land resulting from patrimonial partition would hurt the nobility because, whereas merchants could make money by engaging in business, nobles did not have similar resources. It would prevent them from living a life suitable for their station and eventually ruin them.[25] These scholarly musings were reflected in the *coutume* of 1580 aimed to avoid drastic reforms that might impoverish noble families. In Pasquier's opinion, the protection of the family before the individual was germane to the spirit of French law; for this reason he supported both primogeniture and the exclusion of the endowed daughters from inheritance.[26]

The confluence of the communitarian and egalitarian spirit of the Parisian custom was best exemplified by the rule concerning the endowed children. A child who had been given a marriage portion in the form of dowry or gift was normally not allowed to come to the succession, in which only the children, married or unmarried, who were living in the household at the time of the parents' deaths could take part. The deeply entrenched idea was that a family was a household with children who resided with the parents at the dissolution of the community; only those who contributed their labor to family wealth qualified to share in the succession.[27] The exclusion of the endowed children had feudal origins. Through the rule of mortmain, the feudal lord took possession of the property of a serf who was not living with the heir at the time of his death.[28] Apart from this background, the exclusion of the *enfants dotés* was justified in that the parents should not advantage one child over another through lifetime gifts.[29]

The practice of *rappel*, introduced in 1510 in Paris, allowed endowed children to participate in the parental succession on the condition that they bring back the

literature in favor of primogeniture from the sixteenth century. Joan Thirsk, "The European Debate on Customs of Inheritance, 1500–1700," in Goody et al. (eds.), *Family and Inheritance*, 177–91.

[23] Filhol, *Le premier président Christofle de Thou*, 170–71.

[24] Filhol, "Protestantisme et droit d'aînesse," 197.

[25] In a *factum* (legal brief) likely dating from 1561, Dumoulin vehemently condemned the arguments of Calvinist ministers defending the mutiny by the younger brothers against their older brothers. Ibid., 199–200.

[26] Pasquier, *Lettres*, book 9, letter 1 (to Brisson), *Les œuvres*, vol. 2, cols. 221–28.

[27] Olivier-Martin, *Histoire de la coutume de la prévôté et vicomté de Paris*, vol. 2, 146, and, more generally, vol. 2, 141–62; Lloyd, *The State, France, and the Sixteenth Century*, 34; Diefendorf, *Paris City Councillors*, 227–28.

[28] Mortmain means an inalienable ownership of real estate.

[29] Yver, *Égalité entre héritiers et exclusion des enfants dotés*, 15–23.

property they had received to the estate or that the value of that property be deducted from his or her share of inheritance.[30] Before 1510, this privilege had to be written into the marriage contract of the child; after 1510, returning to succession became the child's default right.[31] Of course, the option of *rappel* was worth exercising only when the endowment was less in value than the share to be expected through inheritance. The revised custom of 1580 inserted the language that a child who had received gifts from parents at marriage or any other occasion could keep them by abstaining from the parental succession.[32] It was part of the general relaxation of customary restrictions dating from feudal privileges.

There were two main principles of succession in the custom of Paris: first, "paterna paternis, materna maternis," and second, "propres ne remontent point."[33] They were intrinsically connected. Under the latter, ascendants were excluded from inheriting *propres* because such an inheritance was deemed unnatural.[34] In the absence of heirs, the inheritance went to the collaterals. Under the rule *paterna paternis materna maternis*, the property coming from the father or the paternal family was separated from the property coming from the mother or the maternal family. If the husband and the wife died childless, the land each spouse had received by inheritance reverted to the closest relatives on each side of the lineage from which the property had come. The *propres* that had originated in the paternal line were not allowed to go to the maternal relatives, and vice versa.[35] The principle *paterna paternis materna maternis* was fastidiously observed in the community property regime, which was another notable characteristic of the Parisian law.

The custom of Paris provided for community property. Barring stipulation in the marriage contract to the contrary, the spouses owned property in common, except for the *propres* given to the husband or the wife through direct or collateral succession or given as gift in direct line. The strict conjugal community rules were modified by the institution of the widow's dower right (*douaire*). At the death of the husband, the widow was entitled to a life annuity (*rente viagère*) on the

[30] Ibid., 54–70. See Jean-Louis Thireau, "Fondements de l'exclusion successorale des filles dotées dans l'ouest de la France," in Bernard d'Alteroche, Florence Demoulin-Auzary, Olivier Descamps, and Franck Roumy (eds.), *Mélanges en l'honneur d'Anne Lefebvre-Teillard* (Paris: Éditions Panthéon-Assas, 2009), 991–1006.

[31] A. C. de Paris, Art. 123, *Nouveau coutumier général*, vol. 3, 10. See Veillon, "Quelques observations," 220.

[32] N. C. de Paris, Arts. 302–304, 307, *Nouveau coutumier général*, vol. 3, 51–52. Jurists assumed that this right had been implicitly allowed in the custom rejecting forced heirship. The adage, "Il ne se porte héritier qui ne veut," reflected this sentiment.

[33] Chénon, *Histoire générale du droit français*, vol. 2, 236.

[34] Brissaud, *A History of French Private Law*, 277.

[35] A. C. de Paris, Art. 147, *Nouveau coutumier général*, vol. 3, 11; N. C. de Paris, Art. 326, *Nouveau coutumier général*, vol. 3, 53. Art. 329 added: "Et sont réputés parents du côté et ligne supposé qu'ils ne soient descendus de celui qui a acquis l'héritage." Ibid. In other words, the persons were presumed to be the relatives, even if they did not descend from the one who had acquired the property. Veillon, "Quelques observations," 221.

propres of the husband. The assets assigned to the dower could not be used to settle the debts of the estate. The size of the dower could be predetermined by the parties' stipulation in the marriage contract; otherwise it was one-half of the hereditary possessions. The property returned to the heirs of the predeceased at the death of the surviving spouse.[36] The rule of *préciput* complemented the customary law device by guaranteeing the surviving spouse the ownership of certain movable property or an amount of money taken out of the community before division. The wife was allowed to renounce the community regime by invoking the prenuptial agreement and recover her *propres*, half of the community property, and her dower and *préciput*.

Bringing in Reason and Equity

Recall royal commissioners were commanded to bring reason into custom (*y pourveoir ainsi que de raison*). The *lettres patentes* repeatedly stated that custom should not be "contrary to reason and equity."[37] Appeal to reason was more than an abstract formula; it meant granting permission to resort to Roman law.[38] The compiled customs included numerous articles derived from non-customary sources like Roman law and legislation.[39] Roman law principles of representation in intestate succession and minimal guaranteed portion for the heirs were incorporated into the new customary law texts of Paris and other regions. One sees a certain legislative agenda in the reformation of customs.

Representation in Succession

The royal commissioners made concerted efforts to extend the rights of children in intestate succession.[40] A number of *coutumes* had disallowed the children to

[36] N. C. de Paris, Art. 229, *Nouveau coutumier général*, vol. 3, 46. See Barbara B. Diefendorf, "Women and Property in Ancient Regime France: Theory and Practice in Dauphiné and Paris," in John Brewer and Susan Staves (eds.), *Early Modern Conceptions of Property* (New York: Routledge, 1995), 170–93.

[37] *Lettres patentes*, March 15, 1498, issued in Amboise, *Nouveau coutumier général*, vol. 4, 639. See supra Chapter 3, note 31 and accompanying text.

[38] "For these jurists nourished by learned law, there was no other path toward the modernity than *raison écrite*." Jacques Poumarède, "Droit romain et rédaction des coutumes dans le ressort du parlement de Bordeaux," in Allinne (ed.), *Itinéraire(s) d'un historien du droit*, 124. The *procès-verbal* of Touraine in 1559 shows that several articles prescribing penalties for crimes were rejected; it was noted, instead, that "the penalties for delicts mentioned in the said article will be remitted to the discretion of the judges, to be decided by their consciences according to royal ordinances and *la raison escrite*." *Nouveau coutumier général*, vol. 4, 701. See Dawson, "French Customs," 794.

[39] The situation was the same in the Netherlands. Gilissen, "Les phases de la codification" (Part 1), 60. See also Bram Van Hofstraeten, "Recording Customs in Early Modern Antwerp, a Commercial Metropolis," *Rechtsgeschichte Legal History* 24 (2016), 288–301.

[40] Filhol, *Le premier président Christofle de Thou*, 223–48.

stand for their deceased parents in a grandparental estate. This custom originated in feudal society where the vassal was required to perform military services for the lord, a consideration that retained little relevance in the sixteenth century.[41] The practice contrasted with Roman law. Roman law allowed representation in direct line indefinitely, as provided in the *Codex*, and in the collateral line to the children of brothers and sisters, as in *Novel* 118.[42] Absence of representation could bring the harsh result of cutting off descendants.[43]

The *coutume* of Paris did not provide for representation before 1510, unless parents had either inserted into a child's marriage contract the stipulation of succession *per stirpes* or created separate instruments *inter vivos* or *causa mortem* to that effect.[44] If such a clause was provided in favor of one child, all other siblings were entitled to the same right.[45] The designation of grandchildren to represent their defunct parents remained a voluntary act of the grandparents, and negligence—if not ill will—on their part could cause serious consequences for grandchildren.[46] It was only in 1510 that the custom of Paris included representation in direct line as a default rule, though not in the collateral line.[47] The children still were not allowed to succeed to their father's right to primogeniture.

There were numerous regional variations in the sixteenth century. Some regions recognized *per stirpes* in both direct and collateral lines to the infinite degree (Touraine); others did not allow it at all (Amiens, Melun, Péronne); yet others allowed representation in the direct line but not in the collateral line (Paris, Orléans, Sens, and Auxerre).[48] Royal commissioners tried to expand representation as much as possible. All the customs reformed by de Thou guaranteed *per stirpes* in the direct line in infinitum and to a limited degree in the collateral line. In 1556, representation was introduced into the *bailliages* of Étampes, Montfort, Mantes, and Vermandois-Laon, and also Melun in 1560. The revised Custom of Paris of 1580 allowed representation in the direct line, and in the collateral line to

[41] Brissaud, *A History of French Private Law*, 600–601.

[42] *Codex*, 58.6.3; *Novel* 118.1 and 118.3 (the children of the predeceased take "such portion of the inheritance as would have fallen to their parents, if living"). In the fourteenth century, Baldus argued that the remoteness of the degree of relationship had no effect in feudal estate. Descimon and Guéry, "Un État des temps modernes?" 229–30.

[43] Veillon, "Quelques observations," 222.

[44] *Per stirpes* means "by stock" or "by branch." Each branch of the family receives an equal share of an estate. Thus, the children of a son or daughter take the share that would have been given to that person.

[45] *Procès-verbal* in *Nouveau coutumier général*, vol. 3, 23.

[46] In the draft custom of 1507, the grandchildren were still excluded from succession when there was no express *rappel* clause in the marriage contract of their parents. Olivier-Martin, *Histoire de la coutume de la prévôté et vicomté de Paris*, vol. 2, 464; Filhol, *Le premier président Christofle de Thou*, 226.

[47] A. C. de Paris, Arts. 133, 134, 138, and 139, *Nouveau coutumier général*, vol. 3, 10; *procès-verbal* in vol. 3, 23. See Olivier-Martin, "Un document inédit," 216. President Thibault Baillet insisted on allowing representation. Veillon, "Quelques observations," 222.

[48] A. C. de Paris, Art. 149; Dawson, "French Customs," 783, note 67.

benefit the children of brothers and sisters.[49] In several localities, de Thou's effort to extend the rule to the collateral line encountered tenacious resistance.[50]

Légitime

Légitime (legitim or legal share) was introduced into the customary laws of Paris and the nearby areas like Chartres and Sens in the first decades of the sixteenth century. Derived from the Roman law principle of equity, the *légitime* protected heirs against the whims of the testator by guaranteeing them a minimum share in the parental estate, which neither a will nor donation could change.[51] Customary law regions had strict systems of limiting the ability to alienate property, called *réserve coutumière*. But these were rules grounded on the need to preserve family estates and thus were different from *légitime*, which was perceived in terms of a moral duty the testator owed to the descendants. A brief discussion of the reserve shares in custom would be helpful.

The *réserve coutumière* varied greatly from region to region. The right to dispose of lineage property was often set by a quota. In the west of France, including Normandy, Brittany, Anjou, and Touraine, the limit was one-third of *propres*. As economic changes turned *acquêts* and *meubles* into an important part of personal fortunes, some customs subjected them to the reserve portion as well. The transmission of property through familial lines could be disrupted by inter vivos gifts or sales. Certain customs thus also regulated gift-giving and sales in order to prevent circumventing succession rules. The revised *coutume* of Paris limited the disposable portion of *propres* to one-fifth, but this pertained to testamentary bequest only.[52] The remaining four-fifths, called the *réserve quatre-quints*, was divided according to the rules of intestate succession. The *coutume* disallowed lifetime gifts exceeding one-half of the intestate share.[53] The complex *réserve coutumière* rules illustrate the intricacy of the French *géographies coutumières* (see Map 5.1). The recognition that the hereditary reserve system was insufficient to ensure the heir's welfare adequately led to the adoption of a form of *légitime*.

How to calculate the guaranteed share under the *légitime* varied. In *Novel* 18 (536) in Roman law, the portion reserved for division was one-third of the

[49] N. C. de Paris, Arts. 314, 319, 320, and 324, *Nouveau coutumier général*, vol. 3, 52–53.

[50] De Thou himself was the party to a lawsuit over the right of representation. His maternal uncle called him and his brothers in 1561 to represent their deceased mother. A suit was filed by de Thou's aunt contesting the succession. The case was decided in favor of de Thou on September 7, 1564. Filhol, *Le premier président Christofle de Thou*, 225–26.

[51] For the origins and evolution of hereditary reserve shares, see Martha Peguera Poch, *Aux origines de la réserve héréditaire du Code civil: La légitime en pays de coutumes (XVIe–XVIIIe siècles)* (Aix-en-Provence: Presses universitaires d'Aix-Marseille, 2015), https://books.openedition.org/puam/885; Brissaud, *A History of French Private Law*, 741–45.

[52] N. C. de Paris, Art. 292, *Nouveau coutumier général*, vol. 3, 51. See Olivier-Martin, *Histoire de la coutume de la prévôté et vicomté de Paris*, vol. 2, 316–17; John P. Dawson, *Gifts and Promises: Continental and American Law Compared* (New Haven: Yale University Press, 1980), 31.

[53] N. C. de Paris, Art. 299, *Nouveau coutumier général*, vol. 3, 51; Olivier Martin, *Histoire de la coutume de la prévôté et vicomté de Paris*, vol. 2, 362–74; Chénon, *Histoire générale du droit français public et privé*, vol. 2, 288–91; Dawson, *Gifts and Promises*, 42.

patrimony when there were up to four children, and "one-half beyond that," meaning one-half of the estate when there were five children or more. This created a bizarre situation in which a child with up to three siblings would get one-twelfth whereas a child with four or more siblings would get one-tenth.[54] Pierre Lizet (1482–1554), *premier président* of the Parlement of Paris from 1529 to 1550, was the chief commissioner at the redaction of the *coutume* of Berry in 1539. He departed from Roman law and laid out the rule that the reserved share to fall under the *légitime* would be half of the estate, deducting debts and funeral expenses. Divided by the number of children, the intestate share of each heir was derived, and the *légitime* was half that share.[55] This rule was upheld in 1548 in a special *enquête par turbe* at the Parlement of Paris. De Thou followed Lizet's scheme in reforming the custom of Paris and extended the institution of legal share to other regions.[56]

Under the revised *Coutume de Paris* of 1580, each child was legally entitled to one-half the share that he or she would have had in the estate of a parent or other ascendant, had there been no donation inter vivos, testamentary bequest, or other special disposition of property, beyond the outlays for the debts and funeral expenses of the deceased.[57] It had the effect of protecting younger children. A parent was free to leave the best part of his assets to a favorite child but was not allowed to disinherit the other children.[58] De Thou insisted that *légitime* cover the fiefs which would normally be governed by the *droit d'aînesse*, so that the impact of undue preference for the first-born would be alleviated. It was one issue on which de Thou disagreed with Dumoulin.[59]

Gifts and Sales

The heads of household were continuously finding ways of treating *propres* as if they were *acquêts*, so the preservation of patrimony could be threatened. The provision of *remploi* was thus inserted into the revised custom of Paris: it required that the proceeds from the alienation of *propres* be reinvested in another property to keep the lineage wealth whole. After 1580, such properties entered the conjugal

[54] Veillon, "Quelques observations," 224.

[55] Filhol, *Le premier président Christofle de Thou*, 178, note 3.

[56] Olivier-Martin, *Histoire de la coutume de la prévôté et vicomté de Paris*, vol. 2, 386–92; Olivier-Martin, "Les manuscrits de Simon Marion," 169; Descimon, "Quelques réflexions à propos des commissaires du roi," # 12. The institution of *légitime* evolved into a contract of *réserve*, to be incorporated later into the Civil Code under the name *of réserve héréditaire*. In modern law, it is called forced heirship.

[57] N. C. de Paris, Arts. 298 and 307, *Nouveau coutumier général*, vol. 3, 51.

[58] N. C. de Paris, Art. 17, also Art. 303, *Nouveau coutumier général*, vol. 3, 31, 51. The customs of Laon, Châlons, Reims, Noyon, Dourdan, Melun, Auxerre, and Péronne adopted, one way or another, the new disposition of *légitime*. Filhol, *Le premier président Christofle de Thou*, 179, note 1.

[59] Veillon, "Quelques observations," 224, note 44.

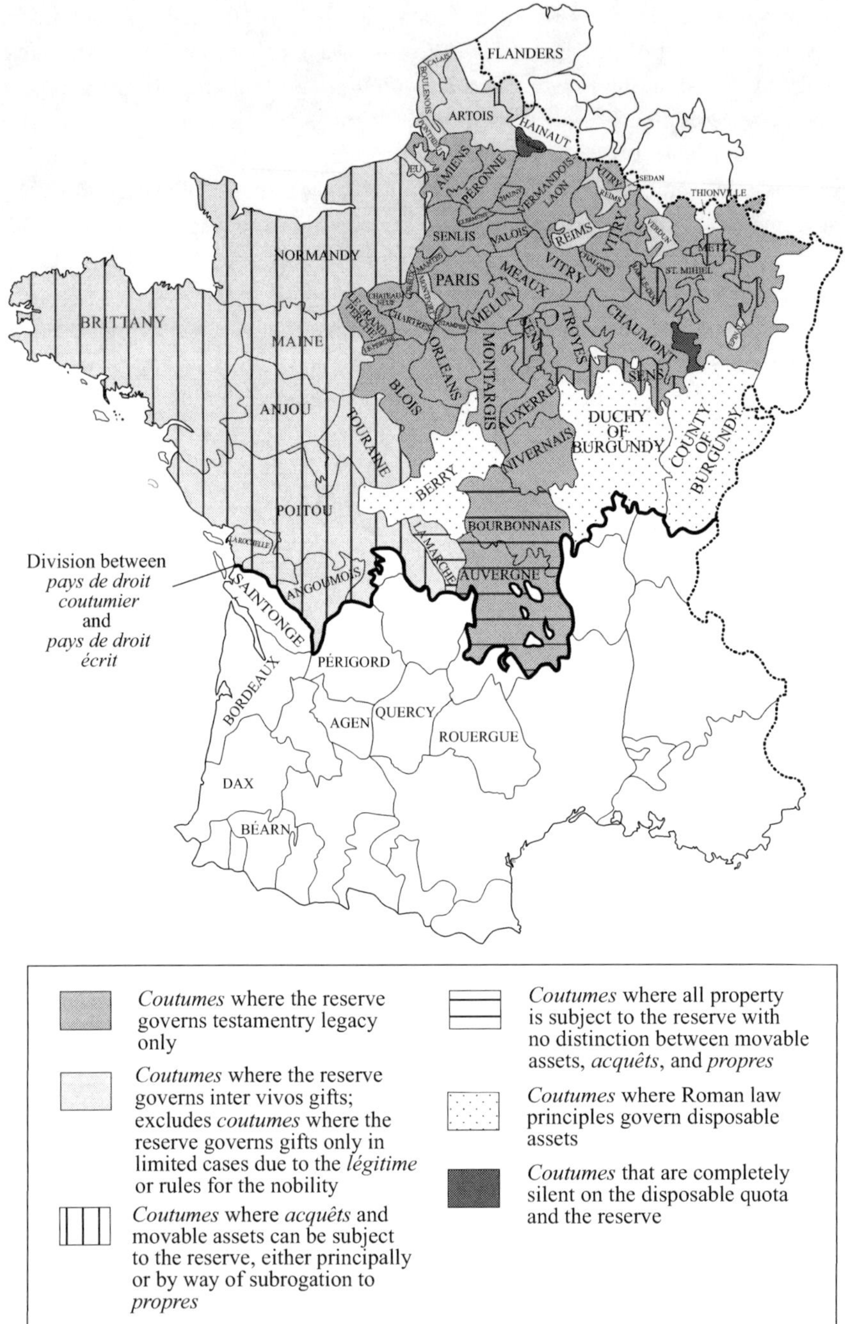

Map 5.1 *Réserve coutumière* after the sixteenth century

Adapted from the map in Jean de Laplanche, *La réserve coutumière dans l'ancien droit français* (1925).

community unless a special stipulation modifying *remploi* had been included in the marriage contract.

The reformed custom of Paris placed spousal donation under restrictions. Once the marriage contract was signed, the spouses could no longer make a mutual donation (*don mutuel*) inter vivos from their community property. Nor could they do so through testamentary gift if there was a surviving child. *Acquêts* entered the community and their value was appraised by an expert at the opening of the succession; they were shared equally between the surviving spouse and the heirs of the predeceased—children and, if none, collaterals.

The *coutume* of Paris also tightened rules governing competency and capacity in donation. The donor had to be in good health when making gifts, to show that he or she still had attachment to worldly concerns. This was a way to limit excessive gifts to the church. Donations of real estate were notarized and insinuated; they were entered on the official registers of the place where the donor resided, not where the property was located.[60]

The customary law guarantee of *retrait lignager* was a safeguard for the blood heirs against the alienation of *propres* by *de cujus* during a lifetime. A redemptive right, it originated from the need to preserve the integrity of fief. Feudal estates consisted of the lands held under the act of fealty and homage. The lord could exercise his redemption right to recover the fief by reimbursing the buyer within forty days of being notified of the sale. He was also allowed to cancel a sale made at an unfavorable price. Stemming from feudal tradition, the practice continued even among commoners, who claimed the repurchase rights of lineage property. Under this mechanism, the *propres* that had been sold to an outsider was subject to recovery by family members. The owner of the land remained free to convey his property within the allowed limits, but his kin, objecting to the alienation of the ancestral lands to strangers, could take it back from the new owner by refunding the purchase price. The old *coutume* of Paris in 1510 allowed a year and a day for redemption, which was preserved in the *coutume* in 1580.[61] This custom confirmed the importance of lineage property in France; *retrait lignager* was not abolished until 1790.

[60] In the revised *coutume* of Paris, the requirements of delivery and of complete surrender by donors of all powers of use or control were tightened and the gift *causa mortis* was eliminated. Olivier Martin, *Histoire de la coutume de la prévôté et vicomté de Paris*, vol. 2, 482–89.

[61] N. C. de Paris, Art. 129, *Nouveau coutumier général*, vol. 3, 40: "When any person has sold and conveyed his family land [*propre héritage*] or *rente* in real estate to a stranger outside the lineage from which the said land or *rente* came to him by succession, it is permitted to the relative of the vendor who is in the lineage which the land or *rente* came from to demand the land or *rente* by way of *retrait lignager*, within a year and a day after the purchaser was seized thereof if the land is held by rent tenure [*en censive*], or after he was received in fealty [*en soy & homage*] if the land is held by feudal tenure [*en fief*], by reimbursing the said purchaser for the principal sum paid and his costs."

Curbing Feudal Privileges

Among the feudal remnants that came under wide criticism was the guardianship for the minor nobles (*garde noble*). Jurists expressed much frustration as the rules were geared for the benefit of the family, not the interest of the minor. Guardianship was conferred on the nearest male relative, who exercised all the rights as to the person and possessions of the minor, with no duty other than restoring the property when the ward reached majority. The minor had no right whatsoever to revenues from the property ("possessions of a minor neither increase nor decrease").[62] Président Thibault Baillet, who carried out some fifteen redactions of customs in the early sixteenth century, devoted sustained effort to eliminate loathsome aspects from the noble custody. He removed from the *coutume* of Paris provisions allowing the collateral relatives to obtain the usufruct on buildings and ownership of movable property.[63] In the late sixteenth century, Baillet's successors renewed attacks. Under the reformed *coutume* of Paris, the medieval wardship, for either a noble or bourgeois, was replaced with a new system of tutelage, in which the *tuteurs* had a fiduciary duty to the minors with their real and personal rights. When necessary, the court could designate the tutor.[64] The introduction of the Roman model of guardianship brought a "complete revolution" of the odious rules in favor of "reason and equity."[65]

The pursuit of the ideals of reason and equity was most vividly played out in areas concerning sundry seigneurial rights. At the time of recording local customs, practitioners in different jurisdictions were charged with investigating and including them in the drafts, but they tended to disregard them systematically. Subsequently in the assemblies, the royal commissioners faced an avalanche of complaints from the lords. It has been well documented that seigneurs reacted to the royal initiative of recording custom by trying to insert even the most ceremonial, bizarre features of their lordship into the written instruments of customary law.[66] Dumoulin pointed out that many unjust and onerous honor-bound rituals, selfish inventions of feudal elites, seeped into the *Coutume de Paris* in 1510. Widely detested, for example, were *droits casuels*, the right of a seigneur, by reason of his "eminent" interest, to receive occasional profits from various acts occurring within his fief. *Lods et ventes* was a tax payable on every change in land ownership. Whenever the sale or mortgage of *censives* took place, the parties, both the buyer and the seller, owed money to the lord.[67]

[62] Brissaud, *A History of French Private Law*, 234.

[63] Poumarède, "Droit romain et rédaction des coutumes," 125.

[64] N. C. de Paris, Arts. 270 and 271, *Nouveau coutumier général*, vol. 3, 49. See Olivier-Martin, *Histoire de la coutume de la prévôté et vicomté de Paris*, vol. 2, 181.

[65] Brissaud, *A History of French Private Law*, 238; Dawson, "French Customs," 782.

[66] See Grinberg, *Écrire les coutumes*.

[67] Dumoulin called *lods et ventes* "burdensome and odious, not to mention sordid," cited from Poumarède, "Droit romain et rédaction des coutumes," 134.

Feudal dues like *lods et ventes* formed an important source of income for the seigneurs, who loudly complained that the parties to land sales refused to pay what they owed to the lords by manipulating the sale prices and tried to escape the taxes as a whole by contracting the sales with a buyout agreement. The lords' strong reactions seemed to show that they, especially the hard-pressed minor nobles, were up against the pervasive atmosphere of antifeudal sentiment during the time of customary law redactions. A rift was developing between the more powerful lords, ecclesiastical or lay, who held the fiefs of dignity, on the one hand, and the rest consisting of the lesser lords, on the other.[68] Whereas the former were concerned about maintaining their exercise of seigneurial justice, the latter were more preoccupied with holding on to whatever remained at their disposal, that is, collecting small fees here and there. There was a premonition of looming changes, which would sooner or later lead to the "shipwreck of customary criminal law."[69]

Grievances of the lords received little sympathy from the royal commissioners, although they were not ignored.[70] Many seigneurial rights underwent assimilation to particular or local custom, inserted awkwardly into ill-suited legal categories of contract, servitude, or the division of real and personal property.[71]

To sum up, most reforms were not the creation of new rules. Rather, they amounted to a reconfiguration, in light of doctrinal and jurisprudential changes, of existing customs that were already in flux. Royal commissioners tended to be cautious or conservative when the customs concerned the preservation of the family and social order; they were more decisive in eliminating obscurities and promoting equity in legal relations. Silence in marriage contracts previously meant no *rappel* or *représentation*; now silence meant the opposite. The inclusion or exclusion of similar rules in the *coutume* translated into broadening or narrowing of the freedom of the parties, in line with legislative policy directions.

How did the reformed customs affect actual lawsuits? The courtroom was the arena in which the provisions of the customs came under real-time scrutiny. Lawyers' pleadings in litigation contributed to the clarification of the contents of

[68] Ibid., 137.

[69] Bernard Schnapper, "Le naufrage du droit pénal coutumier," in *Voies nouvelles en histoire du droit: La justice, la famille, la répression pénale, XVIème–XXème siècles* (Paris: Presses universitaires de France, 1991), 177–85. For seigneurial justice, see Jeremy Hayhoe, *Enlightened Feudalism: Seigneurial Justice and Village Society in Eighteenth-Century Northern Burgundy* (Rochester: University of Rochester Press, 2008).

[70] A. C. de Paris, Arts. 51–55, *Nouveau coutumier général*, vol. 3, 4; N. C. de Paris, Arts. 73–80, *Nouveau coutumier général*, vol. 3, 36. Art. 81 provides "Sales and fees are pursued through [legal] actions only." That is, "the lord cannot hold up the effect of [*retenir*] the contract produced to him by the purchaser, even for want of the payment of the dues from the sales" (Note q).

[71] Poumarède, "Droit romain et rédaction des coutumes," 133–45. Poumarède's study concerns the redaction of customs in the Bordeaux region in the 1510s, but his description captures broadly the situation throughout the sixteenth century.

the customs and their interpretations. Two cases argued at the Parlement of Paris deserve attention.

2. Custom in the Courtroom

The La Rochelle case of 1566 and the Amiens case of 1567 each concerned opposition to a particular aspect of the reformed *coutume*. Those who did not like new rules claimed that royal commissioners had abused their authority in changing the old rules. The lawsuits broadly reflected the tension between the king and his officials on the one hand and the local forces spearheaded by municipal officials on the other. Municipal "oligarchs" and royal *officiers* were often recruited from the same elite group, but a gradual separation developed between them as the latter increasingly postulated themselves as agents of royal authority, continued local ties notwithstanding.[72] The cases below were heard in the heat of the civil war, in the areas particularly hit hard by religious conflicts, and it is safe to speculate that confessional and political questions were at play as well.

The Case of La Rochelle (1566)

A case pleaded at the Parlement of Paris in May 1566 concerned the *coutume* of La Rochelle homologated in 1514.[73] At the time of redaction, presided over by Thibault Baillet, several articles met particularly strong opposition. One of them was Article 43 that forbade *don mutuel*, gifts made between spouses, where children had been born to one or both spouses. Most French *coutumes* providing for the community property regime already did not allow a spouse to benefit the other by inter vivos gifts or by will, because such gifts were feared to let the lineage property be given away, especially when the couple had no children.[74] The only kind of gift allowed between spouses was through the agreement that the survivor would enjoy in usufruct the designated part of the property belonging to the predeceased. The *coutume* of 1514 prohibited mutual gifts in order to prevent the children from being cut off from inheritance by irate parents. Objections from municipal officials such as the mayor and *échevins* were overruled by the commissioners.

[72] Lloyd, *The State, France, and the Sixteenth Century*, 41.

[73] This case is analyzed in René Filhol, "Procès en Parlement de Paris sur la coutume de la Rochelle (20 mai 1566)," in Pierre Andrieu-Guitrancourt (ed.), *Études offertes à Jean Macqueron* (Aix-en-Provence: Faculté de droit et des sciences économiques d'Aix-en-Provence, 1970), 313–18; reprinted in Filhol, *Aux alentours du droit coutumier*, 175–80. The *coutume* of La Rochelle did not undergo reformation.

[74] Olivier Martin, *Histoire de la coutume de la prévôté et vicomté de Paris*, vol. 2, 318–24.

In 1562, the children of one Leveque brought a suit asking the revocation of the donations executed between their parents. After a judge in La Rochelle decided in favor of the children, the case was appealed to the Parlement of Paris. The city officials, who were never happy with the rule disallowing *don mutuel*, seized the opportunity to renew their opposition and joined in the suit as the intervening party, as did *Procureur général du Roi* Baptiste Dumesnil. Some of the most famous lawyers of the time appeared as counsels: Jacques Canaye, Claude Mangot, and Augustin de Thou represented the appellants and the city officials; Pierre Versoris represented the children.[75] The appellants not only disputed the lower court's interpretation of Article 43 but also contested the validity of the article itself. They argued that the royal commissioners in 1514 had overstepped the boundaries of their authority when they forced the provision on the inhabitants.

The key substantive issue was whether allowing *don mutuel* between spouses with children was a "hard, iniquitous, and unreasonable" custom. If it was, the commissioners were justified in advising in 1514, after consultation with the estates, on the need to change it. No one disputed the principle that "bad" customs, against natural reason, should not be observed, but the parties disagreed over whether the provision at hand was one of them. The appellants pointed out that *don mutuel* remained unmodified in neighboring towns and provinces. They also claimed that Article 43 was in conflict with other provisions in the same *coutume*. Article 42 prohibited donation between the spouses in remarriage, a rule that had a clear purpose of preventing the parents from favoring the children from the new union to the detriment of those from the previous marriage. They thus argued that Article 43 made Article 42 redundant and the assembly could not have intended to place comprehensive proscription on interspousal gift.

The appellants claimed, alternatively, that the rule should be declared abrogated by nonuse (*désuétude*), because it had not been observed for a long period of time. They argued that *don mutuel* continued to be practiced by the people despite the prohibition in 1514: "Despite the change [of the old custom], gifts between spouses continued to be made. . . . When some children challenged the gifts, the court upheld the practices. Since 1531 there have been about forty such judgments." Therefore, they asserted, the new provision of 1514 disallowing the practice must be considered to have lost its force.

The appellants then moved to dispute the legality of the redaction process as a whole. Their counsel Mangot reminded the court that in the assembly of estates the three estates "must be of accord, because a law cannot be introduced without the consent of the three estates." The commissioners had been authorized by the king only to reduce to writing the customs, usages, and procedures of every part

[75] For these prominent lawyers at the Parlement of Paris and their interactions, see René Filhol, "Les avocats en Parlement de Paris dans la seconde moitié du XVIe siècle," in Filhol, *Aux alentours du droit coutumier*, 5–38. Augustin de Thou was Christophe de Thou's younger brother.

of the kingdom, in consultation with the practitioners and the people of the locality; they had no power, Mangot contended, to change the rules arbitrarily against the wishes of the estates.

Pierre Versoris, representing the appellees, methodically refuted the arguments of his opponents.[76] First of all, he challenged the municipal officials' legal standing in the case. The appellants' counsel Canaye argued that "the *échevins* were representatives of the three estates in 1514 because they represented the town" and that the commissioners' summary rejection of their objections was a violation of their authority. Versoris countered: "when the king delegated the commissioners, he ordered them to assemble the three estates, and he did not allow the mayors, *pairs*, *échevins* of the town to form a separate group to lodge objection." For Versoris, the municipal officials, as members of a corporate body, had no right to challenge the redaction process independently from the Third Estate, and the commissioners did not transgress their authority in dismissing the objections.

The appellants cited the absence of the *procès-verbal* of the 1514 assembly and its failure to register at the Parlement of Paris. As noted, these supposed procedural defects were brought up repeatedly by those who challenged the validity of the published *coutumes*. Versoris argued, however, that the lack of the proceedings did not render the *coutume* illegitimate or less authentic: "In 1514 this *coutume* was printed in the *coutumiers généraux* and was also registered by the clerk of the city of La Rochelle." Indeed, asserted Versoris, one must conclude laws remained in force even if they had not been formally registered or the registers were lost; if one rejected the legal effect of *coutume* on the grounds of this sort of procedural irregularities, then one would have to deny the validity of all other *coutumes*.

This case is interesting in several accounts. First, one witnesses the emergence of case law as a veritable source of law; the lawyers specifically referred to the postredaction court rulings on *don mutuel* to support their arguments. Secondly, the case demonstrated how deeply the changes in custom affected the inhabitants and how strenuously municipal officials tried to block those changes initiated from outside. It showed the shifting dynamic between the members of a local corporate body and the center. In the sixteenth century, municipal governments were still thriving in major towns, but royal measures continuously reduced their jurisdictions. The Ordinance of Orléans provided that the *bailli* possessed the right of adjudication over civil affairs without assistance or intervention from the *échevins*, deemed incapable of handling these cases.[77] The Ordinance of Moulins of February 1566 formally ended the municipal government's civil jurisdiction,

[76] Pierre Versoris (1528–1588), a counsel for the Guises, was one of the most prominent lawyers of the time. His biographical details are provided in Robert Descimon, *Qui étaient les Seize? Mythes et réalités de la Ligue parisienne (1585–1594)* (Paris: Fédération des sociétés historiques et archéologiques de Paris et de l'Île de France, Librairie Klincksieck, 1983), 226–27.

[77] Art. 50, *Recueil général*, vol. 14, 78.

"nonobstant coutumes, privileges; usances et prescription."[78] Municipal jurisdiction was restricted to police and criminal matters.[79] City officials bitterly protested against the loss of their ancient privileges. The position of *échevins* in La Rochelle, and also in Amiens below, should be seen in this particular context.

Dumesnil, *procureur général*, sided with Versoris. He argued that, even though the *coutume* had failed to be sent to the clerk of the Parlement and there was no *procès-verbal*, such defects were not material enough to render the *coutume* invalid so long as the estates had been duly called and assembled. His pleading in this lawsuit illustrates the function of the king's lawyers. In the sixteenth and seventeenth centuries, the *gens du roi* (*avocat général* or *procureur général*) played a vital role in civil litigation, clarifying customary law texts. Since they normally presented their statements after the private counsels rested their cases, it was their task to provide a comprehensive appraisal of the proffered legal sources and then to submit the government's interpretation of the provisions of custom, drawing on scholarly commentaries, Roman law, or historical and religious writings.[80] In this way, they contributed to the standardization of legal sources and the stabilization of the hierarchy among them which the counsels of private parties tended to flout. When the judgments of the parlements did not include judicial reasoning (*non-motivé*), the government lawyers' pleadings could shed key light on the court decisions. In short, the rationalization and interpretive unification of the redacted customs depended as crucially on the work of the king's lawyers as on the work of private counsels.[81]

The final disposition of the Parlement of Paris on this case is not known. But the fact that the disputed article remained unmodified in the *coutume* of La Rochelle until the end of the ancien régime allows us to conclude the challenges to the homologated custom and the commissioners' authority were not successful. Evidence shows the *modus operandi* of the commissioners was to update custom in accordance with jurisprudence, often to confirm the articles swiftly with a solution to their liking.[82] Recall contested matters that could not reach agreement were shipped off to the Parlement, where the commissioners themselves were

[78] Art. 71, ibid., 208. Article 72 of the Ordinance of Moulins stipulated that in unchartered towns criminal jurisdiction was entrusted to the elected members of the bourgeoisie and citizens, thus reinforcing local communal responsibilities over police and order.

[79] Georges Testaud, *Des juridictions municipales en France: Des origines jusqu'à l'ordonnance de Moulins* (Paris: Librarie de la Société du recueil général des lois et des arrêts, 1901), 189.

[80] Roemier, "Avocat général et coutumes," 168–69.

[81] Dumesnil's statement that "lawyers, separate from the Third Estate, cannot by themselves introduce custom" was at best formulaic. Filhol, *Le premier président Christofle de Thou*, 87, note 4. For the "nonmotivation" of judicial decisions, see Chapter 6.

[82] In Péronne in 1567, a custom dealing with the *rentes*, a rule which had been abolished in other *coutumes*, was included in the first reading of the draft text at the assembly, without opposition or debate. This provision quietly disappeared between the first and the final reading, likely as a result of the intervention of the commissioners. Filhol, *Le premier président Christofle de Thou*, 284–85.

sitting judges.[83] There was little chance that what they had not supported in the assemblies would be heard favorably at the court. Still, disputes were abundant. In Amiens, the parties directly accused the royal commissioners of their allegedly heavy-handed approaches and challenged the validity of the *coutume* reformed under their supervision.

The Case of Amiens (1567)

The *coutume* of Amiens was recorded in 1507 and reformed on September 23 and 24, 1567. Not long after the redaction assembly closed, during which the locals loudly complained about the process, a lawsuit was filed alleging the abuse of power by commissioners de Thou, Faye, and Viole.[84] The case was heard at the Parlement of Paris on August 20, 1568. The issue in contention was the right of *représentation successorale* in the collateral line, a reform which the commissioners had pushed forward against opposition from the nobles.

The case revolved around the succession of Louis d'Ailly, the Vidame d'Amiens. He died without children, leaving a sister and two nephews, sons of the predeceased brother. Under the new rule allowing representation in the collateral line, his nephews were entitled to stand for succession. His surviving sister, Françoise, challenged the rule. Many prominent members of the *bailliage* of Amiens, including the Cardinal of Créquy, the Cardinal of Bourbon, and the Cardinal of Guise, joined in the suit, alongside the municipal government of Amiens, claiming that serious procedural irregularities during the reformation process impaired its legality. When the powerful nobles and the town government came together to challenge the authority of the royal commissioners, it was more or less an act of defiance toward the central government. Note Françoise d'Ailly was the widow of the governor of the duchy of Guise. The Amiens case was a reminder that customary reforms and the attendant legal disputes did not take place separate from religious conflicts during the civil wars.

The complaint in the case listed a number of supposed procedural irregularities. The main issue was the inadequate representation of the estates. It was alleged that the assembly was gathered in haste, preventing the full participation of the deputies. The drafting of the *coutume* had already been done in Paris before the estates were called. The commissioners paid little attention to the preparatory *cahiers* drawn up by local practitioners; they stayed in Amiens for only a short period, quick to overrule the objections of the deputies and tell them to appear later before the Parlement. These grievances were not entirely groundless. The

[83] Grinberg et al., "Rédaction des coutumes et territoires," 44.

[84] This case is analyzed in Filhol, *Le premier président Christofle de Thou*, 94–121; and also in Descimon, "Quelques réflexions à propos des commissaires du roi."

assembly took place in September 1567 in the midst of the crisis of the so-called Surprise of Meaux, a failed attempt by Prince Condé against the royal court.[85] It is indeed remarkable that the king decided to proceed with the assembly in this volatile political situation; it would be surprising if the commissioners had not been in a harried mode. The complainants did not neglect to point out that the copy of the reformed custom was not properly deposited at the court clerk's office.

The lead counsels in the Amiens case were the same lawyers who had appeared in the La Rochelle case. But now, representing new clients, they made arguments completely different from their earlier positions. Pierre Versoris had argued in the La Rochelle case in defense of the authority of the commissioners; now, as the counsel of Françoise d'Ailly, he was ready to dispute their authority vigorously. Claude Mangot, representing the widow of Charles d'Ailly, the predeceased brother of Louis, and the mother of the Vidame's nephews, was this time poised to make arguments to justify the broad authority of the commissioners.

Versoris zeroed in on the oath sworn by the deputies in the assembly. The oath required them to do two things: first, to declare whether they witnessed the custom at hand having been observed in the past, and, second, to determine whether it was a hard and unreasonable custom and against the public good. Versoris argued that the participants had not been given enough means and time to fulfill these important duties required of them under oath. Mangot had a different opinion, however. He claimed his opponent was mistaken in treating the operations of the redaction and the reformation as the same. Most of the time, the initial recording process was more demanding and difficult than its subsequent revision. What seemed like unreasonable haste on the part the commissioners in 1567 was nothing unusual, Mangot argued, because they only needed to revisit the customs already published.

In rebuttal, the plaintiffs' lawyers claimed that the commissioners acted as if they were issuing a law to the locals, rather than reforming the custom in consultation with the estates as required by their commission; they assumed "more power than the king and the *Conseil privé*." Louis Buisson, the counsel of the Cardinal of Guise, reminded the court that custom could not be changed against the wishes and consent of the estates because the new custom was to bind the people in Picardy for generations to come. The recriminations lodged against the commissioners portrayed them as pretentious and arrogant elite jurists who, boasting their knowledge of the science of law, tried to intimidate or at best educate the ignorant people. The commissioners allegedly assumed that their duty was to teach and correct the locals who only minded their private interest, this in the name of the common good.

[85] The "Surprise de Meaux" refers to a conspiracy organized by Louis I de Bourbon Condé to kidnap the king of France, Charles IX, and the royal family. Its failure triggered the Second War of Religion.

Complaining about the commissioners was in all likelihood part of a strategy of the parties who objected to the disposition of particular customs that failed to align with their property interests. Be that as it may, their protest against royal commissioners was a challenge to the legality of the redaction process, causing the legal contest to be framed in terms of popular consent. Lawsuits like this one brought into relief the question of the legislative sovereignty of the crown vis-à-vis the consent of the local representatives of the three orders. The case seemingly pitted the learned jurists against the country folk, royal authority against the rights of the estates, and public interest against private interest.

Considering these weighty issues, the dénouement of the Amiens case was disappointing. It simply fizzled out: Françoise d'Ailly died shortly after, leaving her claim unpursued. The *arrêt* of the Parlement of Paris issued on September 7, 1571, dismissed the appeal and authorized the printing of the reformed *coutume* of Amiens.[86] The result demonstrated that the assertion of the rights of the estates—the right to consent and all—fell short before the reaffirmation of royal authority delegated to the commissioners. This and other similar cases amply demonstrated the changed nature of custom: the force of custom as law was grounded less on popular consent than on royal prerogative.[87]

Much of courtroom duel centered on textual interpretations of custom. Lawyers paid close attention to the meaning of the words and grammars of the written customary provisions in question. These cases showed the recording of custom fostered advances in the techniques of textual construction of law and also had the effect of refining French as a national language.[88] More important, they reaffirmed the idea that the silence or inadequacy of customs must be filled by other sources of law, mainly statutes.[89] As the reformation of customs modified substantive rules of private laws in reflection of doctrine and jurisprudence, a series of royal ordinances and edicts sought their effective implementation. Legislation also addressed private law matters when customary law seemed unable to keep up with rising legal demands.

In the 1560s, there was a sort of division of labor: the reform of the customs was pursued by First President de Thou, and the legislation of royal laws was spearheaded by Chancellor L'Hôpital. Whereas de Thou, as the head of the Parlement of Paris, focused on creating reliable sources of law for everyday legal practice, L'Hôpital, as the highest official of the king, aimed to ensure equitable

[86] De Thou himself presided over the court session in which the final judgment was read out. Filhol, *Le premier président Christofle de Thou*, 118.

[87] Other cases include the one in 1580 in which *avocat* Simon Marion argued on the renunciation to succession by an endowed daughter, analyzed in ibid., 207–208.

[88] Grinberg, "Écrire le droit," 71. Since the Ordinance of Villers-Cotterêts of 1539, French language progressively replaced Latin in law and administration.

[89] Descimon and Guéry, "Un État des temps modernes?" 219.

operation of royal laws by revamping judicial administration throughout the kingdom.[90]

3. L'Hôpital's Laws

A graduate of the law faculty at University of Padua, L'Hôpital was a quintessential humanist jurist (see Figure 5.1).[91] His service of many years as a *conseiller* at the Parlement of Paris allowed him a deep insight into judicial practice. In 1553, L'Hôpital became the chancellor of Marguerite the Duchess of Berry, the sister of Henry II. In this capacity, he was responsible for the administration of the law faculty at the University of Bourges, which enjoyed an international reputation as the center of legal humanism.[92] The biggest names in civil law—Éguiner-François Baron, François Duaren, Hughes Doneau, François Baudouin, Jacques Cujas, and François Hotman—all taught at this celebrated law school at one time or

[90] The chancellor was among the few great officials who were not of noble blood. Often a former *parlementaire*, he was normally well conversant with the inner working of the courts. Hélène Michaud, *La Grande chancellerie et les écritures royales au seizième siècle (1515–1589)* (Paris: Presses universitaires de France, 1967), 34. The chancellor was the only high official who did not participate in mourning at the death of the king because "justice does not die." The office of chancellor was neither venal nor transmissible; the holder was irremovable other than in the case of forfeiture. Only once in the sixteenth century, in 1545, the third chancellor of Francis I, Guillaume Poyet, was condemned and deprived of his office. Barbiche, *Les institutions de la monarchie française*, 81, 154–55. The list of chancellors in the early modern period is in ibid., 159–60.

[91] The coat of arms at the center in Figure 5.1 depicts the Château de la Roche in Chaptuzat near Aigueperse. The Château had long been believed the birthplace of the chancellor, but recent studies suggest that L'Hôpital was born in the Palais des Montpensier in Aigueperse. See Olivier Paradis, "Michel de L'Hospital: du Palais d'Aigueperse à la chancellerie de France," *Sparsae* [Association culturelle d'Aigueperse et ses environs] 57 (2006), 15–34. The caption of Figure 5.1 reads: "Michel de L'Hospital, chevalier, chancellor of France, native of Aigueperse in Auvergne, after having held all the positions of the robe and become commendable by his works, was made Chancellor by the letters of King Francis II, given at St. Leger on the last day of June 1560, after the death of Chancellor Olivier and the demission of Bertrand, *garde des seaux*; while he was in office the famous remonstrances to King Charles IX, in the month of May of the year 1565, were presented by the messieurs of the Parlement Paris; on the 6th of February 1573, he obtained the letters of discharge from the exercise of his office and the royal seals were given to Cardinal de Birague; he died on the following 13th of March at the age of 69, having brought the glory of being regarded as the greatest chancellor France has ever had to the present."

[92] Dupré Lasale, *Michel de L'Hospital*, 179–217. For L'Hôpital, see Crouzet, *La sagesse et le malheu*; Rousselet-Pimont, *Le chancelier et la loi*; Kim, *Michel de L'Hôpital*; Kim, "Civil Law and Civil War"; Marie Seong-Hak Kim, "'Nager entre deux eaux': L'idéalisme juridique et la politique religieuse de Michel de L'Hospital," in Thierry Wanegffelen (ed.), *De Michel de L'Hospital à l'édit de Nantes: Politique et religion face aux Églises* (Clermont-Ferrand: Presses universitaires Blaise-Pascal, 2002), 243–54. L'Hôpital's writings have been edited: *Michel de L'Hospital et ses discours (1559–1562): La plume et la tribune*, ed. Loris Petris (Geneva: Droz, 2002) [hereinafter *Michel de L'Hospital discours I*]; *Michel de L'Hospital, discours et correspondance: La plume et la tribune II*, ed. Loris Petris and David Amherdt (Geneva: Droz, 2013) [hereinafter *Michel de L'Hospital discours II*]; *Carmina: Livre I. Michel de L'Hospital*, ed. and trans. Perrine Galand and Loris Petris (Geneva: Droz, 2014); and *Carmina: Livre II. Michel de L'Hospital*, ed. and trans. David Amherdt, Laure Chappus Sandoz, Perrine Galand, and Loris Petris (Geneva: Droz, 2017).

Figure 5.1 Michel de L'Hôpital (*c.*1505–1573)

Source: gallica.bnf.fr

Bibliothèque nationale de France

another.[93] Reforms L'Hôpital undertook as chancellor of France were solidly grounded on the achievements of legal humanism.

The proliferation of lawsuits was the bane of early modern France. "Since the reign of Charles VII, after the English were chased away from France," opined L'Hôpital in 1566, "people began to plead strenuously in litigation, wanting to recover their property. And even now, after the last troubles, people fight in lawsuits more than ever, and they have come up with more inventions to argue and deceive each other than ever before."[94] The French people were quick to turn to law courts and "there are more lawsuits at the Châtelet of Paris than in all of Italy."[95] Bodin echoed L'Hôpital's sentiment: the French kingdom "has more laws and customs than all the neighboring peoples, and more lawsuits than the rest of Europe."[96] L'Hôpital left extensive writings and speeches, but it is intriguing that references to customary law were rarely found in them. Content to entrust customary law reforms to de Thou, he concentrated on his legislative agenda to reduce the prolixity of processes in litigation.[97]

[93] After the death of Baron, L'Hôpital persuaded Duaren to take up his chair. Duaren brought Baudouin and Doneau to join him. In 1555, a quarrel between Duaren and Baudouin forced the latter to leave the university for a new position in Strasbourg. L'Hôpital soon recruited Jacques Cujas to Bourges. L'Hôpital's letter to the *échevins* of Bourges, recommending Cujas for the position, written July 21, 1555, is included in *Michel de L'Hospital discours II*, 127. Doneau opposed Cujas' appointment. In a letter to Doneau, L'Hôpital rebuked the young professor for his impudence and for causing unwarranted clashes with other faculty members. L'Hôpital's letter of August 3, 1555, ibid., 128–29; Doneau's reply in 130–37. Cujas left Bourges in August 1557.

[94] Remonstrance in the assembly held at Moulins in January 1566, in *Michel de L'Hospital discours II*, 83. L'Hôpital shared the opinion of legal humanists that Bartolus and the Commentators distorted the original meaning of the *Corpus juris civilis* and that rampant glosses brought the multiplication of laws.

[95] Discourse of September 7, 1560, at the Parlement of Paris, in *Michel de L'Hospital discours I*, 376. A party to litigation, he wrote, might come out of the trial either victorious or vanquished, but never with what he or she had hoped for. In one of his Latin epistles, L'Hôpital invited his colleague Charles de Marillac to accompany him to "descend" to the inferno of the tribunal where "there is nothing joyous, gentle, or pleasant that could lighten your eternal pains." *Carmina: Livre II*, 322–23.

[96] It did not help that "King Charles VII and his successors imposed in this kingdom laws written in imitation of Justinian, with a whole train of reasons, against the form of ancient ordinances of the kings and wise legislators." Jean Bodin, *Les six livres de la république* (Lyon: Barthélemy Vincent, 1593), book 6, ch. 6, 1027. This section is not in the 1576 edition.

[97] Lawmaking in early modern France was a collective work and the individual chancellor's personal role could not normally be known. But everyone said, according to Pasquier, that L'Hôpital was the author of the Ordinance of Orléans (1561), the Edict of Roussillon (1564), and the Ordinance of Moulins (1566), "which contained the infinity of articles in matters of police and beautiful regulations." Pasquier, *Lettres*, book 19, letter 14 (to Loisel), in *Les œuvres*, vol. 2, cols. 575–76. L'Hôpital was the "principal entremeteur" of the first ordinance and "instigateur, promoteur & autheur" of the other two. Judicial reform was a subject that had long percolated in L'Hôpital's mind. A document in L'Hôpital's own handwriting lists over sixty draft reform measures. Bibliothèque nationale, Collection Dupuy 491, fols. 59r–60v and 65r–66r. This document, titled "Règlement de justice," is included in *Michel de L'Hospital discours I*, 441–47. It is likely that this manuscript was prepared by L'Hôpital in July 1560, not long after his appointment to the chancellorship. It fully demonstrates that his legal reforms were not makeshift responses to temporary problems but the outcome of a clearly laid-out program that he had in mind for some time. Many items were turned into specific provisions in the edicts and ordinances issued during his chancellorship.

Simplifying Procedures

In August 1560, following the assembly of notables held at Fontainebleau, the government introduced a series of measures to improve the administration of law. While interminable conflicts among the parties clogged the justice system, the hodgepodge of jurisdictions and squabbles among the courts nearly paralyzed it. During the feudal period, seigneurial independence caused the force of a judgment to be limited to the court that had rendered it. The magistrates at royal courts needed to obtain the letter of *pareatis*—meaning "you shall obey"—from the chancellery in order to have their decisions executed in the territory of seigneurial courts. Now the practice created conflicts among the royal courts. Individual parlements claimed jurisdictional autonomy and refused to enforce judgments rendered by other parlements without the letters of *pareatis*.[98] The decisions of the Parlement of Paris for example were not binding outside its jurisdictional boundaries. The Edict of *Pareatis* sought to do away with cumbersome procedures to ensure the across-the-board recognition of *arrêts* of the parlements.[99] The chancellor assured the Parlement of Paris that the edict aimed to facilitate the acceptance of its judgments by the provincial courts of "Toulouse, Brittany, Normandy, and Grenoble."[100]

One of the first measures for which L'Hôpital drew ideas on Roman law principles was the law of *transaction*.[101] *Transaction*, or compromise, allowed the parties to settle a lawsuit in progress or about to commence. Once a settlement was reached by mutual concessions and registered at the court, the arrangement became a legal act. In the Roman rule of *transactio*, "injury," or the lack of consideration, was never a cause for rescinding legal acts between persons of legal age, but French law regularly allowed the parties to undo the settlement on the grounds of "serious injury." As a result, it was not uncommon that people changed their mind and tried to void the settlement, throwing the process into confusion.[102] Preserving the finality of legal settlement was as important, stressed L'Hôpital, as reaching a voluntary resolution of disputes among the parties. "La sévérité et abréviation de justice" were not contradictory notions.[103] The edict issued in Fontainebleau declared that the terms of the settlement, once reached by adults, were irrevocable regardless of the injury alleged afterward; they would have the same force as a judgment of the court.[104]

[98] Brissaud, *A History of French Private Law*, 599; Marcel Marion, *Dictionnaire des institutions de la France aux XVIIe et XVIIIe siècles* (Paris: Picard, 1923), "Paréatis (Lettres de)," 417; Jacques Poumarède and Jack Thomas (eds.), "Introduction," *Les parlements de province: pouvoirs, justice et société du XVe au XVIIIe siècle* (Toulouse: FRAMESPA, 1996), 7–25.

[99] *Recueil général*, vol. 14, 46–49.

[100] Discourse of September 7, 1560, in *Michel de L'Hospital discours I*, 379.

[101] *Recueil général*, vol. 14, 49–50.

[102] Brissaud, *A History of French Private Law*, 517.

[103] Discourse of July 5, 1560, at the Parlement of Paris, in *Michel de L'Hospital discours I*, 367.

[104] The edict issued in April 1561 repeated the measures, *Recueil général*, vol. 14, 104–105. L'Hôpital aimed to prohibit "any restitution against *transactio* made without fraud or force with a person of legal

L'Hôpital told the magistrates in Paris: "The experts of the *Institutes* know that there are three ways in law to end lawsuits: *res iudicata*, *iusiurandum*, and *transactio*, among which the last must be the most agreeable because it is voluntarily reached. While *res iudicata sit sacrosancta velut iusiurandum* (a judged matter should be sacrosanct just like an oath), the nature itself teaches the humans to adhere to what they have agreed."[105] The measures of August 1560 were intended to reduce the formality, delay, expenses, and vexation in litigation.[106] The right to appeal is a "necessary defense," he acknowledged, and "the Romans called it *patronam libertatis*." But "there are certain areas in which one can compel the subjects to resolve their differences, not just without appeals but without legal proceedings."[107] To limit the rights to file a lawsuit or appeal was not his aim; to discourage frivolous proceedings and meritless appeals was.

Other reforms undertaken by the chancellor in the same spirit of encouraging conciliation between the parties and emphasizing the finality of judgement included the creation of consular jurisdiction.[108]

Streamlining Substantive Laws

Reducing lawsuits concerned not just procedural but substantive matters. Private law reforms aimed to fill the gaps in custom, such as marital regime, succession, contract, as well as wills and testaments. Legislative activities in these areas drew broadly from both Roman law and custom, as deemed necessary. The underpinning desire was to have the same laws enforced across the kingdom promoting legal unity under royal authority, an issue arguably more urgent than ever during civil war.[109] Not surprisingly, these efforts met much resistance from provincial parlements.

Edict of Second Marriages (1560)

Jacques-Auguste de Thou was a keen observer of royal legislative efforts. He stated that L'Hôpital began his chancellorship by "publishing a very judicious law on the

age, under the pretext of injury and presumptive fraud." BN, Dupuy 491, printed in *Michel de L'Hospital discours I*, 444.

105 L'Hôpital continued: "Nevertheless there is so much malice that each day there are people who obtain royal letters to rescind the accord. And if one says that he was deceived by settlement, he will say the same thing about judgments and oaths." Discourse of September 7, 1560, in *Michel de L'Hospital discours I*, 376.

106 It is better "to sort out the differences between the parties on their own than to resort to judges who place the matters out of the reach of friendship. Litigation is lengthy and creates enemies. A bad person goes to the court and gets himself in plenty of trouble. Enmity continues forever, while time and money are wasted." Ibid., 377.

107 Ibid., 378.

108 For L'Hôpital's reform of consular courts, see Kim, *Michel de L'Hôpital*, 151–57.

109 See Kim, "Civil Law and Civil War."

topic of the second marriages of women."[110] The Edict of Second Marriages (*secondes noces*), promulgated under Francis II in July 1560, prohibited remarrying widows from giving excessive gifts to their new husbands to the detriment of the children from the first marriage. In the preamble of the edict, the king stated that he decided to intervene in private law in order to ensure justice and peace of the subjects "as the ancient emperors had done."[111] Restricting the rights of the widow to dispose of her property was necessary to prevent the ruination of good families which would cause the decline of the "strength of *l'estat publique*." The reform of *don mutuel* had made it difficult to give gifts between spouses with children, but implementation was far from consistent and the need to protect the interests of the children was seriously felt as scandals continued to arise.[112] Some authors argued that regulations of spousal gift-giving had to do with the collection of royal taxes on similar transactions.[113] Whatever his motives, the king saw the need to act, instead of leaving it to the operation of custom.

The Edict of *Secondes noces* put together two separate Roman laws, issued at different times.[114] Under the first clause, a remarrying widow with children or grandchildren was prohibited from giving her property to her new husband in the marriage contract at a level exceeding the smallest inheritance share of the children from the first marriage. The second clause declared null the grants in which the gifts from the predeceased spouse had been conveyed by the widow or the widower to the advantage of the new spouse, instead of being held for the benefit of the children from the first marriage. These Roman laws were in force in the *pays de droit écrit* and also in some parts of the *pays de droit coutumier*; the royal edict made them apply across the kingdom. Confusion arose, however, over whether the edict covered the actions of widows only (as did the first clause) or the actions of both widows and widowers (as did the second clause). A case heard

[110] De Thou, *Histoire universelle* (1742), vol. 2, 838. Pierre Bayle praised Chancellor L'Hôpital for writing the law, "very just and very necessary," to protect the interests of the children. *Dictionnaire historique et critique*, 4 vols. (Amsterdam: Brunel, 1740), 808.

[111] *Recueil général*, vol. 14, 36.

[112] A public scandal involving a rich widow named Anne d'Allegre erupted. She fell in love with a young man, Georges de Clermont, but he refused to marry her "because she looked too old for him." Eventually he married her, and she turned over all her possessions to her new husband, "her foolish passion preventing her from seeing that he sought only her possessions and not her person." She had seven children from the previous marriage, and almost nothing was reserved of her property for them. De Thou, *Histoire universelle*, vol. 2, 838–89. Olivier-Martin stated that the Edict of Second Marriages was an "exceptional intervention" of legislation, prompted by extraordinary circumstances. *Les lois du roi*, 115. See also Anne Rousselet-Pimont, "Une générosité suspecte: Les libéralités aux proches parents des conjoints d'après la jurisprudence du Parlement de Paris aux XVIe–XVIIe siècles," *Revue historique de droit français et étranger* 83 (2005), 183–213.

[113] François Bourjon, *Le droit commun de la France, et la Coutume de Paris réduits en principes*, 2 vols. (Paris: Grangé, 1770), vol. 2, 126; Claude Duplessis, "Traité des donations," *Les œuvres de Mr Duplessis, ancien avocat au Parlement* (Paris: N. Gosselin, 1726), vol. 2, 195.

[114] The edict was based on two Roman laws, *Faeminae quae* and *Hac edictali*. Brissaud, *A History of French Private Law*, 156–57.

at the Parlement of Paris in 1578 brought to the surface various conflicting interpretations of the law.

The children from the first marriage of one Chabot disputed the validity of their father's gifts to his second wife made through the instrument of their marriage contract. After Chabot's death, the wife's ownership of real property as well as personal possessions was challenged. The wife claimed that the 1560 edict differentiated gift-giving by husbands and wives and that it governed the actions of remarrying widows only, not widowers. After a local judge ruled that the Edict of *Seconde noces* covered widows only, the children appealed. The two renowned lawyers of the time, Étienne Pasquier and Jean Le Maistre, represented the wife and the children respectively. Pasquier argued that the law intended to control the actions by remarrying widows and therefore was not applicable to the case before the court. The preamble of the 1560 edict stated: "the quarrels and rifts between mothers and the children lead to the desolation of good families, and consequently weaken the state."[115] This was the evidence, asserted Pasquier, that the law was issued in consideration of the weakness of the sex.

Pasquier failed to convince the court. The Parlement of Paris decided that the first provision of the edict must be construed to include husbands as well as wives. It ruled: "the motive for the edict was not so much to avoid frivolity, weakness, and infirmity of the female sex as to protect the interests of the children." This was a key example of judicial decision by analogy. The court wrote that the edict used the word "wife" simply as *ratione frequentioris usus* (the reason for frequent use), because the problems targeted by the edict rose more often with a wife than a husband.[116]

The reformed *Coutume de Paris* in 1580 incorporated the provisions of the Edict of *Secondes noces*. Article 279 provided that a wife, in remarriage, could give her new husband a portion of her *propres* not more than what she would have to give to one of her children.[117] It also compelled her to reserve for her children from the first marriage the property she had acquired jointly with her deceased husband. Despite the 1578 court decision, however, the article in the text of the *coutume* still retained the words "woman" and "mother." In 1587, the Parlement of Paris construed the provision to apply to both widows and widowers.[118] These cases show both reformed *coutumes* and royal laws were subject to ongoing judicial construction.

[115] *Recueil général*, vol. 14, 36.

[116] The case, reported in AN X1a 5071, fols. 476–89v, is analyzed in René Filhol, "L'application de l'Édit des secondes noces en pays coutumier," in *Mélanges Roger Aubenas* (Montpellier: Faculté de droit et des sciences économiques de Montpellier, 1974), 295–99.

[117] N. C. de Paris, Art. 279. See Olivier-Martin, *Histoire de la coutume de la prévôté et vicomté de Paris*, vol. 2, 300; Filhol, *Le premier président Christofle de Thou*, 161–63.

[118] The judgment of July 18, 1587, cited from Exupère Caillemer, *Des résistances que les parlements opposèrent à la fin du XVIe siècle à quelques essais d'unification du droit civil. Extrait du livre du centenaire du Code civil publie par la Société d'études législatives* (Paris: A. Rousseau, 1904), 1081.

Substitutions

Laws of substitutions in trust (*substitutions fidéi-commissaires*), also known as trust-entails, illustrate the close intertwinement of custom and legislation. Created through the medium of testamentary bequest or contract, substitutions were a legal device by which members of a family passed properties from one designated heir to another in observance of the method specified by the grantor.[119] The legatee or donee of the gift had full lifetime possession and enjoyment of the property, but he was not allowed to alienate it. The "encumbered" was charged with preserving the property that had been bequeathed to him and giving it upon his death to the new beneficiary substituted for him. The latter, "remainderman," was in his turn charged with keeping it and giving it to another, and so on. Using this conditional instrument, the grantor could control the disposal of his property during one or more generations by creating a succession order, free from the rules of customary or legal devolution. Originally derived from Roman law, it became an important means for the nobles as well as wealthy commoners in the *pays coutumiers* to preserve the bulk of the family fortune by circumventing the principle of equal division.[120]

Entails were justified on the grounds that they protected the interests of posterity; they helped keep patrimony intact in the situation of a family head dying without legitimate male children, or less commonly a family head's prodigality or lack of financial skill. But the system contained serious problems, in particular when it was set up in perpetuity or in secret. This was why Emperor Justinian, in Article 159 of *Novel*, disallowed the creation of substitutions beyond the fourth generation, but the limit was ignored and Baldus approved unlimited entails in the fourteenth century.[121] With the creation of a perpetual trust, the property was effectively taken out of the market, depressing commerce when the estate involved was of substantial size. The major problem was the uncertainty of title and estate settlements. When the trust was set up secretly, the encumbered often passed for the absolute owner. If he alienated the property, he was considered to have forfeited his rights, and the immediate vesting in the remainderman took place. This situation could result in significant harm to innocent parties, purchasers, and

[119] See Cooper, "Patterns of Inheritance and Settlement"; for France see especially 252–76.

[120] Paul Ourliac and Jehan de Malafosse, *Histoire du droit privé*, vol. 3: *Le droit familial* (Paris: Presses universitaires de France, 1968), 406; Michel Petitjean, *Essai sur l'histoire des substitutions du IXe au XVe* siècle *dans la pratique et la doctrine, spécialement en France méridionale* (Dijon: Centre de recherches historiques, Faculté de droit et de science politique, 1975), 519; Lloyd, *The State, France, and the Sixteenth Century*, 32. Brissaud called substitutions "one of the masterpieces of the old organization of the nobility." *A History of French Private Law*, 726.

[121] Jean Domat, *Civil Law in Its Natural Order*, trans. William Strahan, vol. 2 (Boston: Charles C. Little and James Brown, 1850), 645. Emperor Hadrian decreed that substitutions could not be made for *personae incertae*. Justinian initially removed that prohibition, likely with a view to encourage the creation of perpetuities in favor of the church. In 555, however, he forbade the system of entail beyond four generations. Max A. Pock, "The Rule against Perpetuities: A Comparison of Some Common Law and Civil Law Jurisdictions," *St. John's Law Review* 35 (1960), 65–66.

creditors.[122] Publicity was essential in the community property regime. Coquille sympathized with defrauded creditors and disappointed sons-in-law who found that the inheritance they had expected was not there.[123]

There were incessant disputes about interpreting the terms of entails.[124] One question was how to reckon the degree in succession: should the degrees be counted *per capita* (by head, that is, by the number of individuals succeeding to the entail), or *per stirpes* (by stock or *par souche*, that is, by the number of generations of a family succeeding)?[125] The Ordinance of Orléans prohibited perpetual

[122] Domat, *Civil Law in Its Natural Order*, 643–64; Brissaud, *A History of French Private Law*, 731–33.

[123] Coquille, *Les coustumes du pays et comté de Nivernois*, in *Les œuvres*, vol. 2, 349 (Art. 10).

[124] When a testator entailed on his brother so that if the brother died "without legitimate male children" the entail went to the testator's daughters successively under the same condition, what happened if the brother left a grandson by an only daughter? This example is from Cooper, "Patterns of Inheritance and Settlement," 262.

[125] For *per stirpes*, see note 44 in this chapter. In 1549 Dumoulin was consulted in the famous case argued before the Parlement of Dijon involving the seigneury of Arc-en-Barrois. This case is analyzed in René Filhol, "Une consultation de Charles Dumoulin relative à la seigneurie d'Arc-en-Barrois," *Revue historique de droit français et étranger* 26 (1949), 122–132, reconstructed from the documents at Bibliothèque municipale de Besançon, ms. Boisot, 1213. A précis of Filhol's article is in Cooper, "Patterns of Inheritance and Settlement," 263. The testator, Guillaume de Vienne (Guillaume I), seigneur de Saint-Georges, created entails in his testament with the following instructions: (1) in case his son Guillaume de Vienne (Guillaume II) and all his male children in the right line decease without male children, Jean de Vienne, sieur de Paigny, and his male, natural, and legitimate children would receive his succession; (2) in their absence, Girard de Vienne and his male children would be called; (3) in their absence, Jehan de Vienne, sieur de Rollans, and his male, natural, and legitimate heirs would receive the property; and (4) in their absence, Guillaume de Vienne (Guillaume III), sieur de Montbis, would be called in the following terms: "we substitute Guillaume, seigneur de Montbis, and after his death, his natural and legitimate male children descending in the legitimate line." Guillaume III was the last beneficiary named in the testament. Guillaume I died in 1434 and his son Guillaume II inherited the land. After the latter died in 1456, his son Jean de Vienne received it. In 1463, Jean relinquished the land to his cousin Philippe de Vienne, with possibility of repurchase within ten years. The right of repurchase was not exercised, and the son ceded the seigneury to Guillaume III, who was titled the seigneur d'Arc. Jean died without issue. Two of the remaindermen had left no male issue, so the entail went to a collateral Guillaume III. In 1507, the Parlement of Dijon affirmed the rights to the seigneury of François (François I) de Vienne, grandson of Guillaume III, and Philippe, the younger son of Guillaume III. The latter subsequently assigned to his nephew all his rights over the seigneury d'Arc. François II, François I's son, made his sister's son his heir. After François II died without heir in 1537, Claude-Antoine de Vienne, the grandson of Philip, the younger son of Guillaume III, sued the siblings of François II, claiming his right to the seigneury, both in his own name and as the guardian of Marc de Vienne, his nephew. There were both factual and legal disputes in this case. The defendants argued that the property belonged to them by means of the exchange in 1463 and the judgment and transaction of 1507, and not by virtue of the entail created in 1434. Alternatively, if the property was subject to substitution, they argued, the plaintiffs came in at the seventh degree in succession. Since Roman law allowed entails only up to four generations, the entail had run out and the plaintiffs could not benefit from it, unless entail was counted *per stirpes*. This was the gist of the argument of Dumoulin who represented the defendants. The argument against perpetual entails prevailed, and the defendants won at the Parlement of Dijon. The case was then evoked to the Grand conseil, where it stayed until the end of the sixteenth century. The last pieces of the documents date from 1587, and there is no record of the final sentence. From the fact that the seigneury stayed in the line of the defendants of the case, Filhol speculated they eventually prevailed. This case shows that the implementation of the rule of substitution was constantly in dispute. Filhol notes that many famous lawyers of the time were consulted in the case, including Versoris, Brisson, and Choppin at the Parlement of Paris, along with *avocats* at the Parlement of Burgundy. As an added point of interest, Filhol indicates the village of Arc-en-Barrois, in the départemente of Haute-Marne, arrondissement of Châlons, on

substitutions and allowed entails to be created for two degrees, that is, valid for two successive inheritors only, not including the first holder (Article 59). It declared that the regulation was needed "to avoid useless and onerous judicial contestation."[126] The law regulated "substitutions in the future" only; those that had already been set up were not affected.[127] The Ordinance of Moulins in 1566 followed up and required the entails be registered within six months of creation (Article 57).[128] It stipulated that substitutions in existence when the Ordinance of Orléans came into effect be valid up to four occurrences, as in Justinian's law. The Parlement of Paris construed the ordinance to the narrowest extent possible, allowing two degrees *per capita*. By contrast, the Parlement of Toulouse defined it to the broadest extent possible, allowing substitutions for four generations, whether created before or after the Ordinance of Orléans.[129] In the latter method of counting *par souche*, when the trusteeship passed to several brothers successively, all the brothers, no matter how many incidents of succession, formed only one generation, constituting a single occurrence of succession. This was obviously against the intent of the laws. The ordinance of 1629, known as the Code Michaud, expressively condemned the courts' erroneous interpretation of the system, but it did not cause the Parlement of Toulouse to change its jurisprudence.[130]

Michel de Montaigne (1533–1592) stated: "We take these male entails too much to heart. And we look forward to a ridiculous eternity for our names."[131] In the eighteenth century, Montesquieu saw both the utility and drawbacks of the system: "Substitutions, which preserve the estates in families, will be very useful in this government, though not so proper in others"; "since honor is the principle of a monarchical government, the laws must be in line with this principle" and

the border of Burgundy and Champagne, was in all likelihood where Jeanne d'Arc and her father Jacques originated from.

[126] "In order to cut the roots of several proceedings over the matter of substitutions, we prohibit all judges from allowing substitutions beyond and more than two degrees, in all cases arising in the future, either by testament and the last will or by contracts among the living such as marriage contract." *Recueil général*, vol. 14, 80. The reform of entail was proposed by Chancellor L'Hôpital, without solicitation by the deputies in the Estates General at Orléans. Caillemer, *Des résistances*, 1083; Rousselet-Pimont, *Le chancelier et la loi*, 315–17.

[127] Domat, *The Civil Law in Its Natural Order*, 643–47.

[128] "In confirming and extending the article regarding substitutions in our ordinances issued in Orleans, in the hope to remove several difficulties in the said substitutions previously done, . . . we speak, declare, and order that all substitutions done before the Ordinance of Orleans, in whatever disposition it may be, by contract inter vivos or by the last will, and in whatever languages they may be, will be limited to the fourth degree beyond the institution." *Recueil général*, vol. 14, 204.

[129] Ourliac and Malafosse, *Histoire du droit privé*, vol. 3, 528–29.

[130] Caillemer, *Des résistances*, 1084; Cooper, "Patterns of Inheritance and Settlement," 264.

[131] Montaigne, *Les Essais* [Édition de Bordeaux, 1595], ed. Pierre Villey and Verdun-L. Saulnier (Paris: Presses universitaires de France, 1965), book 2, ch. 8, 397. The translation is from Donald M. Frame (ed.), *The Complete Essays of Montaigne* (Stanford: Stanford University Press, 1958), 289. Montaigne was equally opposed to testamentary succession: "In general the soundest distribution of our estate on death seems to me to let it be distributed according to the custom of the *pays*. The laws have thought about this better than we; and it is better to let them err in their choice than rashly run the risk of erring in ours." *The Complete Essays of Montaigne*, 288–89.

"one must endeavor to support the nobility, for whom honor is, in some sense, both child and parent."[132] But he also saw substitutions "hamper commerce" and "the power of redemption by one person of the lineage produces an infinite number of lawsuits." He concluded that "the laws must favor all the commerce that the constitution of this government can allow."[133] During the Revolution, the Convention in 1792 abolished substitution in trust as feudal vestiges.[134]

The legislative efforts to restrict entails demonstrate that economic considerations figured prominently in private law reforms in the ancien régime. In both customary reforms and legislation, encouraging rational management of assets, providing for younger children, and above all promoting certainty in legal transactions were pressing issues. These concerns coexisted with the need to protect and preserve the patrimony of great noble houses in order to stabilize the existing social order.[135]

Instruments of Contract and Testament

The Ordinance of Moulins renewed the requirement in the Ordinance of Villers-Cotterêts that inter vivos gifts be registered in the office of the court clerks at the donor's place of residence (Article 58).[136] Public registration and publication of all gifts, regardless of the size, remained in force throughout the ancien régime and into the Civil Code.[137] When a fictitious transfer with no actual surrender of ownership and a secret transfer of ownership happened frequently, official notice of transactions could prevent lawsuits.[138] Public knowledge of the ownership change was important to protect creditors. The third party could now invoke the failure of registration to challenge the validity of the transfer. As seen above, the reformed custom of Paris in 1580 followed the legislative initiative and inserted into its text the formalities of the registration of property transactions.[139]

[132] Montesquieu, Charles-Louis de Secondat, baron de, *De l'esprit des lois*, book 5, ch. 9 ("Comment les lois sont relatives à leur principe dans la monarchie") (Paris: Lavigne, 1845), 39.

[133] Ibid., 40.

[134] Article 896 of the Civil Code prohibited substitutions as conflicting with the preservation of the interest of agriculture, credit, and the circulation of property. Brissaud, *A History of French Private Law*, 726, 732.

[135] The complex nature of substitutions as a legal instrument exemplifies that "the relationships between the pattern of family settlement and local custom are all further areas of ignorance." Cooper, "Patterns of Inheritance and Settlement," 268.

[136] *Recueil général*, vol. 14, 204–205. The Ordinance of Villers-Cotterêts in ibid., vol. 12, 27. The registration, called *insinuation*, was required (Arts. 132–33) for the donee's acceptance as well as for the donor's act of transfer. See Dawson, *Gifts and Promises*, 29–47.

[137] Edicts of May 1645 (*Recueil général*, vol. 17, 51); November 1690 (vol. 20, 113); December 1703 (vol. 20, 438). In the ordinance of 1731, public registration in one of the forms specified was prescribed in Arts. 1, 2, 26, 27, and 28 (vol. 21, 343–50). See Brissaud, *A History of French Private Law*, 709–10.

[138] Paul Viollet, *Histoire du droit civil français, accompagnée de notions de droit canonique et d'indications bibliographiques* (Paris: L. Larose et Forcel, 1893), 904–905; Brissaud, *A History of French Private Law*, 709.

[139] See note 60 in this chapter. Ricard argued for a requirement that the subject of the gift be physically surrendered, "so that individuals cannot succeed so easily in depriving their heirs of their

The Ordinance of Orléans required all legal acts and contracts be signed by the parties and witnesses and an affidavit to that effect be attached under pain of nullity; if witnesses did not know how to sign, that fact had to be mentioned in the instrument (Article 84).[140] The Ordinance of Moulins in 1566 tightened the admissibility of proof by witnesses and required a written instrument as a normal mode of proof. To avoid "the complication of lawsuits," it decreed that a written contract must be drawn up for transactions exceeding one hundred livres in value (Article 54).[141] The requirement of written proof was a significant departure from the tradition of the Middle Ages that preferred witnesses to writing, as shown in the adage "Tesmoings passent lettres."[142] There was consensus among jurists that preconstituted proof, as embodied in written deeds, was manifestly superior to testimonies after the fact. Proof by witnesses would be allowed only as an exception.

The spread of documentary practices led to a major change in the execution of a will. Jurisprudence extended the specification of writing to testaments. The use of testaments gradually infiltrated the *pays de coutumes* despite various rules discouraging testamentary succession. When lawsuits contesting the wills were on the rise, the observance of the minutest formalities, prescribed in notarial deeds, was essential.[143] A valid will consisted of a declaration made in the presence of two notaries, or of one notary and two witnesses, and put in writing by the notary.[144] In the *pays de droit écrit*, holographic wills were admitted only in favor of children.[145] A nuncupative will, also known as a "deathbed will," was a verbal will consisting in a declaration made in the presence of five or seven witnesses. It had been recognized as a valid will for the distribution of personal property, but its legality became questioned. As Pasquier noted, the Ordinance of Moulins affirmed "writing is preferred to witnesses" and put oral will out of use.[146] In this sense, legislation in the sixteenth century helped reduce the gap between the north and the south in important practices.

In 1580 the reformed Parisian custom required that wills be "signed by the testator and by witnesses, or an explanation must be attached why they could not sign."[147] Legislation and customary law reform complemented each other closely.

property by so facile a contract." Jean-Marie Ricard, *Traité des donations entre-vifs et testamentaires: le traité de la révocation des donations par la naissance & survenance des enfans* (Riom: M. Dégoutte, 1783), vol. 1, 230, cited from Dawson, *Gifts and Promises*, 43–44.

[140] *Recueil général*, vol. 14, 85. [141] Ibid., vol. 14, 203.

[142] Loisel, *Institutes coustumières*, book 5, tit. 5, IIII, 73.

[143] Uniform requirements for the formal execution of wills were introduced to most customs. Dawson, "French Customs," 787; Brissaud, *A History of French Private Law*, 701–702.

[144] Filhol, *Le premier président Christofle de Thou*, 165. The *arrêt* of December 20, 1576, of the Parlement of Paris explicitly required that a nuncupative will be written down by a notary.

[145] Walter Pintens, "Testamentary Formalities in France and Belgium," in Kenneth G. Reid, Marius J. de Wall, and Reinhard Zimmermann (eds.), *Comparative Succession Law*, vol. 1: *Testamentary Formalities* (Oxford: Oxford University Press, 2011), 54.

[146] Pasquier, *L'interprétation des Institutes de Justinian*, 467.

[147] N. C. de Paris, Art. 289, *Nouveau coutumier général*, vol. 3, 50. See Pasquier, *L'interprétation des Institutes de Justinian*, 469; Brissaud, *A History of French Private Law*, 701. The provision was retained in the Civil Code, Art. 971.

Edict of Mothers (1567)

The Edict of Saint-Maur issued in May 1567 was a specimen of royal effort to promote unity in jurisprudence across the kingdom. Commonly known as the Edict of Mothers, it aimed to introduce the rule of *paterna paternis* in the *pays de droit coutumier* to the *pays de droit écrit*.[148] As has been seen earlier, this custom operated to prevent the property of one family from being passed into another family. Under the customary rules of succession, the patrimonies could not be taken away from the stock, stem, or branch from which they had been derived. A widow received the usufruct of half her husband's estate but could not deprive her children of their eventual inheritance. Note that the Edict of Second Marriages of 1560 applied Roman law rules in customary law regions; the Edict of Mothers did the opposite.

The king justified his intervention in private succession matters by professing he "would have tried all the means available to us to ensure the preservation and observation of the laws and customs, which were salutary at the beginning, as was the intention of those who received them, but nevertheless brought, as experience has let us know, much inconvenience and harm to public good." He decided to act because he wanted to prevent "the multitude and vexation of lawsuits from distracting our service."[149] The 1567 edict declared Roman law rule that had been applied in the *pays* and duchies of Guyenne, Languedoc, and Dauphiné was "directly contrary to what is observed in other *pays* of our kingdom," and "it pleases us that the Roman ordinance be neither followed nor practiced anywhere in our kingdom."[150] But the edict attempting to transplant one of the most central principles of succession in the customary law regions to the written law regions met fierce resistance.

The historian de Thou described the different reactions by the parlements to the edict as follows: "The edict . . . was verified and registered at the Parlement of Paris on July 29 and received with great applause by the public. But other Parlements, at which the edict was aimed, rejected it. . . . Despite the repeated *lettres de jussion*, one could not get them to register it."[151] The parlements in the *pays de droit écrit* in unison opposed the introduction of the "alien" concept of *propres* into their territories. In reality, the nature and scope of their allegiance to *droits écrits* varied. The Parlement of Toulouse adhered to the customs of Languedoc and Roussillon, which were in many respects contrary to the rules in the *Corpus juris*; the Parlement of Bordeaux proclaimed the superiority of custom to statute; the Parlement of Aix, the successor to the court of the *sénéchaussée* of

[148] The edict states: "We want, and it pleases us, that mothers from now on do not succeed their children, and that the property of the said children, coming from the father, grandfather, uncles, or relatives, of whatever that may be, from the paternal side, would return to those to which it must return, without letting it happen that the said mothers succeed it." *Recueil général*, vol. 14, 223.

[149] *Recueil général*, vol. 14, 221–22.

[150] Ibid.

[151] De Thou, *Histoire universelle*, vol. 2, book 41, 782.

Provence, defended municipal and provincial statutes, such as the charter of the consulate of Arles and the local laws from the fourteenth century, against both royal legislation and Roman law.[152]

Regardless of these differences, oppositions were uniform. The Parlements of Bordeaux and Toulouse refused to register the law.[153] In the local estates in Dauphiné, strong arguments were made that legislation could not abrogate the customs of the provinces that had recently joined France. The edict was even not sent to the Parlement of Dijon for registration.[154]

Among the parlements that registered the Edict of Mothers, there was divergence in implementation. A certain ambiguity in the language of the edict complicated the matter. The edict stated: "the mothers will succeed the movable property [*meubles*] and the jointly acquired property [*conquêts*] coming from a source other than the paternal side and line."[155] The Parlement of Aix construed this language to mean that the rule of *paterna paternis* applied to both the immovable and movable property. In several *arrêts*, the court thus refused the mother the right to collect movable property of the paternal origin.[156] Another question involved a situation where the mother had already been deceased. Upon the death of her son who was the heir of the paternal *propres*, should the *propres* go to paternal relatives by virtue of *paterna paternis* or should they go to maternal relatives closer in relationship, in accordance with *Novel* 118?[157] Did the Edict of Mothers exclude maternal relatives as it excluded the mother, or can maternal relatives, grandparents through the mother's side for example, succeed the paternal property? Of course, this line of interpretation would defeat the purpose of the edict which aimed to "prevent the property from flowing into other families." But the Parlement of Aix insisted that the edict must be interpreted tightly: since the edict only talked about mothers, it was not permissible to extend the language to maternal relatives, specifically maternal grandparents. It stressed the judicial canon that the judge must interpret the exclusion of succession rights narrowly.

[152] Beaune, *Introduction à l'étude historique*, 453. The Charter of the consulat d'Arles is printed in Giraud, *Essai sur l'histoire du droit français*, vol. 2, 1–4. The *Coutume de Bordeaux* was published between 1520 and 1528. Pierre Jaubert, "A propos de l'ancienne coutume et de la nouvelle coutume de Bordeaux: Bilan et perspectives," in *Extrait d'Annales de la faculté de droit des sciences sociales et politiques et la faculté des sciences économiques* (Bordeaux: Éditions Bière, 1976), 1. For political influence on the formation of territorial customs, see Hilaire, "Coutumes et droit écrit."

[153] Bart, *Histoire du droit privé*, 147.

[154] In 1570, the commissioners reforming the Burgundian customs inserted an express rejection of the edict, confirmed by the *lettres patentes* of Henri III. See Caillemer, *Des résistances*, 1091–92.

[155] "Les meres succederont aux meubles et conquets provenus d'ailleurs que du cote et ligne paternelle."

[156] See Karen Fiorentino, "L'Édit des mères en Provence (1567–1729): Un exemple de la difficile application des ordonnances royales en pays de droit écrit," *Revue historique de droit français et étranger* 85 (2007), 219–46.

[157] Under *Novel* 118, issued in 543, intestacy succession became based on blood-relationship, with females and males on the same footing. In the absence of descendants of her children, the mother was placed in a more equitable position in inheritance.

The edict's reception at the Parlement of Paris had its own difficulties. The jurisdiction of the Parisian court covered both the regions observing *paterna paternis materna maternis* and the regions observing *Novel* 118 as their custom. The Parlement of Paris registered the edict but refused to enforce it in the regions that had customary rules allowing parents to succeed their children as permitted in Roman law. Citing hostilities to the edict from the parlements in the Midi, the *arrêt* of the Parlement of Paris in 1576 decided that the law had no effect in the regions where there was a contrary usage. There were other disputes. Just as in the Edict of Second Marriages of 1560, the 1568 law mentioned the rule *paterna paternis* but not *materna maternis*, entailing the debate among scholars over whether it required the fathers to be subject to the regulation as the mothers.[158] In 1729, the king at last gave in and revoked the law. He reassured his subjects in the written law regions that he did not wish to meddle with their private usages.[159] The attempt to apply the customary rule of *paterna paternis* across the kingdom failed.

These legislative travails show, at least, that the king continually tried to abrogate or modify obsolete or undesirable customary rules. The idea was well established that the king could change customs or ancient ordinances when the discipline and administration of the kingdom—public order—were at stake.[160] The notion of public good became the baseline for the production of norms and the control of legal practices. It affirmed the increasing role of legislation in national life. In 1587, Barnabé Brisson compiled royal ordinances under the title *Code du roy Henry III Roy de France et de Pologne*.[161] The *Code Henry III* consisted of twenty books, and Book 6 included royal laws dealing with private law,

[158] Jean Bouhier, *Traité de la succession des mères, en vertu de l'Edit de Saint-Maur* (Dijon, 1726). Le Brun stated: "In order not to diverge from the usage, it is necessary to conclude that fathers are not included in the Edict." Denis Le Brun, *Traité des successions, devisé en quatre livres* in *Les œuvres de M. Denis Le Brun* (Paris, 1714), vol. 1, book 1, ch. 5, sec. 8 (nos. 6 and 7), 87. There was a proposal to promulgate a new edict regarding the property coming from the side of the mother "which would have been called the Edict of Fathers," but it did not materialize. Paul Viollet, *Précis de l'histoire du droit français* (Paris: L. Larose et Forcel, 1886), 730; Viollet, *Histoire du droit civil français*, 847–48; Rousselet-Pimont, *Le chancelier et la loi*, 324–25.

[159] Olivier-Martin, *Les lois du roi*, 116; Fiorentino, "L'Édit des mères," 245. The text of this edict is in *Recueil général*, vol. 21, 322–26.

[160] Reulos, "Ver la présentation coordonné et logique du droit français," 277; Glasson, *Histoire du droit*, vol. 8, 25, 159.

[161] Barnabé Brisson, *Code du roy Henry III, roy de France et de Pologne* (Lyon: Frères de Gabiano, 1593), first published in Paris in 1587. See Guillaume Bernard, "La codification en France avant le Code civil: Le Code Henri III (1587) du Président Barnabé Brisson (1531–1501)," in Jean Luc Chabot, Philippe Didier, and Jérôme Ferrand (eds.), *Le code civil et les droits de l'homme: Actes du colloque international de Grenoble, 3 et 4 décembre 2003, ancien Palais de justice de Grenoble et Musée de la Révolution française de Vizille* (Paris: L'Harmattan, 2006), 43–69; Éva Jakab, "Brissonius in Context: *De Formulis et solennibus populi Romani verbis*," in du Plessis and Cairns (eds.), *Reassessing Legal Humanism*, 211–43. Henry III had announced in the Ordinance of Blois (1579), issued after the Estates General in 1576, that "certain persons would be commissioned to collect and stipulate the ordinances and reduce them following a systematic order into a volume that would prove useful and necessary" (Art. 207), *Recueil général*, vol. 14, 430.

such as clandestine marriage, second marriage, donation, testament, substitution, succession of mothers, and *retrait lignager*. Brisson's work, published anonymously, was a private venture despite its title, but it vindicated the idea that private law deserved compilation into a corpus.[162]

During the civil war, the standardization of laws and the judicial process became ever more urgent. On more than a few occasions, the holding of the assemblies was delayed due to violence.[163] How did the pervasive religious disturbances and political and social disorder affect legal reforms?

4. Religious Wars and Legal Reforms

Between 1560 and 1565, groups of younger sons of the lesser nobility in various regions seized the disorder during the war to protest against primogeniture, the *droit d'aînesse*. Rallying around the new religion, they denounced the inequity of granting excessive privileges to the first-born and demanded an equal partition of patrimony. The uprisings by discontented youth of the nobility under the banner of the reformed religion did not go unnoticed by those in charge of customary law reform. Royal commissioners tried to reduce the harsh effect of the *droit d'aînesse* by increasing the inheritance share of younger children.[164]

A related question was the parental approval of marriage. In the wake of the spread of the reformed religion, marriage between a Protestant and a Catholic was not uncommon, celebrated before either a priest or a reformed minister. Lawsuits often erupted, disputing the validity of the marriages concluded "à la mode de Genève" and the rights of those married couples to parental succession. In 1557, Henry II issued an edict prohibiting the so-called clandestine marriage; parents were allowed to disinherit children who married without their consent.[165] In February 1563, the Parlement of Paris presented a remonstrance that marriage and baptism must be celebrated uniquely in the Catholic rite.[166] During the religious wars, however, it was politically unwise for the king to exacerbate dissension

[162] Brisson was killed in 1591 by the Seize, the radical members of the Paris *Ligue*, at the age of sixty. A new edition of Brisson's work was published by Charondas Le Caron with the addition of the edicts of Henry IV: *Code du roy Henry III, roy de France et de Pologne* (Paris: Veuve de Sebastien Nivelle, 1605).

[163] The official compilation of the custom of Brittany, a work that started from 1539, saw its completion in 1580. Its final drawing up took place in the midst of crisis during the wars: only ten of the twenty-nine deputies assigned to compile the *coutume* could arrive in Rennes to participate in the assembly. See J. Brejon de Lavergnée, "Les vicissitudes de l'enregistrement des usances locales de Bretagne lors de la rédaction officielle de la Coutume de 1580," *Revue historique de droit français et étranger* 55 (1977), 559–78.

[164] Filhol, "Protestantisme et droit d'aînesse au XVIe siècle."

[165] *Recueil général*, vol. 13, 469.

[166] The same issue had already been raised by the remonstrances of May 1561. Sylvie Daubresse, "Le Parlement de Paris et L'édit du 17 Janvier 1562," *Revue historique* 607 (1998), 529.

within the family. While the law of parental consent on marriage was maintained, the peace treaties and pacification edicts prohibited parents from disinheriting children solely on the grounds of religion. They regularly included the language that "disinheritance or deprivation, either by lifetime or testamentary dispositions, done solely out of spite and because of religion, will not be allowed, as in the past and as in the future, among the subjects of His Majesty."[167]

The *représentation successorale* was also pertinent. By allowing succession *per stirpes*, it could diminish willful disinheritance by parents in their refusal to recall the children to succession. Parents who disapproved of the marriage were unlikely to recall the disobedient children and, where the right to representation was absent, the wrath of parents against the child who defied their wishes could result in the exclusion of all the descendants of that child if he died, survived by siblings.[168] The extension of representation in custom reduced the harsh consequences of the 1557 edict that had required parental consent on marriage and allowed parents to punish disobeying children.[169] This illustrates the extent to which royal religious policy, legislation, and customary law reforms were profoundly interconnected, requiring multifaceted considerations.

Another pressing issue during the raging civil war was whether to allow a spouse to renounce the conjugal community property regime. In the community property system, a conjugal pair was jointly liable for debts incurred by either spouse before or after the marriage, even though a wife could, if properly stipulated in the marriage contract, renounce the community property saddled with debts. She could also withdraw, free and clear, in whole or in part, her contribution to the community property. This restitution required a legal mortgage created on the husband's property by the marriage contract. Without this careful arrangement, the customary law regime could have a disastrous effect. Some edicts during the religious wars ordered the confiscation of the property of heretics and rebels, creating extreme hardship on the wife. Both Dumoulin and de Thou were concerned about this situation. In all reformed customary texts which he directed, de Thou inserted an article expressly allowing the wife of a convicted criminal to renounce the community property arrangement and keep her portion of the marital property.[170]

[167] Art. 31 of the edict of pacification of Paris of May 1576, *Recueil général*, vol. 14, 280. For clandestine marriage and related issues, see infra Chapter 7, note 49 and accompanying text.

[168] Filhol, *Le premier président Christofle de Thou*, 236–37.

[169] It was a roundabout way to find redress for the disinherited. Dawson, *Gifts and Promises*, 39. One may ask whether the Amiens case of 1568, examined above, was not really a dispute between Calvinist and Catholic conceptions of parental authority, which seemed in the process of being crystallized along confessional lines. The localized political struggles within the religious wars were certainly in the background. The extent to which legal disputes reflected particular partisan ends within the religious wars remains an important question for research.

[170] Filhol, *Le premier président Christofle de Thou*, 150–51.

Finally, several general observations can be made regarding the customary law and legislative reforms examined in this chapter. French customs were pervaded with the spirit to preserve the family and patrimony, in the form of the rules of dower, redemption, general and hidden mortgages, ways to transform *conquêts* to new *propres*, and so forth. They had the effect of slowing down economic progress. The reformation of customs aimed to mitigate the problems but the results were mixed. Reforms of the property rights of the feudal nobility were moderate in nature. The king continued to depend on the services rendered by the nobles, and there were growing concerns about the decline and impoverishment of the noble houses due to the fragmentation of their property. For all its desire to rein in feudal vestiges, the crown could not disregard political and societal needs for stability that would be ensured by the integrity of noble lineages.

It is beyond dispute, however, that reforms of customs and legislation shared and promoted the fundamental goals of ensuring clarity, publicity, certainty, and predictability in law. In cases such as the Edict of Second Marriages, the law and the reformed custom moved in the same direction, maintaining a symbiotic relationship. The *Nouvelle Coutume de Paris* closely followed the initiative of the royal edict. In other cases, as in the Edict of Mothers, royal laws failed to change the existing customary rules and reformed *coutumes* simply ignored them. The king was more or less powerless as to the autonomy of the courts in interpreting the laws. At least, nevertheless, one should recognize the royal desire to infuse more efficiency and unity into the kingdom's laws.

There was a broad expectation that customary law solutions and Roman law principles could be reconciled to bring unity in French law for the French people. It is to this issue the next chapter turns.

6
The Idea of "Our French Law"

François Hotman (1524–1590) quipped that a jurist trained solely in Roman law would feel, upon finding himself in a French court, as if "he had landed in the new world in the middle of the savages of America."[1] Having no idea of what *censive*, *retrait lignager*, *saisine*, customary dower, community property regime, and all those other things were, he would think he had never known in his life anything about law or law enforcement.[2] The image of Hotman's hapless jurist captures the pervasive problem in early modern France and indeed across Europe since the renaissance of Roman law. Law education was exclusively based on Roman law and canon law. Graduates, when they finished their studies in university, went back home well equipped with the knowledge of the learned laws. Once they started practicing law, however, they had to plead and render decisions according to local laws, facing a whole new set of questions that had not been foreseen by university doctors. Michel Reulos dubbed the quandary about legal education and practice "*la quaestio vexata* of the sixteenth century."[3]

The compilation of customs helped, to a certain extent, narrow the distance between Roman law and custom. The official texts allowed jurists to write commentaries, clarifying obscurities by drawing on learned law. Authors frequently cited court decisions, and judges in turn referred to scholarly works to develop more rational interpretations of customs.[4] Interactions between doctrine and jurisprudence underscored the need to reduce the multiplicity and diversity of the laws. One can identify three distinct approaches in the efforts to bring more coherence and unity into the sources of law: first, the synthesis of customary texts; second, the harmonization of customs through court decisions; and, third, the creation of a code.

[1] *Antitribonian, ou, Discours d'un grand et renommé iurisconsulte de nostre temps sur l'estude des loix: Fait par l'aduis de feu Monsieur de l'Hospital, Chancelier de France, en l'an 1567* (Paris, 1603; reprint Paris: Éditions de l'Université de Saint-Etienne, 1980), 36.

[2] Ibid., 37.

[3] Reulos, "L'importance des praticiens," 121.

[4] The collaboration "progressed by the same steps along the same routes, each aiding the other, each sanctioning and confirming what the other had elaborated." Édmond Meynial, "Remarques sur le rôle joué par la doctrine et la jurisprudence dans l'œuvre d'unification du droit en France depuis la rédaction des coutumes jusqu'à la Révolution, en particulier dans la succession aux propres" (part I), *Revue générale du droit, de la législation et de la jurisprudence en France et à l'étranger* 27 (1903), 326, note 2. For a survey of the movements for legal unification, see Jean Gaudemet, "Les tendances à l'unification du droit en France dans les derniers siècles de l'ancien régime (XVIe–XVIIIe)," in Società italiana di storia del diritto (ed.), *La formazione storica del diritto moderno in Europa* (Florence: L. S. Olschki, 1977), 157–94.

Custom, Law, and Monarchy: A Legal History of Early Modern France. Marie Seong-Hak Kim, Oxford University Press.
 DOI: 10.1093/oso/9780192845498.003.0006

The first solution relied on doctrine, the work of legal scholars. *La doctrine* called for the unification of law, "half motivated by an innate tendency toward unity, and half by the survival of the religious respect accorded to Roman law."[5] Dumoulin, with his unflinching faith in custom as French law, argued for the creation of a unified body of customs. Coquille and Pasquier espoused the belief that general principles discerned from local *coutumes* would help bring a legal unity. Bodin proposed in his *Methodus ad facilem historiarum cognitionem* (1566) a new system of universal law through a comparative study of history and customs, which would overcome the domination of Roman law.[6] The reformed *Coutume de Paris* was expected by many to become the basis of *le droit commun coutumier*.

The second ideal for legal unity revolved around reconciling customs by means of *la jurisprudence*, the work of judges and lawyers in the courtroom.[7] Court decisions routinely cited past decisions as authorities. Now with the official texts published as law, judges needed to make sure their decisions conformed to them. In the second half of the sixteenth century, the publication of *arrêts notables* demonstrated the full extent of professional competence.[8] The vast jurisdiction of the Parlement of Paris meant its judges and lawyers had to accommodate many disparate customs. Decisions of lower courts that departed from the precedents were quashed on appeal, which promoted unity in judicial decrees. These developments should be distinguished from the creation of the common law in England, yet the weight of case precedents in early modern France approximated that across the Channel.[9] It indicated a pragmatic turn in jurisprudence.

The third solution, the most drastic, envisaged the creation of a national code. This vision consisted of bringing fragmentary doctrinal and jurisprudential progress together, to achieve a legislative coherence through codification. Legal humanists propagated the idea that French law could be gathered and organized into a unified code on the Roman model. There was a steady growth of belief in royal legislative power to create a national law.

This chapter examines the workings of this tripartite vision of "our French law" in the late sixteenth century. Paradoxically, in each conception, Roman law occupied an eminent, imposing place. The *quaestio vexata* persisted until the end of

[5] Meynial, "Remarques sur le rôle joué par la doctrine et la jurisprudence," 455.

[6] Jean Bodin, *Methodus ad facilem historiarum cognitionem* (Paris, 1566); *Method for the Easy Comprehension of History*, trans. Beatrice Reynolds (New York: Columbia University Press, 1945).

[7] Joseph-Claude Ferrière, "Jurisprudence des arrêts," *Dictionnaire de droit et de pratique* (Paris: Brunet, 1769), vol. 2, 90–91. See Guillaume Leyte, "'Le droit commun de la France': Observations sur l'apport des arrêtistes," *Droits: Revue française de théorie juridique* 38 (2003), 53–67; Anne Lefebvre-Teillard, "Naissance du droit français: L'apport de jurisprudence," *Droits: Revue française de théorie juridique* 38 (2003), 69–82; Jean Hilaire, "Questions autour de la jurisprudence des arrêts," in Serge Dauchy and Véronique Demars-Sion (eds.), *Les recueils d'arrêts et dictionnaire de jurisprudence, XVIe–XVIIIe siècles* (Paris: Éditions La Mémoire du Droit, 2005), 21–39.

[8] Geraldine Cazals and Stéphan Geonget (eds.), "Introduction," in *Des "arrests parlans": Les arrêts notables à la Renaissance entre droit et littérature* (Geneva: Droz, 2014), 11.

[9] Caenegem, *Historical Introduction to Private Law*, 1–15.

the ancien régime, yet there was a powerful intellectual reformist spirit on the rise, marshaling the prospect of a more stable and structured law.

1. Doctrine and Humanist Nationalism

Early modern legal scholarship was infused with a distinctive nationalistic vitality.[10] In the sixteenth century many French students still went to study law in Italy, but the majority were educated in Bourges, Orléans, and Poitiers. These French universities evinced a shift from medieval internationalism to progressive nationalism.[11] While legal humanists searched for a veritable spirit of French law in custom, they did not question the intrinsic moral value and technical utility of Roman law. Dumoulin referred to Roman law instinctively, admiring its rationality. As he put it, "[Roman] law, systematized by the authority of the wise men, is suitable for impartiality, is reasonable, and is absolute in many perspectives; so, in general, it was adopted and agreed upon by the Christian people, and became common [law]."[12]

It has been pointed out that Dumoulin's approaches to private law and public law were not of an identical nature.[13] When he wrote on Roman private law or custom, he stayed close to the tradition of the Commentators relying on minute exegesis; when he discussed public institutions of the crown or the church, however, he based his discussion solidly on an independent synthesis of history.[14] The first edition of *Commentarii in Parisienses consuetudines* did not include any criticism of *jus commune*; it was only in the second edition in 1558 that major polemic against the universal authority of the code of Justinian appeared. Thireau has argued that Dumoulin's rejection of the Bartolist thesis that Roman law was the *jus commune* was the result of an intellectual progression which took place in the course of his work on Roman public law, such as *Tractatus de dignitatibus*,

[10] For the rise of national sentiment in the sixteenth century, see Alain Tallon, *Conscience nationale et sentiment religieux en France au XVIe siècle: Essai sur la vision gallicane du monde* (Paris: Presses universitaires de France, 2002); Myriam Yardeni, *La conscience nationale en France pendant les guerres de religion, 1559–1598* (Paris: Béatrice-Nauwelaerts, 1971); Vittorio de Caprariis, *Propaganda e pensiero politico in Francia durante le guerre di religione (1559–1572)* (Naples: Edizioni scientifiche italiane, 1959); André Chastel and Robert Klein, "Humanism, Historical Consciousness and National Sentiment," *Diogène* 44 (1963), 1–18.

[11] From "l'internationalisation des universités du Moyen Âge" to "nationalisation des universités." Jean-Louis Thireau, "Professeurs et étudiants étrangers dans les facultés de droit françaises (XVIe–XVIIe siècles)," *Revue d'histoire des facultés et droit et de la science juridique* 13 (1992), 44.

[12] Dumoulin, *Commentarii*, "De Fiefs," # 110, in *Omnia quae extant opera*, vol. 1, 22–23.

[13] Jean-Louis Thireau, "Une vision du droit public romain au XVIe siècle: Le *Tractatus analyticus de dignitatibus, magistratibus et civibus romanis* de Charles du Moulin," in Jacques Krynen and Michael Stolleis (eds.), *Science politique et droit public dans les facultés de droit européennes (XIIIe–XVIIIe siècle)* (Frankfurt am Main: Vittorio Klostermann, 2008), 393–410. Dumoulin's *Tractatus analyticus de dignitatibus* first appeared in Paris in 1561.

[14] Thireau, *Charles du Moulin*, 197, 208.

written during his stay in Tübingen between November 1553 and October 1554. Before then, Dumoulin treated Roman law as normative rules which contained the solutions that he attempted to discover by virtue of *ratio legis*.[15]

As seen in Chapter 3, Dumoulin argued that custom contained an inner unity because it emanated from the French people who lived under one king. He had a clear formula as to the relationship between custom and Roman law. The custom of each locality constituted common law in its jurisdiction. If local custom was silent, one must refer to the customs of nearby localities. If the resort to customs failed, one should refer to Roman law, but only if it conformed to equity and had direct relevance to the issues in litigation. In other words, Roman law should remain silent until some deficiency arises in specific aspects of custom. Yet, Dumoulin would have no problem imitating and borrowing the superior organization and lucid principles of Roman law to systematize and achieve the "concord" of French customs.

Pasquier enumerated four sources of law in France in a distinct hierarchical order: "first, royal ordinances; second, diverse customs of the provinces; third, general maxims which we transplanted in France, not the entirety of the law of Romans but a part of it; the fourth, the *arrêts* of each parlement."[16] Royal ordinance topped the list. In his letter to Barnabé Brisson, Pasquier complimented him, "a Frenchman and the president at the highest Parlement of France," for composing the "Code Henry" so that "our ordinances can now stand on the same footing as those of the Romans."[17] After royal law, came custom, "the ancient and original law of the French people."[18] There were two kinds of custom, one in the *pays* in the north governed by *droit coutumier* and the other in the *pays* in the south governed by *droit romain*. *Droit écrit* was only a *coutume* and its legal authority in France was neither more nor less than other customs.[19] Pasquier

[15] Thireau, "Une vision du droit public romain," 407.

[16] Pasquier, *L'interprétation des Institutes de Justinian*, book 1, ch. 15 ("Du droict que nous observons en France"), 30. Pasquier repeats his enumeration of the sources of law in one of his letters: he lists "certain moral propositions for which, through a long and ancient usage, we hold faith and give homage to the Romans" before "the general *arrêts* of the sovereign courts." *Lettres*, book 19, letter 15 (to Robert), *Les œuvres*, vol. 2, col. 575.

[17] Pasquier, *Lettres*, book 9, letter 1 (to Brisson), in *Les œuvres*, vol. 2, col. 222. In the same letter, Pasquier mentioned the existing collections made by Pierre Rebuffi, Antoine Fontanon, and Pierre Guénois, and called the king "notre grand Théodose." Rebuffi once served as a professor at Bourges along with Alciato. See Philippe Fabry, *L'État royal: Norms, justice et gouvernement dans l'œuvre de Pierre Rebuffi (1487–1557)* (Toulouse: Presses de l'Université Toulouse 1 Capitole, 2015); Howell A. Lloyd, "Constitutional Thought in Sixteenth-Century France: The Case of Pierre Rebuffi," *French History* 8 (1994), 259–75.

[18] Pasquier, *L'interprétation des Institutes de Justinian*, book 1, ch. 14 ("Ex non scripto"), 29. For Pasquier's nationalistic stance, see Kelley, *Foundations of Modern Historical Scholarship*, 271–309.

[19] Of customs, "we have two types; because there are certain *pays* in which the written law of the Romans is considered *Coustume*; of this kind is the *pays* of Languedoc, Provence, and also Lyonnais and Forestz, under the jurisdiction of the Parlement de Paris; and these are properly called *pays de droict escript*. All the rest of France is called customary, because there are diverse customs, established in ancient times in one or other *présidial* seats, which must be religiously observed by the members and inhabitants of the places." Pasquier, *L'interprétation des Institutes de Justinian*, book 1, ch. 16 ("Des

wrote: "custom is formed in each region, bit by bit, according to the diversity of our *mœurs* [characters], and our *mœurs* are formed from the diversity of our spirit."[20] This opinion is reminiscent of Dumoulin's that beneath the surfaces of different *coutumes* lay the common spirit that inspired them.[21] If some problems remain that cannot be solved by local custom, then, who would question that one should resort to the neighboring region's custom, which is the true common law of that place, rather than Roman law? Roman law was to be used only as reason, as the last resort in the absence of customary rule.[22]

Pasquier's demurrer on Roman law embodied the Gallican spirit pervasive among legal humanists. His letter to Brisson amounted to a manifesto of the independence of French law:

> It is now time that we abandon this false idea occupying our mind which causes us to trample down on our true and innocent law of France and to reduce all our judgments to the judgments of the Romans. Just as God separated us from Italy by a massive range of mountains, so He separated us in almost all things, like mores, laws, characters, and complexions.[23]

Pasquier listed what he saw as the distasteful features of Roman law, among which were patriarchal power (*patria potestas*) and preference for testamentary succession, contrasted with the French concern for the integrity of family property.[24] He lamented that the complexity of Roman law, which overwhelmed the simplicity of French custom, was a breeding pool for litigation.[25]

Pasquier's objection to treating Roman law as the common law in France was shared by his contemporary Guy Coquille. Coquille began his *Les coutumes du pays et comté de Nivernois* as follows:

> The customs of the provinces of France, which are called *coûtumieres*, are their *vray Droit Civil, & Commun*; and those which, according to the consent of the

Coustumes"), 34. Contemporary jurists agreed Roman law had value as custom through the authorization by the king. Jean Bouhier, *Observation sur la coutume de Bourgogne*, in *Les œuvres de jurisprudence*, vol. 1, 390 (ch. 4, no. 41).

[20] Pasquier, *Lettres*, book 9, letter 1 (to Brisson), in *Les œuvres*, vol. 2, col. 225.

[21] See supra Chapter 3, discussion of Dumoulin's *Oratio*.

[22] Pasquier repeated his point in a letter to another recipient: "if there is an obscurity or omission in local customs, one must recource to the general custom of the province, and, if there still remains a problem in the latter, one should recourse to the customs of the neighboring regions instead of referring to Roman law." *Lettres*, book 19, letter 15 (to Robert), in *Les œuvres*, vol. 2, col. 577.

[23] Pasquier, *Lettres*, book 9, letter 1 (to Brisson), in *Les œuvres*, vol. 2, col. 223.

[24] The influence of the Roman concept of paternal power (*patria potestas*) restricted the rights of children during the Middle Ages, but in France *patria potestas* had subsided by the sixteenth century, and children were freed from parental authority by reaching the age of majority or by entering into a marriage. In Paris, one could make a will for the disposable portion of *propres* after reaching twenty-five years of age. N. C. de Paris, Art. 293, *Nouveau coutumier général*, vol. 3, 51.

[25] Kelley, *Foundations of Modern Historical Scholarship*, 285.

> people of the three Orders (which is called *État*), have been established, written down, and authorized by the commissioners delegated by the king may be called written Law. It is just as in Rome where the laws that the people had approved after the proposal of the consul or of the tribune of the plebs were the laws. The difference is: in Rome only the people gave the authority and force of law, because it was a *Republique Democratique*; for us the king inspires the force of law, because this form of government is *Monarchique*. And the *coûtumes* which have not been agreed upon and drawn up in writing are *le Droit Civil non écrit* of the said provinces, just as in Rome unwritten law was introduced by the tacit consent of the people.[26]

By comparing Rome and France, Coquille seemed to say that the people could be no more arbitrary than the king in making laws and popular consent mattered in both democracy and monarchy. In any case, customs of France had nothing in common with the statutes (*les statuts*) of the *ultramontains*.[27] In his *Institution au droit des français*, he wrote:

> Our custom is our civil law; it has the same force and vigor as does the civil law of the Romans in Rome. In my opinion, it is wrong to compare our custom to statutes that Italian doctors talk so much about. In Italy its common law is Roman civil law, but in *France coutumière* Roman civil law is not common law; it does not have the force of law and serves simply as reason, and our custom is our true civil law. That is why it is not necessary to interpret it in the same way as the Italian doctors interpret their statutes.[28]

French customs had been erroneously treated like urban ordinances in Italy, according to Coquille, and the application of the latter's interpretive theories to customs caused many unnecessarily complicated judicial decisions.[29] He reiterated: "our customs are our true civil law, and one must reason and interpret them in accordance with good conscience and equity."[30]

Coquille's assertion that custom was the civil law in France was grounded on his evolutionary and pragmatic view of law. Even after the publication of the

[26] *Les coutumes du pays et comté de Nivernois*, in *Les œuvres de maistre Guy Coquille*, vol. 2, 1.

[27] The *ultramontains* refer to those who supported papal authority in France, as opposed to the *gallicans*.

[28] Coquille, *Institution au droit des français*, in *Les œuvres de maistre Guy Coquille*, vol. 2, 10. The first part of vol. 2 of *Les œuvres* contains *Les coutumes du pays et comté de Nivernois*; the second part of the volume, *Institution au droit des français* and *Questions et responses sur les articles des Coutumes*, restarts pagination at 1.

[29] "In order not to turn ourselves into serfs imitating and admiring foreigners, we will do well by not infringing and obscuring the intelligence of our customs by the aforesaid puzzling references to the Statutes, because our Customs are our Civil and Common Law, and the Statutes are not the *Droit Commun*." *Les coustumes du pays et comte de Nivernois*, in *Les œuvres*, vol. 2, 1.

[30] "Ex bono & aequo." *Questions et responses sur les articles des Coutumes*, 125–26.

coutume of Paris in 1510, he observed, new customs continued to be proffered and proved by *turbes*, and were accepted by the Parlement of Paris.[31] In this context, "when the constitutions and ordinances of our king, unwritten general law of France, or our customs are found deficient," it would be necessary that "we serve ourselves with the laws enacted by the Romans" in accordance with their "appropriateness and reasonableness."[32] While rejecting the force of Roman law in France as the *lois*, Coquille thus fully acknowledged its value in providing solutions to fill the gaps in French law.

What should one do when custom conflicts with *jus commune*? An answer may be found in Coquille's unique interpretive methods. First, he limited the scope of the application of custom, resorting to the instrument of narrow construction of law. A rule contrary to the *jus commune* should be seen as a privilege, exercisable only by those to whom it had been granted.[33] Once inconsistency between local law and the *jus commune* was identified, secondly, Coquille tried to interpret that law in light of an imagined purpose relevant to the local system. When no reference to the *jus commune* could be made, one was to find principles that would unite the divergent French customs, by using methods and principles of the *jus commune*.[34] In this manner, Coquille asserted the primacy of French custom over *jus commune* but at the same time fully subscribed the former to the latter: Roman law should be used to "aid us (I say) by convention and by reason, not by necessity."[35]

Much of the French authors' aversion to Roman law as common law was reflective of the humanist sense of history and also characteristic of Renaissance rhetoric. Their repudiation of the universal authority of *jus commune* was in large part grounded in the confidence they shared in their superb knowledge of the *Corpus juris civilis*. Still, the nationalistic spirit in legal scholarship was genuine, as demonstrated in Dumoulin's *Oratio*. Dumoulin's program of creating common principles of customs carried authentic authority because it came from a practitioner who dealt firsthand with the problems of the patchwork of jurisdictions and the dreadful conflict of laws questions resulting from them. The conflict of laws arises in a case over which two or more contradictory laws have jurisdiction.[36] People owned properties in different places and moved around across jurisdictional lines. Legal transactions involving different *coutumes* were bound to give rise to disputes which could not be solved by the basic principle of "locus regit actum" (the place governs the act). The court before which such cases were

[31] Ibid., 3. The ordinance of Louis XIV, in 1667, officially abolished the use of the *turbes*. *Recueil général*, vol. 18, 123.

[32] Coquille, *Les coutumes du pays et comte de Nivernais*, 2.

[33] Donahue, "Comparative Law before the Code Napoleon," 16.

[34] Ibid., 18–19.

[35] "Nous en aider (dis-je) par bienseance & pour la raison & non par necessite." Coquille, *Les coustumes du pays et comté de Nivernois*, in *Les œuvres*, vol. 2, 2.

[36] The conflict of laws is called private international law in modern law.

brought had to determine which law to apply. Dumoulin and Bertrand d'Argentré (1519–1590) were the two authorities in this field of practice.

The Conflict of Laws

D'Argentré's commentary on the *Coutume de Bretagne* of 1539 prepared the ground for the new *Coutume de Bretagne* of 1580, not unlike what Dumoulin did for the *Coutume de Paris.*[37] D'Argentré developed the following theory. Customary provisions that related to personal status, such as distinctions between nobles and commoners, between legitimate and illegitimate children, and between adults and minors, applied to every person in every place in accordance with the custom of his or her domicile. Therefore, in order to determine whether a person from Normandy had reached the age of majority, for instance, the courts in Paris were required to consult the custom of Normandy. Questions related to property, such as the conditions of fiefs, *censives*, or their hereditary devolution, on the other hand, were governed by the custom of the situs of the property. Rules of *paterna paternis*, *retrait lignager*, *réserve coutumière*, and *droit d'aînesse* were considered to have been established in the interest of fiefs and were governed by the custom *in loco*.

D'Argentré was allegedly partial to the theories favorable to local feudal seigneurs. It put him at odds with Dumoulin. Dumoulin had already garnered substantial reputation for his work on the choice of law cases in contracts, especially concerning the marital property regime.[38] The differences between the two jurists can be illustrated by glancing at one of Dumoulin's court arguments on the marital property issue. Written in 1525, it remains among the most celebrated legal opinions of all times. The case concerned a dispute between the heirs of Jean de Ganay (*c.*1455–1512), chancellor of France under Louis XII.[39] He married his wife in Paris, where the couple lived.[40] M. de Ganay subsequently bought real property in Lyon. Under the *Coutume de Paris*, assets acquired during marriage became community property. By contrast, the marital regime in Lyon, governed by the *droit écrit*, provided for separate property. Dumoulin was retained by the

[37] *Coustumes générales des pays et duché de Bretagne* (Paris: Nicolas Buon, 1608, 1568).

[38] See Stéphane Gruber-Magitot, *Les conflits de coutumes en matière de contrats dans la jurisprudence des parlements: De Dumoulin au Code civil* (Paris: Presses universitaires de France, 1980).

[39] Consilium 53, in Caroli Molinaei, *Consilia et Responsa juris analytica* (Lyon, 1561), 353–60. This case is cited in Henri Batiffol and Paul Lagarde, *Droit international privé*, 6th ed. (Paris: Librairie générale de droit et de jurisprudence, 1974–1976), vol. 2, 307–308; Armand Lainé, *Introduction au droit international privé*, vol. 1 (Paris: F. Pichon, 1888), 228–36; Ernest G. Lorenzen, "The French Rules of the Conflict of Laws," *Yale Law Journal* 38 (1928), 177–78; Friedrich K. Juenger, "Marital Property and the Conflict of Laws: A Tale of Two Countries," *Columbia Law Review* 81 (1981), 1062.

[40] Ernest de Ganay, *Un chancelier de France sous Louis XII Jehan de Ganay* (Paris: Librairie Plon, 1932).

heirs of Madame de Ganay to have the Lyon property declared a community asset. Dumoulin conceded in his brief that the personal law of the spouses could not, of its own force, apply extraterritorially to the land in Lyon. He argued, however, that the parties had the power to enter into an agreement that would control their property rights in foreign real estate. Since the de Ganays had failed to stipulate a specific matrimonial regime other than what was ordained by the customs of Paris, they should be seen as having made a tacit agreement to include all properties acquired during their marriage in the community which was created at the time of their nuptials. Dumoulin's point was that, while the parties could agree to subject their rights to a foreign system of law, the intention to do so must be explicit.

Dumoulin's client prevailed at the Parlement de Paris three years later. His theory that the married couple's property rights are putatively governed by the law of their first marital domicile continues to hold its force in France to this day. The significance of this case is two-fold. First, Dumoulin affirmed that the core spirit of the law resided in contract. Such would become the underlying idea of the articles of the *Nouvelle Coutume de Paris*. Secondly, he declared the supremacy of the customary law of Paris. As he put it: "it is not inappropriate that the law of Paris should thereby, indirectly, have a ubiquitous effect, even with respect to goods and property that are located outside its territory and the parties' domicile." Thanks in large part to Dumoulin, a quintessential practitioner of the law of Paris, the *Coutume* of Paris, and especially his interpretations of its provisions, exerted considerable influence on the judicial process across the kingdom, filling the silence and void in many different *coutumes*. D'Argentré reportedly dismissed Dumoulin's argument, calling it "mirificum Molinaei acumen" (Dumoulin's extraordinary cleverness).[41] The not-so-disguised enmity between these two jurists may be suggestive of the underlying clashes between the custom of the capital and those of the provinces. Dumoulin remained steadfast in his belief that the custom of Paris was the basis for the *droit commun coutumier*.

Le droit commun coutumier

Many legal humanists were convinced that the coordination of customs would be made possible by smoothing out the differences and creating a base of general rules.[42] Their approach consisted of three stages. First, they conducted a

[41] Batiffol and Lagarde, *Droit international privé*, vol. 2, 308. D'Argentré and Dumoulin engaged in the exchange of barbs in which "both sides lacked courtesy." Chénon, *Histoire générale du droit français*, vol. 2, 267–68. The differences in opinion over feudal dues between d'Argentré and Dumoulin are discussed in Church, *Constitutional Thought*, 106–108.

[42] Filhol, *Le premier président Christofle de Thou*, 136; Ourliac and Gazzaniga, *Histoire du droit privé français*, 146–47.

preparatory *conférence* of customs, in order to find similarities and differences among them. Next, they made methodical cross-references to other customs, in accordance with the model of the *Institutes* of Justinian; they usually compared two neighboring customs or compared them with the custom of Paris. Finally, just as Roman law scholars tried to identify major principles from the *Corpus juris civilis*, jurists of customary law attempted to formulate legal principles, interpretive methods, and even rules for the conflict of laws from customs. The distance between custom and Roman law had been reduced, as seen in the inclusion of *légitime* and *représentation successorale* in customary texts.[43] A common law in France would be a customary law illumined by Roman law principles.

A number of comparative commentaries of *coutumes* appeared at the turn of the seventeenth century: among them were *Conférence des coutumes* by Pierre Guénoys (1596), *Institutes coutumières* by Loisel (1607), and *Institution au droit des français* by Coquille (1607).[44] Loisel attempted to extract common precepts from different customs and encapsulate essential elements in the form of adages.[45] Gradually, the notion of French common law of the customs (*droit commun des coutumes de France*) emerged. It was neither a fixed set of rules nor a simple generalization of customary law principles; instead, it referred to an evolving body of opinions of the courts and authors, which aimed to meet the problems of deficiency in individual *coutumes*.[46] The ideal was not to abrogate all contrary customs in order to establish a unified legal system but to delineate common customs that could be used to fill the gaps. Scholars sought to inform judges and lawyers of the general principles of law—or *esprit*—that is most likely adopted in various jurisdictions. In this way, they could address the conflict of customs without resorting to the medieval *jus commune*. Coquille called them the "loix," or "coutumes générales de la France," which would make different customs intelligible to one another.[47]

[43] Meynial, "Remarques sur le rôle joué par la doctrine et la jurisprudence," 329.

[44] Pierre Guénoys, *La conférence des coutumes tant générales, que locales et particulieres du royaume de France . . . avec une briefue explication tirée des loix Romaines* (Paris: Chaudière, 1596). See the modern edition of Loisel, *Institutes coustumières, ou, Manuel de plusieurs et diverses et diverses reigles, sentences, et proverbes*, ed. Reulos.

[45] See Michel Reulos, *Étude sur l'esprit, les sources et la méthode des Institutes coutumières d'Antoine Loisel: Avec 6 photographies du manuscrit original* (Paris: Recueil Sirey, 1935); Paul Henry, "À travers la coutume de Paris et *Les institutes coutumière* de Loisel: Notes de droit civil rétrospectif," *Revue critique de législation et de jurisprudence* 28–39 (1899–1910) (9 parts).

[46] One can say the notion of the *droit commun coutumier* was akin to the creation of the modern American *Restatements of the Law* drafted by the American Law Institute, in that both seek to "restate" the legal rules of secondary authority, heavily annotated with case citations, and to be of use in situations where the law in the jurisdiction is unclear or nonexistent.

[47] "En France sont plusieurs loix generales que chacune Province particulierement a rapportees en ses Coûtumes." *Questions, réponses*, in *Les œuvres*, vol. 2, 126. See Nicolas Warembourg, "Guy Coquille et le droit français: Le droit commun coutumier dans la doctrine juridique du XVIe siècle" (Thèse de doctorat en Droit, Université de Lille 2, 2005).

Loisel titled his book *Institutes coutumières* and Coquille named his *Institution au droit des français*. According to Xavier Martin, the appropriation of the name "Institutes" (textbooks of Roman law) for their works could be either "a profession of faith," affirming their respect for Roman law, or, on the contrary, "a militant act," asserting triumphantly their loyalty to French law.[48] In 1593 Louis Le Caron called his book *Pandectes ou Digeste du droit françois*.[49] In 1605 Pierre de L'Hommeau published *Deux livres de la jurisprudence françoise*.[50] The term *jurisprudence* had been reserved for the science of law—Roman law—so "French jurisprudence" was a novelty.[51] Custom seemingly achieved the intellectual recognition it had long sought.

The *Coutume de Paris* and a Common Law of France

In his *Institution au droit français*, Coquille repeatedly talked about accord among the customs.[52] His examples were rules like *le mort saisit le vif* or *retrait lignager*, in force in many different customs.[53] He thus made a case for the feasibility of creating a law that would be respected across the kingdom. Compared with Dumoulin who argued for a nationwide application of the custom of Paris, however, Coquille was deeply attached to provincial customs. He admired the superb quality of the revised *Coutume de Paris*, a great achievement of learning and

[48] Xavier Martin, "Vie et destinée des coutumes françaises, 1454–1804: Essai de synthèse," *Revue historique de droit français et étranger* 93 (2015), 538.

[49] Louis Le Caron, *Pandectes ou digestes du droict françois* (Lyon: Jehan Veyrat, 1593). He preferred being called Charondas. See Guillaume Leyte, "Charondas et le droit français," *Droit: Revue française de théorie juridique* 39 (2004), 17–33. Le Caron is believed to have been the first author to use the phrase "French law" in the title of a book. See also Louis Le Caron, *Responses ou decisions du droict françois: Confirmees par arrests des cours souveraines de ce royaume et autres; comme aussi des Conseils d'Estat & Privé du Roy, grand Conseil; enrichies de singulieres Observations du droict Romain* (Paris: N. du Fossé, 1605).

[50] Pierre de L'Hommeau, *Deux livres de la iurisprudence françoise* (Saumur: Thomas Portau, 1605).

[51] Martin, "Vie et destinée des coutumes françaises," 537.

[52] "Toutes les Coûtumes de France s'accordent qu'à la haute Justice . . ." (10); "Les coutumes presque toutes s'accordent . . ." (12); "presque toutes les Coutumes s'accordent . . ." (18–19), all in *Institution au droit des François*, in *Les œuvres*, vol. 2.

[53] Many customs agreed on the lord's rights of redemption when the vassal disposed of his fief, except for inheritance or marriage. Coquille stated: "Ainsi dit Paris, art. 26, Melun, article 52 & 53, Sens, artic. 200 & 221, Auxerre, art. 70 & 79, Berry, des fiefs, art. 16 & 41, Orléans, art. 14, Touraine, art. 151 & 190, Blois, art. 87, Troyes, art. 33, Vitry, art. 30, Laon, art. 179, Reims, art. 82." *Institution au droit des François*, in *Les œuvres*, vol. 2, 24. But Coquille would also note discrepancies among the customs: "But Orléans the said art. 14 says that it is not subject to repurchase if the donation was made for God, & in alms. Also Estampes, art. 2, Montfort, art. 17, Reims, article 75 make an exception that, if the descendant donor holds donation without being an heir, it must be subject to repurchase, inasmuch as his donation exceeds the inheritance portion that he would have taken if he had been an heir; the reason for this may be that this excess is not an advance for the heir but is like giving it to a stranger. But Laon, art. 179 says. . . ." Ibid. Numerous analytical comparisons of this kind filled Coquille's treatise. Paulo Slongo, "Genealogie della consuetudine nell'epoca delle guerre di religione in Francia," *Scienza & Politica* 30 (2018), 166.

jurisprudence: "the said articles of the new *coutume* contain for the most part decisions resolving several difficulties and diverse opinions, which have been among French jurisconsults and even decided by solemn judgments."[54] For all this, Coquille remained opposed to recognizing the *Coutume* of Paris as the general custom of the kingdom. Since each province had its own habits and characters, the laws "must also be made in accordance with the taste and sense of each people."[55] He argued:

> Following the same reason that makes us borrow the laws of the Romans, I believe that each province can and should use the *coustumes* of other provinces, even the new *Coustumes de Paris*, by courtesy when domestic *coustumes* fail. It is not because the laws of Paris have any superiority to ours. The estates of each province of Nivernois have as great power and authority in them as the estates of Paris in the Prévôté et Vicomté de Paris.[56]

The notion of the common law of custom was an idea favored mainly by—not unexpectedly—Parisian jurists. Lawyers based in Paris were inclined to support the ideas of a convergence among customs and of an emerging common body of customary law, which the Parlement of Paris was progressively delineating from provincial customs.[57] Because of its vast jurisdiction, the Parlement heard appeals from many districts with different customs. When the local custom was silent, the judges were inspired by the supposed general principles which, in most cases, derived from the custom of Paris.[58] Pasquier, a Parisian lawyer, was unequivocal about the special status of the custom of Paris; it was something "one could resort to in default of other customs, because what Paris is in this kingdom is what Rome was in the Empire."[59]

Yet, custom was local by nature, and many provinces did not wish to give up their autonomy or let their customs be eclipsed by outside customs. The preface

[54] Coquille, *Les coustumes du pays et comté de Nivernois*, in *Les œuvres*, vol. 2, 3. Coquille tended to rate the quality of different local *coutumes* depending on the reputation of the presiding commissioners, and associated the prestige of the *Coutume de Paris* closely with Premier président de Thou, who was "extremely learned, very knowledgeable with French law, and with long and great experiences." Dawson, "French Customs," 789, note 93.

[55] "Puis chacune province a ses mœurs et humeurs diverses; et partant les loix, comme elles ne sont semblables, aussi doivent-elles être faites selon le goût et sens de chacun peuple." *Questions, réponses*, in *Les œuvres*, vol. 2, 125. A similar idea is expressed in ibid., 153.

[56] *Les coustumes du pays et comté de Nivernois*, in *Les œuvres*, vol. 2, 3. Newly published customs of Sens, Melun, Vermandois, Tours, and some other places included "the most beautiful decisions rendered in court judgments." The *coutume* of Nivernais is known for having maintained its French characteristics borrowing only rarely from Roman law. Glasson, *Histoire du droit*, vol. 8, 59–60.

[57] Olivier-Martin, *La coutume de Paris*, 16.

[58] Zink, "Les éditions de coutumes," 488. The custom of Paris was often referred to as a solution when different customs presented a problem of the conflict of laws, from as far away as Toulouse. Chénon, *Histoire générale du droit français*, vol. 2, 317–18.

[59] Pasquier, *Lettres*, book 19, letter 15 (to Robert), in *Les œuvres*, vol. 2, col. 578.

of the reformed *Coutume de Paris* dedicated to the king made note of the strong local sentiments:

> Sir, as in all things, it pleased you to adorn and grace your capital city; it would be the height and perfection of its ornaments if this reduction is done well so that it would prove worthy of being followed and preserved by other provinces of your Kingdom. . . . And should your Majesty find it well to have one sole general custom redacted, promulgated, and compiled for all your provinces, allowing nevertheless each of them to keep its own particular aspects which they never wanted to change, Sir, this would become the greatest work which was ever conceived in these matters by any of your predecessors.[60]

The practitioners in Paris acknowledged that, even though the *Coutume* of Paris could serve as a general custom, it was not *the* customary law and the provinces should keep their own customs. As *avocat* Simon Marion said, "there is no doubt that Paris is the capital city of the kingdom of France; yet it is not a domineering city that has the power to make the laws for others."[61] The creation of a uniform code based on the customary law of Paris was not a proposition to be welcomed by everyone. There was a certain backlash against the fashionable capital that set trends.

The *Coutume de Paris* still held a special place. No less than sixteen commentaries were written on it before 1789, starting from the one by Dumoulin in 1539.[62] Julien Brodeau's *Commentaire sur la coutume de la prévôté de Paris* was reputedly the finest, a classic work marked by erudition, breadth, and originality.[63] For Brodeau (*c.*1585–1563), "the *Coutume de Paris*, of which the sweet and healthy air is breathed by the *messsieurs* of the Parlement, is like the mistress *coutume*, usually extended by their *arrests* to other *coutumes*, for cases that have not been decided there."[64] Besides, the *Coutume de Paris* was based on "the decisions of this great jurisconsult, *Docteur des Docteurs*, who was the powerful genius and learned interpreter of French law, M. Charles du Molin, which one can call with good reason the exemplary and prototype of the *Coutume de Paris*, each article of

[60] *Coutume de Paris* (Paris: Jacques du Puis, 1580). See Reulos, *Étude sur l'esprit, les sources et la méthode des Institutes coutumières d'Antoine Loisel*, 42.

[61] Olivier-Martin, "Les manuscrits de Simon Marion," 45–46.

[62] They include Claude de Ferrière, *Nouveau commentaire sur la coutume de la prévoté et vicomte de Paris*, ed. Sauvan d'Aramon, 2 vols. (Lyon: J. S. Grabit, 1779, 1746); and Eusèbe de Laurière, *Texte des coutumes de la prévôté et vicomte de Paris . . . avec beaucoup de notes nouvelles*, 3 vols. (Paris: Nyon, 1777).

[63] Julien Brodeau, *Commentaire sur la coustume de la prévosté et vicomté de Paris, fait par Maistre Julien Brodeau . . . avec un recueil des arrests cotez sur chaque tiltre et article de ladite coutume . . .*, 2 vols. (Paris: P. Rocolet, 1658). Brodeau did not finish his work before he died in 1653; his commentary covered up to Art. 186 of the *Coutumes*. Glasson, *Histoire du droit*, vol. 8, 46.

[64] Brodeau, *Commentaire sur la coutume de la prévôté de Paris*, vol. 1, 3.

which is truly *un Oracle, & un Arrest*."[65] In 1747 François Bourjon (?–1751) wrote *Le droit commun de la France et la coutume de Paris*, in which he popularized Dumoulin's idea that the custom of Paris was the common law of France.[66] The *Coutume de Paris* was basically the collection of the decisions of the Parlement of Paris, which granted it special weight.[67]

Evidence shows that Dumoulin, an undisputed genius, did not ingratiate himself with others. Not a few contemporary authors were subjected to his intellectual abuse bordering on personal attack. Coquille stridently protested what he saw as Dumoulin's unwarranted criticism of Guillaume Bourgoin, a royal commissioner at the redaction of the custom of Nivernais in 1534, for having drafted an article privileging masculinity in collateral succession. In Coquille's words, Dumoulin "deserved praise for his great and excellent knowledge" but he also "deserved blame for his great and usual slander as in this and several other cases.[68] Coquille attested that he was aware firsthand of the ill-conceived nature of Dumoulin's reproof of Bourgoin because he was Bourgoin's own nephew, son of his sister, and he could vouchsafe that Bourgoin had no personal interest in proposing that rule. Coquille could not restrain himself from pointing out that Dumoulin was a partisan of the "nouvelle opinions de la Religion, non pas de Calvin, mais de Luther" and likely had "some animosity against the said Bourgoin who was an adversary of the said new opinions *ex professo*." Legal opinions were not immune from religious sentiments in the early modern period, no more than academic disputes are independent of ideological clashes in modern times. Dumoulin, it seems, had reason to feel persecuted.

Doctrinal authors' search for the spirit of common law of customs relied on the sustainability of court opinions. Jurisprudence emerged as a veritable source of law in the sixteenth century.

2. Jurisprudence as a Source of Law

In ancien régime France, court decision was a subsidiary source of law applicable only in the absence of other sources. In a lawsuit, the parlement would take a judicial notice that there was neither custom nor legislation that could provide a solution to the case, before proceeding to its *arrêts de règlement*.[69] The obligatory force of these decisions continued so long as the legal void remained unfilled.

[65] Ibid.

[66] Bourjon, *Le droit commun de la France, et la Coutume de Paris réduits en principes*, 2 vols. On Bourjon, see Alain Wijffels, "Ancien Régime France: Legal Particularism under the Absolute Monarchy," in Sean Patrick Donlan and Dirk Heirbaut (eds.), *The Laws' Many Bodies: Studies in Legal Hybridity and Jurisdictional Complexity, c1600–1900* (Berlin: Duncker & Humblot, 2015), 93–99.

[67] Ferrière, *Nouveau commentaire sur la coutume*, vol. 1, 3.

[68] *Les coustumes du pays et comté de Nivernois*, in *Les œuvres*, vol. 2, 359 (ch. 34, art. 14).

[69] Lebrun, *La coutume*, 109.

Alternatively, when the meaning of a customary rule was disputed in litigation and judges upheld a particular construction of the rule, it became the law.

The Parlement of Paris ordered its decrees to be published broadly in the districts "to govern other like cases" or "to serve as law for the future."[70] The idea traced to Aristotle that like cases should be treated alike turned the court rulings into general principles, applicable across its jurisdiction. This led the judge to devise a rational conception of judicial activity and expanded the scope of precedents as case law.[71] The accumulation of *res judicata* prompted a redefinition of the sources of law.

Arrêt de règlement and Judicial Secrecy

There were various reasons for magistrates to resort to precedents. By following precedents, the judge would not have to elaborate a new solution for each case, and the fear of having the decision overturned on appeal would lessen.[72] It also reduced pressure on the judge from the parties who wanted to be treated like the others who came before them. Judicial decisions in France did not provide the "motives," that is, the reasoning that determined the result of the case. The fact that the opinions of the royal courts were not motivated (*motivés*) was one of the most unique aspects of the French judicial system, and it significantly diminished the force of court decisions as precedents.[73] Judges were not only not required to provide reasons for their decisions but were prohibited from doing so. From the first half of the fourteenth century, the court decision consisted of the enumeration of procedural elements and collected proofs, with no reasoning of the court appended. The royal ordinances in 1344 imposed the secrecy of deliberation, and judges and other court officials were threatened with suspension or dismissal from office for violating their oaths of secrecy.[74] The Ordinance of March 1550 forbade the revelation of the "opinions" of the judges, either before or after the judgment.[75] Until the Revolution, the decrees of the Parlement of Paris did not include the reasoning of its rulings.

[70] Dawson, *The Oracles*, 310–11.

[71] Robert Jacob, "Jugement des hommes et jugement de Dieu à l'aube du Moyen Âge," in Robert Jacob (ed.), *Le juge et le jugement dans les traditions juridiques européennes* (Paris: Librairie générale de droit et de jurisprudence, 1996), 44.

[72] *Arrêts de règlement* of the Parlements were observed in inferior jurisdictions. Chénon, *Histoire générale du droit français*, vol. 2, 362.

[73] Beauthier and de Broux, "Un regard historien," 730–34. See Philippe Godding, "Jurisprudence et motivation des décisions des sentences," in Chaim Perelman and Paul Foriers (eds.), *La motivation des décisions de justice* (Brussels: Établissements Émile Bruyland, 1978), 37–67; Tony Sauvel, "Histoire du jugement motivé," *Revue du droit public et de la société politique en France et à l'étranger* 71 (1955), 5–53.

[74] Dawson, *The Oracles*, 288.

[75] Art. 14, Ordinance of March 1550, *Recueil général*, vol. 14, 157.

Why this judicial secrecy? The official reason was that judges of the sovereign courts, whose powers were delegated by the king, were entitled to make a decision at will.[76] The king was not obligated to explain his decisions, and neither were his judges. The decisions of the parlement could not be contested on appeal, even though the parlement could correct its own judgment. If the reason for the decisions had been given, it would be difficult to modify them without undermining the authority of *res judicata* and, above all, the sovereignty of the king from whom they held their power. The secrecy was thus deemed necessary to safeguard judicial duty.[77] Here, one notes the court's reluctance to divulge its reasoning and deliberation was crucially related to the difficulty of the proof of custom: the problem of having to render decisions on the precarious grounds of custom dictated judicial secrecy. In short, judges refrained from stating reasons for their rulings because they could not prove the custom they applied.

Judges understandably were concerned with preserving their liberty to find, modify, and interpret custom, and the rule of nonmotivation was important in maintaining such flexibility. The recording of local customs in the sixteenth century apparently did little to curtail the needs for secrecy.[78] The absence of motivated opinions allowed the parlement, if necessary, to depart from its own precedents, because it was almost impossible for the parties to prove the similarities of cases. Lawyers' arguments could always be rejected on the grounds that the facts were not the same.[79] In this way judicial secrecy may have promoted the autonomy of judges, but it impeded jurisprudential development, rendering it difficult for a lawyer or a judge to make an argument relying on precedents.

The publication of *arrêts* helped resolve these problems in part. From the fifteenth century, some practitioners, called *arrêtistes*, began preparing collections of important decisions of the sovereign courts and wrote commentaries, comparing them with the relevant customary or legislative provisions.[80] They claimed they were creating a theory of jurisprudence on specific questions of law through deduction.[81] The main readers of the published *arrêts* were their fellow legal practitioners.[82] The sovereign courts were not opposed to the publication of *arrêts*; indeed many *arrêtistes* were judges of the court in which the cases had been decided.[83] The collections of decisions included the facts of the cases, procedures, and sometimes arguments of different parties, making it possible for the reader to discern judicial reasoning. This unique literature helped the wide dissemination

[76] Dawson, *The Oracles*, 289. [77] Beauthier and de Broux, "Un regard historien," 732–33.

[78] Sauvel, "Histoire du jugement motivé," 10–25; Dawson, *The Oracles*, 287.

[79] Serge Dauchy and Véronique Demars-Sion, "La non-motivation des décisions judiciaires dans l'ancien droit: Principe ou usage?" *Revue historique de droit français et étranger* 82 (2004), 236.

[80] Dawson, *The Oracles*, 297.

[81] Hilaire, "Questions autour de la jurisprudence des arrêts," 25–29.

[82] In the courtroom, practitioners often referred to the opinions of the *arrêtistes* rather than citing the *arrêts* themselves. See Beauthier and de Broux, "Un regard historien," 735.

[83] Dauchy and Demars-Sion, "La non-motivation des décisions judiciaires," 238.

of court decisions and their development into precedents. Jean-Baptiste Denisart (1713–1765), one of the most famous *arrêtistes* in the eighteenth century, affirmed that "if several *arrêts* judged the same question in the same manner, this forms a usage and jurisprudence which the judges must not break from without reason."[84] Lawyers appearing before the parlement padded their pleadings with the *arrêts* that supported their cases.

Roman Law as *Raison écrite*

While in the *pays de droit coutumier* the custom of Paris was regarded by many as the *coutume générale*, in the *pays de droit écrit* law pivoted around the code of Justinian as the *coutume générale*. Roman law in observance in the south was a Roman law that had been filtered to accommodate each provincial parlement's tradition and sufficiently adapted to local needs.[85] The efforts of the Renaissance jurists to revive a purist Roman law did little to change that. The state of Roman law outside the Midi was complicated. It was the *droit supplétif* in the *pays coutumiers* that bordered the *pays de droit écrit*, such as Berry, Haute Marche, Auvergne, and Bourbonnais. In the *pays coutumiers* proper, it was written reason (*raison écrite*).[86] These designations had different effects in judicial practice.

At least from the fourteenth century, jurists in interpreting laws distinguished between the supplementary authority (*authorité supplétive*) and the doctrinal authority (*authorité doctrinale*) of legal sources. In the *pays de droit coutumier*, where Roman law existed as a purely doctrinal authority in the form of *ratio scripta*, the judge could refer to Roman law only if it was in conformity with the dominant principles of the custom in his jurisdiction and only if it seemed just to him; even when it seemed just to him (that is, *ratio scripta* for him), he could still decide to turn to a different *coutume* instead, the *coutume* of Paris for example if he deemed it preferable. Where Roman law had an authority as *droit supplétif*, on the contrary, the judge was obliged, in the absence of the applicable custom, to apply Roman law even if he found it unreasonable.[87]

Coquille famously reported that *premier président* Pierre Lizet "held Roman civil law to be our common law, and attempted to accommodate our French law to Roman law as much as possible, and considered what was contrary to Roman

[84] *Collection de décisions nouvelles et de notions relatives à la jurisprudence actuelle* (Paris, 1793), cited from Beauthier and de Broux, "Un regard historien," 735. See also Hilaire, "Questions autour de la jurisprudence des arrêts," 35. The practice of *arrêts de règlement* was fiercely condemned at the time of the redaction of the Civil Code in the nineteenth century.

[85] Gruber-Magitot, *Les conflits de coutumes*, 22.

[86] Chénon, *Histoire générale du droit français*, vol. 2, 331–33.

[87] Distinction between *authorité supplétive* and *authorité doctrinale* was laid down in the ordinance of Philip IV in 1312 and affirmed by the edict of Henry IV in 1609. Ibid., vol. 1, 508–10.

law to be *droit étroit* which should be limited in application."[88] By contrast, Coquille went on, Lizet's successor de Thou regarded the customs and French law as "our common law" and called Roman law "raison écrite."[89] This juxtaposition of the supposedly opposing opinions of these two great jurists of sixteenth-century France has been reiterated many times, seen as something akin to the rift between Germanists and Romanists in nineteenth-century Germany. Yet some protested that Coquille's characterization of the views of Lizet and de Thou was inaccurate, overly simplified. Jean Bouhier (1673–1746), *premier président* at the Parlement of Burgundy, expressed doubt, asking how de Thou, an admirer of Roman law, could have "followed the opinion of Dumoulin entirely" or "found customary law in general more equitable than Roman law." Citing a contemporary commentator who viewed the alleged dispute between Lizet and de Thou as "nothing more than a dispute over name," Bouhier concluded: "If de Thou believed that Roman law was followed less as statute [*loi*] than as reason [*raison*], we are still subject to it because reason is the principle of all the laws [*la raison est le principe de toutes les loix*]."[90]

Bouhier's skepticism about what he viewed as Coquille's exaggeration of a semantic dispute seems well grounded. Lizet oversaw the reformation of the custom of Berry with a vision to make it more reasonable, aligned with the jurisprudence of the Parlement of Paris. The conventional reputation of Lizet as the archetype of a magistrate hostile to customary law needs reconsideration.[91] In the same vein, de Thou may have been the last person to question the authority of Roman law. Both Lizet and de Thou shared the belief that Roman law was the foundation of legal science and equitable interpretation. As William Church pointed out, "the very indefiniteness" of interpretation of law allowed jurists to refer to the Roman system.[92] There is little evidence that de Thou perceived his campaign as a movement to stamp out the influence of Roman law from customs.

[88] Coquille, *Les coustumes du pays et comté de Nivernois*, in *Les œuvres*, vol. 2, 2; also *Questions, réponses et méditations*, 126.

[89] "Et ledit de Thou estimoit les Coutumes & le Droit Francois, etre notre Droit Commun, & appelloit le Droit Romain la raison ecrite." Coquille, *Les coustumes du pays et comté de Nivernois*, in *Les œuvres*, vol. 2, 2. Coquille attributed the term "written reason" to de Thou, but obviously it had been in use for some time. Gruber-Magitot, *Les conflits de coutumes*, 29.

[90] Bouhier, *Observation sur la coutume de Bourgogne*, ch. 4, no. 68, in *Les œuvres de jurisprudence*, vol. 1, 396–97.

[91] Lizet did not try to Romanize the custom of Berry, which had already been broadly penetrated by Roman law. Poumarède, "Droit romain et rédaction des coutumes," 125; Thireau, "Le comparatisme et la naissance du droit français," 158. Incidentally, Lizet was one of the many jurists who had to endure Dumoulin's intellectual assault. Dumoulin openly accused Lizet of plagiarizing his writings. Dumoulin, "with his usual self-effacement," wrote in several places in *Le grand coustumier general*: "Lizet took this from my writings and added it"; "This view of mine was imitated by Lizet on this point"; "This is the inequitable addition of Pierre Lizet." See Dawson, "French Customs," 789, note 93. Whether these were valid accusations is open to debate. For Lizet, see Jacqueline Vendrand-Voyer, "Reformation des coutumes et droit romain. Pierre Lizet et la coutume de Berry," *Annales de la faculté de droit et de science politique de Clermont* 18 (1981), 313–81.

[92] Church, *Constitutional Thought*, 276.

The real significance of Coquille's anecdote, then, is that it captured the shift of balance between Roman law and French custom in the wake of the reformation of customs. For Chasseneuz, Tiraqueau, and Cujas in the early and mid-sixteenth century, the authority of Roman law as *lex scripta* was not questioned. For Pasquier and Coquille in the late sixteenth century, by contrast, Roman law was *ratio scripta*; Franco-Germanic customs, not Roman law, were the basis for French law. Coquille did not hide his hostility toward Roman law doctors who tried to cite "an infinite multitude of authorities" or at least "as many laws as other doctors." They pretended to invent some new opinions but in reality they were merely "adherents to the opinions of the glosses and the doctors of their party, even against their own sentiment" and their discourses were "more artifice than substance."[93] By pitting Lizet against de Thou, Coquille highlighted what he perceived as the transition of Roman's authority from *lex* to *ratio*. Here, the historicist perspectives of Coquille and Pasquier, as well as of Dumoulin, and their recognition of the historical significance of the customary law campaign appear evident. Humanist intellectual impulses and insights inspired them to defend French customs but at the same time to resort to Roman law without hesitation. The humanists reaffirmed the practical significance of Roman law in the aftermath of the codification of customs. Based on their firm acknowledgment of its value as a doctrinal, theoretical, and moral authority, they concerned themselves to establish logical relations between Roman law and customary law. Despite their rhetoric, they were too sophisticated to succumb to a rudimentary discourse of clash between national law and foreign law.

The decline of the medieval *jus commune* and the humanist challenge to the primacy of the *Corpus juris* seldom affected the place of Roman law in France.[94] Analysis of the pleadings (*plaidoyers*) at the Parlement of Paris shows that lawyers resorted to Roman law much more frequently than custom or legislation.[95] Because judicial opinions did not disclose judges' reasoning, it is impossible to determine precisely on which law a case was disposed of, but, gathering from lawyers' discourses, judicial practice changed little as far as legal sources were

[93] Coquille, *Les coutumes du pays et comte de Nivernais*, in *Les œuvres*, vol. 2, 3–4.

[94] Krynen, "Le droit romain 'droit commun de la France,'" 23–26; Jean-Louis Thireau, "L'alliance des lois romaines avec le droit français," in Krynen (ed.), *Droit romain, jus civile et droit français*, 354–55. See also Nicolas Warembourg, "Romanisation du droit privé français," in Jacques Krynen and Bernard d'Alteroche (eds.), *L'Histoire du droit en France: Nouvelles tendances, nouveaux territoires* (Paris: Classiques Garnier, 2014), 45–67; Jean Gaudemet, "Les persistances du droit romain dans les traditions juridiques occidentales," in Durand and Mayali (eds.), *Excerptiones iuris*, 227–60.

[95] Marie Houllemare, "La norme dans les plaidoyers d'avocats parisiens du XVIe siècle," in Benoît Garnot and Pascal Bastien (eds.), *Normes juridiques et pratiques judiciaires du Moyen Âge à l'époque contemporaine* (Dijon: Éditions Universitaires de Dijon, 2007), 83–91. See also Marie Houllemare, *Politiques de la parole: Le Parlement de Paris au XVIe siècle* (Geneva: Droz, 2011); Marie Houllemare, "Un avocat parisien entre art oratoire et promotion de soi (fin XVIe siècle)," *Revue historique* 630 (2004), 283–302.

concerned.[96] Often, the Roman law texts cited in legal arguments had nothing to do with the questions at issue in litigation.[97]

Renaissance jurists were men of culture, and they felt compelled to display copious citations from the sources of antiquity. The Ordinance of Villers-Cotterêts of 1539 required the use of French language in both pleadings and court rulings, which nevertheless continued to be inundated with lengthy Latin quotations.[98] An example of the irrepressible enthusiasm of the contemporaries for Roman law materials comes from none other than Christophe de Thou. De Thou's pleadings as an *avocat* exhibited a phenomenal propensity for classical sources. In one such case argued in 1546, de Thou almost "drowned" the audience with citations, three-quarters of which came from the *Corpus juris civilis*.[99] His predilection for humanist eloquence continued after he became the *premier président* of the Parlement. De Thou encouraged the lawyers to follow his examples when they pleaded before the court.[100] Pasquier praised de Thou's ability to render excellent judicial *arrêts* on the spot, extracting effortlessly key solutions from difficult legal passages, but he was much less impressed with the president's affinity to citations.[101] Pasquier lamented that the *avocats*, in imitation of de Thou, tended to "piece together, or rather patch up" passages from literary authors ad nauseam, simply to demonstrate their knowledge and eloquence.[102] De Thou's discourse of May 11, 1565, was a specimen of his rhetorical style, interspersed with an abundance of quotes.[103] His lifetime work of systematizing French customs and his

[96] Houllemare, "La norme dans les plaidoyers," 90.

[97] Gruber-Magitot, *Les conflits de coutumes*, 53. For lawyerly propensity for massive citations, see Marc Fumaroli, *L'âge de l'éloquence: rhétorique et 'res literaria,' de la Renaissance au seuil de l'époque classique*. 2nd ed. (Paris: Albin Michel, 1994), 444–46, 489–90.

[98] See Katie Chenoweth, "The Force of a Law: Derrida, Montaigne, and the Edict of Villers-Cotterêts (1539)," *The Comparatist* 36 (2012), 67–85.

[99] When he defended the property rights of Seigneur de Laval in May 1546, de Thou made 752 citations, whereas normal pleadings included about a dozen references. His sources consisted of the *Digest* (52 percent), the *Code* (15 percent), feudal law (10 percent), canon law (9 percent), commentators (7 percent), customs (5 percent), and literature (1 percent). Houllemare, "La norme dans les plaidoyers," 86. In a pleading in December 1547 on behalf of Francis II de Dinteville, bishop of Auxerre, de Thou cited as authorities "the New and Old Testament, Cicero, Ovid, Aulus-Gellius, Publius Syrus, St. Jerome, Tertullian, the principle *cessante causa*, examples from history of France, popular proverbs, and finally common opinion." Elizabeth A. R. Brown, "Le greffe civil du Parlement de Paris au XVIe siècle: Jean du Tillet et les régistres des plaidoiries," *Bibliothèque de l'École des chartes* 153 (1995), 369, note 148. Brown argues that the legal rhetoric of the time in general and de Thou's style in particular merit a study.

[100] Maugis, *Histoire du Parlement*, vol. 3, 190, 216, 246; Brown, "Le greffe civil du Parlement de Paris," 369, note 147; Filhol, in *Le premier président Christofle de Thou*, 34–35.

[101] Pasquier, *Lettres*, book 7, letter 10 (to M. de La Bite), in *Les œuvres* , vol. 2, col. 187. This letter was written shortly after de Thou's death.

[102] Pasquier deplored French jurists' slavish dependence on citations: "nous seuls entre toutes les autres nations faisons profession de rapiecer, ou pour mieux dire, rapetasser nostre eloquence, de divers passages." *Lettres*, book 7, letter 12 (to Loisel), col. 192.

[103] See Sylvie Daubresse, "Un discours de Christophe de Thou premier président du Parlement de Paris (11 mai 1565)," *Bibliothèque de l'École des chartes* 153 (1995), 373–89.

reputation as the "partisan of the supremacy of custom" did not stop him from being a fervent devotee to Roman law authorities.[104]

National law and custom advocated by humanists laid an important foundation for the philosophical conception of law, but the latter had limited impact in the courtroom. There were differences between theory and practice and also between doctrine and jurisprudence. Commentaries on custom continued to appear but the presence of custom in the pleadings steadily declined.[105] Lawyerly disregard for domestic legal sources was apparently incorrigible. Royal ordinances were rarely cited and, when cited, they were mainly to reject other contradictory royal laws.[106] Judges continued to interpret custom and legislation in light of *jus commune*. It was a universal, accepted tendency in the early modern period.[107] Pasquier once lamented: "*Mon Dieu*, shame on me, we abandon the law of France in order to win cases!"[108]

Roman law remained an undeniable source of inspiration and an indispensable mode of thought. Jurists continuously drew particular solutions as well as general propositions from it. The logic, structure, and terminology of Roman law underpinned French law for centuries, and even diehard nationalists did not imagine doing away with it. As seen in Dumoulin's case, commentaries written on customary texts were not very different in approaches from those authored by the medieval glosssators and Bartolists on *Corpus juris civilis*.[109]

A question arose in the minds of contemporary jurists: if the Romans could compile the *Corpus juris civilis*, could the French not create a French code? The idea started with the modest goal of translating Roman law into French. In 1555, François Némond, a professor of Roman law at the University of Poitiers, eulogized "good king Louis XI" who "wisely contemplated that there should be only *un Droit, et une Loi et Coutume* across the kingdom and that all should be in a common language."[110] Inspired by the royal prescience, Némond embarked on a project of translating the *Institutes* of Justinian into French to "turn all of Roman law into French."[111] Others would go beyond translation or restatement.

Writing more as historian than as jurist, Bodin argued that comparative methods could bring a new system of universal jurisprudence. In his preface to

[104] Houllemare, "La norme dans les plaidoyers," 87. De Thou's knowledge of Roman law was widely admired. Pope Gregory XIII in 1572 commissioned de Thou to undertake bibliographical research on Roman law to correct errors of the Gratian's *Decretum*. Filhol, *Le premier président Christofle de Thou*, 30, note. 3.

[105] Houllemare, "La norme dans les plaidoyers," 89.

[106] Ibid., 87. [107] Reulos (ed.), *Institutes coustumières*, 37.

[108] "Pour sauver nos causes, nous perdions le droit de la France!" Pasquier, *Lettres*, book 9, letter 1 (to Brisson), in *Les œuvres*, vol. 2, col. 224.

[109] Filhol, *Le premier président Christofle de Thou*, 215–18.

[110] See Trevor Peach, "Le droit romain en français au XVIe siècle: Deux Oraisons de François de Némond (1555)," *Revue historique de droit français et étranger* 60 (1982), 40.

[111] Némond declared: "Ignorance of *Droit* is the mother and nurse of all evils." Peach, "Le droit romain en français au XVIe siècle," 29.

Methodus ad facilem historiarum cognitionem, Bodin pointed out the negative influence of the *Corpus juris civilis* on legal education. He implied that jurists were at fault for failing to reform legal science:

> We have almost countless writers who by their commentaries have augmented the civil law of the Romans to such an extent that it seems to suffer from no one thing more, from no more serious malady, than its own huge size. Indeed, the more inept each one was in writing, the more did he pour forth a multitude of books; yet I see no one who has compressed into graceful form the scattered and disjointed material found.[112]

Scholars should "read Plato, who thought there was one way to establish law and govern a state: wise men should bring together and compare the legal framework of all states, or of the more famous states, and from them compile the best kind."[113] It is notable that Bodin's program of a common law of all nations pointed in the direction of a code.

Many of his contemporaries were more impatient. Convinced that the categories employed by the codifiers of the *Corpus juris civilis* caused unnecessary confusion and error, they felt confident in reorganizing the existing material in Roman law by using new improved categories and having them sewn into French law. Linking Roman law and French law was an unambiguous doctrinal current at the end of the sixteenth and the beginning of the seventeenth centuries. The title of Jean Duret's book was *L'Alliance des lois romaines avec le droit français* (1600).[114] In a similar category stood Le Caron's *Responses ou decisions du droict françois confirmées par arrests des cours souveraines* (1605) and Étienne Pasquier's *Interprétation des Institutes de Justinian.*[115] Others, infused with an ever robust nationalism, contemplated reducing all French laws into one body on the model of the *Corpus juris civilis*.

[112] Bodin, *Method for the Easy Comprehension of History*, "Dedication," 2. "When there was no opportunity for the good arts or for culture, their writings have frightened many away from this branch of knowledge," 4. Bodin acknowledged the achievements of legal humanists, but "after investigators started to clear the approach, then the statutes of the Romans seemed to be restored to their early value." He mentioned the names of William Durand, Guy du Faur, Chasseneuz, Bohier, Baron, Connan, Tiraqueau, Brisson, and "the ornament of our college, Du Moulin," from whom he "learned valuable lessons in teaching and judging civil causes" while "from the others almost nothing," 5. Bodin's idea of comparative methods of law was shared by his contemporary François Baudouin in *De institutione historiae universae et ejus cum Jurisprudentia conjunctione prolegomenon* (1698). For Baudouin, see Kelley, *Foundations of Modern Historical Scholarship*, 116–48.

[113] Bodin, *Method for the Easy Comprehension of History*, 2.

[114] *Alliance des Loix Romaines avec le Droict François, contenui aux Ordonnances des Roys, arrests des Cours souveraines et Coustumes provinciales, le tout rapporte aux articles des Coustumes de Bourbonnois* (Paris, 1600). See Thireau, "L'alliance des lois romaines avec le droit français."

[115] For analysis, see Wijffels, "Ancien Régime France." Pasquier's book was edited and published in 1847.

3. Legislation and Legal Unity

France in the mid-sixteenth century radiated a distinctive intellectual current of humanist scholarly engagement. Chancellor L'Hôpital represented an opinion that Roman law provided a model for uniform jurisdiction and coherent application of the laws.[116] There was a reformist circle of jurists in the 1560s around L'Hôpital, who was a sort of *doyen* for legal humanists who shared his literary inspirations and political vision.[117] They strongly denounced judicial corruption.[118] They aspired to a legal unity, turning the humanist achievements into the creation of a more rational legal system. Among them was François Hotman.[119]

Hotman's *Antitribonian*

Hotman proposed that all public and private laws be organized into a single system of code, with legislation superseding incoherent and contradictory customs. His treatise *Antitribonian*, written in 1567, was a critique of the work by Tribonian (*c*.475–545), who had compiled the *Digest* on the order of Justinian. Hotman's analysis of the East Roman minister's alleged distortion of Roman law served as a springboard for his call for the compilation of a national code.

Antitribonian bears on the title page the statement that the book was written on the advice of Chancellor L'Hôpital.[120] Hotman wrote in the last chapter of *Antitribonian*:

> It would give us much pleasure, it seems to me, and principally in this time when God gave us a Solon in our France, who is this great Michel de L'Hôpital, to gather a number of jurists, together with some statesmen and also the most capable lawyers and legal practitioners in this kingdom, and charge them to report together what they have learned and drawn from the books of Justinian (of which they could choose the most beautiful and the best, which would be

[116] "As for the morass of local customs in the sphere of private law, it is likely that L'Hôpital, like Hotman, was ready to design a national code ab initio." Salmon, *Society in Crisis*, 158.

[117] In 1564, when Dumoulin was imprisoned after he published his *Conseil sur le faict du concile de Trente*, L'Hôpital was among those who helped secure his release. Thireau, *Charles du Moulin*, 50–52.

[118] John H. M. Salmon, "France," in J. H. Burns and Mark Goldie (eds.), *The Cambridge History of Political Thought 1450–1700* (Cambridge: Cambridge University Press, 1991), 469.

[119] Ralph E. Giesey and John H. M. Salmon (eds.), *Francogallia by François Hotman* (Cambridge: Cambridge University Press, 1972), "Introduction," 3, 27; Ralph E. Giesey, "When and Why Hotman Wrote the *Francogallia*," *Bibliothèque d'humanisme et Renaissance* 29 (1967), 602; Kelley, "'Second Nature,'" 150–57. François Hotman took refuge in 1567 with the chancellor who had been his patron for the past five years. Donald R. Kelley, *François Hotman: A Revolutionary's Ordeal* (Princeton: Princeton University Press, 1973), 191.

[120] "L'Antitribonian . . . fait par l'advis de feu Monsieur de l'Hospital, Chancelier de France, en l'an 1567." Hotman traveled to Paris in the fall of 1567, around the time of his writing of *Antitribonian*, and paid a visit to Chancellor L'Hôpital. Giesey, "When and Why Hotman Wrote the *Francogallia*," 596.

> truly an invaluable treasure), from the books of philosophy, and finally from the experience which they have acquired in practice. . . . Thus, after such a conference and report, it would follow that the deputies would draw up one or two good volumes, written in the vernacular and in intelligible language, of public law which deals with matters of the state and the crown as well as all the parts of private law. And they should follow, in what might seem desirable to them, the order and continuation of the said books of Justinian, and adjust all things, as has been said necessary from the beginning, to the status and form of the French Republic.[121]

Inspired by his patron, Hotman proposed the creation of a French code, including private as well as public law, with recourse to Roman law principles, this by royal order just as had been done in the East Roman Empire.

Scholars have warned that Hotman's treatment of Roman law in the *Antitribonian* can easily be misconstrued. Like other humanists, Hotman believed that the *Corpus juris civilis* was particular to ancient Rome, with little relevance to French culture and institutions. He defended France's independence from the emperor and asserted Roman law had no authority in France. A full two-thirds of the work was concerned with attack on Roman law and criticism of Tribonian for his alleged hack job.[122] When Hotman's message finally took the form of a positive proposal for his times, however, he was confident that the *Corpus juris* could be the source for legal reform in France. This seemingly paradoxical pro- and anti-Tribonian nature in Hotman was likely due to his understanding of the distinct but related nature of public and private law.[123] For Hotman, public law did not lend itself to universal rules but was peculiar to each nation. It must be derived from historical study and not from philosophical speculation. The public law of Rome, governing the form of its civil institutions, reflected the unique circumstances of that state and thus had no validity for French law.

Hotman elaborated on this opinion in his *Francogallia*, first published in 1573.[124] He devoted the chapters of *Francogallia* to a detailed comparison between Roman law and French law, to show how the terminology and the substance of Roman law were incongruous with those of French law. He studied early Frankish institution in Chapters 3 through 9 of his book, "to illustrate the theme that each nation has its own ancient constitution and custom and that the Franks owed nothing to Roman law." Still, he was reluctant to adhere to an absolute dichotomy between the historical and national nature of public law and the universal nature

[121] Hotman, *Antitribonian*, ch. 18 ("Advis sur l'espérance de quelque réformation"), 153–55.

[122] Giesey, "When and Why Hotman Wrote the *Francogallia*," 598–99. See *Francogallia*, ed. Giesey and Salmon, "Editor's Introduction," 62–72.

[123] Giesey, "When and Why Hotman Wrote the *Francogallia*," 601.

[124] Hotman likely began his first version of the *Francogallia* in late 1567. *Francogallia*, ed. Giesey and Salmon, "Editor's Introduction," 7.

of private law. In *Antitribonian*, Hotman expressed his belief that both public law and private law were amenable to universal as well as historical principles, each to a differing degree.[125] The formation of the French code could borrow from other systems of law what was reasonable, contingent on their being regulated according to the peculiarities of French public law.[126] Public law and the constitution, or political law, were the product of history; in comparison, the stake of history was less prominent in private law, allowing it to be put into a code in imitation of Roman law in form and substance.[127]

The idea that private law could be analyzed according to the universal principles enshrined in the *Corpus juris* was nothing new. Dumoulin offered his bifurcated view of Roman public and private law.[128] The difference between Dumoulin and Hotman resided in their specific programs for how to achieve legal unity. Dumoulin proposed the unification of law as an integral part of the unity of the state, and he elaborated the theory of a customary common law, a compendium of general principles gathered from the customs. Hotman, some two decades junior to Dumoulin, shared a similar vision but took a more extreme stance, proposing a codification of French law on the authority of the crown.[129] Hotman seemed in all aspects to aspire to a task similar to the one that had been given to Tribonian by Emperor Justinian.[130]

Hotman did not doubt that the Justinian Code offered not only principles for the organization of the new code but also some of the best examples of natural equity.[131] He evoked Cicero's ideal of a single code of laws based upon the general principles of equity. Note Hotman articulated his concrete program of codification in the last chapter of *Antitribonian*. Having made amply clear his disapproval of Tribonian's work, Hotman at last acknowledged the significance of the compilation of a single code in the sixth century which, he argued, should be imitated by the French in the sixteenth century. As with other humanists, his loud pronouncements on the irrelevance of Roman law in France should be taken with a grain of salt. Hotman exuded immense intellectual confidence, shared by his contemporary French jurists, that they could do a better job than the East Romans.

[125] Giesey, "When and Why Hotman Wrote the *Francogallia*," 604; Zachary Sayre Schiffman, "An Anatomy of the Historical Revolution in Renaissance France," *Renaissance Quarterly* 42 (1989), 511–14; *Francogallia*, ed. Giesey and Salmon, "Editor's Introduction," 27–28 and 33–34.

[126] Giesey, "When and Why Hotman Wrote the *Francogallia*," 603–604.

[127] *Francogallia*, ed. Giesey and Salmon, "Editor's Introduction," 33.

[128] Thireau, *Charles du Moulin*, 199.

[129] For a comparison of the codification projects proposed by Dumoulin and Hotman, see Henry Cauvière, *L'idée de codification en France avant la rédaction du Code civil* (Paris: A. Rousseau, 1910); van Kan, *Les efforts de codification en France*, ch. 3.

[130] Pierre Mesnard, "François Hotman (1524–1590) et le complexe de Tribonien," *Bulletin de la Société de l'histoire du protestantisme français* 101 (1955), 117–37.

[131] Giesey, "When and Why Hotman Wrote the *Francogallia*," 599; Davis, "Sovereign Subjects, Feudal Law," 232.

Legal Institutions and Political Authority

Scholars agree that Hotman's political and constitutional views turned stringent after *Antitribonian*. Hotman's subsequent Monarchomach political thought located legislative sovereignty not in the royal will but in the Estates General, the successor of the ancient Frankish assemblies. In *Francogallia*, he declared that "the highest administrative authority in the kingdom" was vested in the assembly of the three estates.[132] The laws created by the Estates General and *coutumes* were older than the kings, he contended, and the prince could not pretend that he was the author of them and violate them. All in all, Hotman's slipshod historical arguments for the sovereignty of the people seemed a particular outcome of a particular time in French history.

The radical shift in Hotman indicated that by this time he had parted company with the thought of his former patron L'Hôpital, who died in 1573. L'Hôpital unfalteringly upheld the power of the crown to make and execute law and insisted that the Estates, along with the parlements, had a purely advisory and consultative role. Here it would be helpful to examine how the monarchy in the 1560s and 1570s dealt with the two institutions in its quest for legislative authority.

The old medieval idea that the king governs *par grand conseil* persisted in the ancien régime.[133] In theory, major legislative actions in the sixteenth century were undertaken in consultation with the Estates General. The Ordinance of Orléans (1561) and the Ordinance of Blois (1579) were two such examples. The drawing up of the text of the Ordinance of Orléans was not completed until August 1561, but its promulgation was backdated to January to make a point that it was done at the behest of the Estates General that had ended in the previous December.[134] In no way, however, was the king bound by the deputies' demands. He made laws as he wished, regardless of the *cahiers de doléance* of the Estates.[135] As the Estates General as consultative body gradually declined, the void in national politics was filled by judicial institutions, most notably the Parlement of Paris. Well before 1614, when the last meeting of the Estates General was held prior to the Revolution, the Parlement already maintained that it was the body speaking for different orders, corps, and communities vis-à-vis the king. Legally

[132] *Francogallia*, ed. Giesey and Salmon, 291.

[133] Barbiche, *Les institutions de la monarchie française*, 89.

[134] Greengrass, "A Day in the Life of the Third Estate," 74. The Ordinance of Moulins (1566), one of the greatest legislative monuments in the ancien régime, was issued at the conclusion of the assembly of the notables, the convocation of which had been specifically called for by Chancellor L'Hôpital. See Kim, *Michel de L'Hôpital*, 148–50.

[135] Michel Reulos, "L'action législative d'Henri III," in Robert Sauzet (ed.), *Henri III et son temps: Actes du colloque international du Centre de la Renaissance de Tours, Octobre 1989* (Paris: J. Vrin, 1992), 178. The deputies of the three estates did not participate in the elaboration of the text of the ordinances, which was done in the royal council with no need for their consent. Chénon, *Histoire générale du droit français*, vol. 2, 348. See also Krynen, "Réflexion sur les idées politiques aux États généraux de Tours de 1484."

speaking, judges were only *officiers* appointed by the king and holders of their posts; they represented no one other than themselves.[136] Regardless, the judges arrogated to themselves the role of standing for the country.

The registration of the Ordinance of Orléans sheds light on the complex relationship between the Parlement of Paris and the Estates General on the one hand and each institution's respective relationship with the crown on the other hand. At the conclusion of the assembly, the deputies of the Estates General took an unprecedented action of forwarding their *cahiers de doléances* to the Parlement of Paris, asking that they be registered. This was apparently a move intended to seek the Parlement's approbation on getting their demands to be incorporated into the ordinance.[137] It caught the royal government by surprise. Originally, the registration of royal ordinances by the parlements was largely a formality, designed to bring them to the knowledge of the law courts and ensure their authenticity, even though the parlements increasingly claimed that an ordinance was not enforceable unless it went through the process of registration in the respective jurisdiction.

From the early fifteenth century, the Parlement of Paris had declined to send deputies to the Estates General on the ground that it could not act both as judge and as plaintiff. When the royal government pressed the Parlement to register the Ordinance of Orléans without delay, reminding it that the articles had already been deliberated at length in the royal council and the Estates General, the Parlement replied that the court was not part of the Estates General and that it had the duty to examine the ordinance and express its opinions. This development caused persistent "misunderstandings" regarding the locus of the proper legislative authority, between the Estates General, the royal government, and the Parlement of Paris.[138] The precedent of Orléans was followed by the Estates General at Blois in 1576, and the verification of the *cahiers de doléances* by the Parlement became a regular practice. By asserting its right to scrutinize and verify ordinances, the Parlement augmented its legislative role and confirmed its superior position over the Estates General.[139]

In the sixteenth century, the king tried to pit these two institutions against each other in the hope to better maneuver them.[140] Charles IX in the 1560s appealed to the Estates General to check the power of the Parlement of Paris. In his opening speech to the Estates General in November 1560, Chancellor L'Hôpital distinguished between the parlements, which judged the private suits of individuals,

[136] Barbiche, *Les institutions de la monarchie française*, 109.

[137] G. F. Denault, "The Legitimation of the Parlement of Paris and the Estates General of France, 1560–1614" (PhD diss., Washington University, 1975), 263–64. See also Sylvie Daubresse, "The Parlement of Paris and the Ordinances of Blois (1579)," *French History* 23 (2009), 446–66; Greengrass, "A Day in the Life of the Third Estate."

[138] Daubresse, "The Parlement of Paris and the Ordinances of Blois (1579)," 448.

[139] Maugis, *Histoire du Parlement*, vol. 1, 670.

[140] Denault, "The Legitimation of the Parlement of Paris and the Estates General."

and the Estates General, which deliberated on the "general grievances" of the people.[141] Emphasizing the link between the people and the royal laws was a way of circumventing the law courts' claim to intervene. Often the king preferred handpicked assemblies of notables to the unwieldy Estates General. The Ordinance of Moulins was issued in February 1566 at the conclusion of the assembly of the notables, in which the king referred to "the complaints and grievances that were brought to us by our subjects in different places in the provinces of the kingdom during our tours for the last two years."[142] After the Estates General in Blois in 1576, Henry III attempted to moderate the Estates' demands by enlisting the cooperation of the Parlement of Paris.[143]

Contemporary jurists were divided. Hotman in *Francogallia* dismissed the Parlement of Paris as an invention of the kings who wished to keep the members of this "spurious senate" to be "dependent on them and accommodating to their wishes."[144] Hotman did not hide his contempt for *les praticiens*.[145] His faith in the Estates General and open animosity to the magistracy seemed somewhat in line with Coquille's. Writing toward the end of the reign of Henry III, Coquille, three times a deputy of the third estate of Nivernais to the Estates General (1560, 1576, and 1588), called the Estates General "the primary institution of this monarchy," the best and the most informed councilors of the sovereign. The Estates were the "incarnation of the body of the king, that is, the collective instance of the sovereignty, or yet the king in majesty."[146] *Avocat* Pasquier, by contrast, was far more skeptical about its role. For him, the law court, not the Estates General, was the legitimate institution representing the ancient assemblies, with the authority to maintain the law.[147] The Parlement of Paris was the principal "retenail," a force that sustained and restrained the monarchy.[148] This clash of opinions revealed the shifts in the institutional balance hitherto in place; it presaged the "eventual collapse" of the medieval constitutional system.[149]

[141] Chancellor L'Hôpital's opening speech to the Estates of Orléans on November 13, 1560, outlining the role of the Estates General as the deliberation on the "plaints générales qui concernoyent l'universel." *Michel de l'Hospital discours I*, ed. Petris, 386. See Kim, *Michel de L'Hôpital*, 121–24. L'Hôpital was well aware of the danger the crown would face in the case of collusion of the Estates General and the Parlement of Paris: the former could refuse to vote for any subsidy and the latter could refuse to register ordinances.

[142] *Recueil général*, vol. 14, 189–90.

[143] Daubresse, "The Parlement of Paris and the Ordinances of Blois (1579)," 456.

[144] *Francogallia*, ed. Giesey and Salmon, 505.

[145] Ibid., "Introduction," 33.

[146] Arlette Jouanna, "Noblesse, Noblesses," in Lucien Bély (ed.), *Dictionnaire de l'Ancien Régime: Royaume de France, XVIe–XVIIIe siècle* (Paris: Presses universitaires de France, 1996), 516.

[147] Pasquier began his career as an *avocat* at the Parlement of Paris and was named *avocat général* at the Chambre des comptes in 1585.

[148] Pasquier, *Les recherches de la France*, book 2, ch. 4, in *Les œuvres*, vol. 1, col. 66. "Our kings, to whom God has given *toute puissance absolue*, wanted to reduce their wills under the civility of the law and in doing so had their edicts and decrees filtered through the alembic of this public order," in which the laws were published and verified by the Parlement. Ibid.

[149] Church, *Constitutional Thought*, 295.

In sum, one can conclude that the sixteenth century witnessed the emergence of the Parlement of Paris as the central institution in national life at the expense of the Estates General.[150] The Parlement sought to enhance its image as the protector of the law of the realm and the "voice" of reason; it claimed that it was the intermediary between the crown and its subjects.[151] Hotman's invocation of custom and the Estates General as the touchstone of constitutionalism seemed strangely out of place, especially when the legal field was in flux. Toward the end of the sixteenth century, the expanding worldview of humanists increasingly turned them to general sources of law like natural law. During the Wars of Religion, legal pleadings tended to be filled with historical references and literary sources. It resulted in a "desacralization of positive law": the objective of justice was no longer merely to apply the law but to "implement the idea of justice, in the Platonic sense of the term, embodied in various legal systems."[152] In this context, the so-called fundamental laws of positive law elaborated by Hotman and others, justifying the primacy of the corporate will of the realm uniquely in reliance on custom, lacked sufficient theoretical abstractions.[153] By contrast, Bodin's theory of sovereignty was grounded in natural, not positive, law.[154] In his system, the people's rights rested on reason and equity rather than customary law.

During the last decades of the sixteenth century, the Valois monarchy was deep in the crisis of civil war. The crown faced serious constitutional and political turmoil. How the monarchy dealt with the challenges—and opportunities—of the times is the subject of the next chapter.

[150] The relationship between the local parlements and the provincial estates in the *pays d'état* pointed in the same direction. In the late seventeenth and eighteenth centuries, the Parlement of Dijon posed as defender of provincial rights over the estates of Burgundy. See Swann, *Provincial Power and Absolute Monarchy*.

[151] See Sylvie Daubresse, *Le Parlement de Paris ou la voix de la raison (1559–1580)* (Geneva: Droz, 2005).

[152] Houllemare, "La norme dans les plaidoyers," 90.

[153] Chénon, *Histoire générale du droit français*, vol. 2, 411. Hotman merely "invented an ancient assembly with enough authority to make a mockery of consuetudinary mystique." *Francogallia*, ed. Giesey and Salmon, "Editor's Introduction," 3.

[154] Church, *Constitutional Thought*, 237.

7
The Crown and the Constitution

In sixteenth-century France, there was no distinction between administration (*gubernatio*) and justice (*jurisdictio*). Far from being limited to adjudicating disputes between the parties, *jurisdictio* included legislating and regulating all measures necessary to assure order. The term *justice* designated reestablishing peace, equity, and concord so people could live without litigation, and legislation was one of the essential elements of this "preventive justice."[1]

A principal prerogative of the parlements was the power to judge in *équité*.[2] "Équité" and "equity" in French and English legal lexicology have dissimilar meanings. Equity law which developed in England refers to a judge-made law, aimed to overcome the shortcomings induced by the formalism of common law. In France, unlike England, equitable solutions had been incorporated into the law at the Parlement of Paris, and there was no need to set up separate courts to develop a body of special rules based on equity.[3] Glossators and canonists in the Late Middle Ages devised the theory that the Parlement of Paris, which originated in the Curia regis, shared in the authority of the prince, and this organic identification with the crown granted the court the liberty of legal interpretation. Legislation and jurisprudence were not in opposition to each other as if they were two rival instruments.[4] The power to judge in *équité* did not in theory disturb or destabilize the authority of the king.[5] As theoretical separation between the authority to make laws and the authority to implement them began to take shape, however, especially during the crisis of civil war, constitutional questions loomed.

The parlements' position revealed layers of complexity. On the one hand, judges prided themselves on their role of dispensing royal justice as part of the king's person (*pars corporis principis*). On the other hand, they were part of corporate elites, with strong desire to defend their interests and privileges and resist

[1] Reulos, "L'importance des praticiens," 130; Barbiche, *Les institutions de la monarchie française*, 345.

[2] Jacques Krynen, "Le problème et la querelle de l'interprétation de la loi, en France, avant la Révolution (Essai de rétrospective médiévale et moderne)," *Revue historique de droit français et étranger* 86 (2008), 161–97; Olivier Beaud, *La puissance de l'État* (Paris: Presses universitaires de France, 1994), 192 ("Equity is nothing other than another way of designating the faculty of interpretation of magistrates").

[3] John P. Dawson, "The Equitable Remedies of the French Chancery before 1789," in Hans Dölle, Max Rheinstein, Konrad Zweigert, Wolfgang Kunkel, and Hans Julius Wolff (eds.), *Festschrift für Ernst Rabel* (Tübingen: Mohr, 1954), vol. 1, 99–140.

[4] Krynen, "The Absolute Monarchy," 40.

[5] Krynen, "Entre science juridique et dirigisme," 183.

Custom, Law, and Monarchy: A Legal History of Early Modern France. Marie Seong-Hak Kim, Oxford University Press.
 DOI: 10.1093/oso/9780192845498.003.0007

interference from the outside. The sale of offices, the uniquely French institution of allowing judges to obtain a hereditary share in royal office, was a critical element in this power dynamic, straddling the realms of public and private. The king exercised power through state officials who owed him their positions and public authority, but in turn he owed them protection of their private interests and privileges he had created. The king would not—could not—abuse his power infringing upon their property rights he had granted because, simply put, he needed continued credit in the form of venality to run the state.

This chapter discusses the operation of the early modern state from the perspectives of civil law and constitutional law. The relationship between the crown and venal *officiers* delineated the contours of royal prerogatives, which Jean Bodin termed "the true marks of sovereignty."[6] Exploration of the sale of offices at the nexus of the law of obligations and constitutional principles sheds important light on the theory and practice of the monarchy.

1. The King and His Judges

Équité, meaning judging by interpreting law (*interpretatio legis*), is a legal method to soften the harsh effects of judicial decisions resulting from the strict application of statutes or custom. According to Tiraqueau, *équité* attenuates the rigidity of law, in particular for the benefit of the unfortunate, the poor, and the weak.[7] Claude-Joseph de Ferrière (*c*.1680–*c*.1748) defined *équité*, "which can be called natural justice," as "a benign interpretation which one renders to the *loi* in order to soften its rigor, in relation to a particular situation which requires not to follow exactly its disposition in certain cases." It refers to the power of the sovereign courts "to break the rigor of law in their judgments, no matter whether its commands are clear and precise, when just reasons seemed to require it."[8]

Judging in *équité* is different from rendering a sentence at the discretion of the adjudicator, however. It is "not a hazy, impressionist judgment"; instead, *équité* refers to judicial fairness, going beyond the law in the interest of justice by means of "a rigorous demonstration which cannot be rebutted, denied, overturned by contrary evidence."[9] Only the parlements, not lower courts, had the power to rule

[6] "Des vraies marques de souveraintė" is the title of book I, ch. 11 of Bodin, *Les six livres de la république* (ch. 10 in the 1593 edition).

[7] Boyer, "La notion d'équité," 259.

[8] "Droit étroit" in Ferrière, *Dictionnaire de droit et de pratique*, vol. 1, 504.

[9] Magdi Sami Zaki, "Définir l'équité," *Archives de philosophie du droit* 35 (1990), 87. There is no equity law in civil law systems and *équité* has no official place in the French legal system, but judges have rendered creative and equitable decisions. See A.-F. Debruche, "What is 'Equity'?: Of Comparative Law, Time Travel and Judicial Cultures," *Revue générale de droit* 39 (2009), 203–28. The term *équité* is mentioned sparingly in the Code civil of 1804, most notably in Article 1135: "Agreements obligate a party, not only as to what is expressly undertaken, but also as to all the

in *équité*. The *parlementaires* zealously guarded their exclusive right to this "soul of the law."[10] *Équité* functioned precisely as part of royal justice, through which a "transfer of sovereignty" of the king to the parlements took place. François Connan observed: "It is not our practice to consult the king concerning all the private controversies that present difficulty, as the Romans formerly were accustomed to do. In these matters the authority of the Parlement and of all the judges is supreme, and from the judges the appeal is to the Parlement; from the Parlement no one can appeal, not even to the king."[11] Connan may be oversimplifying a bit, because it was possible for the parties to petition the king through *maîtres de requêtes* regarding the parlement's judgment. Yet Connan, himself a member of the Conseil privé of Francis I, was making the point that the king would not disrupt arbitrarily the regular course of justice.

The judges could take into account particular conditions of the parties, places, and the time, derogating from harsh custom and legislation or simplifying Roman law rules. If a law was unreasonable or inadequate, justice required that it be modified in application. The specific consideration of *équité* in a number of related judicial decisions was regarded as jurisprudential custom, capable of substituting for written law.

Interpretatio legis, or *Équité*

Two decisions on *équité* from the Parlement of Toulouse are illuminating. After Toulouse was annexed by the king of France in 1271, property matters were governed by the code of Justinian, though municipal justice still adhered to some local practices. The custom of Toulouse, promulgated in 1286, was subject to the control of the royal courts, and the interpretive competence of consuls was dismissed.[12] Following the creation of the Parlement of Toulouse in 1443, the influence of Roman law was predominant in parlementary circles. Conflicts between the *jus commune* and the local custom, containing 144 articles, often emerged in matters of family relations institutions.[13]

consequences which equity, custom or rules of law [*l'équité, l'usage ou la loi*] give the obligation according to its nature."

[10] The power of equity "was not extended to lower jurisdictions thanks to the vigilance of the sovereign courts which, jealous of their privileges, never allowed them to be regarded as equal to themselves." Boyer, "La notion d'équité," 258.

[11] Connanus, *Commentariorium iuris civilis* (1724), book 1, ch. 2, 47, cited from Dawson, "French Customs," 792, note 102.

[12] *Consuetudines Tolosae* in *Nouveau coutumier général*, vol. 4, 1037–70. See Henri Gilles, *Les coutumes de Toulouse (1286) et leur premier commentaire (1296)* (Toulouse: Académie de législation, 1969); Yabumoto Masanori, "*Voluntas domini regis in suo regno facit jus*: 'Toruzu kanshū-hō' ni miru Kape cho nanfutsu shihai no jissō–Kanshū-hō o baikai to suru rippō zettai shugi no kakuritsu" [The Image of "Roi législateur" in the *Coutumes de Toulouse* under the Capets in the Midi–The Establishment of Legislative Absolutism through Customary Law], *Hōgaku seijigaku ronkyū* 73 (2007), 77–108.

[13] Poumarède, "Droit commun *versus* coutume de Toulouse," 145.

The custom of Toulouse granted a preferential status to fathers and husbands in inheritance. Its Article 124 did not allow a mother to succeed her sons who died intestate, whose property would rather go to his father or his closest relatives in the paternal side. This rule, derogating from *Novel* 118 of the Justinian code, was a cause for much financial hardship for surviving mothers.[14] In the face of this problem, the Parlement of Toulouse, instead of openly abrogating the custom, devised a judicial instrument that could moderate the harsh consequences from its literal application. The Parlement created the "*légitime de grace*" and allowed the mother one third of what she would have obtained under the Justinian code. It was a bold construction of case law based on a presumption that the son, if he had not died intestate, would have willed in favor of the mother, which would have enabled her to assert her right of *légitime*.

Normally a solution of this sort would not be justified because it introduced into intestate succession the institution of the *légitime*, which uniquely concerned testamentary law. But it had the practical advantage of determining in advance precisely what the mother would receive, without leaving it to the judge's discretion to decide in each case how much should be given to the mother. Neither the parties nor the king opposed this judicial expediency of diverging from the custom. Toward the end of the sixteenth century, a series of judicial decrees were rendered applying this solution.[15]

Another example concerned deviation from royal law in the name of *équité*. The royal edicts issued between 1539 and 1551 ordered the forced sale of the land seized from a debtor. Those were highly unpopular laws because they went against the deeply entrenched sentiment in old France that the integrity of the family land must be preserved. Often poorly organized auctions resulted in proceeds far below the property's market value. In response, the Parlement of Toulouse devised a new procedure: it allowed the debtor to rescind the sale and retake the seized property within ten years from the judgment of the property's confiscation. Royal officials did not protest the Parlement's action, and no parties complained about it to the Conseil du Roi. These examples showed that the equity power by the parlements was considered a legitimate source of law, not an abuse of power.[16]

The kings for long had no reservation about the law courts' interpretation of law and judgment in *équité*. Law was the expression of the sovereign will, serving the interest of the community, and its elaborations by the courts formed the substance of *gubernatio*. Confident in the courts' legal expertise, the monarchs regularly indicated that application of laws implied interpretation, which conformed

[14] For *Novel* 118, see supra Chapter 5, note 157.

[15] Boyer, "La notion d'équité," 260–61; Poumarède, "Droit commun *versus* coutume de Toulouse," 150–51.

[16] Boyer, "La notion d'équité," 262–64. A royal declaration of 1736 expressly recognized the validity of this institution originating from the jurisprudence of the Parlement of Toulouse.

to good administration of justice.[17] In time, however, the king grew less open to the idea of the courts' freedom of interpretation.[18] The notion of *équité* meant adjudicators weighing the benefit of granting a remedy against the damage it could cause, something modern law calls the "balance of convenience."[19] The judges' discretion could be seen as excessive when the result was something other than what the king had intended. The law courts' claim of their presumptive right of judging in *équité* became increasingly incompatible with the prevailing constitutional ideology of the sovereignty of the ruler.

From the beginning of the fourteenth century, the crown issued *lettres patentes*, or *lettres de déclaration*, which "declared" the meaning of legislative texts, ordinances, or edicts that had been published. *Déclaration* was a technical term, in use until the end of the ancien régime, referring to interpretive royal laws. As time went on, declarations became more frequent, lengthy, and specific.[20] Originally responses issued at the solicitation from the courts, they increasingly served the purpose of limiting the magistrates' interpretive power. Royal letters and orders issued by Louis XI reproached the courts for construing ordinances and edicts "at will" (*à leur intention*), defeating the intention of the legislator. The Parlement of Paris long compared itself to the Roman Senate.[21] Historical and philological research of legal humanists in the sixteenth century had the effect of allowing the law court a new realm of legal norms and interpretations, drawing on the abstract conception of natural law, or fundamental law of the kingdom.[22] The courts, more boldly than before, claimed themselves the guardian of justice.

When the king first began prohibiting the interpretation of the ordinances and edicts, he reasoned the courts stood in the way of improving judicial administration. He suspected judges of inciting litigation by reading the laws in a manner less than straightforward. In the preamble of the ordinance of July 1493, Charles VIII deplored the fact that "the laudable and ancient ordinances of the kings our predecessors are not entirely guarded and observed"; the king commanded an oath from the judges of the Parlement that they maintain ordinances "point to point."[23] In the ordinance of March 1498, Louis XII ordered the courts to preserve the record of royal ordinances and read them to the public twice a year.[24] Under

[17] Charles VI (r. 1368–1422) committed his councilors at the *Cour des aides* to "correct, augment, increase, diminish or clarify" his new ordinances, to "interpret…all as if it was done by us in our person." Krynen, "Le problème et la querelle," 171.

[18] Dawson, "The Equitable Remedies of the French Chancery," 126.

[19] Debruche, "What is 'Equity'?" 224.

[20] Krynen, "Le problème et la querelle," 170.

[21] Jacques Krynen, "Droit romain et État monarchique. À propos du cas français," in Joël Blanchard (ed.), *Représentation, pouvoir et royauté à la fin du Moyen Âge* (Paris: Picard, 1995), 13–23.

[22] Houllemare, "La norme dans les plaidoyers," 91.

[23] *Recueil général*, vol. 11, 220 and 248; Krynen, "Le problème et la querelle," 171.

[24] In the preamble of the ordinance issued in Lyon in 1510, Louis XII complained that "through the subtleness and craftiness of some lawyers and other practitioners . . . and various interpretations made on these [ordinances], the path to justice became . . . obstructed and perverted." Cited from Krynen, "Le problème et la querelle," 171–72.

François I, Chancellor Guillaume Poyet (*c.*1473–1538) declared at the promulgation of the Ordinance of Villers-Cotterêt that the law, once issued by the king, stood outside the power of any court to "interpret, add to, or diminish it."[25]

Major conflicts erupted during the religious wars. The king explicitly forbade judges to interpret the pacification edicts. In August 1563, Chancellor L'Hôpital chided the *parlementaires* of Rouen for taking royal ordinances apart.[26] In January 1566 in his opening speech at the assembly of notables in Moulins, the chancellor declared: "Justice belongs to the king and not to private individuals; . . . in this monarchy interpretation belongs to the king who makes the laws, and not to anyone else."[27] The judge's job was not to interpret the law but to assure that it be observed. The chancellor's message would see its full theoretical exposition by Jean Bodin.[28]

For Bodin, the word *équité* had different meanings for the prince and for magistrates: "*équité* for a prince is to declare or correct the law; *équité* for a magistrate is to assuage and mitigate the rigor, or aggravate the leniency [*aigrir la douceur*] thereof when it is necessary, or to address the problem in the case that had not been foreseen in the law."[29] *La loi* without *équité* is "a body without a soul" (*un corps sans âme*); whereas *la loi* concerns general matters, *équité* searches for particular circumstances.[30] The correct interpretation of the law is nothing other than the law itself. Bodin stressed, in words highly reminiscent of L'Hôpital's, that the judge was obligated to apply the law in accordance with the intention of the legislator and the general spirit of the law, because "the magistrate's power is not to judge the law but to judge according to the law."[31] When the magistrates interpreted the law not in harmony with the will and intention of the king, such interpretations were conclusively against the law and their decisions abusive.

Other sixteenth-century jurists also voiced warnings against the unbridled use of the notion of *équité*, which would defeat the intent of the legislator and eventually destroy the law.[32] Pasquier stated:

[25] Bernard Chevalier, "La réforme de la justice: Utopie et réalité (1440–1540)," in Stegmann (ed.), *Pouvoirs et institutions en Europe au XVIe siècle*, 242.

[26] Discourse of August 17, 1563, at the Parlement of Rouen, in *Michel de L'Hospital discours II*, ed. Petris and Amherdt, 51; Kim, *Michel de L'Hôpital*, 128–29.

[27] Discourse of January 24, 1566, *Remonstrance de Moulins*, in *Michel de L'Hospital discours II*, ed. Petris and Amherdt, 84–85.

[28] Scholars have long taken notice of Bodin's intellectual debt to L'Hôpital. Denis Crouzet doubts Bodin's *Les six livres de la république* would have been written but for L'Hôpital's intellectual enterprise which, in the early years of the religious troubles, rediscovered and recognized the monarchical authority as the unique force to restore civil peace. Crouzet, *La sagesse et le malheur*, ch. 5. According to Salmon, Bodin's *Methodus ad facilem historiarum cognitionem* was composed in the context of L'Hôpital's reformist regime. Salmon, *Society in Crisis*, 217. See Kim, "Civil Law and Civil War," 804.

[29] Bodin, *Les six livres de la république*, book 6, ch. 6, 734.

[30] Ibid.

[31] "Il n'appartient pas au magistrat de juger de la loy, mais selon la loy," ibid., 735.

[32] Krynen, "Le problème et la querelle," 182. See also Jean-Louis Thireau, "Le bon juge chez les juristes français du XVIe siècle," in Jean-Marie Carbasse and Laurence Depambour-Tarride (eds.), *La*

> We observe a distinction in our France that, while a lower court judge, in rendering the sentence, must be bound by the ordinances, the Courts, which hold the title of sovereign and consequently represent the Prince, can, though they cannot judge expressly against the ordinance (because in this case the *arrêt* would be null), modify it *ex variis rerum causis et figuris* [from the various causes and forms of cases]. This is a very true proposition. In this, however, I hope that one treats jurisprudence wisely: the authority of a sovereign court is great but not so great as to be above the law.[33]

Équité was considered a source of unwritten law alongside custom, but it should not become confused with arbitrariness. At stake was thus not *équité* per se but its proper use. Neither Bodin nor Pasquier denied the magisterial prerogative of *équité* which, as Pasquier noted, meant not so much to contradict a given law as to circumvent it. The king had the final power to decide whether judges abused *équité*.

Concerns about the seemingly ever-expanding interpretive power of the judges were captured in the popular adage, "Dieu nous garde de l'équité des parlements" (God save us from the *équité* of the parlements).[34] Public outcry against equity power in early modern France "pointed to more than suspicion and hatred of lawyers"; it "suggested a larger distrust of the devices and engines of modern 'justice.'"[35] As seen in Chapter 3, early on Louis XI griped about judges keeping the laws in a disorganized mess so that more lawsuits would arise. They were suspected of intentionally prolonging trials and encouraging unnecessary appeals, hoping that they could collect more *épices*. *Épices* were originally gifts in kind given by the parties to the judges presiding over their cases. By the sixteenth century they had been converted into a standardized money payment as an obligatory fee.[36] Since judges were inadequately paid by the crown in fixed salary, *épices* became an important source of supplemental income for them.

Legal practitioners were fair game for early modern writers. They were blamed for rampant lawsuits, delays, high costs, and corruption in the judicial system. Unscrupulous lawyers allegedly resorted to convoluted arguments and intricacies. In *Antitribonian*, Hotman sneered at lawyers' abject abidance of legal "jargons": for them "using certain words is like using magic with charms, pictograms,

conscience du juge dans la tradition juridique européenne (Paris: Presses universitaires de France, 1999), 131–54.

[33] Pasquier, *Lettres*, book 19, letter 15 (to Robert), in *Les œuvres*, vol. 2, col. 579.

[34] This phrase is featured in Henri Roland and Laurent Boyer (eds.), *Adages du droit français contemporain*, 2nd ed. (Lyon: L'Hermès, 1986), vol. I, 233–38.

[35] Kelley, "Lord Deliver Us from Justice," 160–61. See Vernon Valentine Palmer, "From Embrace to Banishment: A Study of Judicial Equity in France," *American Journal of Comparative Law* 47 (1999), 277–301.

[36] Laurie Freger, "Le cout de la justice civile à travers les archives judiciaires: L'exemple des épices des magistrats," *L'Atelier du Centre des recherches historiques* 5 (2009), https://journals.openedition.org/acrh/1738.

and secret spells, which must be strictly and superstitiously observed, because missing a syllable would spoil the entire mystery." They must have learned them from the books of the Romans or at the law faculties, but their actual practices in the courtroom were "as remote from the style and form of pleadings of the ancient Romans as the mores of the French people are from those of Tartars or Troglodytes."[37]

In Thomas More's Utopia, all lawyers were banished.[38] With no similar solutions at their disposal, French kings tried to systematize laws in order to rein in legal professionals. As Hotman's patron L'Hôpital pointed out, the real problem was not the laws but the people who abused them. The chancellor deplored: "we have turned the laws, which had been created to come to the aid of the mortals, into dreadful and fateful ruins of the good people."[39] Many cases of the travesty of justice were caused when the laws were manipulated by those at the Palais for their financial gains, whereas "such monstrosities exist in neither the laws of the Romans nor ours."[40]

Various interests—parochial, corporate, and individual—jousted in recurring incidents of the contest of will between the crown and the law courts. Challenges to royal legislative power could arise during the registration of royal edicts, well before their implementation stage.

Parlements and Royal Legislation

Registration of laws at the parlements dated from the mid-fifteenth century. The process consisted of three separate phases: first, the reading and verification of the acts by the court; second, *enregistrement*, meaning transcription in the register of the court with mentions attesting to its accord; and third, publication, meaning proclamation and distribution in a printed form. Its main function was to give public notice of new law. Despite its original purpose, the ritual of registration became a powerful instrument for law courts to voice their discontent, if any. When the parlement deemed the proposed laws to be against the public good and fundamental laws, it formulated its reservations in *remontrances*.[41] These amounted, in the modern context, to introducing amendments to legislation.

[37] Hotman, *Antitribonian*, ch. 9, 68–69.

[38] "Furthermore they absolutely exclude and banish all attorneys, proctors, and sergeants at the law: which craftily handle matters and subtly dispute of the law." Thomas More, *Utopia* (1516), trans. Ralph Robinson (London: Blackie and Son, 1908), book 2, 157.

[39] *Carmina: Livre II*, ed. and trans. Amherdt et al., 112–15.

[40] Ibid., 112–13. There were too many lawyers who were "depraved, lazy, ignorant, rapacious, hypocritical, [and] avaricious," 134–35.

[41] There were three forms depending on the degree of solemnity: *remontrances* (could be formulated by the courts and also by the assemblies of the estates); *répresentations* (could be presented also by inferior tribunals), and the *lettres*. Barbiche, *Les institutions de la monarchie française*, 109–10.

Upon receiving an ordinance for registration, the law court probed the text, article by article. The delay caused by the scrutiny often tested royal patience. Most of the time the king accepted the parlement's remonstrances; other times, the king issued a *lettre de jussion* ordering the court to proceed to registration. The court still addressed to the king *itératives* and *réitératives remontrances.* Repeated remonstrances could have crippling effects on royal policy. After several rounds of rebuke and defiance, normally some compromise was attained. If not, the impasse was ultimately broken when the king decided to exercise his prerogatives as *le roi justicier* in person and held a *lit de justice.*[42] The court then had no choice but to surrender to royal will, though it still recorded its objections in the registers by describing the constraints to which it had been submitted. If the law court could not thwart royal will, it could at least cause public embarrassment to the king, who would have enough motivation to prevent that from happening.[43]

The *lit de justice* has traditionally been understood as the occasion of the invocation of the king's retained justice (*justice retenue*). According to Krynen, however, the concept of retained justice, along with its companion concept of delegated justice (*justice déléguée*), did not exist in the sixteenth century. The actual forma in use was that the authority of the king was communicated (*communiquée*) to the parlement.[44] Bodin observed that the king "communicated the authority, force, and power to command."[45] Sovereign justice, inseparable from the crown, was not subject to delegation. It was on this ground, argued Krynen, that the royal council practiced *évocations* of recalling cases, normally at the request of a litigant, from the parlements to the Conseil privé and quashing their decisions when necessary.[46]

[42] See Sarah Hanley, *The Lit de Justice of the Kings of France: Constitutional Ideology in Legend, Ritual, and Discourse* (Princeton: Princeton University Press, 1983). According to Richard Bonney, the belief that the *lit de justice* was a constitutional forum in the Middle Ages is far from the truth. "The apparent link between reigns provided by the *lit de justice* is in fact no link at all, since the term had different meanings, and the assembly was used for different purposes, between 1527 and 1673." Bonney, "Absolutism: What's in a Name?" 97–98.

[43] Chénon, *Histoire générale du droit français*, vol. 2, 350.

[44] Jacques Krynen, "Qu'est-ce qu'un Parlement qui 'représente le roi'?" in Durand and Mayali (eds.), *Excerptiones iuris*, 357–58. Christophe de Thou states in his discourse in May 1565, as part of the Parlement's remonstrances, that the king "communicated to and bestowed on" his magistrates and officials "the power that God had bestowed on him" ("il a communicqué et baillé puissance que Dieu luy a baillee"). Daubresse, "Un discours de Christophe de Thou," 383.

[45] Bodin, *Les six livres de la Republique*, book 3, ch. 4, 333. The title of Chapter 4 is "De l'obeissance que doit le magistrat aux loix & au Prince souverain." The Parlement was the mouth of the king who spoke in the judicial *arrêts*; in other words, it was the king who spoke, not the judges. Krynen, "Qu'est-ce qu'un Parlement qui 'représente le roi'?" 362.

[46] The Conseil privé's power of *cassation* was officially confirmed by the Ordinance of Blois in 1579. But *évocation* of cases was not frequent, even during the reign of Louis XIV. The royal council normally transferred such exceptional cases to another parlement. See Albert Hamscher, *The Conseil Privé and the Parlements in the Age of Louis XIV: A Study in French Absolutism* (Philadelphia: American Philosophical Society, 1987); Tony Sauvel, "Les demandes de motifs adressées par le conseil du roi aux cours souveraines," *Revue historique de droit français et étranger* 35 (1957), 529–48.

In the sixteenth century, most strenuous opposition to royal legislation was directed at the pacification edicts during the religious wars. Those cases, to be discussed in Chapter 8, involved grand constitutional issues. In many other cases, however, main issues concerned corporate interest and local privileges.

The courts in the Midi with strong Roman law tradition resisted interference from the center in the form of sweeping ordinances and edicts, as illustrated in their opposition to the Edict of Mothers in 1567.[47] There was also a collective reason to challenge the jurisprudence of the Parlement of Paris. Local parlements were not keen on accepting the superior status of the court in the capital. They preferred the notion of the "union des classes," that all the parlements of France formed equal parts of the union as a single parlement under royal authority. This idea undermined the Parlement of Paris' claim as the oldest and most illustrious court representing royal justice above the provincial courts.[48] Rejection of the Parisian court's preeminence impeded unity in jurisprudence among the sovereign courts. As important, if not more, as the courts' commitments to local liberties were the judges' private interests.

Parlements and Patriarchy

Competing regional particularism and strong esprit de corps stood side by side. Judges formed one of the most definable, prominent corporate bodies in old France. Their common stake in officeholding shaped their behaviors in a distinct direction. Some historians have argued that the prevalent patriarchal culture, combined with the judges' desire to protect their social and economic interests, seriously influenced the court jurisprudence. Sarah Hanley has contended that royal legislation and case law in early modern France aimed at augmenting patriarchal authority in private law and royal authority in public law simultaneously. According to her, the monarchy and the corporation of magistrates struck a covenant—the "family-state compact"—to exert control over the nation's social and economic production and reproduction. Hanley's focus is on a series of laws

[47] See Chapter 5. See Guillaume Leyte, "Le provincialisme juridique dans la France d'ancien régime: Quelques remarques," *Revue d'histoire des facultés de droit et de la science juridique* 23 (2003), 95–117; Jonathan K. Powis, "Order, Religion, and the Magistrates of a Provincial Parlement in Sixteenth-Century France," *Archiv für Reformationsgeschichte* 71 (1980), 180–97.

[48] Robert Villers' communication, "Les origines de la théorie parlementaire dite de 'l'union des classes,'" in "Société d'histoire du droit, 1983–1984," *Revue historique de droit français et étranger* 62 (1984), 718–19. Chancellor L'Hôpital stated: "If the king could administer his sovereign justice, as was done in earlier times, through one parlement, he would do so. Different parlements are only various divisions [*classes*] of the parlement of the king. It is odd that some prevent the execution of others' judgments." Discourse of September 7, 1560, in *Michel de L'Hospital discours* I, 379. He was advocating the new edict of *Pareatis* which ordered the implementation of *arrêts* across the kingdom. The idea of *the union des classes* was put into practice when the *lit de justice* declaring the king's majority was held at the Parlement of Rouen in 1563.

issued in the 1550s and the early 1560s to regulate marriage and also judicial decisions on inheritance laws in the late sixteenth and early seventeenth centuries.

The edict of 1557 under Henry II forbade clandestine marriage.[49] The Ordinance of Orléans of 1561 reinforced this measure and declared that those who surreptitiously sequestrated the girls and let the couple be married without the consent of their parents or guardians were punished for the crime of kidnapping.[50] The Ordinance of Blois (1579) reaffirmed the solemnities required for the celebration of marriage and the prohibition of marital union without parental agreement; those who violated the law were culpable of the crime of abduction (*rapt*) and punishable by death.[51] From these laws Hanley theorized that the early modern French state made concerted efforts to reshape families through the medium of law. She equated the French family with the state, and the power of the male head of a household over his wife and children with the absolute power of the king; in each realm, the king and the father shared the goal of maintaining "patriarchal hegemony."[52] The implementation of royal laws regulating marriage and the development of a distinct jurisprudence protecting agnatic interests together widened "the gap in social entitlement by empowering male heads and placing females at risk."[53] They were evidence, Hanley argued, of royal measures to preserve the patrimony of the ruling class. This innovative thesis of Hanley epitomized gender analysis which, as one scholar noted, has since pushed the early modern historiography of family "conspicuously in a political direction."[54]

There is little dispute that the French monarchy was concerned to shore up the social and material interests of the ruling houses. The argument that in the late sixteenth century the king and legal professionals made conscious efforts to turn the family into a political institution through legislation and jurisprudence seems somewhat overwrought, however. The protection of the family institution was

[49] *Recueil général*, vol. 13, 469. See supra Chapter 5, note 165 and accompanying text.

[50] Art. 111, in ibid., vol. 14, 91.

[51] Arts. 40–44, in ibid., vol. 14, 391–92. When the Council of Trent opened the session to discuss the sacrament of marriage in November 1563, the French ambassadors submitted the petition that "the marriage of sons and daughters of the family not be recognized to be legitimate without the consent of their parents." Despite the efforts of the Cardinal of Lorraine, however, the Council declared that clandestine marriage was not any less valid. This decree was met with much hostility in France. Charles Dumoulin called it "monstrous" in his "Consultation sur le fait du Concile de Trente," cited from Filhol, *Le premier président Christofle de Thou*, 234. While parental consent was not made mandatory, post-Tridentine church administrators promoted parental involvement by acknowledging dowry exchange as a vital component of social reproduction. See Jutta Sperling, "Marriage at the Time of the Council of Trent (1560–70): Clandestine Marriages, Kinship Prohibitions, and Dowry Exchange in European Comparison," *Journal of Early Modern History* 8 (2004), 67–108.

[52] Hanley, "Endangering the State," 15.

[53] Ibid., 21. Hanley has argued that the first royal marital edict of 1557 was a result of years of determined lobbying by jurists who, between 1550 and 1650, developed a body of distinct jurisprudence in French marital law.

[54] Gerber, "Family, the State, and Law," 474–75.

always one of the most fundamental duties of the monarchy. Just as God alone reigns over the universe, the old maxim went, so the king rules the commonwealth and the father the family.[55] Drawing an analogy between fatherhood and kingship and between paternal authority and royal prerogative was hardly a new idea, in France or elsewhere.[56] The family stood universally as the legal edifice, and patriarchy equated to kingly authority. Gender ideology, while relevant, would need to be explored without overshadowing juristic and other sociocultural elements that affected legal development and shaped jurisprudence in early modern France. The appearance of state laws regulating marital formation, so far the domain of church law, was also closely related to complex situations in the wake of the Reformation.[57]

Most contemporary jurists supported requiring parental consent on marriage. Pasquier said that it would be a desirable thing to have a marriage blessed by the father and the mother.[58] Dumoulin emphatically opposed clandestine marriage. As to the custom denying representation in direct line, he fully agreed that its harsh results needed to be redressed, but he also stated that "custom of this kind can be justified if it let the children know that they should not dare to enter into marriage and give birth to grandchildren without the consent of their parents, who can empower them to succeed."[59] When jurisconsults and magistrates supported royal laws on marriage formation, they likely were revealing their conservative mindset. Yet, it is also possible that they were mindful of the effects of the civil requirements, separate from the canonic requirements, of juristic acts on economic transactions. Parental approval of marriage provided for notice, an essential element in marital property relations. Adequate notice and publicity

[55] See André Burguière, "L'État monarchique et la famille (XVIe–XVIIIe siècle)," *Annales. Histoire, sciences sociales* 56 (2001), 313–35. Overseeing the family under the trusteeship of the father and society under the supervision of the state was an idea that formed the gist of the French Civil Code. See Jean-Louis Halpérin, *Histoire des droits en Europe, 1750 à nos jours* (Paris: Flammarion, 2004).

[56] In 1559, the Cortes in Castile extended the law so that children under the age of twenty-five could be disinherited for getting married without their father's consent. Cooper, "Patterns of Inheritance and Settlement," 251. In many premodern cultures, the spheres of political power and familial power were inseparably connected. In Confucian culture in East Asia, the distinction between the sovereign–father–husband–senior member, on the one hand, and the minister–son–wife–junior member, on the other, underpinned all family, social, and political relations. See Jérôme Bourgon, "Lapsus de Laïus. Entre régicide et parricide, l'introuvable meurtre du père," *Extrême-Orient Extrême-Occident* (2012), 313–39, https://doi.org/10.4000/extremeorient.229.

[57] See Saskia Lettmaier, "Marriage Law and the Reformation," *Law and History Review* 35 (2017), 461–510 (arguing that the Protestant Reformation played an important role in bringing the laws of marriage formation and dissolution under state control). See also Anne Lefebvre-Teillard, "Marriage in France from the Sixteenth to the Eighteenth Century: Political and Juridical Aspects," in Silvana Seidel Menchi and Emlyn Eisenach (eds.), *Marriage in Europe, 1400–1800* (Toronto: University of Toronto Press, 2016), 261–93 (arguing that growing state control over the formation of the matrimonial bond from the sixteenth century contributed to the secularization of marriage which culminated during the Revolution).

[58] Pasquier, letter to Messieurs Robert & Rournier, docteurs, regents of droit at the université d'Orléans, book 3, letter 1, *Les œuvres*, vol. 2, col. 49.

[59] Cited from Filhol, *Le premier président Christofle de Thou*, 234–35.

were crucial as creditors needed to know whom and what kind of property they were dealing with, especially in a community property system.[60] It was for similar concerns that the king required that baptisms, marriages, and burials be recorded by parish clergy and deposited at the *bailliage* court.[61]

Preserving parental authority had effects on regulating entails as well. Broader testamentary disposition under the influence of Roman law promoted both *patria potestas* and perpetual entails.[62] In response, reformed customs brought in a variety of mechanisms intended to prevent individual fathers and husbands, acting as administrators of lineal property, from abusing their power to defeat the rights of their family and offspring. In a house-based society (*société à maisons*), royal edicts frequently mentioned the concerns of financial ruins of the "bonnes maisons et familles anciennes."[63] The importance of sustaining the integrity of family estates by male heirs was widely recognized. But measures restricting substitutions and enhancing representation and reserved shares, as examined in Chapter 5, were geared to abate unfettered testation and the arbitrary authority of the family heads. The laws had their own logic of the times.

To recapitulate, reforms attempted by the monarchy deserve exploration from multifaceted perspectives, beyond the reductive class and gender models in property relations. First, the underlying desire in custom for the preservation of patrimony should not be underestimated. Second, the case of trust-entails plainly showed that parental and patriarchal authority did not always coincide. Third, for many contemporary authors, obedience to parental power at home dovetailed with the observance of law and public order. After all, Dumoulin was unapologetic in defending primogeniture and parental power, but we would not dismiss him as a stalwart of the feudal hierarchy or a hopeless misogynist. Jurists like him reveled in complex legal questions in the sixteenth century which concerned more than paternal privileges. In the same vein, Bodin viewed *patria potestas* as integrally related to the well-ordered state, but that does not make him a defender of tyrannical patriarchy.

Arguably the most insightful aspect of the family compact thesis is that royal laws and jurisprudence reinforced, in conjunction, the property rights of magistrates who purchased their offices. The gendered construction of family law posits that the judicial elites created by venality formed the lynchpin of the ruling class in early modern France and that they expanded the monarch's political power as well as their own familial and social interests. It thus underscores in part the

[60] Donahue, "Comparative Law before the Code Napoleon," 18.

[61] Art. 181, Ordinance of Blois (1579), *Recueil général*, vol. 14, 423.

[62] Cooper, "Patterns of Inheritance and Settlement," 201.

[63] The preambles of the Edict of Second Marriages ("la désolation des bonnes familles") and the Edict of the Mothers ("la perte et destruction des bonnes maisons et familles anciennes"), *Recueil général*, vol. 14, 36 and 222.

classic class arguments highlighting the bourgeois ambitions to obtain and preserve their ennobling offices.

2. Venality of Offices

The sale of offices was practiced in many European countries, but no country developed an apparatus on the French scale.[64] French kings entered the credit markets in full force in the early sixteenth century, somewhat later than other monarchs. Francis I amassed huge debts in vain effort to secure conquests in Italy and desperately needed to raise money. Chief means of credit were the creation of *rentes* and the sale of offices. In 1523, Francis created a special fund (*trésor*), called the *finances extraordinaires et parties casuelles*, to receive the loans and extraordinary taxes.[65] It specialized in handling the proceeds from the sale of offices, thereby fully regularizing the practice. Selling posts to highest bidder was made a matter of public policy. Demands for office were high because of the immense power, privileges, and prestige that came with it. A contemporary saying went, "every time it pleased the king to create an office to sell, it pleased God to create a fool to buy it."[66] Francis' successors were reduced to creating swarms of new offices, as the monarchy entered the period of religious wars with staggering royal debt. By the end of the sixteenth century, nearly all judicial offices had become open to sale, including the judgeships at the parlements.[67]

The nature of the venality system, obtaining private interest in public authority, was at once political (legitimation of forms of domination), social (recruitment of state servants), and economic (alienation of public power and remuneration for state servants).[68] The purchased office was considered fictitious real property, its

[64] For the sale of offices in Spain and the Netherlands, see K. W. Swart, *Sale of Offices in the Seventeenth Century* (The Hague: M. Nijhoff, 1949); for Britain, see Douglas W. Allen, "Purchase, Patronage, and Professions: Incentives and the Evolution of Public Offices in Pre-Modern Britain," *Journal of Institutional and Theoretical Economics* 161 (2005), 57–79.

[65] Christopher Stocker, "Public and Private Enterprise in the Administration of a Renaissance Monarchy: The First Sales of Office in the Parlement of Paris (1512–1524)," *Sixteenth Century Journal* 9 (1978), 4–29; Knecht, *Francis I*, 129–31.

[66] Marion, *Dictionnaire des institutions de la France*, "Offices," 406.

[67] Classic studies on the sale of offices include Roland Mousnier, *La vénalité des offices sous Henri IV et Louis XIII*, 2nd ed. (Paris: Presses universitaires de France, 1971, 1946); William Doyle, *Venality: The Sale of Offices in Eighteenth-Century France* (Oxford: Oxford University Press, 1996); Paul Louis-Lucas, *Étude sur la vénalité des charges et fonctions publiques* (Paris: Challamel et Thorin, 1882), 2 vols.; Franklin Ford, *Robe and Sword: The Regrouping of the French Aristocracy after Louis XIV* (Cambridge, MA: Harvard University Press, 1953); François Bluche, *Les magistrats du Parlement de Paris au XVIIIe siècle (1715–1771)* (Paris: Les Belles Lettres, 1960); Shennan, *The Parlement of Paris*.

[68] Descimon, "Power Elites and the Prince," 101–102. For social ramifications of the venality system and various socioeconomic strategies among the elites, see Robert Descimon, "The Birth of the Nobility of the Robe: Dignity versus Privilege in the Parlement of Paris, 1500–1700," in Michael Wolfe (ed.), *Changing Identities in Early Modern France* (Durham, NC: Duke University Press, 1997), 95–123; Robert Descimon, "Conflits familiaux dans la robe parisienne aux XVIe et XVIIe siècles: Les

material foundation resting on the *lettre de provision* from the king. It was akin to *rentes* created on the Hôtel de Ville de Paris, with the office functioning as *rente constitute*, a capital in a legal fiction.[69] It was a royal debt, in simple terms. For aspiring candidates, venality was basically acquiring status on investment on credit. Not all could afford the large capital sum needed for purchase, and many borrowed to procure the funds. In this way, the venality system extended the network of credit across society.[70] The king's ability to dominate the ruling class heavily depended on his power to control their financial investment in offices and manipulate personal and corporate privileges attached to them. The supposed permanence of this system required a special status in law, with important implications in constitutional law as well as civil law.

The system of venality reinforced, and was reinforced by, the principle of the irremovability of judges. The rule of *inamovibilité* was affirmed for the first time by Louis XI. The ordinance of 1467 prescribed that the king could not discharge officials except "par mort, forfaicture ou incompatibilité d'offices."[71] Some maintained that the perpetuity of offices was a fundamental law, but the king's main motive in 1467 was likely more mundane, that is, to facilitate the sale of the offices he had created.[72] The whole enterprise would have a gaping hole without the guarantee of tenure, as the fear of losing offices would dampen the enthusiasm of potential buyers. Charles Loyseau (1564–1627) stated that the ordinance of 1467 prescribing irremovability turned into dead letters such clauses in the letters of provision of office as "tant qu'il nous plaira" and "que le Roy est suffisamment informé de la capacité de l'officier."[73] But what really protected and sustained the security of the officials were commercial transactions between them and the king.

In the sixteenth century royal ordinances and edicts denounced venality and regularly stipulated the suppression of all judicial offices created since the reign of Louis XII.[74] Needless to say, the king's fiscal situation did not allow him to redeem the offices by paying back the money. The king routinely disregarded his own

paradoxes de la transmission du statut," *Cahiers d'histoire* 45 (2000), https://journals.openedition.org/ch/399.

[69] Descimon, "Power Elites and the Prince," 115.

[70] "The officiers were not the only ones to have a stake in venal office-holding." Bien, "Offices, Corps, and a System of State Credit," 96.

[71] Jacques Kubler, *L'origine de la perpétuité des offices royaux: L'origine de la perpétuité des offices royaux* (Nancy: Société d'impressions typographiques, 1958). For the Ordinance of 1467, see Christopher Stocker, "Office and Justice: Louis XI and the Parlement of Paris (1465–1476)," *Mediaeval Studies* 37 (1975), 360–86.

[72] Louis-Lucas, *Étude sur la vénalité des charges et fonctions publiques*, vol. 2, 17.

[73] Charles Loyseau, *Les cinq livres du droit des offices*, in *Les œuvres de Maistre Charles Loyseau* (Lyon: La Compagnies des libraries, 1701), book 1, ch. 3 ("De la provision des offices"), 21, and book 1, ch. 10 ("Des vacations irregulieres des offices"), 66; see also book 3, ch. 1 ("De la vénalité des offices"). Loyseau cited Bodin, *Les six livres de la république*, book 3, ch. 3 ("Des magistrats") and book 4, ch. 4 ("S'il est bon que les officiers d'une Republic soient perpetuels").

[74] Ordinance of Orléans, Arts. 30–39, *Recueil général*, vol. 14, 72–74; Ordinance of Moulins, Arts. 9 and 11, ibid., 192.

prohibition, rendering his laws "édicts de parade sans effect" in Pasquier's words.[75] The *parlementaires*, on their part, opposed any reform of the system that they feared would diminish the value of their offices and their income.[76] The price of offices kept going up rapidly until 1635, before it began to drop toward the end of the century, continuing the slide in the next century.[77] The system continued through the end of the ancien régime.

Jurisprudence on Venality

Selling and buying offices was a market-based economic transaction. It was closely linked to the conjugal property regime because under the custom of Paris spouses owned their property in common.[78] The rules regulating marriages and those governing the transaction of offices both remained in an ambiguous zone between public law and discretionary private law.[79]

How did the customary law reforms deal with venal offices? The *Coutume de Paris* of 1510 had no mention of venality because offices had not yet been fully regarded as a private property to enter the patrimony. The *coutumes* of 1580 included a new provision, which came from a judgment of the Parlement of Paris rendered in 1557. Article 95 provided:

> Venal office is deemed immovable property, and can be held by mortgage when it is seized from the debtor by the authority of justice before resignation is accepted and provision is made for the benefit of a third party. It can be put on public notice for sale and awarded by decree. All the amounts resulting from the adjudication are subject to taxation as movable property and are shared among

[75] Pasquier, *Les recherches de la France*, book 4, ch. 17, *Les œuvres*, vol. 1, col. 404.

[76] Henry II in April 1554 doubled overnight the number of offices to sell by issuing the Edict of Semester. He claimed that the edict aimed to reduce *épices* and avert judicial malversation by establishing a mutual control between the two semestral sections. Few took that explanation seriously, and the edict met serious opposition from the *parlementaires*. See supra Chapter 4, note 10.

[77] The price of some offices, such as *secrétaire du roi*, rarely dropped. Barbiche, *Les institutions de la monarchie française*, 81; see William Doyle, "The Prices of Offices in Pre-Revolutionary France," *Historical Journal* 27 (1984), 831–60.

[78] Marriage laws no doubt had strong ramifications for property relations. See Lefebvre-Teillard, "Marriage in France from the Sixteenth to the Eighteenth Century."

[79] Robert Descimon and Simone Geoffroy-Poisson, "La construction juridique d'un système patrimonial de l'office: Une affaire de patrilignage et de genre," in Élie Haddad and Robert Descimon (eds.), *Épreuves de noblesse. Les expériences nobiliaires de la haute robe parisienne (XVIe–XVIIIe siècle)* (Paris: Les Belles Lettres, 2010), 58. The boundaries between public and private law were fluid in the sixteenth century. A study of bastards shows that lawyers in the seventeenth century argued that excluding bastards from inheritance was "a '*public law*' (*droit public*) that could not be abrogated by 'the rights or dispositions of a particular province.'" Gerber, *Bastards*, 21. As he notes, this claim was not successful: the argument was rejected by the Parlement of Grenoble, much as other courts of the Midi had rejected the Edict of Mothers and the Edict of Second Marriages.

the competing creditors who in this regard receive the proceeds in proportion to their claims.[80]

A venal office was thus real property (*immeuble*) in the event of seizure; in all other cases it was a movable asset as part of the community property. As movable property, like cash and liquid wealth, it could be given freely inter vivos and was not subject to the *réserve des quatre quints* in testamentary bequest.[81]

This new provision in the *coutume* compelled parents to insert in marriage contracts the stipulation that the office was lineage property, or *propres*. The stake was high because the value of offices increased rapidly. The acquisition of an office was a major investment venture, which often required the mobilization of financial resources from both the groom's and the bride's families. When bought by the parents, it normally was considered *propres*. The office was commonly given to the groom as a dowry, just like a seigneurie or any other real property. Since it often happened that the couple was forced to sell the wife's *propres* as well as the husband's, with or without the *remploi* clause, the family that funded the purchase of the office wanted to protect the investment by characterizing it as *propres*. This way the officeholder was not free to alienate it, since it was guaranteed to future generations.[82] The designation of venal office as patrimonial property was particularly critical to *roturier* (non-noble) families. Local customary laws had done little to prevent the division and alienation of non-noble property.[83] The *coutume* of Paris reformed in 1580 left unanswered many questions regarding the property rights as to the offices.[84]

In 1604, Henry IV guaranteed the hereditary transmission of offices in return for the payment of annual dues, known as the *paulette*.[85] Judgeship now could be passed along without the danger of forfeiture, exempt from the rule of *quarante jours*.[86] As the venality system matured with the legalization of hereditary succession, the courts developed a series of case law regarding the legal state of the offices. Descimon and Geoffroy-Poisson have shown that a distinctive jurisprudence

[80] "Office vénal est reputé immeuble, & à suitte par hypothèque quand il est saisi sur le débiteur par authorité de justice paravant résignation admise & provision faite au profit d'un tiers: & peut estre crié & adjugé par decret: & toutesfois les deniers provenants de l'adjudication, sont sujets à contribution, comme meubles, entre les créanciers opposans qui viennent pour ce regard a desconfiture au sol la livre." *Nouveau coutumier général*, vol. 3, 37. A wife's property rights established by matrimonial agreements preceded those of other creditors, but Article 95 of the *Coutume* excluded the value of the office from the common property scheme.

[81] Descimon and Geoffroy-Poisson, "La construction juridique," 53. For *réserve coutumière*, see supra Chapter 5, notes 52 and 53 and accompanying text and also Map 5.1.

[82] Giesey, "Rules of Inheritance." [83] Bien, "Offices, Corps, and a System of State Credit," 95.

[84] Henry III, under whose reign the reformation of the *Coutume de Paris* took place, was vocal in wanting to abolish venality. It may have helped the trend of treating offices as lineage property. Descimon and Geoffroy-Poisson, "La construction juridique," 51.

[85] Mousnier, *La vénalité des offices*, 239–41.

[86] Under the rule of "quarante jours," no resignation in favor of another was valid unless the resigning party survived forty days after the completion of the transaction. Ibid., 44–46.

emerged on the property rights to office, which were fully reflective of the social perceptions and economic forces of the patrimony of the officials.[87] Their main thesis is that the case law effectively denied the female property ownership of offices and that the consolidation of the venality system disrupted equality between husband and wife, the fundamental spirit of the custom of Paris. This, argued the authors, was in departure from the practices in the sixteenth century when court judgments had treated the office as an *acquêt* of the conjugal community, barring stipulations otherwise in the marriage contract. A wife used to have the same rights as her children, but no longer so in the seventeenth century.

A few examples of the new jurisprudence are instructive. When a father gave an office to his son, it was his *propres*; when he gave it to his daughter, to be occupied by her husband, the office was an *acquêt* and the office entered conjugal property.[88] Whether the office was community property depended on who, husband or wife, died first. If the wife predeceased the husband, the office was treated as movable property and the widower split the value of the office with his children. When his children died after their mother, the father could inherit their portion of the office. If the husband predeceased the wife, by contrast, the office or its *remploi* was regarded as immovable property. Since *propres* did not ascend, the mother could not inherit from her children who died after her husband's death, and the share of the deceased child went to his or her siblings.[89]

The case law further established that, when an office was held in community property, the *mi-denier* the widower owed to the heirs of his wife was calculated on the value of the office at the time of its purchase, not at the time of succession. This was not a matter of small concern at a time of stupendous inflation of the values of the offices. All the capital gains from the increase in the price of the offices thus went to the surviving husband. If the office had been treated as immovable property and as hereditary possessions, its value would have been included in the calculation of the customary dower and counted as the basis of the predetermined dower. But the office was considered movable property for the purpose of the dower, before being considered "in the alternative" and added to the immovable property when there was not enough real property on which the dower could be set up. The office was included in the dower for the children in full extent as *propres*.[90] All these court decisions solidified the nature of the office as a property of males, creating an uneven relationship in marriage alliance. Eventually it thwarted the essence of the community property regime in customary law; a wife ceased to be the equal partner and collaborator of her husband.[91] Gender equity was not something that early modern jurisprudence could boast about.

[87] Descimon and Geoffroy-Poisson, "La construction juridique." [88] Ibid., 50.
[89] Ibid., 51. [90] Ibid., 52–53. [91] Ibid., 57.

Contemporary jurists uniformly decried the venality of offices. Hotman in *Francogallia* called it "base commerce and public robbery."

> It damages any kind of esteem in which other nations may hold France when a magistracy is offered at a single price and later its administration is divided up among individual claimants, just as a fine ox is bought from a butcher at a single price and is afterwards sold in pieces at a meat-market.[92]

It was like buying in bulk and selling in retail to make a high profit. In his *Epitre envoyée au Tigre de la France* (1560), Hotman accused the Guises of perverting justice by expanding the venality system.[93] The undertone of resentment against venal *robins* is unmistakable in Hotman's propaganda.[94] For Pasquier, selling and buying offices among private persons was a "calamité."[95] Dumoulin had a personal gripe: he fretted that he did not receive in France the recognition he deserved when foreigners were showering him with honors. "Why have I been neglected in my own country? The reason is simple: I did not want to purchase a judicial office or put up the state for auction."[96] Some expressed concerns that sale of offices slowed the industry and commerce of France by deflecting money and talent from entrepreneurial pursuits. Many young men, infatuated with a law career, bought offices but some became imprudent, Chancellor L'Hôpital regretted in 1566, as they "treated their offices as temporal goods and their own patrimonies and worried more about how to make a profit than about how to be of service to the king."[97]

Bodin methodically analyzed why sale of offices was harmful for the state. When princes "put on sale the estates, offices, and benefices, it is impossible ever to see a just distribution of punishments and rewards"; this lesson, well heeded in the past, was abandoned during the reign of King Francis and ignored by his

[92] *Francogallia*, ed. Giesey and Salmon, 518–19 (ch. 20 "The parlements as courts of law"). Hotman issued two new editions of *Francogallia* in 1576 and 1586, featuring substantial modifications from the earlier versions. So the precise chapter number for this section on the parlements varies.

[93] François Hotman, *Le Tigre de 1560*, ed. Charles Read (Geneva: Slatkine Reprints, 1970). See Rodolphe Peter, "Le 'Tigre' de François Hotman: Une énigme bibliographique résolue," *Bulletin de la Société de l'histoire du protestantisme français* 124 (1978), 113–18.

[94] Salmon, *Society in Crisis*, 125–26.

[95] Pasquier, *Les recherches de la France*, livre 4, ch. 17, *Les œuvres*, vol. 1, col. 405.

[96] Thireau, *Charles du Moulin*, 269. Dumoulin's personal grievance against venality is worth noting. His career was in stark contrast with de Thou's. The two were colleagues when de Thou was an *avocat* at the Parlement of Paris. They had daily contact, likely sharing their ideas on reforming customs, and one can speculate de Thou was deeply influenced by Dumoulin's intellect and vision. Salmon, *Society in Crisis*, 157–58. Unlike de Thou who became a president of the Parlement in 1554 by purchasing the office, Dumoulin was unable to advance his career. The two remained good friends, nevertheless. Dumoulin designated de Thou as the executor of his will. See Peguera Poch, *Aux origines de la réserve héréditaire du Code civil*, part 2, ch. 2, # 63.

[97] Remonstrance in the assembly at Moulins, January 24, 1566, in *Michel de L'Hospital discours II*, ed. Petris and Amherdt, 82.

successors.[98] By selling offices, the kings "sell the most sacred thing in the world, which is justice, they sell the Republic, they sell the blood of the subjects, they sell the laws, and they take away all the rewards of honor, virtue, learning, piety, and religion; they open the gates to theft, corruption, avarice, injustice, ignorance, impiety, in short, all vice and villainy."[99] The king claimed that his fiscal situation required the venality, but "there is no veritable excuse or real semblance to seek the ruin of the state under the pretense of poverty. And it is a ridiculous thing for a prince to pretend poverty, as he would have so many means to prevent it if he wanted to."[100]

Fortunately for historians, Bodin's frustration with these practices did not stop him from undertaking a full analysis of the legal attributes of venal offices. Bodin placed the system under scrutiny within the framework of private law. For the king as well as his subjects, buying and selling an office was a commercial enterprise, conducted in accordance with the law of obligations and subject to changing market forces, as much as any other contractual exchange of property.[101] We now turn attention to these legal issues in royal transactions.

Public Office and Private Law of Obligations

Bodin conceptualized the sale of offices in terms of a civil law contract between the king and his officials. For him, the office was a property loaned—not sold—by the king to the officeholder, for the consideration of the price the latter paid to the royal treasury. As a commercial contract, the transaction was governed by the laws of obligations: the king could not break the terms of the agreement without the consent of the other party. It meant the king, the owner of the office, could not demand it back until he could return the money. From a legal point of view, what were transferred were the revenues from the office, on loan, and not the office itself. The officeholders could dispose of their offices like their own property, within limitations, but they never owned them outright.

This formulation conformed to the opinions of contemporary legists that all royal officials merely exercised a part of the crown's prerogative that remained undivided and their appointment could be revoked at any time by the king. Dumoulin saw an office as an entity of private rights in nature, as guaranteed in custom, but he stressed that the officeholders' rights were limited because the offices emanated from the king to whom they must ultimately revert. Their rights did not constitute full proprietary rights of ownership for the reason that the

[98] Bodin, *Les six livres de la république*, book 5, ch. 4 ("De loyer, et de la peine"), 572.

[99] Ibid., 573.

[100] Ibid.

[101] Ralph E. Giesey, "State-Building in Early Modern France: The Role of Royal Officialdom," *Journal of Modern History* 55 (1983), 204.

power to command, *merum imperium*, belonged to the king alone. "When the common good and the necessity of the public weal require it," Dumoulin argued, "everything is the king's."[102] Still, the king could not arbitrarily encroach upon the rights of the officeholders and must respect them like any other private property rights.[103] Likewise, he insisted that the king, in attempting to restrict seigneurial powers, must follow proper legal procedures.

Is a prince subject to the laws of his country which he had sworn to keep? For Bodin, these are actually two separate questions that must be distinguished. "If the prince swears unto himself that he will keep his law, he is no more bound by his law than by the oath made unto himself."[104] Bodin continued:

> We must not confound *la loy* with *le contrat. La loy* depends on the one who has the sovereignty, which can bind all his subjects but cannot bind himself. The *convention* is mutual between the prince and his subjects, which reciprocally bind the two parties; one of the parties cannot violate it with prejudice and without the consent of the other. The prince in this case has nothing above his subject.[105]

In the case of *contrat* involving the sale of offices, the king was held to the obligation to respect the terms that he had agreed on: without reimbursement of the purchase value, the king could not dismiss the *officier*.[106] On this premise Bodin concluded that "the office is like a borrowed thing, which the owner cannot demand back before the time it was lent for be expired."[107] The king promised to operate within the bounds of the civil law principles of the contract he had entered into, this while he continued to harry the *parlementaires* with demands for forced loans.

It is helpful to recall that France was a society of *corps*, or corporate bodies. The king addressed himself less to individuals than to bodies. Examples were the three estates, the *corps* of officials, the communities of different professions, and the territorial and local communities, provinces, *pays*, cities, towns and villages, and their inhabitants. "The French kingdom was a motley conglomerate of particularism" and "it was the king who assured the cohesion of its fabric."[108] When the

[102] "Quando commune bonum, & reipublicae necessitas," "omnia sunt Regis." Tit. 1, art. 3, gloss 6, no. 65, in *Omnia*, vol. 1, 81.

[103] Ibid., 239. Thireau, *Charles du Moulin*, 269; Salmon, "France," 466.

[104] Bodin, *Les six livres*, book 1, ch. 9 ("De la souverainete"), 133.

[105] "Le Prince en ce cas n'a rien par dessus le sujet." Ibid., 134.

[106] Chénon, *Histoire générale du droit français*, vol. 2, 345.

[107] "L'office est comme une chose empruntée, que le propriétaire ne peut demander que le temps prefix ne soit expiré." Bodin, *Les six livres*, book 3, ch. 2, 319. See Lee, "'Office Is a Thing Borrowed.'"

[108] Barbiche, *Les institutions de la monarchie française*, 4–5.

competing *corps* and institutions wanted to obtain the most benefit, they turned to the crown.[109] The king was the ultimate arbiter between them. Yet the king was himself dependent on corporate institutions from which he could draw financial advantages. Corporate society imposed legal as well as fiscal restraints on royal discretion, which prompted the king to abide by custom and the law. Above all, the market forces did. Turning to the exercise of his arbitrary power in the seventeenth and eighteenth centuries would thus have destroyed royal credibility in fiscal matters, alienating future clients in contracting loans. Obtaining steady and cheap credit was crucial as the king went on with his foreign wars in earnest.[110]

One can argue that the French monarchy was perpetually engaged in franchising public authority, whether to feudal seigneurs, venal magistrates, or tax farmers. As mentioned in Chapter 2, the term *franchises* in the Middle Ages was synonymous with *libertés* or simply *coutumes*. In the early modern period, the link between franchise and immemorial custom was broken when customary law was homologated by the king, allowing the royal enterprises of venality of offices and tax farming to reach an unprecedented level.

The king and his ministers were remarkably resourceful in utilizing the credit system built on venal offices to their gains. In fact, one of the most salient challenges to the revisionist view of limited monarchical power is the argument that the king was fully capable of making magistrates pay, repeatedly, by threatening the creation of new offices and imposing forced loans.[111] The parlements naturally resisted the increase in the number of offices because it would depress the prices of existing offices and the value of their investment. At the same time, the king periodically bluffed them into accepting his demands by saying that he would finally revoke existing offices in accordance with the edicts (with the option of recreating them at a higher price). In either case, the magistrates invariably fell in line.

Another effective measure of extracting wealth was the so-called *augmentations de gages*, or a salary increase. This meant increased *gages* were to be the interest payment on the additional capital the *officier* had to place in the office.[112] Royal demands for forced loans from the magistrates were not unusual in the sixteenth century. In 1542, L'Hôpital, a young *conseiller* at the Parlement of Paris, was assessed for two hundred *écus*, his share of the loan the king demanded from the magistrates. The future chancellor asked why this disproportionate sum should be levied on him, while his richer colleagues escaped rather easily.[113] The

[109] Cremer, "La genèse de la notion de noblesse de robe," 25–26.

[110] See Hilton Root, "Tying the King's Hands: Credible Commitments and Royal Fiscal Policy during the Old Regime," *Rationality and Society* 1 (1989), 240–58. Farming out tax collection in the seventeenth and eighteenth centuries was an important state commercial venture.

[111] Bien, "Offices, Corps, and a System of State Credit," 97; Hurt, *Louis XIV and the Parlements*, 7–8, 68–74.

[112] Mousnier, *La vénalité des offices*, 308, 400–15.

[113] Kim, *Michel de L'Hœpital*, 18.

government in the seventeenth century made financial extraction into an art form. The demonstrated power of Louis XIV to secure loans from the parlements contradicted revisionist historians' argument that the king was compelled to reach a social compromise with officeholders.[114]

The significant point seems to lie not so much in whether the king cared about the economic and social interests of the elites as in the fact that their relationship was forged over the king's commitment to their venal interests and privileges. Whether he did so willingly or reluctantly is of secondary importance. Preservation of the elites' privileges can be called "feudal," but it was an essential measure to sustain the finance of the "modern" state. As David Bien aptly put it, "many of the privileges were surprisingly modern in origin, not medieval," and "they had little to do with domination by an agrarian elite."[115] The state credit system, with attendant personal and corporate entitlements, operated under the written law.

Early modern corporatism has been portrayed as evidence of a continuation of medievalism. But the existence of corporate bodies like the judicial officials led the king to adhere to his commitment to upholding the individual subject's property rights and fulfilling his obligations, namely, the rule of law. It was in the same spirit of imposing the binding written law of customs. When various interest groups jockeyed for privileges and social supremacy, the existence of clear, settled laws and the presence of a powerful king to enforce them were essential.[116] Maintaining partnership with them required the king's guarantee to his constituency of their rights in law. The king used the instrument of law to manage both the corporate groups and their components.

Here is the paradox of absolutism, an obviously loaded term. When the king claimed full power, he had less real power; when he claimed *not* to be above the law, he had less difficulty in governing the state. The king could enhance royal authority and derive strength by assuring his subjects that he was willing to honor his legal obligations. The result was a far more refined concept of sovereignty, compatible with the absolute *imperium* of the king. Considered in terms of a legal contract, the venality of offices had significance beyond the privatization of public power; it served as a mechanism that sustained the coexistence of the contractual theory of kingship and the rhetoric of the divine right of rulers.

What about the venal *officiers*? Were they more concerned with their social interests than with official duty? To what end did they wield their power and authority? "Traditional" historiography tended to find public mindedness among

[114] Hurt, *Louis XIV and the Parlements* 75; Swann, *Provincial Power and Absolute Monarchy*, 16 (the revisionist scholarship of absolutism "exaggerates the extent to which the monarchy was in thrall to vested interests").

[115] Bien, "Offices, Corps, and a System of State Credit," 111.

[116] Henshall, "Early Modern Absolutism," 19.

royal judges than more skeptical-minded scholars of late.[117] There is much truth in the view that public office in the sixteenth and seventeenth centuries was a source of profit rather than a duty to the king or to the country, at least judged by Enlightenment standards. A typical *parlementaire* family was more interested in enjoying the privileges of nobility than in destroying them. Without importing too much of a modern bureaucratic state into the early modern period, one can nevertheless argue that the *jus commune* training of officials, who identified the laws they applied with the royal will and common good, might have inculcated in them a sense of public duty and the commitment to the rule of law.[118] The spirit of law as a science of *gouvernance publique* spilled over to customary law in the sixteenth century through royal campaign.[119] It was an enterprise which legal humanists eagerly supported as responses to the need of society to make the heterogeneous diversity of law in medieval society more homogeneous and controllable.

Throughout history, law often functioned as a privileged instrument of power. Yet, subsuming judicial function under the narrow class or gender paradigm or reducing individual judges to the role of male heads-of-household serving as trustees of their patrimony may be oversimplifying matters. Would pursuing private interest be conclusively detrimental to the commonwealth? To quote Montaigne, "the common interest must not require all things of all men against the private interest."[120] Or, more simply, it would be worth recalling that people can have many different reasons for doing something, and they are not always reducible to their perceived socioeconomic interests. There is no sense in thinking that public officials in the sixteenth century were necessarily worse guardians of law than they are in our own.

Recognition of the role of legal professionals in sustaining—or disrupting—the rule of law highlights the importance of law in historiography. It has been rightly pointed out that many early modern historians, "having distinguished 'law' from 'practice,'" now "treat the former with a skepticism bordering on indifference."[121] The theme of the appropriation of legal norms in social practices has downplayed the importance of the sources of law. But codified customs and royal ordinances and doctrinal considerations of them could be seen as honest reflections of

[117] This allegedly semi-romantic, nostalgic royalist historiography was less punctilious in its use of the term absolutism.

[118] Lloyd, *The State, France, and the Sixteenth Century*, 42, 47.

[119] The "positivization" of the law, of both customs and legislation, had the effect of reducing the potential of Roman law as an art of governance. Wijffels, "Une très brève histoire du droit," 404. See also Descamps and Wijffels, "Approches historiques," 70–73.

[120] Montaigne put it in terms of a dilemma, in *Les Essais*, book 3, ch. 1 ("Of the useful and the honorable"); *The Complete Essays of Montaigne*, 609. "Our country does not come before all other duties; and it is good for it to have citizens who are dutiful to their parents" (citing Cicero); "Let us abandon this monstrous and deranged justice and stick to more human imitations," 609–10.

[121] The quote is from Gerber, "Family, the State, and Law," 481.

society, revealing perceptions of individuals of early modern France, no less than the unfolding of practices of law in the courtroom.[122] It is still important to look at juristic and jurisprudential arguments as well as the actions of legislators or judges in the public realm, separate from their motivations suggested in a cultural paradigm. After all, one would like to think that lawyers and judges were interested not so much in engendering a particular social order as in providing solutions to the specific questions before them.[123]

When the parlements resisted the registration of royal edicts, they were asserting their time-honored institutional role in the legislative process. Efforts to explain their actions do not need to be confined to a narrow perspective of the socioeconomic interest of the robe nobility. It seems clear that neither the king nor local elites could dominate the early social structure with their brute feudal or patriarchal interest alone.

3. Custom and Constitutional Theory

At the beginning of the sixteenth century, Claude de Seyssel (1458–1520) set forth the boundaries of royal authority in terms of *loi fondamentale*: the king was obligated to preserve the "libertez, priuileges et louables coustumes" of the estates in society.[124] "La civilité," which demanded observance, was custom, which meant the right to property.[125] The king also needed to correct or abolish the customs that no longer had value, which constituted the check of "la police."[126] When Seyssel declared that the law court performed the role of the *frein de justice*, he was referring to the duty of the court to protect the rights of a given party in accordance with law.[127] Seyssel's theory signaled changes in the medieval tradition of respect reserved for custom. Historical inquiries into the origin and nature of custom had already lifted much of the mystique surrounding custom as *loi fondamentale*. Roman law theories of royal prerogatives to make and unmake the law diminished the role of custom as a constraint on royal authority.

In the early sixteenth century, Chasseneuz affirmed that the recording of custom meant not so much making new law but confirming extant usage; royal approval turned the latter into law. His contemporary Rebuffi similarly stated that the written customs approved by the prince had the force of *leges*, and that the prince was bound to observe custom only if it contained natural law and

[122] See Jérôme-Luther Viret, "La reproduction familiale et sociale en France sous l'Ancien Régime: Le rapport au droit et aux valeurs," *Histoire & sociétés rurales* 29 (2008), 165–88.

[123] These are the words of Gerber, "Family, the State, and Law," 483.

[124] Claude de Seyssel, *La grande monarchie de France* (Paris: Galiot du Pré, 1557), part 2, ch. 18, 36v. On Seyssel, see Nannerl O. Keohane, "Claude de Seyssel and Sixteenth-Century Constitutionalism in France," *Nomos* 20 (1979), 47–83.

[125] Seyssel, *La grande monarchie*, part 2, ch. 2, 19v.

[126] Ibid., part 1, ch. 10, 12r.

[127] Ibid., part 1, ch. 10, 11v–12v. See Church, *Constitutional Thought*, 25–27.

reason.[128] In the same vein, Tiraqueau believed that, even though the prince should not infringe a person's legal right without just cause, the prince was not bound by custom as positive law so long as it was not based on divine or natural law or *jus gentium*. In William Church's summation, Tiraqueau's opinion represented "the transition from the medieval identification of law as custom to the later concepts subordinating both law and popular rights to the prince."[129] Again, it was Dumoulin who decidedly reaffirmed royal authority over custom. For him, equity was the key criterion in evaluating the merit of individual customs; by identifying equity with royal power, he subjugated custom under the king's authority.[130]

Pasquier lent support to the idea of custom as the law made by the people, but he still attributed superior authority to ordinances. He wrote that the king, who "owes us justice," had the duty to "administer justice according to where we live and where our property is located."[131] In other words, the king had the obligation to respect the diversity of local custom. However, "there is a big difference between *la loi* and *la coustume*," and "we never accept *la coustume* that directly contravenes *la loi*." Collected customs were published and registered at the parlements, but it was not the same as the homologation of ordinances, because the registration process for customs aimed merely to give notice to the public and make them more readily available in the jurisdictions of *bailliages*.[132] Thus:

> No one can be excused for ignorance of *la loy commune*, which was established by the king, yet one can be excused for his ignorance of a *coustume* which is, just like a *statut*, more a matter of the fact than of the law.[133]

Pasquier underscored the general principle that the king had the right to approve or abolish custom: "it has always been the general rule that the law of the prince can depart from custom."[134] Custom can be changed by royal ordinance, moral or natural precepts, religion, or public necessity. Any custom that contradicted a

[128] Church, *Constitutional Thought*, 64–65, 110. [129] Ibid., 67, 105.

[130] Dumoulin was not always consistent. In his annotation on Article 447 of the custom of Maine that legal actions to rescind contracts could be brought within thirty years, Dumoulin referred to an ordinance of Louis XII, issued in 1512, as an example that the king did not intend to override a contrary custom: "The custom indeed was not only sanctioned in perpetuity by the three estates of the district, but it was enrolled at the Parlement of Paris, and from their authority the good king Louis XII could not, and did not wish or intend to, derogate." Dumoulin, *Le grand coustumier general*, vol. 2, 102. In his notes to other customs, however, he argued that royal ordinances were effective in abrogating customary rules. Julien Brodeau, pointing to Dumoulin's similar annotation on the custom of Anjou, said that the royal ordinance in question was in force in both jurisdictions. See *Nouveau coutumier général*, vol. 4, 511–12, note h, and 575, note d. See Dawson, "French Customs," 792–93, note 103.

[131] The king "owes us justice [*nous est debiteur de la Justice*]." Pasquier, *Lettres*, book 6, letter 2 (to Choppin), *Les œuvres*, vol. 2, cols. 156–57.

[132] *Plaidoyé d'Estienne Pasquier pour Monsieur le Duc de Lorraine*, *Les œuvres*, vol. 1, col. 1092.

[133] Ibid. *Statut* here refers to Roman law observed in Italian cities.

[134] Pasquier, *L'interprétation des Institutes de Justinian*, book 1, ch. 16, 34.

royal ordinance was presumptively invalid; conversely, nothing precluded an ordinance from deviating from custom. "It is a very clear rule," he concluded, that "the general law of the prince can efface, at the stroke of a pen, all the private customs of every province."[135]

Pasquier's opinion was shared by Choppin. Choppin placed emphasis on the historical process of the homologation of customs. The king authorized the writing of local custom at the assembly of the estates; the *procès-verbal* of the reformation proceedings was justly its soul (*l'âme*).[136] "The king alone gives laws to his people or is the sole author who gathers and establishes customs for his subjects"; "this sovereign right was never communicated to inferior seigneurs."[137]

In comparison with Pasquier and Choppin, Coquille was reluctant to characterize the published *coutumes* as virtual royal ordinances and was more insistent on the authority of the people to make their law. In Coquille's writings there was a complete absence of "the precept unanimously supported by the Parisian legists, namely, that the king might abolish individual local customs through royal ordinance."[138] Specific characteristics of Coquille's thoughts—emphasis on the contractual character of custom and confidence on the independence and self-sufficiency of customary law—have been ascribed to his career in relative isolation in the province, largely separated from the contemporary intellectual trends in the capital.[139] Coquille held a genuine aversion to centrally driven royal interference with local custom and to the claim that the *coutume* of Paris was the de facto *coutume* of the entire France. In this regard, he was at the opposite end of the spectrum from Dumoulin. A quintessential Parisian, Dumoulin had no reservation in declaring that the custom of Paris was the basis of a common law, a ready reference in the conflict of laws, and eventually the foundation of a unified French law.[140] Coquille's deep knowledge of local customs also left him unconvinced of Dumoulin's enchantment with Roman law; the custom of Nivernais was known for its strong French characteristics with relatively little borrowing from Roman law. Coquille's defense of local customs was an oddity, one can conclude, in the general climate of opinion of the time, and this is in part why he has received so much attention from historians. It attests that juristic opinions of legal humanists were in large part shaped by their personal and professional backgrounds.

[135] "La Loy generale du Prince efface par un seul trait de plume, toutes les Coustumes particulieres de chasque Province." Pasquier, *Lettres*, book 19, letter 15 (to Robert), *Les œuvres*, col. 577.

[136] Choppin, *Commentaires sur la coustume d'Anjou*, "Avant-Propos," part 2, question 6, *Les œuvres*, vol. 1, 43.

[137] Ibid., part 3, question 2, in *Les œuvres*, vol. 1, 48.

[138] Church, *Constitutional Thought*, 286. [139] Ibid., 276, 301.

[140] Kelley, *Foundations of Modern Historical Scholarship*, 172; Kelley, "Civil Science in the Renaissance," 266.

The recording of customs rendered the notion of royal legislative power in private law less extraordinary. The groundwork was laid for promoting the concord of *coutume* in public law. Bodin and Le Caron each provided theoretical justifications for the supremacy of royal legislation, an expression of sovereignty, which formed the foundation for the constitution of France.

Bodin and the True Marks of Sovereignty

Historians agree that Bodin's constitutional thought underwent a metamorphosis, likely in reaction to the Monarchomach theory of popular sovereignty.[141] In 1566, Bodin wrote in his *Methodus ad facilem historiarum cognitionem* that the king was not properly above the law. The king "cannot destroy the laws peculiar in the entire kingdom or alter any of the customs of the cities or ancient ways without the consent of the Three Estates."[142] Concerning the parlements, he stated "those who have been trying to overthrow the dignity of these courts seek the ruin of the state, since in them is placed the safety of civil order, laws, customs, and the entire state."[143] In *Les six livres de la république*, ten years later, Bodin moved away from his earlier constitutional position and accepted an unlimited monarchy as the only means of restoring political unity and peace.

For Bodin, a key element of royal power was exclusive legislative power. It signaled a departure from the medieval tradition of kingship, which tended to treat the ruler primarily as a judge. Bodin refuted as absurd the argument that the sovereign prince could not make law without the consent of the estates or the parlements. The only restraints came from God and nature:

> As for divine and natural laws, all princes of the earth are subject to them, and it is not in their power to contravene them, if they do not want to be culpable of divine lèse-majesté, making war on God, under whose greatness all monarchs of the world must make yoke and lower the head in all fear and reverence. And by this the absolute power of the princes and sovereign lordships does not extend beyond the laws of God and nature.[144]

This means no law, except for divine and natural law, is binding on the sovereign. Royal laws deserved obedience. When the prince chose the laws for the benefit of the public, some individuals gained profits and others suffered losses but, in either

[141] Monarchomachs refer to French Huguenot theorists who opposed monarchy during the religious wars, justifying tyrannicide. See J. H. M. Salmon, "Bodin and the Monarchomachs," in Horst Denzer (ed.), *Jean Bodin: Verhandlungen der internationalen Bodin Tagung in München* (Munich: C. H. Beck, 1973), 359–78.

[142] Bodin, *Method for the Easy Comprehension of History*, ch. 6, 204.

[143] Ibid., ch. 6, 257.

[144] Bodin, *Les six livres de la république*, book 1, ch. 9, 133.

case, "it is not lawful for a subject to oppose the laws of his prince under the color of honesty or justice."[145]

In his characteristic analytical style, Bodin expounded on the relationship between custom and royal authority. He declared: "custom has force only by sufferance and only so long as it pleases the sovereign prince, who may make a law from it by putting thereupon his own affirmation"; thus "all the force of civil laws and customs lies in the power of the sovereign prince."[146] The king's lawmaking power was not limited by custom. The coronation oath, stated Bodin, did not bind the monarch to keep the laws and customs of the land.[147] Some people might say that "not only the magistrates have the power to make edicts and laws, each one according to his authority and jurisdiction, but private individuals make customs, both general and particular" and that "custom has no less power than the law, and just as the sovereign prince is the master of the law so are private individuals masters of the customs."[148] But these were misconceptions, which he quickly set out to correct.

Bodin wrote: "For general and private laws and customs, which do not concern the establishment of the kingdom, we are not used to changing them, before we have properly assembled the three estates in France in general, or in each *bailliage* in particular." It was "not because it is necessary to abide by their advice or the king may not do the contrary to what they demand when natural reason and justice of his wishes require it." Rather, it was because "in doing so the greatness and majesty of a true Prince sovereign is recognized when the estates of all the people gathered and present requests and supplications to their prince in all humility, without any power of commanding or discerning or deliberative voice." In brief, "what pleases the king to consent, dissent, command, or prohibit becomes law, edict, or ordinance."[149] The king has his laws consented to and verified in the three estates and the parlements, not because he cannot make laws without them but simply because it is a good thing to do:

> As to the verification of the edicts by the Estates or the Parlements, it plays a role of great consequence in having the laws observed; not that the sovereign prince cannot make law, but that, as Theodosius says, *humanum esse*, meaning that the consent of the Senate was obtained, not so much of necessity as of courtesy, for it is said in a similar case that it is good that the senate makes the prince keep his law. There is nothing that arouses more awe and reverence among the subjects than the authority of his law; on the contrary, there is nothing more dangerous than the contempt the sovereign holds in his own law.[150]

[145] Book 1, ch. 9, 147.
[146] Book 1, ch. 11, 198.
[147] Book 1, ch. 9, 135.
[148] Book 1, ch. 11, 198.
[149] Book 1, ch. 9, 136–37.
[150] Book 1, ch. 9, 145.

Custom draws its weight from the prince alone and has force only so long as it pleases him; the king may quash it through a simple royal act if he so desires.[151] When the three estates present humble petitions, "the king may accept or reject them as he sees fit."[152] Bodin contrasted custom with the law:

> Custom takes force little by little, and it takes many years before the common consent of all or of most people becomes known; but the law comes forth instantly and takes the vigor of the one who has the power to command all. Custom flows gently and without force, whereas the law is commanded and published through power, and oftentimes contrary to the subjects' liking. This is why Dio Chrysostom compared custom to a king and the law to a tyrant. Moreover, custom can be abolished by the laws but not the laws by custom. It is always within the authority and power of the magistrate and those who are charged with having the laws observed, to execute them when they deem it desirable.[153]

La coutume and *la loy* have different origins, but both depend on the power of the sovereign prince. Bodin's exposition of royal sovereignty transcended the traditional boundaries in existence between local law and national law, between public law and private law, and between the customs and ordinances. Bodin's contemporary Louis Le Caron pushed these ideas forward with his own royalist and positivist overtones.

Le Caron Defines *Coutume* and *Loy*

Le Caron stood out from his contemporaries for his polemic against Roman law and at the same time intense distrust of custom.[154] Critical of the tendency of French scholars to adhere to Roman law, he reminded the readers that Roman law in France was, as declared in the famous ordinance of Philip IV, a "custom and common usage," resorted to as "reason, as one uses the precepts and rules of other sciences."[155] But "the subtlety of Roman law has changed and corrupted the simplicity of the ancient French law so much that it only promotes new lawsuits regarding questions and diverse interpretations or contradictions of Roman law."[156]

[151] Book 1, ch. 11, 198. [152] Book 2, ch. 1, 226–27.

[153] Book 1, ch. 11, 198. Dio Chrysostom (40–120) was a Greek orator and historian of the Roman Empire.

[154] See Slongo, "Genealogie della consuetudine," 166–70.

[155] Le Caron, *Pandectes ou digestes du droit françois*, book 1, ch. 25 ("De la Coustume"), 398. See supra Chapter 2, note 29.

[156] Ibid., book 1, ch. 2, 11. Le Caron expressed a similar opinion in his *Responses ou decisions du droict françois*: Roman law is not the *droict commun de la France*. Wijffels, "Ancien Régime France," 90.

While he advocated French custom over Roman law, Le Caron still viewed it as an inadequate choice to be the legitimate basis of French law. He distinguished custom from the king's law: "custom, even if it has the force of law because it is regarded as law by those who use it and have long used, is nevertheless not properly law." In a language quite similar, but with a twist, to that of Bodin, Le Caron argued:

> There is a great difference between *la loy* and *la coutume*: *la loy* is a general ordinance and, to define it precisely, we must say it should not be considered law unless it is just or has been produced by reason. But *la coutume* is a common observance, which is passed on gently by tacit consent of those who have used it, and sometimes rather for the benefit or convenience of the most powerful people than by just and right reason. Often it is not general but particular to the region where it has taken force and authority. So, in opposition to Dio's opinion, I compare *la loy* to the king and *la coutume* to the tyrant. The tyrant (as Plato says) creeps up gently and gradually establishes himself, refusing the name of tyrant: but having empowered himself he turns to force and command. On the contrary, the king rules with full power, not by force but by the laws. *La coutume* often has reason for usage alone, but *la loy* is founded on natural and civil reason.[157]

In sum, law is the work of the prince and is necessarily equitable, founded upon justice and reason; custom, on the other hand, is but fortuitous usages. It lacked the two elements vital to a true law, namely, conformity with justice and creation by sovereign authority.[158]

According to Le Caron, most odious about custom, apart from its diversity, was its supposedly mysterious character—immemorial nature, popular consent, and so forth—which only gave rise to all kinds of abuses and privileges. Scholars and legal practitioners were equally to blame:

> Different schools and factions of Roman jurisconsults (not to mention philosophers) brought great confusion to jurisprudence, and furthermore they brought these practitioners who were for the most part ignorant of good letters. Customs were secretly preserved by them and, having not been written down and published to anyone, customs depended on their responses and testimonies, or rather oracles, as if they were some venerable Druids.[159]

[157] Le Caron, *Pandectes ou digestes du droit françois*, book 1, ch. 25, 391. [158] Ibid.

[159] *Nouveau commentaire de L. Charondas le Caron . . . sur la coustume de la Ville, Prevosté, & Vicomté de Paris, ou droict civil parisien* (Paris: P. Mettayer, 1613), "Avant-Propos" [n.p.].

Sovereign courts often corrected evil customs that were "contrary to the law of nature": the Parlement of Rouen successfully quashed the "barbaric, uncivil and unreasonable custom" of Normandy which prohibited the children of those who had been condemned to death from succeeding their ascendants or other relatives.[160] In most cases, however, "the conflicting and different opinions of judges and legal practitioners" perpetuated the hopeless diversity of customs.[161]

At last, the king ordered the reformation of the *coutume* of Paris, which was carried out "by some hidden providence of God reserved for our times in the aftermath of the great troubles and civil wars of France." France, "which recognizes but one king . . . must have only one and the same law or *coustume* . . . that conforms to the law of Paris."[162] But Le Caron could not hide his discontent, and puzzlement, that the reformed customs at the end of the sixteenth century were still called *les coutumes* when, in reality, they bore no distinction from *la loi*. He observed:

> Now that all the customs of major provinces of the *pays* of France which we used to call *coustumier* are recorded in writing, it seems that the distinction of *droit escrit* and *non escrit* no longer exists; it is even considered that when we speak of law we mean that which is general for all the *pays*, and not the mores and *coustumes* of particular provinces.[163]

When *un droit* which had drawn its force and authority from the mutual consent of the people "*accoustumé* to it" comes to be "written down and authorized by the sovereign to have the force of *loy* and perpetual edict," he claimed, "it loses the name *coutume* and must be understood under the name of *droict escrit*," which was precisely the case of "the *coutumes* of France that had been reformed and redacted in writing."[164] He contended that the *pays de coutumes* in the north and the center of the kingdom became the veritable *pays de droit écrit* after the customary law campaign, governed by the codified rules, and that the *pays* in the Midi became in effect the *pays de coutumes*, where the use of Roman law had been allowed by the king to have the force of law only in the form of custom and common usage.[165]

Le Caron's protest notwithstanding, the old designations of *pays de coutumes* in the north and *pays du droit écrit* in the south persisted. Yet, one hardly fails to see the point he tried to get across: the promulgated customs became quasi-legislation. Le Caron may have exaggerated, but he clearly saw the semantic confusion surrounding the term "custom." He seemed to have a sense of foreboding

160 Le Caron, *Pandectes ou digestes du droit françois*, book 1, ch. 25, 394.
161 Ibid., book 1, ch. 25, 389–90.
162 Le Caron, *Nouveau commentaire*, "Avant-Propos" [n.p.].
163 Le Caron, *Pandectes ou digestes du droit françois*, book 1, ch. 2, 12–13.
164 Ibid., book 1, ch. 6, 60.
165 Lebrun, *La coutume*, 82–85.

about custom's ambiguous and polysemic nature, which would indeed cause grief to generations of historians over the next several hundred years, continuing to this day.

Both Bodin and Le Caron, who watched the customary law campaigns first-hand, were convinced that the opinions of the estates or the parlements did not limit the king's authority to make law. Bodin achieved the completion of his theorization of sovereignty when, according to Church, he confirmed "the subordination of customary law to the ruler, and the separation of that law from the inviolable legal rights of the subjects."[166] Positive law no longer bound the king; he could now be bound only by divine and natural law, which inhered in the extraconstitutional realm. The immunities of the subjects on the basis of natural law "proved to be but a step toward their subjection to the ruler" as they lacked "those stabilizing qualities inherent in the older constitutionalism."[167] The obligation of the king to promote the common interest (*intérêt commun* or *intérêt public*) in law was the gist of fundamental laws, or constitutional restraints, that the law courts would try to harness on the monarch.[168]

A lawful government ruled by the sovereign with the established law became the crux of the new constitutional consciousness. The shift, emerging from the abyss of civil war, consolidated through civil law.

[166] Church, *Constitutional Thought*, 237. [167] Ibid., 328, 335.

[168] François Saint-Bonnet, "L'intérêt général dans l'ancien droit constitutionnel," in Bertrand Mathieu, Michel Verpeaux, Josseline de Clausade, and Michel Charasse (eds.), *L'intérêt général, norme constitutionnelle* (Paris: Dalloz, 2007), 9–21.

8

De la Coutume au Code Civil

The adage of one king, one law, and one religion became a veritable article of faith during the religious wars. When the country was ravaged by confessional conflicts and its survival was in doubt, the idea of civil law was articulated by jurists and state administrators with a keen sense of urgency, as a means to stop the forces threatening political unity and to bring civil peace. Discussion of how they responded to the trials and tribulations of civil war underscores the importance of making sense of the role of individuals in the face of the inexorable forces of history. The first part of this chapter focuses on two prominent judicial officials of the time, Chancelier L'Hôpital and Premier président de Thou, and examines how they endeavored to restore the ideals of law during the national crisis.

After the wars were over, the recovery and consolidation of the monarchy began. The idea of French law matured with the increasing stability of the state, but with less of its earlier vitality. The monarchy in the seventeenth century grew more competent but more complacent. Now that the crown enjoyed unobstructed power of legislation, there seemed to be no pressing reason for discussing the various sources of law. The orthodox mentality in the reign of Louis XIV paradoxically lessened the imperativeness of one king and one law. Doctrinal jurists turned more skeptical about the project of unifying customs. Complaints against the maze of conflicting jurisdictions and pervasive arbitrariness in the administration of the law were loudly voiced by exasperated *philosophes* in the eighteenth century, but the last decades of the ancien régime arguably lacked sufficient political impulse to bring meaningful changes.

The demise of custom as law at the outbreak of the Revolution was swift and decisive. It marked the passing of a distinct perception in law. The force of custom came from the past; now the role of the past in shaping the contents of the law was consciously and comprehensively rejected by the revolutionaries. Amidst the revolutionary euphoria, history no longer seemed a destiny. The last part of the present chapter provides a very brief overview of the French law's trajectory through this pivotal phase in history, with some reflections on its implications in modern French law.

Custom, Law, and Monarchy: A Legal History of Early Modern France. Marie Seong-Hak Kim, Oxford University Press.
 DOI: 10.1093/oso/9780192845498.003.0008

1. Civil Law and Civil War

One can cut through the complex mesh of constitutional pretensions and political contentions between the king and the Parlement of Paris in the second half of the sixteenth century by focusing on L'Hôpital and de Thou.[1] As discussed in the preceding chapters, each played a central role in creating a rational and unified legal system, L'Hôpital through the legislative reform of judicial administration and de Thou through customary law reform. The chancellor of France and the first president of the Parlement of Paris were two of the most important royal officials in early modern France.[2] Each post was a commissioned office at the pleasure of the king, never venal or transmissible. Both L'Hôpital and de Thou were known for their moderate religious views. They were Ciceronian stoics, opposed to persecution and violence.[3] They shared a belief in the ideal of justice and the reforming spirit of law. They were both convinced that the key solution for the calamities of war that splintered the kingdom resided in the restoration of *l'État de droit*. They were deeply attached to Gallicanism. All these affinities notwithstanding, they had institutional—historical—roles to play, representing different dimensions of royal justice. During the civil war, they faced down each other over the religious pacification policy.

Two Perceptions of Royal Justice: L'Hôpital and de Thou

In 1560, shortly after his elevation to the chancellorship, L'Hôpital told the Parlement of Paris that the magistrates, as councilors to the king, should help him in state policy with their advice, but made it clear the king never shared with them his indivisible authority. It was the duty of the king's subjects to observe all royal commands: "his laws, edicts and ordinances" must be obeyed by all, "except

[1] See Marie Seong-Hak Kim, "Michel de L'Hôpital and Christophe de Thou: Two Perceptions of Royal Justice during the French Religious Wars," in Kjell Å Modéer and Matin Sunnqvist (eds.), *Suum Cuique Tribuere: Legal Contexts, Judicial Archetypes and Deep-Structures Regarding Courts of Appeal and Judiciaries from Early Modern to Late Modern Europe* (Stockholm: Institutet för Rättshistorisk Forskning/Olin Foundation, 2018), 131–73.

[2] Olivier-Martin, *Les lois du roi*, 319.

[3] Cicero's dictum, *suum cuique tribuere* (rendering each one his due), was frequently cited in their public statements, for example, de Thou's discourse of May 11, 1565, discussed below in this chapter. For L'Hôpital's religious views, see Seong-Hak Kim, "Dieu nous garde de la messe du chancelier: The Religious Belief and Political Opinion of Michel de L'Hôpital," *The Sixteenth Century Journal* 24 (1993), 595–620; for de Thou's, see Roelker, *One King, One Faith*. In 1555, the Parlement of Paris quashed the lower court's capital punishment verdicts for heresy. The Parlement ruled that the case of a Pierre Lormeau was "badly judged" and reprimanded royal officials in Blois for using unauthorized methods in interrogation. President de Thou chastised the judge and the royal prosecutor for failing to follow the procedures that needed to be observed "even with things that concern matters of religion," and warned them they would be suspended if they repeated such blunders. William Monter, *Judging the French Reformation: Heresy Trials by Sixteenth-Century Parlements* (Cambridge, MA: Harvard University Press, 1999), 152–53.

for the king alone."[4] The king, the sole legislator, would not accept the courts' attempts to limit the scope of his law by repeated remonstrances. The law court's role was to dispense justice according to the law; the court merely applied the law, nothing more. In November 1561, L'Hôpital again reminded the magistrates that their business was deciding cases between private parties.[5] It was wrong that the Parlement, in deliberating on an edict, "always chopped up the whole thing or tore it in pieces; having presented remonstrances and learned the wishes of the king, it did the contrary." Some, like the chancellor himself, knew this was done with good intention, but others thought the court transgressed its power. Remonstrances were always well received by the king but, once they had been submitted, the judges must accept the laws made in the king's council.[6]

The Edict of January in 1562 legalized Protestant worship, and the Parlement of Paris was in full defiance mode. This was the first occasion that Chancellor L'Hôpital and President de Thou were pitted against each other in their official capacities. At the time of the issuance of the edict, Premier Président Gille Le Maistre was ill and de Thou took over his duties.[7] De Thou, charged with the unenviable task of presenting the Parlement's dissent to the king, carefully explained why it opposed the edict: the unity of religion was a foundation for the monarchy and should not be compromised. This was an opinion that fully demonstrated the "mentalités unanimistes" of the time, grounded in the fear that the edict would create calamitous rifts in the family and the state and rend the whole fabric of society.[8] The remonstrance summed up that the maintenance of peace and order was inseparable from upholding Catholicism as the only religion in France and it was the Parlement's duty to protect it.

The Parlement again delayed the registration of the Edict of Amboise in 1563, prompting the chancellor to call "malicious" its attempt to interpret the peace treaty approved by the king. He asked the judges: "Which is more important: the judgment of the king and his council or your own judgment? The peace treaty or your opinion?" The magistrates were acting as if they were "tutors and curators of the king."[9] Rarely had a chancellor before L'Hôpital used such harsh and stern language in addressing the sovereign courts, openly berating them for disobeying the king.[10] The common image of the French chancellors as monolithically concerned with promoting the unlimited power of the king must be taken with

[4] Discourse of December 13, 1560, at the Estates General in Orléans, in *Michel de L'Hospital discours I*, ed. Petris, 395–96.

[5] Discourse of November 12, 1561, at the Parlement of Paris, in ibid., 430.

[6] Ibid., 431.

[7] Sylvie Daubresse, "Christophe de Thou et Charles IX: Recherches sur les rapports entre le Parlement de Paris et le prince (1560–1574)," *Histoire, économie et société* 17 (1998), 393.

[8] Daubresse, "Le Parlement de Paris," 532; Thierry Wanegffelen, *L'édit de Nantes: Une histoire européenne de la tolérance du XVIe au XXe siècle* (Paris: Le Livre de poche, 1998), 103.

[9] *Remonstrance* to the Parlement of Paris, after the peace of Amboise, in *Michel de L'Hospital discours I*, ed. Petris, 459.

[10] Michaud, *La grande chancellerie*, 27.

nuance. Yet L'Hôpital occupied a conspicuous place even among the most ardent royalist ministers. In a meeting between L'Hôpital and de Thou on May 9, the court was bluntly ordered to withdraw the requirement that its members make a profession of faith.[11]

The Parlement of Paris was not the only court that received rebukes from the chancellor for stepping outside of its duties. In August 1563, L'Hôpital castigated the *parlementaires* of Rouen in 1563 for failing to obey the royal will:

> You say you are above the ordinances and are not obliged to follow them if they displease you. Messieurs, messieurs, let the ordinance be above you. You say you are sovereign courts but the ordinance is the king's command and you are not above the king. There is no one, princes or others, who is not bound to keep the ordinances of the king.... The will of judges must accord with the intention of the legislator. The king makes an ordinance; by interpreting it you corrupt it.[12]

Here one sees the chancellor making a clear separation between jurisprudential and normative competence. A key theme in L'Hôpital's admonishment to judges was that their job was restricted to "private justice," deciding cases between private parties in accordance with royal law. Judging "in accordance with law" meant just that, to follow the language of royal edicts faithfully. The prince was the administrator of both the *loi* and the *droit*; the parlement could not interpret, that is, modify, royal law, without being insubordinate to the king. The logic of governing was not identical with the logic of judging.[13]

It has been argued that lawmaking in the early modern period was a "pedagogical instrument intended to convince the population of the interest of recognizing royal authority."[14] The issuance of legislation, motivated often to compensate for the crown's material weaknesses, was as important as the success of its implementation, if not more so. The major significance of the sixteenth-century legislative efforts resided not so much in bringing actual administrative changes as articulating new ways the king's power to authorize them would be defined and legitimated in law. L'Hôpital's counsel to the *parlementaires* that they should only mind their judicial functions presented a new frame of reference: by relegating law courts to a narrowly defined realm of adjudicative duty, he separated *la justice*

[11] Roelker, *One King, One Faith*, 289; Kim, *Michel de L'Hôpital*, ch. 5.

[12] Discourse of August 17, 1563, at the Parlement of Rouen, in *Michel de L'Hospital discours II*, ed. Petris and Amherdt, 51. "Judges who do not want to conform to the legislator are like sailors who go against their captain and cause the ship to founder." If an ordinance is seen as hard, difficult, improper, or inconvenient, "you must still guard it until the prince corrects it." Ibid.

[13] François Saint-Bonnet, "Le Parlement, juge constitutionnel (XVIe–XVIIIe siècle)," *Droits: Revue française de théorie, de philosophie et de culture juridiques* 34 (2001), 179; Saint-Bonnet, "L'intérêt général dans l'ancien droit constitutionnel."

[14] Bernard Durand, "Royal Power and Its Legal Instruments in France, 1500–1800," in Antonio Padoa Schioppa (ed.), *Legislation and Justice* (Oxford: Clarendon Press, 1997), 304.

from *la législation*. For him, as Denis Crouzet put it, "royal authority, in order not to be contested (by the passions of men), must be moderate, but the prince alone can determine this moderation. Power cannot be appreciated except by the one who holds it."[15] L'Hôpital's pronouncements summed up a belief in the absolute power of the king, who must be absolutely obeyed.

In November 1563, the chancellor came to the Parlement of Paris unannounced. He was point-blank with his disapproval of the court. The judges implemented some laws and refused to do so with others; this set "a bad example creating confusion in justice" because the parties, holding in their hands the written laws, did not know why those laws were not followed in their cases.[16] If the judges failed to observe the ordinances, warned the chancellor, the record of the *mercuriales* would be sent to the king. The Parlement should pay more attention to petitions from lower courts, as he did not wish to receive any more complaints from the *présidiaux* and *prévots des maréchaux*.[17] L'Hôpital flatly declared that the judges were impeding pacification by obstructing royal efforts. He stated: "I think the judges are in part responsible for civil wars because they add audacious and wicked spirit."[18]

The chancellor's tirades were met by an improvised remonstrance by Premier président de Thou. In one of his rare public pronouncements, de Thou professed that the court "did not aim to do anything other than to observe [the royal ordinances] and to have them observed, knowing how much harm their infractions could bring." Yet, he added, it "sees that some ordinances are like spiders' webs, which can catch minor things but get broken by big things."[19] By this remarkable analogy, de Thou conveyed in an oblique way the sentiment in the law court questioning the overall wisdom and efficacy of the royal laws: they might have been able to compel and restrain the lowly but proved completely ineffective because they were ignored by the powerful; they merely focused on achieving instant results, without paying attention to broader consequences. But he also made a

[15] Crouzet, *La sagesse et le malheur*, 375.

[16] Discourse of November 12, 1563, at the Parlement of Paris, *Michel de L'Hospital discours II*, ed. Petris and Amherdt, 67. The chancellor also broadly chastised the law court for the laxity of discipline among its members. The abuse of *épices* "has become more serious today than ever before." Ibid., 68.

[17] Daubresse, *Le Parlement de Paris*, 162. The *mercuriale* referred to a general assembly of the *chambres* of the Parlement, held to monitor the internal discipline of judges. It was first prescribed by Charles VIII in 1493, to take place every two weeks on Wednesday. The *gens du roi* reprimanded judges for misbehavior or failure to fulfill their duties. See Jean Gaudemet, "Mercuriale," in *Encyclopedia universalis*, n.d., http://www.universalis.fr/encyclopedie/mercuriale/. In the sixteenth century, the *mercuriales* took place once a trimester, and eventually once a semester (Ordinance of Blois of 1579, Article 144).

[18] "Pense que les juges en partie sont cause des guerres civilles *quia addidere animos audacibus et improbis*." Discourse of November 12, 1563, *Michel de L'Hospital discours II*, ed. Petris and Amherdt, 69. For the chancellor's tumultuous dealings with the Parlement of Paris, see [Marie] Seong-Hak Kim, "The Chancellor's Crusade: Michel de L'Hôpital and the Parlement of Paris," *French History* 7 (1993), 1–29.

[19] BN, ms. fr. 4398, fol. 499. Filhol, *Le premier président Christofle de Thou*, 23.

point that the Parlement was always divided over remonstrances: there are some who favor resorting to them by "affection and duty" toward the king and not the spirit of "contradiction," and there are others who reject them thinking that, in the past, they did not bring "any fruit."[20]

The Ordinance of Moulins demonstrated the king's determination to stop the Parlement's abuse of remonstrance. Its Article 1 forbade magistrates to address remonstrances to the king which would amount to "interpretation, declaration, or moderation" of the king's law.[21] The sweeping prohibition on repeated remonstrances can be seen as the first official negation of the law court's *équité* power.[22] Article 208 of the Ordinance of Blois, issued in May 1579, ordered that all the laws issued "at Orléans, Roussillon, Moulins, and Amboise be kept and observed precisely" and enjoined "all our judges, magistrates, officials and others, as well as the ecclesiastical and lay seigneurs to observe them and make them observed, without violating them . . . under the pretext of *équite*, or whatever it may be."[23]

L'Hôpital disapproved what he saw as the court's unreasonable conservatism, but conservatism was the defining spirit of the Parlement of Paris.[24] It has been argued that the chancellor and the Parlement of Paris did not have the same concept of time. As a law court, the Parlement "sought assured, not contingent, truth" and valued prudence in the exercise of stable and enduring justice.[25] Everything moved slowly and cautiously. L'Hôpital could not afford such complacencies. He needed the immediate implementation of pacification edicts to stop violence. The ideal of religious unity must yield, temporarily, to political exigency. L'Hôpital believed that the law needed to change in conformity with the "condicio temporum" (conditions of the times).[26] In times of crisis, it was imperative to adapt the law to the reality. He declared in 1561 before the extended assembly of notables and *parlementaires*: "Human laws and policy cannot always remain the same; one must change them sometimes according to what people are."[27] He reiterated it the following year: "One should consider not merely if the law is just in itself but if it is suitable for the times and the people for whom it was made."[28]

In a striking passage evoking Aristotle, Cicero, and Thomas Aquinas, L'Hôpital contemplated on positive law and natural law: "The definition of justice is a constant and perpetual will to protect and offer each person what is his own and what

[20] Daubresse, "Christophe de Thou et Charles IX," 403.

[21] *Recueil général*, vol. 14, 191. The Ordinance of Moulins was registered at the Parlement of Paris on March 1, 1566. Maugis, *Histoire du Parlement*, vol. 1, 615.

[22] Krynen, "Le problème et la querelle," 182.

[23] *Recueil général*, vol. 14, 430.

[24] Rousselet-Pimont, *Le chancelier et la loi*, 212.

[25] Daubresse, *Le Parlement de Paris*, 262–63.

[26] *Michel de L'Hospital discours I*, ed. Petris, 298–99. See Kim, "Civil Law and Civil War," 819–20.

[27] Discourse of June 18, 1561, at the Parlement of Paris, in *Michel de L'Hospital discours II*, ed. Petris and Amherdt, 411. See Daubresse, *Le Parlement de Paris*, 260–67.

[28] Discourse of January 3, 1562, at the Assembly at Saint-Germain-en-Laye, in *Michel de L'Hospital discours I*, ed. Petris, 438.

belongs to him, even in this time so corrupt that, in order to arrive at what is right, one must bend to the opposite, like the bow or the bent rod."[29] When the circumstances change, duty changes, and what constitutes a good judgment changes. The law must move along with the evolution of things and beings. He stated: "There is no law so holy that leaves no regret in a private case," but "the legislator must look *ad id quod plerumque accidit* [to what happens most often]."[30] The same applied to public law. This was an opinion that was bound to clash with the *parlementaires*' belief in the immutability of law.

The Parlement worked hard to build its image as the representative of the king and at the same time the executor of the judgments of God. The judges claimed that they were "*la loi vivante*," whose duty was to help ensure positive law to conform to divine and natural law. De Thou declared in 1565 that the Parlement received its authority from "God whose judgments we dispense."[31] The grace of God "*est avec nous et nous avec luy*." All the while, the court did not have anything on its own, because everything came from the king "to whom God wanted, commanded, and ordered that all the souls of his kingdom render honor and obedience, without exception." When God commanded that the king be honored, "he commanded that he be honored either directly in his own person or indirectly in the persons of his magistrates and officials, to whom he communicated and bestowed the power that God had bestowed on him, desiring that *majus imperium post eum in regno haberent* [they have the greatest authority after him in the kingdom]."[32]

Chancellor L'Hôpital had his hands full. He had to deal with religious dissent, political anarchy, and state bankruptcy. An edict issued at Moulins in 1566 affirmed that the royal domain could be temporarily alienated in times of need under the supervision by the Parlement and the Chambre des comptes, and that the leasing of domain rights should take place at public auction to the highest bidder.[33] Viewed by some as a violation of fundamental law, this was a measure grounded on the scheme to "buy back the domain and to ensure that the crown could do so without legal impediment."[34] It was in line with the royal policy toward venality of offices. L'Hôpital held a principled opposition to the private ownership of public offices and stressed, as often as he could, that the security of the magistrates' position would be guaranteed so long as they properly observed royal ordinances.[35] This may have been something that foreshadowed

[29] "Mémoire à Charles IX," BN Dupuy 491, fol. 48–49v, in *Michel de L'Hospital discours I*, ed. Petris, 461–62. The date of this *mémoire* has been in dispute. Petris believes it was written in 1562, not in 1568 as has been believed.

[30] Discourse of September 7, 1560, in *Michel de L'Hospital discours I*, ed. Petris, 376–77.

[31] Daubresse, "Un discours de Christophe de Thou," 383. [32] Ibid.

[33] "Edit sur l'inalienabilité du domaine de la couronne," February 1566, *Recueil général*, vol. 14, 185–89.

[34] Salmon, *Society in Crisis*, 155.

[35] See Kim, "The Chancellor's Crusade."

Bodin's conceptualization of the offices. Bodin testified that the chancellor had endeavored to change all the offices into commissions, to be held only at the king's pleasure, and that he "never had any other thing in his mouth"—it was his unvarying objective.[36]

One can conjecture that L'Hôpital's and de Thou's respective attitudes to the practice of venality were in part influenced by their personal backgrounds. The de Thous were one of the most eminent judicial dynasties, carefully built on the system of the sale of offices. L'Hôpital, the son of an exile, did not have any of it and remained largely an outsider to the capital's judicial corporative culture, mentality, and wealth.[37] As the chancellor, he was compelled to preside over the reaffirmation and systematic organization of the venality system despite his philosophical objection to the practice.

The relationship between L'Hôpital and de Thou allows insight as to how underlying political, cultural, and social elements intertwined to create distinctive constitutional arguments and professional values in the sixteenth century.[38] De Thou often clashed with the extremist party in the Parlement, including his predecessor François de Saint-André who supported a harsh policy against Protestants.[39] De Thou was regarded as a consensus-builder in the court who tried to persuade his hardline colleagues to accept royal edicts of pacification.[40] The differences in opinion between de Thou and L'Hôpital were above all reflective of the exigency of politics and commitment to official duties. L'Hôpital advocated royal legislative power and tried to educate the magistracy in the French national image, in terms of "French law."[41] The goal of judicial reforms was that "our justice be administered *purement et nettement* [purely and smoothly]."[42] L'Hôpital reminded his readers that laws were there to show "how to be more mindful of others, rather than how to deceive them."[43] The duty of the judge to serve as their austere guardian was ever under challenge.[44]

L'Hôpital believed in innovation through legislation, whereas de Thou and judges believed in renovation through jurisprudence, defending the sanctity of

[36] Bodin, *Les six livres de la république*, book 4, ch. 4, 465.

[37] L'Hôpital started his career as *conseiller* at the Parlement of Paris, the office his wife Marie Morin brought as dowry. He duly acknowledged it in his testament. Kim, *Michel de L'Hôpital*, 15. Evidence shows he did not amass wealth. After he was disgraced in 1568, L'Hôpital retired to his modest estate in Vignay and spent his last years most likely in financial uncertainty. Ibid., 171–90.

[38] On this point, see Kim, "Michel de L'Hôpital and Christophe de Thou."

[39] During the *mercuriales* in February 1560, Saint-André called de Thou "le petit avocat," deriding the latter's supposedly lowly career start. Maugis, *Histoire du Parlement*, vol. 1, 364.

[40] Roelker, *One King, One Faith*, 183–84. Historians agree that the eventual acceptance of the Edict of January by the Parlement, after much resistance, was the result of de Thou's moderate leadership in mediating its relationship with the king. Daubresse, "Le Parlement de Paris," 533; Daubresse, "Christophe de Thou et Charles IX," 389.

[41] Salmon, "France," 469. For L'Hôpital, the irreducibility of royal law is a fact of reason. Crouzet, *La sagesse et le malheur*, ch. 5.

[42] Ordinance of Moulin, 1566, Art. 14, *Recueil général*, vol. 14, 194.

[43] *Carmina: Livre II*, ed. and trans. Amherdt et al., 114–15. [44] Ibid., 112–13.

precedents and judicial practices. In all respects, the predicaments of the religious wars imposed immense burden on them, and everyone else. It was the paradox of history that the scourge of civil war catalyzed new conceptions of civil law and civil peace.

Judges and the Religious Wars

Judges had much to lose from the destruction and disorder of the religious wars, in particular from the social clashes that swept France. The world of the legal profession in the late sixteenth century saw a gradual separation of magistrates from the rest—*avocats*, *procureurs*, and municipal officials. Whereas the former group enjoyed exalted status as the *noblesse de robe*, the latter found themselves relegated to the rank of second-class citizens and were increasingly resentful of the others' pretensions. Uneasiness about the growing animosity from the social groups beneath them, from whom many had been recruited, led the *parlementaires* to exaggerate their distinct identity. Lest they should lose their carefully cultivated image, judges tried to enhance professional probity, doctrinal purity, and high moral standards of behavior.[45] Most important among the values it projected was religious orthodoxy. The Parlement of Paris emphasized its position as the staunch defender of Catholicism. Individual judges embraced the norm of a "perfect Catholic judge." The era of the religious wars witnessed a "phenomenon of acculturation," in which the judicial elites effected a "transformation of the image of judge" as the protector of law, justice, and religion.[46] The reformist culture in the sixteenth century to stem disorder, violence, fraud, and chicanery was shaped by the externalization of judicial values amid religious conflicts.

In the midst of the renewal of judicial conscience and duty, some judges perceived possible conflicts between public morality and private interest governing relations among citizens.[47] But most became convinced that the public interest they represented and identified with would be the best protection against the threat of violence and anarchy. They were careful to insist that unorthodox thoughts were no crime. The result was a growing schism between them and popular attitudes. It is important to recall that nowhere in sixteenth-century Europe did the idea of religious toleration exist, however limited in practice. With their natural conservative bent, judges feared a change in religious belief would rend

[45] Colin Kaiser, "Les cours souveraines au XVIe siècle: Morale et Contre-Réforme," *Annales. Économies, Sociétés, Civilisations* 37 (1982), 15.

[46] Ibid. 15–16.

[47] Jonathan Powis, "Aristocratie et bureaucratie dans la France du XVIe siècle: État, office et patrimoine," in Philippe Contamine (ed.), *L'État et les aristocraties (France, Angleterre, Écosse), XIIe–XVIIe siècle: Actes de la table ronde, 26 et 27 septembre 1986* (Paris: Presses de l'École normale supérieure, 1989), 240–42; see also Robert Descimon, "La haute noblesse parlementaire parisienne: La production d'une aristocratie d'État aux XVIe–XVIIe siècles," in ibid., 357–86.

the whole fabric of society, yet their sense of due process separated them from crowd fanaticism. Eventually, moral and political pressure thrust on the elite *parlementaires* drove them to rally around the royal authority as the guarantor of the rule of law. Mob rule was the last thing they wanted. They would rather see the monarchy strengthened than weakened.

With the backing of royal officials, Henry IV brought the war to an end in 1598. The authorization of the hereditary transmission of offices in 1604 completed the formation of the *noblesse de robe*.[48] In the seventeenth century, judges largely became subdued partners in the new political order under the absolutist tendency of the crown. The magistrates' private and public interests were merged to bring forth a redefinition and redirection of the law profession. The judicial model grounded on venality could be viewed as being in contradiction to the ideal of a "perfect magistrate." Yet it may be, as Ralph Giesey explained, that venality only concerned the way the office was acquired, not the way the judicial function was performed. The royal official who purchased an office was a professional bureaucrat, who was "educated into" the exercise of his authority as "the impersonal representative of a higher power of rulership."[49] The venal aspect of an office should not obscure the public aspect of the exercise of judicial authority.

The "oldest preoccupation of monarchs" was "persuading elites with local authority to govern according to the wishes of the centre, or at least recognise a common interest," and the French kings were largely successful at it.[50] There were times when the crown collided with the sovereign courts openly. The entire reign of Charles IX, the Fronde *parlementaire* (1648–1649) under Louis XIV, and the later years (especially after 1754) of the long reign of Louis XV (r. 1715–1774) saw a definite downturn in their dealings.[51] Even during those times, however, the relationship between the king and his judges was not one of sustained confrontation and hostility but one of symbiosis.

The competence of jurisdiction over the affairs concerning the royal person or his rights continuously expanded, and the principle of fundamental law served mainly as a moral restriction to the power of the king. As one historian quipped, this moral injunction may have actually meant something when someone nicknamed Saint Louis was on the throne, but not so much when the king was Louis

[48] Denis Richet, "Élite et noblesse: La formation des grands serviteurs de l'État (fin XVIe–début XVIIe siècle)," in Denis Richet (ed.), *De la Réforme à la Révolution* (Paris: Aubier, 1991), 143–54; Robert Descimon, "Modernité et archaïsme de l'État monarchique: Le Parlement de Paris saisi par la vénalité (XVIe siècle)," in Jean-Philippe Genet (ed.), *La genèse de l'État moderne. Bilans et perspectives* (Paris: Édition du CNRS, 1990), 147–61.

[49] Giesey, "State-Building," 197. The parlements' assertion of autonomy unfolded within the framework of national law.

[50] Henshall, "Early Modern Absolutism," 38. Early modern absolutism "is no 'zero sum' model, in which more authority for the crown meant less for everyone else," 42.

[51] The "revolt of the judges" during the Fronde was an aberration, prompted by political rather than legal issues. See A. Lloyd Moote, *The Revolt of the Judges: The Parlement of Paris and the Fronde, 1643–1652* (Princeton: Princeton University Press, 2015, 1972).

XIV.[52] Yet, during the several hundred years that came between the two Louis, the crown and the judges both understood the importance of the more rational sources of law for the effective administration of justice. The early modern monarchy was more collaborative than has generally been believed, this without militating against the absolute monarchy.

What was the state of *la coutume* in the aftermath of the religious wars and the recovery of the monarchy? The following sections survey, *à toute vitesse*, the sources of law in the seventeenth and eighteenth centuries and in the wake of the Revolution in 1789.

2. The Life and Destiny of the *Coutumes*

Xavier Martin separated the 350 years of the "vie et destinée" of the French customs into three parts: first, the period of "promotion," from 1454 to 1635, during which custom caught up with Roman law in importance in doctrine; second, the period of "resistance," from 1635 to 1789, during which custom was on the defensive in the face of the high culture of the seventeenth century and the Enlightenment of the eighteenth century; and finally, the period of "extinction," from 1789 to 1804, during which custom met its final fate.[53]

Following the redaction of the customs in the *pays de droit coutumier*, a large number of commentaries appeared, cementing the diversity of customs in the kingdom. In the last two centuries of the ancien régime, Dumoulin's work was valued more for its collection of the different customs—his *Le grand coustumier général* was republished in 1681—than the vision for the concord of customs he had articulated in *Oratio*. His idea of extending the *coutume* of Paris nationwide became less convincing, or compelling, as the monarchy entered a more stable period of royal power. The ordinances of Louis XIV, prepared by Colbert between the 1660s and 1680s, revealed that the monarchy still continued efforts to bring the laws to systematic compilations.[54] The king and his ministers had little political stake in private property disputes, and it was nothing unusual that the seventeenth-century reforms focused on codifications in civil and criminal procedures rather than substantive matters. But the need for coherent private laws in the kingdom was real. Between 1731 and 1747, Henri-François D'Aguesseau (1668–1751), chancellor of France under Louis XV, issued ordinances

[52] Chénon, *Histoire générale du droit français*, vol. 2, 345.

[53] Martin, "Vie et destinée des coutumes françaises."

[54] "Ordonnance civile touchant la reformation de la justice" (1667) prescribed the unified set of rules for civil procedure for all royal courts. The Ordinance of Commerce (1673) and the Ordinance of the Navy (1681) were also issued. *Recueil général*, vol. 18, 103–90.

standardizing laws on gifts, wills, and entails.[55] D'Aguesseau stated: "There are many good laws in France . . . but the public is not served any better than when there were none, because they are not enforced or are poorly enforced."[56] For all these laudable concerns, and despite the existence of a more advanced administrative organization, the French monarchs lacked the verve and flexibility to push forward the unification of law.[57]

Meanwhile, custom, having achieved its intellectual status vis-à-vis Roman law in the sixteenth century, gradually lost its appeal as a doctrinal subject from the mid-seventeenth century. The king established the chair of French law in each university, but it did not reverse the decline of scholarly interests in custom.[58] It may have been the predictable consequence of *le classicisme* and *les lumières*.[59]

The Classical Age

Authors at the turn of the seventeenth century fully acknowledged the significance of the customary law reforms. Once written down and homologated by the king, customs became in all aspects indistinguishable from royal laws. Antoine le Maistre (1608–1658), *avocat* at the Parlement of Paris, declared: "The *Roy*, under whose name justice is exercised, can abolish an *Ordonnance* and a *Coustume*. *Il est le suprême Législateur*."[60] Loyseau affirmed that in order for the customs to become law they needed to be "not only decreed [*arrestées*] under the order of the king before his commissioners but also approved and verified by him in his Parlement like his other *loix*."[61] He added: "As for the decisions [*arrests*] of the

[55] The laws on donations (1731), testaments (1735), and substitutions (1747). These ordinances were received by the parlements with little resistance. See Henri Regnault, *Les ordonnances civiles du chancelier Daguesseau*, 2 vols. (Paris: Recueil Sirey, 1929–1938); Isabelle Storez, "La philosophie politique du chancelier d'Aguesseau," *Revue historique* 265 (1981), 381–400; Isabelle Storez, *Le chancelier Henri-François d'Aguesseau, 1658–1751: Monarchiste et libéral* (Paris: Publisud, 1996).

[56] "Mémoire sur les vues générales que l'on peut avoir pour la Réformation de la Justice," in *Les œuvres complètes du chancelier d'Aguesseau*, ed. Jean-Marie Pardessus (Paris: Fantin et Cie, 1819), vol. 13, 225. D'Aguesseau deplored, "the procedures multiply every day, the instructions become more loaded with incidents and difficulties, and the costs of the trials increase instead of decreasing." Ibid., 215.

[57] In Spain, the Decrees of Nueva Planta, issued by Philip V in the wake of the War of the Spanish Succession (1701–1714), imposed the law of Castile as the common law (*derecho común*) in the entire Spanish kingdom, but Aragon still maintained its proprietary legal institutions, underpinned by *jus commune* and case law. For a view that custom could never be completely displaced under the absolute monarchs of Spain, see Aniceto Masferrer, "The Decline and Displacement of Custom in Early Modern Spain," *Tijdschrift voor Rechtsgeschiedenis* 87 (2019), 1–46.

[58] Edict of Saint-Germain, 1679, established a chair of "droit français contenu dans les ordonnances et dans les coutumes."

[59] Martin, "Vie et destinée des coutumes françaises," 541.

[60] *Les plaidoyez, et harangues de Monsieur Le Maistre, cy-devant advocat au Parlement . . .* (Paris: Pierre Le Petit, 1657), no. 36, 713.

[61] Charles Loyseau, *Traité des seigneuries* (Paris: Abel L'Angelier, 1608), "Des droicts des seigneuries souveraines," ch. 3, 51–52.

Parlements and other sovereign courts, they are not *loix*; thus rather it is the observation and execution of *loix*."[62] In a similar spirit Pierre de L'Hommeau wrote "it is not the presence and consent of the three estates of the province that give force to custom, but the king acting through the commissioners he had delegated for this purpose."[63]

The renewed doctrinal appreciation of Roman law in the seventeenth century made the commanding authority of the *coutume* of Paris less certain, however. The evolving relationship between custom and Roman law is always an important reference point in measuring the law in the ancien régime. Loyseau observed the French were compelled to regard Roman law principles as competitors but "we are still constrained to turn to them in cases which our usage has not yet penetrated."[64] He acknowledged, "if our jurisprudence is today better ordered than that of the Romans, it is because it has been easy for us to add to what has already been invented."[65] By the mid-century, the opinion that Roman law was part of "our common law," alongside local custom and royal law, had become the mainstream idea in doctrine.

The Enlightenment

In the eighteenth century, Claude-Joseph de Ferrière revisited the old debate, first brought up by Coquille, pitting Lizet against de Thou over the authority of Roman law in France.[66] Ferrière largely repeated Coquille's assessment: Lizet, for whom "Roman law must serve as common law, in default of custom," argued that in the silence of the custom of the locality one needed not look for solution elsewhere than in Roman law; on the contrary, de Thou, for whom Roman law should serve only as *raison écrite*, believed it was possible to depart from it and, in default of custom on a given question, the judge should resort to neighboring customs before reaching out to Roman law.[67] But Ferrière proposed a third approach.

[62] Ibid., 52. [63] L'Hommeau, *Deux livres de la iurisprudence françoise*, book 1, 8.

[64] Charles Loyseau, *Traité du déguerpissement et délaissement par hypothèque* (1597), "Préface," in *Les œuvres* (1678), 1.

[65] "We have taken and learned from [Roman law] the most beautiful solutions & the most secure maxims we now practice"; "the Romans are the only people in the world who reduced law to a science." Ibid.

[66] Claude-Joseph de Ferrière, *Histoire du droit romain, contenant son origine, ses progrès; comment et en quel tems les diverses parties, dont est composé le corps du droit civil, ont été faites: L'usage que l'on fait en France du droit romain, son excellence, et la manière de l'étudier* (Paris: Saugarin, 1734). Claude-Joseph was the son of Claude de Ferrière (1639–1715); both were celebrated professors of law of their times. See Jacqueline David-Moreau, "Claude-Joseph de Ferrière, un précurseur?" in Jacques Poumarède and Anne Lefebvre-Teillard (eds.), *Histoire de l'histoire du droit: Actes des journées internationales de la Société d'histoire du hroit, Toulouse, 1–4 juin 2005* (Toulouse: Presses de l'Université de Toulouse 1 sciences sociales, 2006), 97–109.

[67] Ferrière, *Histoire du droit romain*, ch. 28 ("De l'usage du Droit Romain en France"), 342. For an extended discussion of this chapter of Ferrière, see Arnaud Vergne, "Coutumes de France et droit

According to him, the opinions of de Thou and Lizet need not be viewed in contradiction if one distinguished the subject matter in litigation. If the legal question at issue arose from a matter governed by customary law and the custom of the locality was silent, one must resort to neighboring customs or the *coutume* of Paris. If the legal question concerned a subject that was not customary in nature, on the other hand, the judge must refer to Roman law.[68] In the latter case, Roman law as written reason is the dispositive rule in judgment and the judge has to limit at the outset any possibility to seek a solution elsewhere. In either situation, judges would still heed Roman law, not by necessity but by reason.

There was widespread skepticism in the eighteenth century as to the unification of law. After long efforts toward a unified French law, and with such modest results, there was weariness among jurists who were not so sure about its practicality or desirability.[69] Some dreaded the possible destructive consequences from having diverse customs supplanted by a code. Opinions of the *philosophes* were divided. Montesquieu, with his belief in legal pluralism, saw the advantages of the diversity of customs and questioned the value of legal unity. He summed up the 600 years of French legal history leading up to his time: "one sought to make the customs more general, as far as this could be done without injuring the interests of individuals which were protected"; "thus, our customs assumed three characteristics: they were written down, they were more general, and they received the stamp of royal authority."[70] Making them general did not mean making them uniform. He remained unconvinced of the wisdom of changing the received laws and usages for the dubious goal of unity.[71]

Montesquieu's reservation was grounded primarily in his belief that legal diversity was a shield against tyranny; the multiplicity of customs and laws would serve as a safeguard against arbitrary power. He wrote:

> Monarchies do not permit of so great a simplicity of laws as despotic governments. . . . The monarch who knows each of his provinces may establish different laws, or tolerate different customs. But as the despotic prince knows nothing and can attend to nothing, he must take general measures and govern by a rigid

romain selon Pierre Taisand, Claude-Joseph de Ferrière et Antoine Terrasson (1678–1750)," *Slovenian Law Review* 4 (2007), 240–43.

[68] Ferrière, *Histoire du droit romain*, ch. 28, 343.

[69] Xavier Martin, "L'unité du droit français à la veille de 1789: Une aspiration modérée?" *Pensiero Politico* 19 (1986), 321. See Joseph van Kan, "Unification du droit et les résistances des jurisconsultes sous l'ancien régime," in Le Bras (ed.), *Mélanges Paul Fournier*, 363–74.

[70] Montesquieu, *L'esprit des lois*, book 28, ch. 45, 391.

[71] "To make a general custom of all the particular customs would be rash, even in these times when princes find only obedience everywhere. Because, if it is true that one should not make changes when inconveniences equal advantages, one should even less do so when advantages are small and inconveniences immense." Ibid., book 28, ch. 37, 383.

> and inflexible will, which throughout his whole dominions produces the same effect; in short, everything bends under his feet.[72]

The territorial variety of the legal system would be an important deterrence to despotism. A *parlementaire* from Bordeaux, Montesquieu may have been unpersuaded by the supposed universality of the custom of Paris. He asked: "When the citizens observe the laws, what does it matter if they observe the same ones?"[73]

During the resurgence of the aristocracy under Louis XV, Montesquieu's nuanced opinion suffered a sort of intellectual hijacking by those who, equating rather crudely provincialism with particularism in custom, made specious arguments invoking the "spirit of the laws."[74] Montesquieu, even though he was not favorably disposed toward legislative uniformity, would not have approved this questionable use of his theory, in particular by the nobles who were mainly preoccupied with preserving their privileges of tax exemption.[75]

The views of Voltaire (1694–1778), as one could expect, were something else. Voltaire did not hide his prodigious aversion to the hodgepodge of French customs.[76] His many caustic remarks on laws and customs immortalized what he saw as the hideous reality of law in France: "We have no laws, but we have five or six thousand volumes on the laws";[77] "your custom of Paris is interpreted by twenty-four different commentaries; therefore it proves that it was ill-conceived twenty-four times. It contradicts one hundred and forty other customs, all of them having the force of law in the same nation, and all these contradict one another."[78] Voltaire poured his frustration about the sorry state of French law into his *Dialogue entre un plaideur et un avocat* (1751).[79] This hilarious satire, quintessentially Voltairean, deserves to be revisited at length.

A lawyer and his client discuss their case involving the wards of several orphans. The lawyer smugly chides the client for impatience when the latter asks about the progress of the case, reminding him that "*only* eighteen years" have

[72] Book 6, ch. 1, 51–52. [73] Book 29, ch. 18, 402.

[74] Martin, "L'unité du droit français à la veille de 1789," 325.

[75] Montesquieu called for abolishing major feudal customs: "The laws must abolish the *droit d'aînesse* among the nobles, so that fortunes may always be restored to equality through continual division of inheritances. There must be no *substitutions, retraits lignages, majorats*, or adoptions. All the measures that had been invented in order to perpetuate the grandeur of families in monarchical states cannot be of use in the aristocracy." Montesquieu, *De l'esprit des lois*, book 5, ch. 8, 39.

[76] "Le fatras de nos différentes coutume," Voltaire to M. Élie de Beaumont, June 7, 1771, *lettre* 285, in *Recueil des lettres de M. de Voltaire, 1769–1771*, *Œuvres complètes de Voltaire* (Paris: Imprimerie de la société littéraire-typographique, 1785), vol. 61, 501. De Beaumont (1732–1786) was a Protestant *avocat* at the Parlement of Normandy and then of Paris. He consulted on the *causes célèbres* of the time such as *l'affaire Jean Calas* (1762) and *l'affaire Pierre-Paul Sirven* (1762).

[77] Voltaire to André Destouches à Siam, 1767, in *Mélanges*, cited from Martin, "Vie et destinée des coutumes françaises," 541, note 37.

[78] Voltaire, "Lois," *Dictionnaire philosophique*, in *Œuvres complètes de Voltaire*, nouvelle édition (Paris: Thomine et Fortic, 1821, 1764), vol. 36, 389.

[79] Voltaire, "Dialogue entre un plaideur et un avocat, " in *Œuvres complètes de Voltaire* (Paris: Librairie Hachette, 1876–1900), vol. 24 (1892), 317–19.

passed and "*only* one third of their fortune has dissipated in court fees." Still the attorney tries to cheer him up by saying that he and his wards have a good chance to prevail because there is a crucial article in their favor written by Charondas. Is this Charondas the chancellor of our past king who made a law to help orphans, asks the client. *Point du tout*, answers the lawyer, "he is a private author who stated his opinion in a thick book, a tome that nobody reads but is cited by *avocats* and relied on by judges," and, because they do so, "you win the case." He cautions, nevertheless, that Jean Tournet and Julien Brodeau also wrote something on the issue that could be used against their case.

The lawyer thoughtfully clarifies that "with no Roman law sufficiently explicit in a case, we turn to several different opinions." The client is skeptical: "Why are you talking about Roman law? Are we living under Justinian or Theodosian?" "No, but our ancestors really loved hunting and tournaments; they would run around with their mistresses. You see, when you have such important occupations, it does not leave you much time to establish a universal jurisprudence." The client seems to get it: "Ah, I see; you don't have the laws, and you go ask Justinian and Charondas what should be done when you have an inheritance to divide." "You are wrong," the lawyer corrects him: "we have more laws than all of Europe combined; almost every town has its own laws." He laments that the orphans would have easily won the lawsuit if they had been born in Guignes-la-Putain instead of Melun near Corbeil, because the custom of Guignes, a town just a few steps down the road from their hometown, is much more favorable to their case. "But are Guignes and Melun not both in France? Is it not an absurd and terrible thing that what is true in one village is false in another? What kind of barbarism is it that fellow countrymen do not live under the same law?" The lawyer coolly explains:

> A long time ago the people of Guignes and the people of Melun were not compatriots. These two beautiful towns were, in the good old days, two separate empires. The noble sovereign of Guignes, though a servant of the King of France, gave laws to his subjects; these laws depended on the will of his butler, who did not know how to read, and their respectable tradition was passed down to the Guignois, from father to son, so that although the line of the barons of Guignes became extinct for the misfortune of the humankind, the way of thinking of their first valets still continues and takes the place of fundamental law. It is like going from post to post in the kingdom; you change the jurisprudence as you change horses. Judge for yourself what it is like for a poor *avocat* when he has to plead, for example, for a Poitevin against an Auvergnat![80]

[80] "Il en est ainsi de poste en poste dans le royaume; vous changez de jurisprudence en changeant de chevaux." Ibid., 318. In *Dictionnaire philosophique*, Voltaire writes: "A man who travels in this

One cannot miss Voltaire's high opinion of customs and of the learned judges who applied them. In *Dictionnaire philosophique* (1764), he relayed the predicament of the judges who, facing so many different commentaries on the *coutume* of Paris, "do not know which one to listen to." "But to put them at ease, we have just turned the custom of Paris into verses. This is how the priestess of Delphi used to deliver her oracles."[81]

Voltaire was merciless in exposing the appalling chaos of legal sources and the impudence of legal practitioners who took advantage of it for their profit. Behind the mordant derision lay his ardent desire for a unified law. In the *Dialogue*, the client asks why France could not have one law and one measure system as in England, to which the lawyer has a ready answer: "Don't you see that the English are barbarians? They use the same measuring system, but they have in return twenty different religions." The hapless client avers:

> I feel I would have nothing to complain about an Anabaptist who would be baptized when he is thirty years old; but I would find it very bad if he would not pay me a bill of exchange. Those who commit sins solely against God must be punished in the other world; those who sin against the people must be punished in this world.[82]

Where are the reasonableness, coherence, and stability of law, he asks. Voltaire, ever helpful, has a suggestion. London became "worthy of being inhabited" because it had been destroyed and rebuilt after the great fire; just like that, "if you want good laws, burn the ones you have and make new ones."[83] In a sense, the French did just that. Meanwhile, Denis Diderot (1713–1784) sounded resigned: "France is condemned to never having a code."[84] Voltaire's prognosis was not uplifting: "I am afraid reforming our laws will be as difficult as reforming our finances."[85]

One can guess that the revival of interest in customary law in the eighteenth century did not amuse Voltaire. To watch partisans of aristocratic resurgence and provincial particularism linking their agenda to the dubious social contract theory and its democratic fervor must have been doubly irksome for him. Some contemporaries eagerly recalled that the redaction and reformation of custom had been carried out in the assemblies of the three orders, representing all the population, and the customs that came out of these assemblies were the veritable social

country changes laws almost as many times as he changes horses at travel stations." "Coutume," *Dictionnaire philosophique*, *Œuvres complètes*, vol. 35, 417.

81 "Coutume," *Dictionnaire philosophique*, 417.

82 Voltaire, "Dialogue entre un plaideur et un avocat," 319.

83 Voltaire, "Lois," 388–89.

84 Denis Diderot, *Mémoires pour Catherine II* (Paris: Garnier frères, 1966), 3.

85 Voltaire to Guyton de Morveau, May 29, 1775, in *Corréspondance*, cited from Martin, "Vie et destinée des coutumes françaises," 546, note 54.

pacts of the provinces.[86] Custom was exalted for its virtue and values grounded in free and general consent, from which it derived its imperative power and approbation for seigneurial privileges. Yet this voluntarist conception of custom—"contractualisme contumier"—had the strange effect of subjecting the progressive idea of popular sovereignty to the archaic essence of custom.[87] Jean-Jacques Rousseau (1712–1778) would rather stay away from this self-serving, counterintuitive concoction. Rousseau unambiguously advocated the creation of a state law replacing the multiple local legal sources:

> We must make three codes: political, civil, and criminal. All three, clear, short, and precise as much as possible.... With regard to Roman law and customs, all this, if it exists, must be removed from schools and law courts. No other authority should be known there than the laws of the State; they must be uniform in all provinces to dry up a source of lawsuits.[88]

When the nobility tried to reassert seigneurial claims and reintroduce the long-forgotten feudal dues, peasants and their lawyers in some provinces "reflexively" took refuge behind the texts of customs, viewed as a bulwark against seigneurial abuses.[89] The irony was ripe. Custom, ever malleable, seemed to be transfigured into whatever was needed in the midst of ubiquitous clamors for popular rights and liberty. One could feel Dumoulin's exasperation two centuries earlier ("sometimes white, sometimes black, sometimes of a changing color").[90]

Speaking of irony, writings on custom by the Renaissance jurists, such as Dumoulin, Loisel, Coquille, and Pasquier, came into full vogue in the decades preceding the Revolution.[91] Dumoulin's defense of seigneurial property rights and contractual obligations in customary law had a special appeal to the nobility. Sixteenth-century works on *droit coutumier* were invoked by the robe nobility—not to be outdone by the sword—as a justification not only for the increasingly cumbrous corporate structure of the parlements but also for the reassertion of its constitutional role as the mediator between the crown and people. As the elites tried to mobilize public opinion to their side, jurisprudence on customary law proliferated and the judges made grand gestures of postulating themselves as the defender of *la peuple*. But the robe nobles' embracement of custom as the embodiment of popular rights was no less bewildering than the swords' invocation of

[86] Martin, "L'unité du droit français à la veille de 1789," 326.

[87] Ibid.

[88] *Considérations sur le gouvernement de Pologne et sur la réformation projetée* (London, 1782), ch. 10, 104–105.

[89] Martin, "L'unité du droit français à la veille de 1789," 326–27.

[90] Dumoulin, *Oratio*, in *Omnia quae extant opera*, vol. 2, 690. See supra Chapter 3, note 97.

[91] John H. M. Salmon, "Renaissance Jurists and 'Enlightened' Magistrates: Perspectives on Feudalism in Eighteenth-Century France," *French History* 8 (1994), 388.

custom as the expression of popular sovereignty which they supposedly safeguarded in the provinces.

The incongruity of the ancien régime was on full display. The crown sought to undermine seigneurial privileges but did not wish to disrupt the existing social hierarchy grounded on liberties and entitlements. The elites' adoption of the rhetoric of natural rights and personal liberty was bound to have consequences. Having opposed for over 150 years the convocation of the Estates General, fearing it would lessen their political role, judges at the Parlement of Paris changed their mind and supported its gathering. They had reason to feel aggrieved by what they viewed as the crown's attempt to undermine long-established institutional arrangements. The magistrates resorted to custom, a French constitution, as some "borrowed ammunition to fight their cause," but "it blew up in their faces."[92] The revolutionaries lumped custom and feudalism together and sent them both to their summary demise.

3. The French Deviation

The Decree of August 4, 1789, issued by the National Assembly, abolished the feudal system.[93] Custom lost the force of law. The venality of offices, blamed for being the main cause of the abuse of power, was put to an end. During the preparatory work for the national code, there was discussion to recognize custom as a supplementary source of law. The draft code, known as the *Projet de l'an VIII* (1800), included provisions stipulating that custom be used in the silence of the positive *loi*, but they were abandoned in the final version of the code.[94] The law of 30 *ventôse* of Year XII (1804) brought the Code Napoléon into effect. Its Article 7 nullified all preexisting laws. Royal law and customary law—including Roman

[92] Joseph H. Shennan, *Liberty and Order in Early Modern Europe: The Subject and the State, 1650–1800* (London: Longman, 1986), 40.

[93] Jean Baptiste Henri Duvergier (ed.), *Collection complète des lois, décrets, ordonnances, règlemens, avis du Conseil d'État (1788 à 1830)* (Paris: Guyot et scribe, 1834), vol. 1, 33–35. The Law of March 15–28, 1790, laid out the scope of this monumental declaration. Ibid., 114–21. The debates in the Constitutional Assembly are summarized in Edmond Seligman, *La justice en France pendant la Révolution* (Paris: Plon-Nourrit et Cie, 1901–1913), vol. 1, 280–307.

[94] *Projet de L'An VIII* [*Projet* of 1800], *Livre préliminaire*, in Pierre-Antoine Fenet, *Recueil complet des travaux préparatoires du Code civil* (1968, 1827). "Preliminary Title. Of the General Definitions of Law and the Promulgation of the Laws" (Arts. 1–23) reads in part: "4. When no rule for a particular situation can be derived from legislation or custom, the court is bound to proceed according to equity. To decide equitably, resort is made to justice, reason, and prevailing usages. 5. Custom results from a long series of actions constantly repeated, which acquired the force of a tacit and common agreement. . . . 11. In civil matters, where there is no express law, the judge must act as a minister of equity. Equity is a return to natural law, or to received usages where positive law is silent." Witold Wolodkiewicz, "Livre préliminaire 'titre préliminaire' dans le projet et dans le texte définitif du Code Napoléon," *Revue historique de droit français et étranger* 83 (2005), 441 (arguing the removal of these provisions was prompted by the consideration that the power to define the sources of law belonged to the legislature, not legal scholars).

law and the published *coutumes*, general and local—were declared null and void and removed from the law books.[95] The code became the only legitimate source of law.

Was custom an unintended casualty of the unfolding politics? The revolutionaries professed a desire to efface the social values of the ancien régime, but when Napoleon's jurists rejected the customs as law they were renouncing not so much individual customs as the prerevolutionary legal system equated with the feudal order.[96] The customary law order was rejected because it had become, despite its name, a system impervious to popular control and monopolized by the legal elite. Judges at the parlements had earned so much notoriety in the last years of the monarchy that dismantling the law courts and their entrenched power in the provinces altogether seemed justified.[97] France was preoccupied as much with doing away with egregious feudal privileges surviving in the form of custom as with nullifying the idea that judges could make law.[98] By rejecting custom as a source of law, it extinguished the tradition of judicial interpretation of law, reducing the judge to a function of mechanical and syllogistic application of *la loi*.

Article 5 of the Civil Code forbade judges to rule on cases in a manner intended to be binding in future cases with similar facts. It rejected the Anglo-American doctrine of *stare decisis*; decisions of high courts were treated not as a source of law but merely as sources of authority regardless of the facts in the case.[99] The limitation on the application of precedents creates a problem for the judge, however, when the applicable statute is unclear, when there is a conflict between two or more applicable laws, or when there are no applicable rules. Article 4 of the code prohibited the judge from refusing to decide a case on the grounds of the silence, obscurity, or insufficiency of the written law. The judge who refused to render a decision because of the absence of applicable rules could be prosecuted as guilty of denying justice. The judge, obeying Article 4, was thus required to fill in gaps left by incomplete statutory materials without liberty to interpret them. Jean-Étienne-Marie Portalis (1746–1807), the leading draftsperson of the Civil Code, foresaw this problem when he stated: "In the absence of a precise text on a

[95] The abolition of the customs during the revolutionary period was piecemeal, creating countless cases of litigation. This confusing state is well-documented in Jean-Louis Halpérin, *L'impossible Code civil* (Paris: Presses universitaires de France, 1992).

[96] Numerous stalemates in the codification efforts were caused not over the contents of laws but by the political climate. Ibid.

[97] For the distinctly antijudicial ideology of the French Revolution, see Albert Soboul, *La Revolution française* (Paris: Éditions sociales, 1982), 124–33.

[98] See Marie Seong-Hak Kim, "'Government des juges' ou 'juges du gouvernement'? The Revolutionary Traditions and Judicial Independence in France," *Korean Journal of International and Comparative Law* 26 (1998), 1–42.

[99] Jacques Ghestin, *Traité de droit civil* (Paris: Librairie générale de droit et de jurisprudence, 1977), vol. 1, 434–40. According to Damaska, the rejection of precedents is representative of the belief that society is "governed by a few unalterable principles from which clear rules can be deduced so that the law can be made surveyable." Mirjan R. Damaska, *The Faces of Justice and State Authority: A Comparative Approach to the Legal Process* (New Haven: Yale University Press, 1986), 34.

matter, an old usage, consistent and well-established, an uninterrupted series of similar decisions, an opinion, or a received maxim takes the place of the statute."[100] His call for a transaction between written law and custom went largely unheeded, yet it gave rise to *jurisprudence constante*.

Jurisprudence constante (stable jurisprudence) is a legal doctrine in civil law jurisdictions that, when a certain legal point has consistently been decided in the same way in a long series of cases, those decisions applying that particular legal principle obtain persuasive force and are followed by the courts in subsequent cases dealing with similar or identical issues of law.[101] This was an inevitable consequence of Article 5, which restricted judicial role to applying the law by rote, and Article 4, which compelled judges to refer to precedents and case law. Article 12 of the Civil Procedure Code stated judges could decide cases "in accordance with the rules which are applicable." This can be taken as a reference to and recognition of the existence of case law rules. It becomes clear, then, that the revolutionary solution, despite its supposed novelty, was not a new invention; it stood on the rubric of law in the ancien régime, during which a legal custom, especially a general custom generated by means of *jurisprudence constante*, functioned under the legislative prerogative of the crown.

The revolutionary legislators eagerly embraced Montesquieu's dictum that the judge is *la bouche de la loi*.[102] But their mobilization of Montesquieu was as selective and patchy as the eighteenth-century judges' invocation of Dumoulin. While they adopted Montesquieu's logic of a strict separation of governmental powers, they dismissed both his reservation about a uniform law and his vision of an independent judiciary.[103]

[100] Jean-Étienne-Marie Portalis, *Discours préliminaire du premier projet de Code civil [le 21 janvier 1801]* (Bordeaux: Éditions Confluences, 2004), 18.

[101] See Joseph Dainow, "The Civil Law and the Common Law: Some Points of Comparison," *American Journal of Comparative Law* 15 (1966), 419–35; Vincy Fon and Francesco Parisi, "Judicial Precedents in Civil Law Systems: A Dynamic Analysis," *International Review of Law and Economics* 26 (2006), 519–35. *Jurisprudence constante* does not carry controlling authority. Article 1351 of the Civil Code explains the principle of the "decided matter" (*chose jugée* or *res judicata*) as follows: "The force of res judicata takes place only with respect to what was the subject matter of a judgment. It is necessary that the thing claimed be the same; that the claim be based on the same grounds; that the claim be between the same parties and brought by them and against them in the same capacity."

[102] "The judges of the nation are, as we have said, only the mouth that pronounces the words of the law, inanimate beings who can moderate neither its force nor its rigor." Montesquieu, *L'esprit des lois*, book 11, ch. 6, 111. Judicial power does not have its own will but a duty to discern a "more precise text of the law" (*Les jugements ne soient jamais qu'un texte plus précis de la loi*). See Karel Menzo Schönfeld, *Montesquieu en "la bouche de la loi"* (Leiden: New Rhine Publishers, 1979), ch. 5. On the rise of the School of Exegesis, see Jean-Louis Halpérin, *Histoire du droit privé français depuis 1804* (Paris: Presses universitaires de France 1996), 45–81.

[103] The strong judicial tradition in ancien régime France and its absence in colonial America resulted in contrasting interpretations of Montesquieu's idea of "la bouche de la loi" in postrevolutionary France and the United States. Montesquieu's impact on his French readers was conditioned by their memories of the Parlements, to which his American readers were indifferent. Judith N. Shklar, *Montesquieu* (Oxford: Oxford University Press, 1987), 113. The result was the development of two different judicial systems. Kim, "'Gouvernement des juges' ou 'juges du gouvernement'?," 7–15.

Scholars have long debated on the Revolution's stupefying legacy in French law, bolstered by the ascendancy of state law and resistance to the monopoly of jurists. Dawson dubbed the revolutionaries' negation of custom and judge's power to make law "the French deviation."[104] John Henry Merryman was more blunt, calling it an aberration. They both regretted that French jurists, in their quest for intellectual abstraction, blithely ignored and sorely misinterpreted the core tradition of ancien régime France and *jus commune.*[105]

Gripes against the revolutionary law are an expression of faith in Europe's common legal past. *Jus commune* has been presented as a language and a method of reference in continental Europe, transcending national borders from the Middle Ages. It was not a set of positive rules; the expression *jus commune* was rather a technical term constructed by legal science in order to create a workable framework that would subsume pluralistic legal norms.[106] Jurists in early modern Europe established a legal hierarchy in which primacy was given to legislation. While royal laws and customs superseded *jus commune* by virtue of the principle that special laws override general laws, however, those special laws were still narrowly construed. Coquille's interpretive system exemplified this method.[107] *Jus commune* as a supplementary law, applicable in all places, continued its solid presence. A confluence of universal natural law and positive law was not an alien idea from the late seventeenth century.

Codification in the wake of the French Revolution should be seen in the context of this legal heritage of Europe. Portalis accorded Roman law, the matrix of *jus commune*, almost religious respect, as he declared "The majority of authors who censure Roman law with as much bitterness as skittishness blaspheme what they do not know."[108] But obstinate adherence by the French to their revolutionary tradition and the subsequent misconception in historiography distorted the meaning of *jus commune*, argued Merryman, hampering the country's subsequent legal development. Outside France, countries within the civil law tradition regularly listed custom as a source of law after statutes and regulations. The Spanish Civil Code of 1889 stated: "The sources of the Spanish legal system are statutes, customs, and general legal principles."[109] The Swiss Civil Code of 1907 was another example, providing: "In the absence of an applicable statute, the judge must decide according to customary law and, in the absence of custom, according to the rules which he would enact were he a legislator. He must follow the

[104] Dawson, *The Oracles*, ch. 4, titled "The French Deviation," 263.

[105] John Henry Merryman, "The French Deviation," *American Journal of Comparative Law* 44 (1996), 109–19.

[106] Descamps and Wijffels, "Approches historiques," 59–61.

[107] See supra Chapter 6, note 35 and accompanying text.

[108] Portalis, *Discours préliminaire du premier projet de Code civil*, 28.

[109] Código Civil, art. 1, sec. 1.

solutions recognized by doctrine and jurisprudence."[110] This language, putting forward with precision the nature and the hierarchy of sources of law, inspired legislators around the world and became a prototype in many national codes. In France, however, "legal institutions and practices that had long existed as part of the European *jus commune*" were characterized as "improper and deviant," while the French post-revolutionary reforms were exalted as "just and proper."[111]

Jus commune has proved resilient, nevertheless. During the last two centuries, scholars and legal practitioners have continued to moderate the seemingly impregnable Civil Code, tempering the rigid legicentrist framework.[112] There is consensus that the revolutionary attempts to tame the judiciary by making the law judge-proof have largely failed.[113] *Jus commune* has had its ups and downs. In the 1990s following the fall of the Soviet Union, there was widespread enthusiasm for the prospect of expanding the European Union and postulating the common law as its foundation, but ironically this type of historical contextualization has proved a handicap and obstacle.[114] Still, discussion of *jus commune* as an indelible part of Europe's historical unity continues powerfully. For custom, there is a rise of doctrinal interest in recent years and judicial opinions regularly recognize it as a source of law, though there is little agreement over its scope or kinds.[115]

Finally, the old debate over the relative dangers of "gouvernement des juges" and "juges du gouvernement" has ample relevance today.[116] The constitutional amendment of 2008 in France authorized concrete constitutional review.[117] The earlier system of allowing only abstract review of statutes had separated constitutional review from the adjudication of individual cases, but now the Conseil constitutionnel can conduct ex post review of the statutes in particular cases. It seems governing *with* judges has become a regular feature for the foreseeable future. The ideal of unintimidated justice is never questioned, but at the same time the

[110] Schweizerisches Zivilgesetzbuch (ZGB), art. 1, sec. 2 and 3. There was opposition that custom was vague and varied in different parts of the country, but Eugen Huber, the redactor of the code, persuasively asserted that custom could be applied only in the case of a gap in the code and therefore could not possibly contravene any provisions in the text. His argument prevailed and the provision in question was inserted in the code that took effect in 1912. Ivy Williams, *The Sources of Law in the Swiss Civil Code* (London: Oxford University Press, Humphrey Milford, 1923), 38.

[111] Merryman, "The French Deviation," 114.

[112] Beauthier and de Broux, "Un regard historien," 717, 736.

[113] Mitchel de S.-O.-l'E. Lasser, "Judicial (Self-) Portraits: Judicial Discourse in the French Legal System," *Yale Law Journal* 104 (1995), 1325–1410.

[114] The Anglo-American influence in rejuridicizing the countries of Eastern Europe has also discouraged the idea of a common tradition centered on the civil law. Descamps and Wijffels, "Approches historiques," 63–64, note 22.

[115] Jean Carbonnier, *Droit civil: Introduction* (Paris: Presses universitaires de France, 2002); Pascale Deumier, "Coutume ou coutumes: Existe-t-il une notion uniforme de la 'coutume' en droit français?" in Garnier and Vendrand-Voyer (eds.), *La coutume dans tous ses états*, 217–34.

[116] Édouard Lambert, *Le gouvernement des juges et la lutte contre la législation sociale aux Etats-Unis* (Paris: M. Giard & cie, 1921).

[117] Loi constitutionnelle, no. 2008–24 of July 23, 2008 ("Modernisation des institutions de la Ve république").

seemingly ever-expanding interpretive power of judges, namely the growing trend of the judicialization of politics, may signal yet different—familiar, some may rather say—concerns.

Voltaire said: "I don't like arbitrary power anywhere and I especially hate it in judges."[118] Some 250 years later, he still speaks for us.

[118] Voltaire to M. Élie de Beaumont, June 7, 1771, in *Recueil des lettres de M. de Voltaire*, 500.

9
Conclusion

A key question in legal history is the relationship between popular consensus and state authority. Surely every traditional society has ways of resolving disputes, and people follow those rules in the belief that they have been in observance from time immemorial and therefore are binding. When left to themselves, however, people often cannot agree on the content of the rules, that is, what they had consented to. *Consensus populi* thus gives way to the legislative powers of the state to decide which among competing rules should govern them. The law of the state compels different groups to act against their own self-interest. This is how custom in European history came to be distinguished from social or cultural practices and became part of a national law. It underwent three distinct stages: legal thought captured social conduct by writing it down, reconstructed it by incorporating custom into formal legal tradition, and then marginalized it by relegating customary law to the bottom of the legal hierarchy of norms.[1] The king's control of the sources of law including custom was aided by "judges, legislators, and scholars."[2] The preceding chapters have attempted to make sense of this historical process in monarchical France.

Ernest Désiré Glasson, a French jurist at the turn of the twentieth century, argued that the French redaction of customs was an extraordinary event, compared with which the compilation by Justinian's commissioners was "une œuvre d'enfant" (child's play). A specimen of Gallic hyperbole, one may say, yet Glasson put his finger on the prime feature of the French venture—it was "a legislative and juridical effort all at once, perhaps unique in history."[3] The local assembly of the

[1] H. Patrick Glenn, "The Capture, Reconstruction and Marginalization of 'Custom,'" *American Journal of Comparative Law* 45 (1997), 617–18.

[2] Raoul C. Van Caenegem, *Judges, Legislators and Professors: Chapters in European Legal History* (Cambridge: Cambridge University Press, 1987). An important work of scholars of medieval law is to track down the authors of court decisions which had been rendered as a collective body, in order to determine individual contributions. The sociologist and the anthropologist, and perhaps the historian, too, may wince at a legal historian's statement: "The question then is: Who made customary law. Of course, not the population at large, though in theory the 'people' are credited with being the makers of customary law. In reality however, custom manifests itself through the courts and their decisions." Dirk Heirbaut, "Who Were the Makers of Customary Law in Medieval Europe? Some Answers Based on Sources about the Spokesmen of Flemish Feudal Courts," *Tijdschrift voor Rechtsgeschiedenis* 75 (2007), 257–58. Heirbaut concludes: "lords, bailiffs, judges, arbiters and legal advisers were the key-figures of customary law in their region and, as such, they were the real makers of customary law, or to paraphrase the title in Italian (*I signori del diritto*) of R. C. Van Caenegem's *Judges, Legislators and Professors*, the 'lords of customary law.'" Ibid., 273.

[3] Glasson, *Histoire du droit*, vol. 8, 21.

Custom, Law, and Monarchy: A Legal History of Early Modern France. Marie Seong-Hak Kim, Oxford University Press.
 DOI: 10.1093/oso/9780192845498.003.0009

estates in the *bailliage*, convoked by the king, was initially an extended *turbe à temoin* to prove the law, with the king presiding as judge through his commissioners. The monarchy had good reason to frame the process of redaction as consultative. But royal commissioners modified customs deemed iniquitous and unreasonable to conform to doctrinal and jurisprudential developments.[4] There was no essential antagonism between customs promulgated in the king's name and customs defined as the expressions of popular consent, because the campaigns involved not so much making or unmaking the laws as certifying by central authority the points on which learned consensus had taken place in the legal community. The line between legislation and adjudication became more clearly drawn: adjudication is retrospective, legislation prospective; while the judge adjudicates in particular, the legislator legislates in general. Through the homologation of customs, the king reaffirmed his lawmaking sovereignty, while coopting broader popular support.

The development of the legal system in France took place in response to popular demand rather than on the state's own initiative. Royal justice spread because the people wished to avoid being subject to arbitrary decisions, whether by the seigneurs or by municipal officials. There were ever-growing expectations from the population at large, from the individual parties caught in a lawsuit to the deputies of the Estates General, for a speedy and efficient justice. The recorded customs, now put in a more reliable but more abstract form, allowed disputes to be resolved without depending on questionable traditions, and with finalizing results. Convenience and competency of judicial administration rendered the litigant's burden lighter, the judge's job smoother, and the king's *dur métier* less arduous.[5] Royal customary law policy seemed to attest to the old-fashioned idea that the law, reinforced by royal authority, afforded better protection for the less-than-mighty subjects. The rule of law made the king "the ultimate recourse of his subjects against injustice."[6]

This book has suggested several correctives to the common understanding of law in the ancien régime. A quaint view of custom as pristine, folksy popular norms sustaining a self-produced social order is of little utility, no matter how much universal legitimacy it may command. Historians are inclined to privilege custom with certain nostalgia and at the same time highlight the representative nature of the local assemblies flavored with a democratic appeal. When the people defended their custom, however, they did so "because it granted them privileges, not because it contained the good old norms derived from their

[4] The dynamic in the assemblies of the estates, where competing claims were presented and debated, was vividly captured in the *procès-verbaux*. They are potentially rich sources for social, anthropological, political, and legal inquiries alike.

[5] Michel Antoine, *Le dur métier de roi: Études sur la civilisation politique de la France d'Ancien Régime* (Paris: Presses universitaires de France, 1986).

[6] Barbiche, *Les institutions de la monarchie française*, 10, citing Michel Antoine.

habitual behaviour."[7] The assembly of the three estates was a representative body mainly in the sense that the nobles and their agents gathered to defend their privileges, whose claims were neutralized and mitigated by royal commissioners. The theme of the redaction of the customs as an act of popular sovereignty needs to be balanced against the fact that the provincial *coutumes* were approved and issued exclusively upon royal permission. We have no reason to think there was greater consensus in the medieval and early modern times about what social or moral values were acceptable in the community and how individual behavior could be made to conform to them than there is in our own.

Early modern legal history has shown that state formation was intrinsically tied with the control of the sources of law. In sixteenth-century France, the baffling and daunting complexity of customs animated legal scholars and practitioners with the desire to systematize them, and to reconcile them with Roman law, another general custom in the kingdom. The Renaissance quest for rational order shifted regional matters into a national framework. Dumoulin, armed with sheer intellectual force, called for the concord of customs as the epitome of individual liberty and public order. The efflorescence of eclectic juristic interpretations of law gave rise to a new notion of state sovereignty embodied in the royal person.

The crown's success in making the kingdom's laws more systematic and equitable vindicates an important aspect of the meaning that historians and theorists have attached to the idea of a *monarchie absolue*. It is essential not to overlook the underlying reality of politics. During the chaos of the Italian Wars and the Wars of Religion, the monarchy relied heavily on the sale of offices as a form of credit in royal finances. The *parlementaire* families who bought offices were also the chief creditors of royal *rentes*. The king often failed to pay salaries to judges who had purchased offices, which was akin to reneging interest payments for the long-term loans they had extended to him, but he did not repudiate his outstanding legal obligations in the form of the posts he had sold. Contemporary authors argued that royal authority rested on natural law; since private property rested on natural law, the king had to respect the property of his subjects. The king's promise to observe, and to have observed, the law and custom ensured the support of the elite *parlementaires*. The fear of lawless disorder drove this important sector in society into the royal ambit. The Valois, deeply mired in civil war, made things easy for the Bourbons.

In the seventeenth and eighteenth centuries, the crown continued financial exploitation of the *officiers*. Keen on the state-based extraction of wealth to fund foreign wars, the king, from Francis I through Louis XVI, functioned more as an arbiter of privileges than an arbitrary tyrant; he refereed among the different *corps*

[7] Watson, "The Evolution of Law: Continued," 546.

in the kingdom, instead of humiliating and silencing them and suppressing local autonomies.[8] Concessions made by the crown were deemed legitimate insofar as they were within the bounds of law. The problem was that this system worked so well, with so many privileges sold, over the centuries that eventually it could no longer produce sufficient means for the monarchy.

To his credit, the king, while he never recognized the judges' political pretensions, rarely interfered with their judicial decisions. With few exceptions, the absolute monarch would not overrule his own judges. In the theory of sovereignty the king could not be bound by his own laws, but he still needed to take care not to undermine the rights of the subjects arbitrarily and flout their confidence. This apparent paradox explains how a strong monarchy could, and eventually did, function through the end of the ancien régime. Royal sovereignty was grounded on *puissance de la justice*. The king did not have to be in endless war with his subjects in order to become an absolute ruler. The history of custom and law shows that there was no sharp break in passage from feudal to absolute monarchy. The notion of gradual transition implies that order grows out of chaos, and it reveals a sort of rhythm in the evolution of the French monarchy.

The once dynamic vision of a unified body of law came to stagnate after the sixteenth century. Few attempts were made after 1600 to record or reform custom. The Bourbon monarchs, arguably competent enough to legislate in all areas of law, turned to edicts and ordinances, instruments far more pliable than customs. As the personal embodiment of legal unity, the king had little incentive to work toward a uniform law. The monarchy, in all likelihood, perceived legal unification as a desirable but distant premise. Of course, there were always skeptics who feared the unifying impulse of royal law and defended the primordial virtue of provincial laws. A civil code would come only with the radical solutions of the Revolution, replacing particularism with centralization and superimposing equality over liberty and privileges. This history of France serves as a reminder that modernism in law is not always synonymous with modernism in politics.

Study of legal history offers a clear path to grasping the past on a continuum. From a rounded appreciation of French law, one can expect to gain a deeper insight into the European legal tradition. There is little agreement on the *jus commune* and European unity in the twenty-first century, no more than there was consensus among medieval doctors and Renaissance legal humanists on *le droit commun*. A more engaged dialogue between historians and jurists will help us better understand the laws and politics of our own times and make prudent and knowledgeable choices for the future.

[8] Barbiche, *Les institutions de la monarchie française*, 9.

Bibliography

Ableiges, Jacques d'. *Le grand coutumier de France*. Edited by Édouard Laboulaye and Rodolphe Dareste. Paris: Auguste Durand et Pedone-Lauriel, 1868.

Akehurst, F. R. P. *The Etablissements de Saint Louis: Thirteenth-Century Law Texts from Tours, Orléans, and Paris*. Philadelphia: University of Pennsylvania Press, 1996.

Allen, Douglas W. "Purchase, Patronage, and Professions: Incentives and the Evolution of Public Offices in Pre-Modern Britain." *Journal of Institutional and Theoretical Economics* 161 (2005), 57–79.

Andersen, Per, and Mia Münster-Swendsen, eds. *Custom: The Development and Use of a Legal Concept in the Middle Ages: Proceedings of the Fifth Carlsberg Academy Conference on Medieval Legal History 2008*. Copenhagen: DJØF Publishing, 2009.

Anderson, Perry. *Lineages of the Absolutist State*. London: Verso, 2013 [1974].

Antoine, Michel. *Le dur métier de roi: Études sur la civilisation politique de la France d'Ancien Régime*. Paris: Presses universitaires de France, 1986.

Antoine, Michel. "La monarchie absolue." In *The Political Culture of the Old Regime*, Vol. 1 of *The French Revolution and the Creation of Modern Political Culture*. Edited by Keith M. Baker, 3–24. Oxford: Pergamon Press, 1987.

Arabeyre, Patrick. "Aspects du 'nationalisme culturel' dans le domaine du droit au début du XVIe siècle: Les grands juristes français selon Barthélemy de Chasseneuz." *Annales de Bourgogne* 74 (2002), 161–88.

Arabeyre, Patrick. "Culture juridique et littérature européennes chez les derniers bartolistes français (première moitié du XVIe siècle)." *Clio@Themis: revue électronique d'histoire du droit* 2 (2009). https://www.cliothemis.com/Culture-juridique-et-litterature.

Arabeyre, Patrick, Jean-Louis Halpérin, and Jacques Krynen, eds. *Dictionnaire historique des juristes français (XIIe–XXe siècle)*. Paris: Presses universitaires de France, 2007.

Assier-Andrieu, Louis. "Penser le temps culturel du droit. Le destin anthropologique du concept de coutume." *L'homme. Revue française d'anthropologie* 160 (2001), 67–90.

Assier-Andrieu, Louis. "De l'idéologie à la culture: Les géographies coutumières." *Clio@Themis: revue électronique d'histoire du droit* 9 (2015). http://www.cliothemis.com/De-l-ideologie-a-la-culture-les.

Astaing, Antoine, and François Lormant, eds. *Le juriste et la coutume du Moyen Âge au Code civil: Actes du colloque international organisé à Nancy, les 1er et 2e juillet 2010*. Nancy: PUN-Éditions universitaires de Lorraine, 2014.

Aubépin, Henri. *De l'influence de Dumoulin sur la législation française. Extrait de la Revue critique de législation et de jurisprudence*. Paris: Cotillon, libraire du Conseil d'État, 1855.

Aubert, Félix. "Les sources de la procédure au Parlement de Philippe le Bel à Charles VII." *Bibliothèque de l'École des chartes* 51 (1890), 477–515.

Aubert, Félix. *Histoire du Parlement de Paris de l'origine à François I*. 2 vols. Paris: A. Picard et fils, 1894.

Aubert, Félix. *Le Parlement de Paris au XVIe siècle. Extrait de Nouvelle revue historique de droit français et étranger*. Paris: Sirey, 1906.

Aubert, Félix. "Recherches sur l'organisation du Parlement de Paris au XVIe siècle (1515–1589)." In *Extrait de Nouvelle revue historique du droit français et étranger*. Paris: Sirey, 1912.

Aubert, Félix. "Les sources de la procédure au Parlement au XIVe siècle." *Bibliothèque de l'École des chartes* 80, no. 1 (1919), 122–44.

Austin, John. *The Province of Jurisprudence Determined*. London: Murray, 1832.

Babeau, Albert. "La représentation du tiers état aux assemblées pour la rédaction des coutumes au XVIe siècle." *Revue historique* 21, no. 1 (1883), 91–100.

Bakos, Adrianna E., ed. *Politics, Ideology, and the Law in Early Modern Europe: Essays in Honor of J. H. M. Salmon*. Rochester: University of Rochester Press, 1994.

Barbiche, Bernard. *Les institutions de la monarchie française à l'époque moderne: XVIe–XVIIIe siècle*. Paris: Presses universitaires de France, 1999.

Bart, Jean. *Histoire du droit privé: De la chute de l'Empire romain au XIXe siècle*. Paris: Montchrestien, 1998.

Bart, Jean. "Transcrire, rédiger, réformer les coutumes." In *L'écriture des juristes: XVIe–XVIIIe siècle*. Edited by Laurence Giavarini, 35–55. Paris: Classiques Garnier, 2010.

Batiffol, Henri, and Paul Lagarde, *Droit international privé*, 6th ed. 2 vols. Paris: Librairie générale de droit et de jurisprudence, 1974–1976.

Baumgartner, Frederic J. *Henry II, King of France 1547–1559*. Durham, NC: Duke University Press, 1988.

Baumgartner, Frederic J. *France in the Sixteenth Century*. New York: St. Martin's Press, 1995.

Bayle, Pierre. *Dictionnaire historique et critique*. 4 vols. Amsterdam: Brunel, 1740.

Beaud, Olivier. *La puissance de l'État*. Paris: Presses universitaires de France, 1994.

Beaumanoir, Philippe de. *Les coutumes de Beauvaisis*. Edited by Amédée Salmon. 2 vols. Paris: A. Picard et fils, 1899–1900.

Beaumanoir, Philippe de. *The Coutumes de Beauvaisis of Philippe de Beaumanoir*. Translated by Frank R. P. Akehurst. Philadelphia: University of Pennsylvania Press, 1992.

Beaune, Henri. *Introduction à l'étude historique du droit coutumier français jusqu'à la rédaction officielle des coutumes*. Lyon: Briday, 1880.

Beauthier, Régine, and Pierre-Olivier de Broux. "Un regard historien: Sources du droit, sources du pouvoir?" In *Les sources du droit revisitées*, vol. 4: *Théorie des sources du droit*. Edited by Isabelle Hachez et al., 715–54. Brussels: Facultés universitaires Saint Louis, 2012.

Bederman, David J. *Custom as a Source of Law*. Cambridge: Cambridge University Press, 2010.

Beignier, Bernard, ed. *La codification: Actes du colloque organisé les 27 et 28 octobre 1995 à Toulouse*. Paris: Dalloz, 1996.

Beik, William. *Absolutism and Society in Seventeenth-Century France: State Power and Provincial Aristocracy in Languedoc*. Cambridge: Cambridge University Press, 1985.

Bell, David A. *Lawyers and Citizens: The Making of a Political Elite in Old Regime France*. Oxford: Oxford University Press, 1994.

Bellomo, Manlio. *The Common Legal Past of Europe, 1000–1800*. Translated by Lydia G. Cochrane. Washington, DC: Catholic University of America Press, 1995.

Benton, Lauren A. *Law and Colonial Cultures: Legal Regimes in World History 1400–1900*. Cambridge: Cambridge University Press, 2002.

Berman, Harold J. *Law and Revolution: The Formation of the Western Legal Tradition*. Cambridge, MA: Harvard University Press, 2009.

Bernard, Guillaume. "La codification en France avant le Code civil: Le Code Henri III (1587) du Président Barnabé Brisson (1531–1591)." In *Le Code civil et les droits de l'homme: Actes du colloque international de Grenoble, 3 et 4 décembre 2003, ancien Palais de justice de Grenoble et Musée de la Révolution française de Vizille*. Edited by Jean-Luc Chabot, Philippe Didier, and Jérôme Ferrand, 43–69. Paris: L'Harmattan, 2006.

Berroyer, Claude, Eusèbe Laurière, and Charles Du Moulin. *Bibliothèque des coutumes: Contenant la préface d'un nouveau coutumier général; une liste historique des coutumiers généraux; une liste alphabétique des textes & commentaires des coutumes, usances, statuts, fors, chartes, stiles, loix de police, & autres municipales du royaume*. Paris: Gosselin, 1699.

Beseler, Georg. *Volksrecht und Juristenrecht*. Leipzig: Weldmann, 1843.

Bezemer, Kees. "Jacques de Révigny (d. 1296): Roman Law as a Means to Shape French Law." *Clio@Themis: revue électronique d'histoire du droit* 10 (2016). http://www.cliothemis.com/Jacques-de-Revigny-d-1296-Roman.

Bien, David D. "Offices, Corps, and a System of State Credit: The Uses of Privilege under the Ancien Régime." In *The Political Culture of the Old Regime*, Vol. 1 of *The French Revolution and the Creation of Modern Political Culture*. Edited by Keith M. Baker, 89–114. Oxford: Pergamon Press, 1987.

Bien, David D. "Manufacturing Nobles: The Chancelleries in France to 1789." *Journal of Modern History* 61, no. 3 (1989), 445–86.

Bluche, François. *Les magistrats du Parlement de Paris au XVIIIe siècle (1715–1771)*. Paris: Les Belles Lettres, 1960.

Blume, Fred H., et al. *The Codex of Justinian: A New Annotated Translation, with Parallel Latin and Greek Text Based on a Translation by Justice Fred H. Blume*. Cambridge: Cambridge University Press, 2016.

Bodin, Jean. *Les six livres de la république*. Paris: Jacques du Puys, 1576; *Les six livres de la république*. Lyon: Barthélemy Vincent, 1593.

Bodin, Jean. *Method for the Easy Comprehension of History*. Translated by Beatrice Reynolds. New York: Columbia University Press, 1945.

Bodin, Jean. *The Six Bookes of a Commonweale*. Edited by Kenneth D. McRae. Translated by Richard Knolles. Cambridge, MA: Harvard University Press, 1962.

Bonney, Richard. *Political Change in France under Richelieu and Mazarin, 1624–1661*. Oxford: Oxford University Press, 1978.

Bonney, Richard. "Absolutism: What's in a Name?" *French History* 1, no. 1 (1987), 93–117.

Bonney, Richard. *L'absolutisme*. Paris: Presses universitaires de France, 1989.

Bonney, Richard. "Review of Nicholas Henshall, *The Myth of Absolutism: Change and Continuity in Early Modern European Monarchy* (London: Longman, 1992)." *English Historical Review* 110 (1995), 1253–55.

Bordier, H.-L. "Commentaires sur un document relative à quelques points de la coutume de Paris et de la jurisprudence du Parlement au quatorzième siècle." *Bibliothèque de l'École des chartes* 1 (1844), 396–435.

Bossuat, André. "La formule 'Le roi est empereur en son royaume': Son emploi au XVe siècle devant le Parlement de Paris." *Revue historique de droit français et étranger*, 4th ser., 39, no. 4 (1961), 371–81.

Bouhier, Jean. *Traité de la succession des mères, en vertu de l'Édit de Saint-Maur*. Dijon, 1726.

Bouhier, Jean. *Observation sur la coutume de Bourgogne*. In *Les œuvres de jurisprudence*. Edited by Joey de Bevy, vol. 1. Dijon: Louis-Nicolas Frantin, 1787.

Bourdot de Richebourg, Charles A., et al. *Nouveau coutumier général, ou Corps des coutumes générales et particulières de France, et des provinces: connues sous le nom des Gaules; exactement vérifiées sur les originaux conservez au greffe du Parlement de Paris & des autres cours du royaume*. 4 vols. Paris: Brunet, 1724.

Bourgon, Jérôme. "La coutume et le droit en Chine à la fin de l'empire." *Annales. Histoire, Sciences Sociales* 54 (1999), 1073–1107.

Bourgon, Jérôme. "Lapsus de Laïus. Entre régicide et parricide, l'introuvable meurtre du père." *Extrême-Orient Extrême-Occident*, no. Hors-série (2012), 313–39. https://doi.org/10.4000/extremeorient.229.

Bourjon, François. *Le droit commun de la France, et la Coutume de Paris réduits en principes*. 2 vols. Paris: Grangé, 1770.

Boyer, Georges. "La notion d'équité et son rôle dans la jurisprudence des Parlements." In *Mélanges offerts à Jacques Maury*, vol. 2: *Droit comparé: Théorie générale du droit et droit privé*, 257–82. Paris: Dalloz & Sirey, 1960.

Boyer, Georges. *Mélanges d'histoire du droit occidental*. Paris: Sirey, 1962.

Brand, Paul. "Law and Custom in the English Thirteenth Century Common Law." In *Custom: The Development and Use of a Legal Concept in the Middle Ages*. Edited by Per Andersen and Mia Münster-Swendsen, 17–32. Copenhagen: DJØF Publishing, 2009.

Braudel, Fernand. *La méditerranée et le monde méditerranéen à l'époque de Philippe II*. 2nd ed. Paris: A. Colin, 1966 [1949].

Breen, Michael P. "Patronage, Politics, and the 'Rule of Law' in Early Modern France." *Proceedings of the Western Society for French History* 33 (2005), 95–113.

Breen, Michael P. *Law, City, and King: Legal Culture, Municipal Politics, and State Formation in Early Modern Dijon*. Rochester: University of Rochester Press, 2007.

Breen, Michael P. "Law, Society, and the State in Early Modern France." *Journal of Modern History* 83, no. 2 (2011), 346–86.

Breen, Michael P. "Law and Social History in Early Modern France." In *Social Relations, Politics, and Power in Early Modern France: Robert Descimon and the Historian's Craft*. Edited by Barbara B. Diefendorf, 42–60. Kirksville: Truman State University Press, 2016.

Bréjon, Jacques. *Un jurisconsulte de la Renaissance: André Tiraqueau (1488–1558)*. Paris: Recueil Sirey, 1937.

Bréquigny, Louis George Oudard Feudrix de, ed. *Ordonnances des roys de France de la troisième race*. Paris: Imprimerie royale, 1790.

Brissaud, Jean. *A History of French Private Law*. Translated by Rapelje Howell. Boston: Little, Brown, 1912.

Brisson, Barnabé. *Code du roy Henry III, roy de France et de Pologne*. Lyon: Frères de Gabiano, 1593.

Brodeau, Julien. *Commentaire sur la coustume de la prévosté et vicomté de Paris, fait par Maistre Julien Brodeau...avec un recueil des arrests cotez sur chaque tiltre et article de ladite coutume. Ensemble les Coustumes notoires du Chastelet de Paris et les Décisions de messire Jean Des Mares*. 2 vols. Paris: P. Rocolet, 1658–1669.

Brooks, Christopher W. *Lawyers, Litigations and English Society since 1450*. London: Hambledon, 1998.

Brown, Elizabeth A. R. "Le greffe civil du Parlement de Paris au XVIe siècle: Jean du Tillet et les régistres des plaidoiries." *Bibliothèque de l'École des chartes* 153 (1995), 325–92.

Burguière, André. "L'État monarchique et la famille (XVIe–XVIIIe siècle)." *Annales. Histoire, Sciences Sociales* 56, no. 2 (2001), 313–35.

Caenegem, Raoul Charles van. *Judges, Legislators and Professors: Chapters in European Legal History*. Cambridge: Cambridge University Press, 1987.

Caenegem, Raoul Charles van. *An Historical Introduction to Private Law*. Cambridge: Cambridge University Press, 1992.

Caillemer, Exupère. *Des résistances que les parlements opposèrent à la fin du XVIe siècle à quelques essais d'unification du droit civil*. Paris: A. Rousseau, 1904.

Carbasse, Jean-Marie. "Contribution à l'étude du processus coutumier: La coutume de droit privé jusqu'à la Révolution." *Droits* 3 (1986), 25–37.

Carbasse, Jean-Marie. "Unité et diversité de l'ancienne France." In *L'unité des principaux États européens à la veille de la Révolution*. Edited by P. Vilard and Jean-Marie Carbasse, 1–11. Paris: Université René Descartes, 1992.

Carbasse, Jean-Marie, ed. *Histoire du parquet*. Paris: Presses universitaires de France, 2000.

Carbasse, Jean-Marie. "Philippe de Beaumanoir, Coutumes de Beauvaisis." *Revue d'histoire des facultés de droit et de la science juridique* 22 (2002), 135–54.

Carbasse, Jean-Marie. "Le roi législateur: Théorie et pratique." *Droits* 38 (2003), 3–19.

Carbonnier, Jean. *Droit civil: Introduction*. Paris: Presses universitaires de France, 2002.

Castaldo, André. "Pouvoir royal, droit savant et droit commun coutumier dans la France du Moyen Âge. Le roi est-il le maître du droit privé, via le droit romain? À propos de vues nouvelles I." *Droits* 46 (2007), 117–58.

Castaldo, André. "Pouvoir royal, droit savant et droit commun coutumier dans la France du Moyen Âge. Le droit romain est-il le droit commun? À propos de vues nouvelles II." *Droits* 47 (2008), 173–248.

Castaldo, André. "Droit coutumier et droit écrit: Encore l'Auvergne (Parlement, 22 décembre 1386)." *Revue historique de droit français et étranger* 90, no. 2 (2012), 161–78.

Cauvière, Henry. *L'idée de codification en France avant la rédaction du Code civil*. Paris: A. Rousseau, 1910.

Cazals, Géraldine. "Molinaeus Noster Charles du Moulin (1500–1566), oracle du droit, praticien engagé et fondateur de l'école juridique française, un modèle de jurisconsulte dans la France au XIXe siècle." In *Liber amicorum, Mélanges réunis en homage au professeur Jean-Louis Thireau*. Edited by Anne Dibigny-Reverso, Xavier Prévost, and Nicolas Warembourg, 57–100. Paris: Mare & Marin, 2019.

Cazals, Géraldine, and Florent Garnier, eds. *Les décisionnaires et la coutume: Contribution à la fabrique de la norme*. Toulouse: Presses de l'Université Toulouse 1 Capitole, 2017.

Cazals, Géraldine, and Stéphan Geonget, eds. *Des "arrests parlans": Les arrêts notables à la Renaissance entre droit et littérature*. Geneva: Droz, 2014.

Champeaux, Émile. "Coutumes de Bourgogne et coutumes du duché de Bourgogne." *Mémoires de la Société pour l'histoire du droit et des institutions des anciens pays bourguignons, comtois et romands* 2 (1935), 49–76.

Chastel, André, and Robert Klein. "Humanism, Historical Consciousness and National Sentiment." *Diogène* 44 (1963), 1–18.

Chénon, Émile. "Les Marches séparantes d'Anjou, Bretagne, et Poitou." *Nouvelle revue historique de droit français et étranger* 16 (1892), 18–62; 165–211.

Chénon, Émile. *Histoire générale du droit français public et privé des origines à 1815*. 2 vols. Paris: Sirey, 1926.

Chenoweth, Katie. "The Force of a Law: Derrida, Montaigne, and the Edict of Villers-Cotterêts (1539)." *The Comparatist* 36 (2012), 67–85.

Chevalier, Bernard. "La réforme de la justice: Utopie et réalité (1440–1540)." In *Pouvoir et institutions en Europe au XVIe siècle, vingt-septième colloque internationale d'études humanistes, Tours*. Edited by André Stegmann, 227–35. Paris: J. Vrin, 1987.

Cheyette, Fredric L. "La justice et le pouvoir royal à la fin du Moyen Âge français." *Revue historique de droit français et étranger* 3 (1962), 373–94.

Cheyette, Fredric L. "Custom, Case Law, and Medieval 'Constitutionalism': A Re-Examination." *Political Science Quarterly* 78, no. 3 (1963), 362–90.

Cheyette, Fredric L. "Choice of Law in Medieval France." In *Essays in Legal History in Honor of Justice Felix Frankfurter*. Edited by Morris D. Forkosch, 481–96. Indianapolis: Bobbs-Merrill, 1966.

Cheyette, Fredric L. "Suum Cuique Tribuere." *French Historical Studies* 6, no. 3 (1970), 287–99.

Choppin, René. *Les œuvres de René Choppin*. Paris: Jacques d'Allin, 1643.

Church, William Farr. *Constitutional Thought in Sixteenth-Century France: A Study in the Evolution of Ideas*. New York: Octagon Books, 1969.

Cohen, Esther. *The Crossroads of Justice: Law and Culture in Late Medieval France*. Leiden: Brill, 1993.

Collins, James B. *Fiscal Limits of Absolutism: Direct Taxation in Early Seventeenth-Century France*. Berkeley: University of California Press, 1988.

Collins, James B. *Classes, Estates, and Order in Early Modern Brittany*. Cambridge: Cambridge University Press, 1994.

Collins, James B. *The State in Early Modern France*, 2nd ed. Cambridge: Cambridge University Press, 2009 [1995].

Commines, Philippe de. *Les mémoires de messire Philippe de Commines, chevalier, seigneur d'Argenton sur les principaux faits et gestes de Louys XI, et Charles VIII, son fils, rois de France*. Rouen: Jean Berthelin, 1634.

Connan, François. *Francisci Connani Commentaria Juris civilis*. Paris, 1553.

Conte, Emanuele. "Roman Law vs Custom in a Changing Society: Italy in the Twelfth and Thirteenth Centuries." In *Custom: The Development and Use of a Legal Concept in the Middle Ages*. Edited by Per Andersen and Mia Münster-Swendsen, 33–50. Copenhagen: DJØF Publishing, 2009.

Cooper, J. P. "Patterns of Inheritance and Settlement by Great Landowners from the Fifteenth to the Eighteenth Centuries." In *Family and Inheritance: Rural Society in Western Europe, 1200–1800*. Edited by Jack Goody, Joan Thirsk, and E. P. Thompson, 192–327. Cambridge: Cambridge University Press, 1976.

Coquille, Guy. *Les œuvres de Maistre Guy Coquille, Sieur de Romenay, contenans plusieurs traitez touchant les libertez de l'eglise gallicane, l'histoire de France & le droict françois*. 2 vols. Bordeaux: Claude Labottière, 1703.

Cosandey, Fanny, and Robert Descimon. *L'absolutisme en France: histoire et historiographie*. Paris: Seuil, 2002.

Coudert, Jean. "La dernière rédaction de coutume avant la Révolution: La difficile réformation des usages de Hattonchâtel (1784–1788)." *Revue historique de droit français et étranger* 67, no. 2 (1989), 237–72.

Cremer, Albert. "La genèse de la notion de noblesse de robe." *Revue d'histoire moderne et contemporaine* 46, no. 1 (1999), 22–38.

Crouzet, Denis. *La sagesse et le malheur: Michel de L'Hospital, chancelier de France*. Seyssel: Champ Vallon, 1998.

Crouzet, Denis, Élisabeth Crouzet-Pavan, Loris Petris, and Clémence Revest, eds. *L'humanisme au pouvoir? Figures de chanceliers dans l'Europe de la Renaissance*. Paris: Classiques Garnier, 2020.

Cuttica, Cesare. "A Thing or Two about Absolutism and Its Historiography." *History of European Ideas* 39, no. 2 (2013), 287–300.

D'Aguesseau, Henri-François. "Mémoire sur les vues générales que l'on peut avoir pour la réformation de la justice." In *Les œuvres complètes du chancelier d'Aguesseau*. Edited by Jean-Marie Pardessus. Paris: Fantin et cie, 1819.

Dainow, Joseph. "The Civil Law and the Common Law: Some Points of Comparison." *American Journal of Comparative Law* 15, no. 3 (1966), 419–35.

Damaska, Mirjan R. *The Faces of Justice and State Authority: A Comparative Approach to the Legal Process*. New Haven: Yale University Press, 1986.

D'Argentré, Bertrand. *Coustumes générales des pays et duché de Bretagne*. Paris: Nicolas Buon, 1608 [1568].

Daubresse, Sylvie. "Un discours de Christophe de Thou premier président du Parlement de Paris (11 mai 1565)." *Bibliothèque de l'École des chartes* 153 (1995), 373–89.

Daubresse, Sylvie. "Charles IX et le Parlement de Paris: À propos de cinq discours du pouvoir." *Revue historique* 602 (1997), 435–55.

Daubresse, Sylvie. "Christophe de Thou et Charles IX: Recherches sur les rapports entre le Parlement de Paris et le prince (1560–1574)." *Histoire, économie et société* 17 (1998), 389–422.

Daubresse, Sylvie. "Le Parlement de Paris et l'édit du 17 janvier 1562." *Revue historique* 607 (1998), 515–47.

Daubresse, Sylvie. "Henri III au Parlement de Paris: Contribution à l'histoire des Lits de justice." *Bibliothèque de l'École des chartes* 159 (2001), 579–607.

Daubresse, Sylvie. *Le Parlement de Paris ou la voix de la raison (1559–1589)*. Geneva: Droz, 2005.

Daubresse, Sylvie. "The Parlement of Paris and the Ordinances of Blois (1579)." *French History* 23, no. 4 (2009), 446–66.

Dauchy, Serge, and Véronique Demars-Sion. "La non-motivation des décisions judiciaires dans l'ancien droit: Principe ou usage?" *Revue historique de droit français et étranger* 82, no. 2 (2004), 223–39.

Dauchy, Serge, and Véronique Demars-Sion, eds. *Les recueils d'arrêts et dictionnaires de jurisprudence, XVIe–XVIIIe siècles*. Paris: Éditions La Mémoire du Droit, 2005.

David-Moreau, Jacqueline. "La coutume et l'usage en France de la rédaction officielle des coutumes au Code civil: Les avatars de la norme coutumière." *Revue d'histoire des facultés de droit et de la science juridique* 18 (1997), 125–57.

David-Moreau, Jacqueline. "Claude-Joseph de Ferrière, un précurseur?" In *Histoire de l'histoire du droit: Actes des journées internationales de la Société d'histoire du droit, Toulouse, 1–4 juin 2005*. Edited by Jacques Poumarède and Anne Lefebvre-Teillard, 97–109. Toulouse: Presses de l'Université de Toulouse 1 sciences sociales, 2006.

Davis, Kathleen. "Sovereign Subjects, Feudal Law, and the Writing of History." *Journal of Medieval and Early Modern Studies* 36, no. 2 (Spring 2006), 223–61.

Dawson, John P. *Comparative Law*. Ann Arbor: University of Michigan, 1937.

Dawson, John P. "The Codification of the French Customs." *Michigan Law Review* 38 (1940), 765–800.

Dawson, John P. "The Equitable Remedies of the French Chancery before 1789." In *Festschrift für Ernst Rabel zu seinem 80. Geburtstag*. Edited by Hans Dölle, Max Rheinstein, Konrad Zweigert, Wolfgang Kunkel, and Hans Julius Wolff, vol. 1, 99–140. Tübingen: Mohr, 1954.

Dawson, John P. *The Oracles of the Law*. Ann Arbor: University of Michigan Law School, 1968.

Dawson, John P. *Gifts and Promises: Continental and American Law Compared*. New Haven: Yale University Press, 1980.

De Caprariis, Vittorio. *Propaganda e pensiero politico in Francia durante le guerre di religione*. Naples: Edizioni scientifiche italiane, 1959.

Debruche, A.-F. "What is 'Equity'? Of Comparative Law, Time Travel and Judicial Cultures." *Revue générale de droit* 39 (2009), 203–28.

Decock, Wim. "Charles Dumoulin (1500–1566)." In *Great Christian Jurists in French History*. Edited by Olivier Descamps and Rafael Domingo, 97–116. Cambridge: Cambridge University Press, 2019.

Dedek, Helge. "When Law Became Cultivated: 'European Legal Culture' between *Kultur* and Civilization." In *Towards a European Legal Culture*. Edited by Geneviève Helleringer, 351–74. Munich: Beck, 2014.

Delachenal, Roland. *Histoire des avocats au Parlement de Paris, 1300–1600*. Paris: E. Plon Nourrit et cie, 1885.

Denault, G. F. "The Legitimation of the Parlement of Paris and the Estates General of France, 1560–1614." PhD dissertation, Washington University, 1975.

Derouet, Bernard. "Les pratiques familiales, le droit et la construction des différences (15e–19e siècles)." *Annales. Histoire, Sciences Sociales* 52, no. 2 (1997), 369–91.

Desan, Suzanne, and Jeffrey Merrick, eds. *Family, Gender, and Law in Early Modern France*. University Park: Pennsylvania State University Press, 2009.

Descamps, Olivier, and Alain Wijffels. "Approches historiques de la notion de ius commune en Europe occidentale." In *Sur les chemins d'un jus commune universalisable*. Edited by Mireille Delmas-Marty, Kathia Martin-Chenut, and Camila Perruso, 53–73. Paris: Mare & Martin, 2021.

Descimon, Robert. *Qui étaient les Seize? Mythes et réalités de la Ligue parisienne (1585–1594)*. Paris: Fédération des sociétés historiques et archéologiques de Paris et de l'Île de France, Librairie Klincksieck, 1983.

Descimon, Robert. "La haute noblesse parlementaire parisienne: La production d'une aristocratie d'État aux XVIe–XVIIe siècles." In *L'État et les aristocraties (France, Angleterre, Écosse), XIIe–XVIIe siècle: Actes de la table ronde, 26 et 27 septembre 1986*. Edited by Philippe Contamine, 357–86. Paris: Presses de l'École normale supérieure, 1989.

Descimon, Robert. "Modernité et archaïsme de l'État monarchique: Le Parlement de Paris saisi par la vénalité (XVIe siècle)." In *La genèse de l'État moderne. Bilans et perspectives*. Edited by Jean-Philippe Genet, 147–61. Paris: Édition du CNRS, 1990.

Descimon, Robert, ed. *Discours pour la majorité de Charles IX et trois autres discours*. Paris: Imprimerie nationale, 1993.

Descimon, Robert. "Power Elites and the Prince: The State as Enterprise." In *Power Elites and State Building*. Edited by Wolfgang Reinhard, 101–21. Oxford: Oxford University Press, 1996.

Descimon, Robert. "The Birth of the Nobility of the Robe: Dignity versus Privilege in the Parlement of Paris, 1500–1700." In *Changing Identities in Early Modern France*. Edited by Michael Wolfe, 95–123. Durham, NC: Duke University Press, 1997.

Descimon, Robert. "Conflits familiaux dans la robe parisienne aux XVIe et XVIIe siècles: Les paradoxes de la transmission du statut." *Cahiers d'histoire* 45, no. 4 (2000). https://journals.openedition.org/ch/399.

Descimon, Robert. "Quelques réflexions à propos des commissaires du roi dans la rédaction et la réformation des coutumes au XVIe siècle." *Les cahiers du Centre de recherches historiques* 26 (2001), 93–106. http://journals.openedition.org/ccrh/1393.

Descimon, Robert. "Declareuil (1913) contre Hauser (1912): Les rendez-vous manqués de l'histoire et de l'histoire du droit." *Annales. Histoire, Sciences Sociales* 57 (2002), 1615–36.

Descimon, Robert. "Review of John J. Hurt, *Louis XIV and the Parlements: The Assertion of Royal Authority* (Manchester: Manchester University Press, 2002)." *Annales. Histoire, Sciences Sociales* 57, no. 6 (2002), 1655–58.

Descimon, Robert. "Review of Anne Rousselet-Pimont, *Le chancelier et la loi au XVIe siècle, d'après l'œuvre d'Antoine Duprat, de Guillaume Poyet, et de Michel de L'Hospital* (Paris: De Boccard, 2005)." *Annales. Histoire, Sciences Sociales* 62 (2007), 1204–1205.

Descimon, Robert, and Simone Geoffroy-Poisson. "La construction juridique d'un système patrimonial de l'office: Une affaire de patrilignage et de genre." In *Épreuves de noblesse. Les expériences nobiliaires de la haute robe parisienne (XVIe–XVIIIe siècle)*. Edited by Élie Haddad and Robert Descimon, 47–59. Paris: Les Belles Lettres, 2010.

Descimon, Robert, and Alain Guéry. "Un État des temps modernes?" In *L'État et les pouvoirs*. Edited by Jacques Le Goff, 181–256. Paris: Seuil, 1989.

Deumier, Pascale. "Coutume ou coutumes: Existe-t-il une notion uniforme de la 'coutume' en droit français?" In *La coutume dans tous ses états: Actes du colloque international des 15 au 17 juin 2010 à l'occasion de la célébration du 500e anniversaire de la rédaction de la coutume d'Auvergne Clermont-Ferrand-Riom*. Edited by Florent Garnier, Albert Rigaudière, Jacqueline Vendrand-Voyer, and Centre Michel de l'Hospital (Clermont-Ferrand), 217–34. Paris: Éditions La Mémoire du Droit, 2013.

Dewald, Jonathan. "The Perfect Magistrate: Parlementaires and Crime in Sixteenth-Century Rouen." *Archiv für Reformationsgeschichte* 67 (1976), 284–300.

Dewald, Jonathan. "Social Groups and Cultural Practices." In *Renaissance and Reformation France*. Edited by Mack P. Holt, 22–57. Oxford: Oxford University Press, 2002.

Dickinson, John A. "New France: Law, Courts, and the Coutume de Paris, 1608–1760." *Manitoba Law Journal* 23 (1995), 32–54.

Diderot, Denis. *Mémoires pour Catherine II*. Paris: Garnier frères, 1966.

Diefendorf, Barbara B. "Women and Property in Ancien Régime France: Theory and Practice in Dauphiné and Paris." In *Early Modern Conceptions of Property*. Edited by John Brewer and Susan Staves. London: Routledge, 1995.

Diefendorf, Barbara B. *Paris City Councillors in the Sixteenth-Century: The Politics of Patrimony*. Princeton: Princeton University Press, 1983.

The Digest of Justinian. Edited by Alan Watson, Theodor Mommsen, and Paul Krueger, 4 vols. Philadelphia: University of Pennsylvania Press, 1985.

Dolan, Claire. "Entre les familles et l'État: Les procureurs et la procédure au XVIe siècle." *Journal of the Canadian Historical Association/Revue de la Société historique du Canada* 10 (1999), 19–36.

Domat, Jean. *The Civil Law in Its Natural* Order. Edited by Luther S. Cushing. Translated by William Strahan. Vol. 2. Boston: Charles C. Little and James Brown, 1850.

Donahue, Charles. "Comparative Law before the Code Napoleon." In *The Oxford Handbook of Comparative Law*. Edited by Mathias Reimann and Reinhard Zimmermann, 3–32. Oxford: Oxford University Press, 2006.

Doucet, Roger. *Les institutions de la France au XVIe siècle*. 2 vols. Paris: A. et J. Picard et cie, 1948.

Doyle, William. "The Prices of Offices in Pre-Revolutionary France." *Historical Journal* 27 (1984), 831–60.

Doyle, William. *Venality: The Sale of Offices in Eighteenth-Century France*. Oxford: Oxford University Press, 1996.

Dubber, Markus Dirk, and Christopher L Tomlins, eds. *The Oxford Handbook of Legal History*. Oxford: Oxford University Press, 2018.

Dugas de La Boissonny, Christian. "Barthélemy de Chasseneuz (1480–1541)." In *Le juriste et la coutume du Moyen Âge au Code civil: Actes du colloque international organisé à Nancy, les 1er et 2 juillet 2010*. Edited by Antoine Astaing and François Lormant, 91–100. Nancy: PUN-Éditions universitaires de Lorraine, 2014.

Dumoulin, Charles. *Prima pars commentariorum in consuetudines parisienses authore D. Carolo Molendineo*. Paris: P. Le Preux, 1539.

Dumoulin, Charles. *Oratio de concordia et unione consuetudinum Franciae*. Paris, 1546.

Dumoulin, Charles. *Le grand coustumier general: Contenant toutes les coustumes generalles & particulieres du Royaume de France & des Gaulles: mesmement toutes celles qui ont esté redigees par les trois Estats, & homologuees, corrigees & annotees de plusieurs decisions & arrests, diligemmét & fidellement par Messire Charles Du Molin*. 2 vols. Paris: Jacques du Puys, 1567.

Dumoulin, Charles. *Caroli Molinaei, Omnia quae extant opera*. Edited by François Pinsson. 5 vols. Paris, 1681.

Duplessis, Claude. *Les œuvres de Mr Duplessis, ancien avocat au Parlement*. Paris: N. Gosselin, 1726.

Dupont-Ferrier, Gustave. *Les officiers royaux des bailliages et sénéchaussées et les institutions monarchiques locales en France à la fin du Moyen Âge*. Paris: E. Bouillon, 1902.

Dupont-Ferrier, Gustave. "Le rôle des commissaires royaux dans le gouvernement de la France spécialement du XIVe au XVIe siècle." In *Mélanges Paul Fournier. De la Bibliothèque d'histoire du droit, publiée sous les auspices de la Société d'histoire du droit*. Edited by Gabriel Le Bras, 171–84. Paris: Recueil Sirey, 1929.

Dupré Lasale, Émile. *Michel de L'Hospital avant son élévation au poste de chancelier de France*. Paris: Thorin et fils, 1875.

Durand, Bernard. "Royal Power and Its Legal Instruments in France, 1500–1800." In *Legislation and Justice*. Edited by Antonio Padoa Schioppa, 291–312. Oxford: Clarendon Press, 1997.

Durand, Bernard, and Laurent Mayali, eds. *Excerptiones iuris: Studies in Honor of André Gouron. Studies in Comparative Legal History*. Berkeley: Robbins Collection, 2000.

Duve, Thomas. "Legal History and Comparative Law: A Dialogue in Times of the Transnationalization of Law and Legal Scholarship." *American Journal of Comparative Law* 66 (2018), 727–31.

Duve, Thomas. "Legal Traditions: A Dialogue between Comparative Law and Comparative Legal History." *Comparative Legal History* 6, no. 1 (2018), 15–33.

Duvergier, Jean Baptiste Henri, ed. *Collection complète de lois, décrets, ordonnances, réglemens, avis du Conseil d'État (1788 à 1830)*. Vol. 1. Paris: A. Guyot et scribe, 1834.

Ehrlich, Eugen. *Fundamental Principles of the Sociology of Law*. Translated by Walter Lewis Moll. Cambridge, MA: Harvard University Press, 1936.

Emmanuelli, François-Xavier. *Un mythe de l'absolutisme bourbonien: L'intendance, du milieu du XVIIème siècle à la fin du XVIIIème siècle (France, Espagne, Amérique)*. Aix-en-Provence: Publications Université de Provence, 1981.

Esmein, Adémar. *Cours élémentaire d'histoire du droit francais: À l'usage des étudiants de première année*. Paris: Larose & Forcel, 1892.

Esmein, Adhémar. "La coutume doit-elle être reconnue comme source du droit civil français?" *Extrait du Bulletin de la Société d'études législatives*. Paris: Arthur Rousseau, 1905.

Esmein, Adhémar. *Eléments de droit constitutionnel français et comparé*. 6th ed. Paris: Recueil Sirey, 1914.

Esmein, Adhémar. "L'originalité du Code civil." In *Le Code civil 1804–1904: Livre du Centenaire*. Edited by Jean-Louis Halpérin, 5–21. Paris: Dalloz, 2004.

Ewald, William. "Comparative Jurisprudence (II): The Logic of Legal Transplants." *American Journal of Comparative Law* 43, no. 4 (1995), 489–510.

Fabry, Philippe. *L'État royal: Norms, justice et gouvernement dans l'œuvre de Pierre Rebuffi (1487–1557)*. Toulouse: Presses de l'Université de Toulouse 1 Capitole, 2015.

Ferrière, Claude de. *Nouveau commentaire sur la coutume de la prévôté et vicomté de Paris*. Edited by Sauvan d'Aramon. 2 vols. Lyons: J. S. Grabit, 1779.

Ferrière, Claude-Joseph de. *Histoire du droit romain, contenant son origine, ses progrès; comment et en quel temps les diverses parties, dont est composé le corps du droit civil, ont été faites: L'usage que l'on fait en France du droit romain, son excellence, & la manière de l'étudier*. Paris: Saugarin, 1734.

Ferrière, Claude-Joseph de. *Dictionnaire de droit et de pratique*. 2 vols. Paris: Brunet, 1769.

Filhol, René. *Le premier président Christofle de Thou et la réformation des coutumes*. Paris: Recueil Sirey, 1937.

Filhol, René. "Une consultation de Charles Dumoulin relative à la seigneurie d'Arc-en-Barrois." *Revue historique de droit français et étranger* 26 (1949), 122–32.

Filhol, René. "Dumoulin." In *Dictionnaire de droit canonique*. Edited by R. Naz, vol. 5, 41–67. Paris: Letouzey, 1953.

Filhol, René. *Le vieux coustumier de Poictou*. Bourges: Éditions Tardy, 1956.

Filhol, René. "La rédaction des coutumes en France aux XVe et XVIe siècles." In *La rédaction des coutumes dans le passé et dans le présent: Colloque organisé les 16 et 17 mai 1960 par le Centre d'histoire et d'ethnologie juridiques*. Edited by John Gilissen, 63–85. Brussels: Université libre de Bruxelles, Institut de sociologie, 1962.

Filhol, René. "La preuve de la coutume dans l'ancien droit français." In *La preuve*, 357–73, *Recueils de la Société Jean Bodin pour l'histoire comparative des institutions* 17. Brussels: Édition de la librairie encyclopédique, 1965.

Filhol, René. "Procès en Parlement de Paris sur la coutume de La Rochelle (20 mai 1566)." In *Études offertes à Jean Macqueron*. Edited by Pierre Andrieu-Guitrancourt, 313–18. Aix-en-Provence: Faculté de droit et des sciences économiques d'Aix-en-Provence, 1970.

Filhol, René. "Protestantisme et droit d'aînesse au XVIe siècle." *Recueil de mémoires et travaux de la Société d'histoire du droit écrit* 7 (1970), 195–205.

Filhol, René. "The Codification of Customary Law in France in the Fifteenth and Sixteenth Centuries." In *Government in Reformation Europe, 1520–1560*. Edited by Henry J. Cohn, 265–83. London: Macmillan, 1971.

Filhol, René. "L'application de l'Édit des secondes noces en pays coutumier." In *Mélanges Roger Aubenas*, 295–99. Montpellier: Faculté de droit et des sciences économiques de Montpellier, 1974.

Filhol, René. "Les avocats en Parlement de Paris dans la seconde moitié du XVIe siècle." In *Aux alentours du droit coutumier: Articles et conférences du doyen René Filhol*, 5–38. Poitiers: Université de Poitiers Faculté de droit et des sciences sociales, 1988.

Fiorentino, Karen. "L'Édit des mères en Provence (1567–1729): Un exemple de la difficile application des ordonnances royales en pays de droit écrit." *Revue historique de droit français et étranger* 85 (2007), 219–46.

Fon, Vincy, and Francesco Parisi. "Judicial Precedents in Civil Law Systems: A Dynamic Analysis." *International Review of Law and Economics* 26, no. 4 (2006), 519–35.

Ford, Franklin L. *Robe and Sword*. Cambridge, MA: Harvard University Press, 1953.

Forsyth, William. *The History of Lawyers, Ancient and Modern*. New York: James Cockcroft, 1875.

Foster, Nicholas H. D., William Twining, Andrew Halpin, and Gordon Woodman. "A Fresh Start for Comparative Legal Studies? A Collective Review of Patrick Glenn's Legal Traditions of the World, 2nd Edition." *Journal of Comparative Law* 1 (2006), 100–76.

Franklin, Julian H. *Jean Bodin and the Sixteenth-Century Revolution in the Methodology of Law and History*. New York: Columbia University Press, 1963.

Franklin, Julian H. *Jean Bodin and the Rise of Absolutist Theory*. Cambridge: Cambridge University Press, 1973.

Freger, Laurie. "Le cout de la justice civile à travers les archives judiciaires: L'exemple des épices des magistrats." *L'Atelier du Centre des recherches historiques* 5 (2009). https://journals.openedition.org/acrh/1738.

Fujita, Takahiro. "Deyu Mūran to Kokiyū no kanshūhō ron" [Customary Law Theories of Dumoulin and Coquille]. *Dokkyō hōgaku* 78 (2009), 303–17.

Fujita, Takahiro. "Furansu kanshū hōgaku to Rōmahō: Furansu kyōtsūhō to wa nanika (I)" [French Customary Law and Roman Law: What is French Common Law]. *Dokkyō hōgaku* 78 (2009), 163–218.

Fumaroli, Marc. *L'âge de l'éloquence: Rhétorique et 'res literaria,' de la Renaissance au seuil de l'époque classique*. 2nd ed. Paris: Albin Michel, 1994.

Ganay, Ernest de. *Un chancelier de France sous Louis XII Jehan de Ganay*. Paris: Librairie Plon, 1932.

Gandilhon, René. "L'unification des coutumes sous Louis XI." *Revue historique* 194, no. 4 (1944), 317–23.

Garnier, Florent, and Jacqueline Vendrand-Voyer, eds. *La coutume dans tous ses états: Actes du colloque international des 15 au 17 juin 2010 à l'occasion de la célébration du 500e anniversaire de la rédaction de la coutume d'Auvergne Clermont-Ferrand-Riom*. Paris: Éditions La Mémoire du Droit, 2013.

Gaudemet, Jean. "Les tendances à l'unification du droit en France dans les derniers siècles de l'ancien régime (XVIe–XVIIIe)." In *La formazione storica del diritto moderno in Europa*. Edited by Società italiana di storia del diritto, 157–94. Florence: L. S. Olschki, 1977.

Gaudemet, Jean. "Les persistances du droit romain dans les traditions juridiques occidentales." In *Excerptiones iuris: Studies in Honor of André Gouron, Studies in Comparative Legal History*. Edited by Bernard Durand and Laurent Mayali, 227–60. Berkeley: Robbins Collection, 2000.

Gaudemet, Jean. "Mercuriale." In *Encyclopedia universalis*, n.d. http://www.universalis.fr/encyclopedie/mercuriale/.

Gazzaniga, Jean-Louis. "Quand les avocats formaient les juristes et la doctrine." *Droits* 20 (1994), 31–41. https://books.openedition.org/putc/12979.

Gazzaniga, Jean-Louis. "Rédaction des coutumes et codification." *Droit: Revue française de théorie, de philosophie et de culture juridique* 26, no. 2 (1997), 71–80.

Gazzaniga, Jean-Louis. "Avocats, littérateurs et érudits au XVIe siècle." In *Excerptiones iuris: Studies in Honor of André Gouron, Studies in Comparative Legal History*. Edited by Bernard Durand and Laurent Mayali, 261–81. Berkeley: Robbins Collection, 2000.

Geertz, Clifford. "Local Knowledge: Fact and Law in Comparative Perspective." In *Local Knowledge*, 167–234. London: Fontana, 1983.

Gény, François. *Méthode d'interprétation et sources en droit privé positif: Essai critique*. Paris: Librairie générale de droit et de jurisprudence, 1932 [1899].

Gephart, Werner. *Law, Culture, and Society: Max Weber's Comparative Cultural Sociology of Law*. Recht als Kultur 7. Frankfurt am Main: Vittorio Klostermann, 2015.

Gerber, Matthew. "Family, the State, and Law in Early Modern and Revolutionary France." *History Compass* 7 (2009), 474–99.

Gerber, Matthew. *Bastards: Politics, Family, and Law in Early Modern France*. Oxford: Oxford University Press, 2012.

Ghestin, Jacques. *Traité de droit civil*. Vol. 1. Paris: Librairie générale de droit et de jurisprudence, 1977.

Giavarini, Laurence, ed. *L'écriture des juristes: XVIe–XVIIIe siècle*. Paris: Classiques Garnier, 2010.

Giavarini, Laurence. "Autour de *L'écriture des juristes*. Sur la question de l'action de l'écriture et du droit." *Clio@Themis, Revue électronique d'histoire du droit* 7 (2014). http://www.cliothemis.com/Autour-de-L-ecriture-des-juristes.

Giesey, Ralph E. "When and Why Hotman Wrote the *Francogallia*." *Bibliothèque d'humanisme et Renaissance* 29 (1967), 581–611.

Giesey, Ralph E. "Rules of Inheritance and Strategies of Mobility in Prerevolutionary France." *American Historical Review* 82, no. 2 (1977), 271–89.

Giesey, Ralph E. "State-Building in Early Modern France: The Role of Royal Officialdom." *Journal of Modern History* 55, no. 2 (1983), 191–207.

Gilissen, John. "Les phases de la codification et de l'homologation des coutumes dans les XVII Provinces des Pays-Bas." *Tijdschrift voor Rechtsgeschiedenis* 18 (1950), 36–67 (Part I) and 239–90 (Part II).

Gilissen, John. "Loi et coutume: Quelques aspects de l'interpénétration des sources du droit dans l'ancien droit belge." *Tijdschrift voor Rechtsgeschiedenis* 21 (1953), 257–96.

Gilissen, John, ed. *La rédaction des coutumes dans le passé et dans le présent: Colloque organisé les 16 et 17 mai 1960 par le Centre d'histoire et d'ethnologie juridiques*. Brussels: Université libre de Bruxelles, Institut de sociologie, 1962.

Gilissen, John. *Introduction historique au droit*. Brussels: Bruylant, 1979.

Gilissen, John. *La coutume*. Typologie des sources du Moyen Âge occidental 41. Turnhout: Brepols, 1982.

Gilissen, John, ed. *La coutume=Custom*. Vol. 1: *Antiquité, Afrique noire, Amérique, Australie*. Recueils de la Société Jean Bodin pour l'histoire comparative des institutions 51. Brussels: De Boeck-Wesmael, 1989.

Gilles, Henri. *Les coutumes de Toulouse (1286) et leur premier commentaire (1296)*. Toulouse: Académie de législation, 1969.

Giordanengo, Gérard. "Le pouvoir législatif du roi de France (XIe–XIIIe siècle), travaux récents et hypothèses de recherche." *Bibliothèque de l'École des chartes* 147 (1989), 283–310.

Giordanengo, Gérard. "Jus commune et 'droit commun' en France du XIIIe au XVe siècle." In *Droit romain, jus civile et droit français*. Edited by Jacques Krynen, 219–47. Toulouse: Presses de l'Université des sciences sociales de Toulouse, 1999.

Giordanengo, Gérard. "Roma nobilis, orbis et domina. Réponse à un contradicteur." *Revue historique de droit français et étranger* 88 (2010), 91–150.

Girard, Étienne, and Jacques Joly. *Trois livres des offices de France*. Paris, 1658.

Giraud, Charles-Joseph-Barthélemy. *Essai sur l'histoire du droit français au Moyen Âge*. 2 vols. Paris: Videcoq, 1846.

Glasson, Ernest Désiré. *Histoire du droit et des institutions de la France*. 8 vols. Paris: F. Pichon, 1887.

Glenn, H. Patrick. "The Capture, Reconstruction and Marginalization of 'Custom.'" *American Journal of Comparative Law* 45 (1997), 613–20.

Glenn, H. Patrick. "Are Legal Traditions Commensurable?" *American Journal of Comparative Law* 49 (2001), 133–45.

Glenn, H. Patrick. "Commensurability and Translatability." In *Law and Justice in a Multistate World: Essays in Honor of Arthur T. von Mehren*. Edited by James A. R Nafziger and Symeon C. Symeonides. Ardsley-on-Hudson: Transnational Publishers, 2002.

Glenn, H. Patrick. "Eason-Weinmann Lecture: The Common Laws of Europe and Louisiana." *Tulane Law Review* 79 (2005), 1041–63.

Glenn, H. Patrick. "Comparative Legal Families and Comparative Legal Traditions." In *The Oxford Handbook of Comparative Law*. Edited by Mathias Reimann and Reinhard Zimmermann, 421–39. Oxford: Oxford University Press, 2006.

Glenn, H. Patrick. "A Concept of Legal Tradition." *Queen's Law Journal* 34, no. 1 (2008), 427–45.

Glenn, H. Patrick. *Legal Traditions of the World: Sustainable Diversity in Law*. 5th ed. Oxford: Oxford University Press, 2014 [2000].

Godding, Philippe. "Jurisprudence et motivation des décisions des sentences." In *La motivation des decisions de justice*. Edited by Chaim Perelman and Paul Foriers, 37–67. Brussels: Etablissements Émile Bruylant, 1978.

Godefroy, Frédéric. *Dictionnaire de l'ancienne langue française et de tous ses dialectes du IXe au XVe siècle*. Paris: F. Vieweg, 1881–1902.

Gonzalez de Gaspard, Philippe. "Le discours sur la concorde et l'union des coutumes de France de Charles Du Moulin (Présentation et traduction)." DEA de philosophie du droit, Université Panthéon-Assas Paris II, 2000.

Goody, Jack, Joan Thirsk, and E. P. Thompson, eds. *Family and Inheritance: Rural Society in Western Europe, 1200–1800*. Cambridge: Cambridge University Press, 1976.

Gouron, André. "Aux origines de l'émergence du droit: Glossateurs et coutumes méridionales (XIIe siècle–milieu du XIIIe siècle)." In *Religion, société et politique: Mélanges en hommage à Jacques Ellul*. Edited by Étienne Bravasa, Claude Emeri, and Jean-Louis Seurin, 255–70. Paris: Presses universitaires de France, 1983.

Gouron, André. "La coutume en France au Moyen Âge." In *La coutume=Custom*, Vol. 2: *Europe occidentale médiévale et moderne*. Edited by Jacques Vanderlinden, 193–217. Recueils de la Société Jean Bodin, vol. 52. Brussels: De Boeck-Wesmael, 1990.

Gouron, André. "Sur les origines de l'expression 'droit coutumier.'" In *Droit et coutume en France aux XIIe et XIIIe siècles*. Aldershot: Variorum, 1993.

Gouron, André. "Les ordonnances royales dans la France médiéval." In *Justice et législation*. Edited by Antonio Padoa-Schioppa, 81–100. Paris: Presses universitaires de France, 2000.

Gouron, André, and Albert Rigaudière. *Renaissance du pouvoir législatif et genèse de l'État*. Montpellier: Société d'histoire du droit et des institutions des anciens pays de droit écrit, 1988.

Gouron, André, and Odile Terrin. *Bibliographie des coutumes de France, éditions antérieures à la Révolution*. Travaux d'histoire éthico-politique 28. Geneva: Droz, 1975.

Grandilhon, René. "L'unification des coutumes sous Louis XI." *Revue historique* 194, no. 4 (1944), 317–23.

Greengrass, Mark. "A Day in the Life of the Third Estate: Blois, 26th December 1576." In *Politics, Ideology, and the Law in Early Modern Europe: Essays in Honor of J. H. M. Salmon*. Edited by Adrianna E. Bakos, 73–90. Rochester: University of Rochester Press, 1994.

Grinberg, Martine. "La rédaction des coutumes et les droits seigneuriaux: Nommer, classer, exclure." *Annales. Histoire, Sciences Sociales* 52, no. 5 (1997), 1017–38.

Grinberg, Martine. "Les interprètes et le droit coutumier. Les éditions des coutumes du bailliage d'Amiens." *Les cahiers du Centre de recherches historiques*, no. 26 (2001). https://doi.org/10.4000/ccrh.1493.

Grinberg, Martine. *Écrire les coutumes: Les droits seigneuriaux en France, XVIe–XVIIIe siècle*. Paris: Presses universitaires de France, 2006.

Grinberg, Martine. "Écrire le droit: Les coutumes, la langue et le 'bon usage.'" In *L'écriture des juristes: XVIe–XVIIIe siècle*. Edited by Laurence Giavarini, 57–71. Paris: Classiques Garnier, 2010.

Grinberg, Martine, Simone Geoffroy-Poisson, and Alexandra Laclau. "Rédaction des coutumes et territoires au XVIe siècle: Paris et Montfort-l'Amaury." *Revue d'histoire moderne et contemporaine* 59, no. 2 (2012), 7–55.

Gruber-Magitot, Stéphane. *Les conflits de coutumes en matière de contrats dans la jurisprudence des parlements: De Dumoulin au Code civil*. Paris: Presses universitaires de France, 1980.

Guénoys, Pierre. *La conférence des coutumes tant générales, que locales et particulières du royaume de France...avec une briefue explication tirée des loix Romaines*. Paris: Chaudière, 1596.

Guillot, Olivier, Yves Sassier, and Albert Rigaudière. *Pouvoirs et institutions dans la France médiévale*. 2 vols. Paris: A. Colin, 1994.

Haferkamp, Hans-Peter. "The Science of Private Law and the State in Nineteenth Century Germany." *American Journal of Comparative Law* 56, Special Symposium Issue: "Beyond the State: Rethinking Private Law" (2008), 667–89.

Halpérin, Jean-Louis. *L'impossible Code civil*. Paris: Presses universitaires de France, 1992.

Halpérin, Jean-Louis. *Histoire du droit privé français depuis 1804*. Paris: Presses universitaires de France, 1996.

Halpérin, Jean-Louis. "Adhémar Esmein et les ambitions de l'histoire du droit." *Revue historique de droit français et étranger* 75, no. 3 (1997), 415–33.

Halpérin, Jean-Louis. *Histoire des droits en Europe, 1750 à nos jours*. Paris: Flammarion, 2004.

Halpérin, Jean-Louis. *Profils des mondialisations du droit*. Paris: Dalloz, 2009.

Halpérin, Jean-Louis. "The Concept of Law: A Western Transplant?" *Theoretical Inquiries in Law* 10 (2009), 333–54.

Halpérin, Jean-Louis. "Est-il temps de déconstruire les mythes de l'histoire du droit français?" *Clio@Themis: revue électronique d'histoire du droit* 5 (2012). http://www.clio-themis.com/Est-il-temps-de-deconstruire-les.

Halpérin, Jean-Louis. "La détermination du champ juridique à la lumière de travaux récents d'histoire du droit." *Droit et société* 81 (2012), 403–23.

Halpérin, Jean-Louis. "Histoire comparée du droit." In *L'histoire du droit en France: Nouvelles tendances, nouveaux territoires*. Edited by Jacques Krynen and Bernard d'Alteroche, 183–203. Paris: Classiques Garnier, 2014.

Hamon, Philippe. "La chute de la maison de Thou: La fin d'une dynastie robine." *Revue d'histoire moderne et contemporaine* 46, no. 1 (1999), 53–85.

Hamscher, Albert N. *Conseil Privé and the Parlements in the Age of Louis XIV: A Study in French Absolutism*. Philadelphia: American Philosophical Society, 1987.

Hanley, Sarah. *The Lit de Justice of the Kings of France: Constitutional Ideology in Legend, Ritual, and Discourse*. Princeton: Princeton University Press, 1983.

Hanley, Sarah. "Endangering the State: Family Formation and State Building in Early Modern France." *French Historical Studies* 16 (1989), 4–27.

Hanley, Sarah. "'The Jurisprudence of the Arrêts': Marital Union, Civil Society, and State Formation in France, 1550–1650." *Law and History Review* 21, no. 1 (2003), 1–40.

Hardwick, Julie. *The Practice of Patriarchy: Gender and the Politics of Household Authority in Early Modern France*. University Park: Pennsylvania State University Press, 1998.

Hardwick, Julie. *Family Business: Litigation and the Political Economies of Daily Life in Early Modern France*. Oxford: Oxford University Press, 2009.

Hart, Herbert Lionel Adolphus. *The Concept of Law*. Oxford: Clarendon Press, 2012 [1961].

Hayhoe, Jeremy. *Enlightened Feudalism: Seigneurial Justice and Village Society in Eighteenth-Century Northern Burgundy*. Rochester: University of Rochester Press, 2008.

Heirbaut, Dirk. "Who Were the Makers of Customary Law in Medieval Europe? Some Answers Based on Sources about the Spokesmen of Flemish Feudal Courts." *Tijdschrift voor Rechtsgeschiedenis* 75, no. 3 (2007), 257–74.

Henry, Paul. "À travers la coutume de Paris et *Les institutes coutumière* de Loisel: Notes de droit civil rétrospectif." *Revue critique de législation et de jurisprudence* 28–39 (1899–1910) (9 parts).

Henshall, Nicholas. *The Myth of Absolutism: Change and Continuity in Early Modern European History*. London: Longman, 1992.

Henshall, Nicholas. "Early Modern Absolutism 1550–1700: Political Reality or Propaganda?" In *Der Absolutismus-Ein Mythos? Strukturwandel Monarchischer Herrschaft in West- und Mitteleuropa (ca. 1550–1700)*. Edited by Ronald G. Asch and Heinz Duchhardt, 25–53. Cologne: Böhlau Verlag, 1996.

Hepburn, Jasmin. "A Lawyer and His Sources: Nicolas Bohier and Legal Practice in Sixteenth-Century France." In *Reassessing Legal Humanism and Its Claims: Petere Fontes?* Edited by Paul J. du Plessis and John W. Cairns, 244–81. Edinburgh: Edinburgh University Press, 2016.

Hilaire, Jean. "Coutumes et droit écrit: Recherche d'une limite." *Mémoires de la Société pour l'histoire du droit et des institutions des anciens pays bourguignons, comtois et romands* 40 (1983), 153–75.

Hilaire, Jean. "Coutumes rédigées et 'gens des champs' (Angoumois, Aunis, Saintonge)." *Revue historique de droit français et étranger* 65, no. 4 (1987), 545–73.

Hilaire, Jean. "La procédure civile et l'influence de l'État autour de l'appel." In *Droits savants et pratiques françaises du pouvoir (XIe–XVe siècle)*. Edited by Jacques Krynen and Albert Rigaudière. Bordeaux: Presses universitaires de Bordeaux, 1992.

Hilaire, Jean. "Le Roi et nous. Procédure et genèse de l'État aux XIIIème et XIVème siècles." *Histoire de la justice* 5 (1992), 3–18.

Hilaire, Jean. *La vie du droit coutumes et droit écrit*. Paris: Presses universitaires de France, 1994.

Hilaire, Jean. "Questions autour de la jurisprudence des arrêts." In *Les recueils d'arrêts et dictionnaires de jurisprudence, XVIe–XVIIIe siècles*. Edited by Serge Dauchy and Véronique Demars-Sion, 21–39. Paris: Éditions La Mémoire du Droit, 2005.

Hilaire, Jean. "La France méridionale avait-elle une frontière sous l'Ancien Régime?" *Bulletin Académie des sciences et lettres de Montpellier* (February 2008), 45–54.

Hildebrandt, Mireille. "The Precision of Vagueness, Interview with H. Patrick Glenn." *Rechtsfilosofie & Rechtstheorie* [Netherlands Journal of Legal Philosophy] 35, no. 3 (2006), 346–60.

Hoeflich, Michael H. "Law, Society and Reception: The Vision of Alan Watson." *Michigan Law Review* 85 (1987), 1083–94.

Hofstraeten, Bram Van. "Recording Customs in Early Modern Antwerp, a Commercial Metropolis." *Rechtsgeschichte Legal History* 24 (2016), 288–301.

Holt, Mack P. *The French Wars of Religion, 1562–1629*. Cambridge: Cambridge University Press, 1995.

Homais, Maurice. *De la vénalité des offices sous l'Ancien Régime*. Paris: L. Larose, 1903.

Hooker, Michael Barry. *Legal Pluralism: An Introduction to Colonial and Neo-Colonial Laws*. Oxford: Clarendon Press, 1975.

Hotman, François. *Le Tigre de 1560*. Edited by Charles Read. Geneva: Slatkine Reprints, 1970.

Hotman, François. *Francogallia*. Edited by Ralph E. Giesey and J. H. M. Salmon. Cambridge: Cambridge University Press, 1972.

Hotman, François. *Antitribonian, ou, Discours d'un grand et renommé iurisconsulte de nostre temps sur l'estude des loix*. Paris: Éditions de l'Université de Saint-Etienne, 1980.

Houllemare, Marie. "Un avocat parisien entre art oratoire et promotion de soi (fin XVIe siècle)." *Revue historique* 630 (2004), 283–302.

Houllemare, Marie. "La norme dans les plaidoyers d'avocats parisiens du XVIe siècle." In *Normes juridiques et pratiques judiciaires du Moyen Âge à l'époque contemporaine*. Edited by Benoît Garnot and Pascal Bastien, 83–91. Dijon: Éditions universitaires de Dijon, 2007.

Houllemare, Marie. *Politiques de la parole: Le Parlement de Paris au XVIe siècle*. Geneva: Droz, 2011.

Hurt, John J. *Louis XIV and the Parlements: The Assertion of Royal Authority*. Manchester: Manchester University Press, 2002.

Ibbetson, David. "Custom in Medieval Law." In *The Nature of Customary Law: Legal, Historical and Philosophical Perspectives*. Edited by Amanda Perreau-Saussine and James B. Murphy, 151–75. Cambridge: Cambridge University Press, 2007.

The Institutes of Justinian. Translated by J. B. Moyle. 5th ed. Oxford: Clarendon Press, 1913.

Isambert, François A., Nicolas Decrusy, and Alphonse Honoré Taillandier, eds. *Recueil général des anciennes lois françaises, depuis l'an 420 jusqu'à la Révolution de 1789*. 29 vols. Paris: Belin-Le-Prieur, 1822.

Jacob, Robert. "Jugement des hommes et jugement de Dieu à l'aube du Moyen Âge." In *Le juge et le jugement dans les traditions juridiques européennes: Études d'histoire comparée*. Edited by Robert Jacob, 43–86. Paris: Librairie générale de droit et de jurisprudence, 1996.

Jacob, Robert. "Beaumanoir versus Révigny: The Two Faces of Customary Law in Philip the Bold's France." In *Essays on the Poetic and Legal Writings of Philippe de Remy and His Son Philippe de Beaumanoir of Thirteenth-Century France*. Edited by Sarah-Grace Heller and Michelle Reichert, 221–76. Lewiston: Edwin Mellen Press, 2001.

Jacob, Robert. "La coutume, les mœurs et le rite. Regards croisés sur les catégories occidentales de la norme non écrite." In *La coutume et la norme en Chine et au Japon*. Edited by Jérôme Bourgon, 145–66. Extrême-Orient Extrême-Occident 23. Saint-Denis: Presses universitaires de Vincennes, 2001.

Jacob, Robert. "Les coutumiers du XIIIe siècle ont-ils connu la coutume?" In *La coutume au village dans l'Europe médiévale et moderne: Actes des XXe journées internationales d'histoire de l'Abbaye de Flaran, septembre 1998*. Edited by Mireille Mousnier and Jacques Poumarède, 103–19. Toulouse: Presses universitaires du Mirail, 2001.

Jacob, Robert. "Philippe de Beaumanoir et les clercs. Pour sortir de la controverse du Ius commune." *Droits: Revue française de théorie, de philosophie et de culture juridiques* 50 (2011), 163–88.

Jacquart, Jean. *François Ier*. Paris: Fayard, 1981.

Jakab, Éva. "Brissonius in Context: *De Formulis et solennibus populi Romani verbis*." In *Reassessing Legal Humanism and Its Claims: Petere Fontes?* Edited by Paul J. du Plessis and John W. Cairns, 211–43. Edinburgh: Edinburgh University Press, 2016.

Jaubert, Pierre. "À propos de l'ancienne coutume et de la nouvelle coutume de Bordeaux: Bilan et perspectives." In *Extrait d'Annales de la faculté de droit des sciences sociales et politiques et la faculté des sciences économiques*. Bordeaux: Éditions Bière, 1976.

Jeanclos, Yves. "Coutume et loi, une approche logistique du droit." In *De code en code: Mélanges en l'honneur du doyen Georges Wiederkehr*. Edited by Marc Puech, 429–42. Paris: Dalloz, 2009.

Jeanclos, Yves. "Si la loi était une coutume qui a réussi?" In *Le juriste et la coutume du Moyen Âge au Code civil: Actes du colloque international organisé à Nancy, les 1er et 2 juillet 2010*. Edited by Antoine Astaing and François Lormant, 239–60. Nancy: PUN, Éditions universitaires de Lorraine, 2014.

Johnson, Jerah. "La Coutume de Paris: Louisiana's First Law." *Louisiana History* 30, no. 2 (1989), 145–55.

Jouanna, Arlette. "Noblesse, Noblesses." In *Dictionnaire de l'Ancien Régime: Royaume de France, XVIe–XVIIIe siècle*. Edited by Lucien Bély. Paris: Presses universitaires de France, 1996.

Jouanna, Arlette. *Le pouvoir absolu: Naissance de l'imaginaire politique de la royauté*. Paris: Gallimard, 2013.

Jouanna, Arlette. *La France du XVIe siècle: 1483–1598*. 3rd ed. Paris: Presses universitaires de France, 2016.

Journès, Claude, ed. *La coutume et la loi: Études d'un conflit*. Lyon: Presses universitaires de Lyon, 1986.

Juenger, Friedrich K. "Marital Property and the Conflict of Laws: A Tale of Two Countries." *Columbia Law Review* 81, no. 5 (1981), 1061–79.

Kadens, Emily. "Custom's Two Bodies." In *Center and Periphery: Studies on Power in the Medieval World in Honor of William Chester Jordan*. Edited by Katherine L. Jansen, G. Geltner, and Anne E. Lester, 239–48. Leiden: Brill, 2013.

Kagan, Richard L. *Lawsuits and Litigants in Castile, 1500–1700*. Chapel Hill: University of North Carolina Press, 1981.

Kahn-Freund, Otto. "On Uses and Misuses of Comparative Law." *Modern Law Review* 37 (1972), 1–27.

Kaiser, Colin. "Les cours souveraines au XVIe siècle: Morale et Contre-Réforme." *Annales. Économies, Sociétés, Civilisations* 37 (1982), 15–31.

Kan, Joseph van. *Les efforts de codification en France: Étude historique et psychologique*. Paris: Rousseau & cie, 1929.

Kan, Joseph van. "Unification du droit et les résistances des jurisconsultes sous l'ancien régime." In *Mélanges Paul Fournier: De la Bibliothèque d'histoire du droit*. Edited by Gabriel Le Bras, 363–74. Paris: Recueil Sirey, 1929.

Kelley, Donald R. "Fides Istoriae: Charles Dumoulin and the Gallican View of History." *Traditio* 22 (1966), 347–402.

Kelley, Donald R. *Foundations of Modern Historical Scholarship: Language, Law, and History in the French Renaissance*. New York: Columbia University Press, 1970.

Kelley, Donald R. *François Hotman: A Revolutionary's Ordeal*. Princeton: Princeton University Press, 1973.

Kelley, Donald R. *The Beginning of Ideology: Consciousness and Society in the French Reformation*. Cambridge: Cambridge University Press, 1981.

Kelley, Donald R. "Civil Science in the Renaissance: Jurisprudence in the French Manner." In *History, Law and the Human Sciences: Medieval and Renaissance Perspectives*, 261–76. London: Variorum Reprints, 1984.

Kelley, Donald R. "Second Nature': The Idea of Custom in European Law, Society, and Culture." In *Transmission of Culture in Early Modern Europe*. Edited by Anthony Grafton and Ann Blair, 131–72. Philadelphia: University of Pennsylvania Press, 1990.

Kelley, Donald R. *The Human Measure: Social Thought in the Western Legal Tradition*. Cambridge, MA: Harvard University Press, 1990.

Kelley, Donald R. "Lord Deliver Us from Justice." *Yale Journal of Law & the Humanities* 5 (1993), 159–68.

Keohane, Nannerl O. "Claude de Seyssel and Sixteenth-Century Constitutionalism in France." *Nomos* 20 (1979), 47–83.

Keohane, Nannerl O. *Philosophy and the State in France: The Renaissance to the Enlightenment*. Princeton: Princeton University Press, 1980.

Kim, Marie Seong-Hak. "The Chancellor's Crusade: Michel de L'Hôpital and the Parlement of Paris." *French History* 7, no. 1 (1993), 1–29.

Kim, Marie Seong-Hak. "'Dieu nous garde de la messe du chancelier': The Religious Belief and Political Opinion of Michel de L'Hôpital." *Sixteenth Century Journal* 24 (1993), 595–620.

Kim, Marie Seong-Hak. *Michel de L'Hôpital: The Vision of a Reformist Chancellor during the French Religious Wars*. Kirksville: Sixteenth Century Journal Publishers, 1997.

Kim, Marie Seong-Hak. "'Government des juges' ou 'juges du gouvernement'? The Revolutionary Traditions and Judicial Independence in France." *Korean Journal of International and Comparative Law* 26 (1998), 1–42.

Kim, Marie Seong-Hak. "'Nager entre deux eaux': L'idéalisme juridique et la politique religieuse de Michel de L'Hospital." In *De Michel de L'Hospital à l'édit de Nantes: Politique et religion face aux Églises*. Edited by Thierry Wanegffelen, 243–54. Clermont-Ferrand: Presses universitaires Blaise-Pascal, 2002.

Kim, Marie Seong-Hak. "Christophe de Thou et la réformation des coutumes: L'esprit de réforme juridique au XVIe siècle." *Tijdschrift voor Rechtsgeschiedenis* 72 (2004), 91–102.

Kim, Marie Seong-Hak. "Lawyers." In *Europe, 1450 to 1789: Encyclopedia of the Early Modern World*. Vol. 3, 459–64. New York: Charles Scribner's Sons, 2004.

Kim, Marie Seong-Hak. "Michel de L'Hospital: Un célébre aiguepersois, combatant pour la justice et la paix civile." *Sparsae* [Association culturelle d'Aigueperse et ses environs] 57 (2006), 5–14.

Kim, Marie Seong-Hak. "Custom, Community, and the Crown: Lawyers and the Reordering of French Customary Law." In *Between the Middle Ages and Modernity: Individual and Community in the Early Modern World*. Edited by Charles H. Parker and Jerry H. Bentley, 169–86. Lanham: Rowman & Littlefield, 2007.

Kim, Marie Seong-Hak. "Civil Law and Civil War: Michel de L'Hôpital and the Ideals of Legal Unification in Sixteenth-Century France." *Law and History Review* 28 (2010), 791–826.

Kim, Marie Seong-Hak. "L'Hôpital's Laws." *Law and History Review* 28 (2010), 843–48.

Kim, Marie Seong-Hak. *Law and Custom in Korea: Comparative Legal History*. Cambridge: Cambridge University Press, 2012.

Kim, Marie Seong-Hak. "La coutume et la raison comme sources de droit dans la première moitié de l'ère Meiji." In *Droit japonais, droit français, Quel dialogue?* Edited by Beatrice Jaluzot, 57–77. Geneva: Schulthess, 2014.

Kim, Marie Seong-Hak. "Can There Be Good Colonial Law?: Korean Law and Jurisprudence under Japanese Rule Revisited." In *The Spirit of Korean Law: Korean Legal History in Context*. Edited by Marie Seong-Hak Kim, 129–54. Leiden: Brill Nijhoff, 2016.

Kim, Marie Seong-Hak. "Charles Dumoulin's *Commentarii in consuetudines Parisienses*." In *The Formation and Transmission of Western Legal Culture: 150 Books That Made the Law in the Age of Printing*. Edited by Serge Dauchy, Georges Martyn, Anthony Musson, Heikki Pihlajamäki, and Alain Wijffels, 82–85. Studies in the History of Law and Justice 71. Heidelberg: Springer, 2016.

Kim, Marie Seong-Hak. "Michel de L'Hôpital and Christophe de Thou: Two Perceptions of Royal Justice during the French Religious Wars." In *Suum Cuique Tribuere: Legal Contexts, Judicial Archetypes and Deep-Structures Regarding Courts of Appeal and Judiciaries from Early Modern to Late Modern Europe*. Edited by Kjell Å Modéer and Matin Sunnqvist, 131–73. Stockholm: Institutet för Rättshistorisk Forskning/Olin Foundation, 2018.

Kim, Marie Seong-Hak. "Custom as a Source of Law in European and East Asian Legal History." In *Comparative Legal History*. Edited by Olivier Moréteau, Aniceto Masferrer, and Kjell Å Modéer, 186–211. Cheltenham: Edward Elgar, 2019.

Klimrath, Henri. *Travaux sur l'histoire du droit français*. Edited by Leopold August Warnkönig, 2 vols. Paris: Joubert, 1843.

Knecht, Robert J. *Francis I*. Cambridge: Cambridge University Press, 1982.

Knecht, Robert J. *The French Civil Wars, 1562–1598*. Harlow: Longman, 2000.

Kochkina, Svetlana. "Listening to the Dead with Our Eyes: François Olivier-Martin's Library, a Mirror Image of a Legal Historian." *Library & Information History* 32, no. 3 (2016), 203–18.

Krigel, Blandine. "Historiographie et histoire du droit aux XVIIème et XVIIIème siècles." In *Histoires de France, historiens de la France: Actes du colloque international, Reims, 14 et 15 mai 1993*. Edited by Yves-Marie Bercé and Philippe Contamine, 189–207. Paris: Honoré Champion, 1994.

Krygier, Martin. "Law as Tradition." *Law and Philosophy* 5, no. 2 (1986), 237–62.

Krynen, Jacques. "Réflexion sur les idées politiques aux États généraux de Tours de 1484." *Revue historique de droit français et étranger* 62 (1984), 183–204.

Krynen, Jacques. "'De Nostre certaine science…' Remarques sur l'absolutisme législative de la monarchie médiéval française." In *Renaissance du pouvoir législatif et genèse de l'État*. Edited by André Gouron and Albert Rigaudière, 31–44. Montpellier: Sociéte d'histoire du droit et des institutions des anciens pays de droit écrit, 1988.

Krynen, Jacques. *L'empire du roi. Idées et croyances politiques en France XIIIe–XVe siècle*. Paris: Gallimard, 1993.

Krynen, Jacques. "Droit romain et État monarchique. À propos du cas français." In *Représentation, pouvoir et royauté à la fin du Moyen Âge*. Edited by Joël Blanchard, 13–23. Paris: Picard, 1995.

Krynen, Jacques. "Voluntas domini regis in suo regno facit ius: Le roi de France et la coutume." In *El dret comú I Catalunya*. Edited by Aquilino Iglesia Ferreirós, 59–89. Barcelona: Fundació Noguera, 1998.

Krynen, Jacques, ed. *Droit romain, jus civile et droit français*. Études d'histoire du droit et des idées politiques 3. Toulouse: Presses de l'Université des sciences sociales de Toulouse, 1999.

Krynen, Jacques. "Entre science juridique et dirigisme: Le glas médiéval de la coutume." *Cahiers de recherches médiévales* 7 (2000), 171–87. https://journals.openedition.org/crm/892.

Krynen, Jacques. "Qu'est-ce qu'un Parlement qui représente le roi?" In *Excerptiones iuris: Studies in Honor of André Gouron*. Edited by Bernard Durand and Laurent Mayali, 353–66. Berkeley: Robbins Collection, 2000.

Krynen, Jacques. "The Absolute Monarchy and the French Unification of Private Rights." In *Privileges and Rights of Citizenship: Law and the Juridical Construction of Civil Society*. Edited by Julius Kirshner and Laurent Mayali, 27–55. Berkeley: Robbins Collection, 2002.

Krynen, Jacques. "Le droit romain 'droit commun de la France.'" *Droits: Revue française de théorie, de philosophie et de cultures juridiques* 38, no. 2 (2003), 21–35.

Krynen, Jacques. "Le problème et la querelle de l'interprétation de la loi, en France, avant la Révolution (Essai de rétrospective médiévale et moderne)." *Revue historique de droit français et étranger* 86, no. 2 (2008), 161–97.

Krynen, Jacques. *L'État de justice: France (XIIIe–XXe siècle)*, vol. 1: *L'idéologie de la magistrature ancienne*. Paris: Gallimard, 2009.

Krynen, Jacques, and Bernard d'Alteroche, eds. *L'histoire du droit en France: Nouvelles tendances, nouveaux territoires*. Paris: Classiques Garnier, 2014.

Krynen, Jacques, and Albert Rigaudière, eds. *Droits savants et pratiques françaises du pouvoir (XIe–XVe siècle)*. Bordeaux: Presses universitaires de Bordeaux, 1992.

Kubler, Jacques. *Recherches sur la fonction publique sous l'ancien régime: L'origine de la perpétuité des offices royaux*. Nancy: Société d'impressions typographiques, 1958.

Kuskowski, Ada-Maria. "The Development of Written Custom in England and in France: A Comparative Perspective." In *Law, Governance, and Justice: New Views on Medieval Constitutionalism*. Edited by Richard W. Kaeuper, Paul Dingman, and Peter Sposato, 101–20. Leiden: Brill, 2013.

Kuskowski, Ada-Maria. "Inventing Legal Space: From Regional Custom to Common Law in the Coutumiers of Medieval France." In *Space in the Medieval West: Places, Territories, and Imagined Geographies*. Edited by Meredith Cohen and Fanny Madeline, 133–58. Farnham: Ashgate, 2014.

La Roche-Flavin, Bernard de. *Treze livres des parlemens de France, esquels est amplement traicté de leur origine et institution et des présidens conseilliers, gens du roy, greffiers, secrétaires... et de leur charge, devoir et jurisdiction*. Bordeaux: Millanges, 1617.

Lainé, Armand. *Introduction au droit international privé*. 2 vols. Paris: F. Pichon, 1888–1892.

Lambert, Édouard. *La fonction du droit civil comparé*. Paris: V. Giard & E. Brière, 1903.

Lambert, Édouard. *Le gouvernement des juges et la lutte contre la législation sociale aux États-Unis: L'expérience américaine du contrôle judiciaire de la constitutionnalité des lois*. Paris: M. Giard & cie, 1921.

Laplanche, Jean de. *La réserve coutumière dans l'ancien droit français*. Paris: Recueil Sirey, 1925.

Lasser, Mitchel de S.-O.-L'E. "Judicial (Self-) Portraits: Judicial Discourse in the French Legal System." *Yale Law Journal* 104 (1995), 1325–1410.

Lasser, Mitchel de S.-O.-L'E. *Judicial Deliberations: A Comparative Analysis of Judicial Transparency and Legitimacy*. Oxford: Oxford University Press, 2009.

Laurière, Eusèbe de. *Texte des coutumes de la prévôté et vicomté de Paris... avec beaucoup de notes nouvelles*. 3 vols. Paris: Nyon, 1777.

Laurière, Eusèbe de, Louis Georges Oudart-Feudrix de Bréquigny et al., eds. *Ordonnances des rois de France de la troisième race recueillies par ordre chronologique* [1051–1514]. 21 vols. Paris: Imprimerie royale, 1723–1849.

Lavergnée, J. Brejon de. "Les vicissitudes de l'enregistrement des usances locales de Bretagne lors de la rédaction officielle de la Coutume de 1580." *Revue historique de droit français et étranger* 55, no. 4 (1977), 559–78.

Le Bras, Gabriel, ed. *Mélanges Paul Fournier. De la Bibliothèque d'histoire du droit, publiée sous les auspices de la Société d'histoire du droit*. Paris: Recueil Sirey, 1929.

Le Brun, Denis. *Traité des successions, devisé en quatre livres* in *Les œuvres de M. Denis Le Brun*. Vol. 1. Paris, 1714.

Le Caron, Louis. *Pandectes ou digestes du droit françois, par Loys Charondas le Caron*. Lyon: Jean Veyrat, 1593.

Le Caron, Louis. *Responses ou decisions du droict françois: Confirmees par arrests des cours souveraines de ce royaume et autres: Comme aussi des Conseils d'Estat & Privé du Roy, grand Conseil; enrichies de singulieres observations du droict Romain*. Paris: N. du Fossé, 1605.

Le Caron, Louis. *Nouveau commentaire de L. Charondas le Caron... sur la coustume de la Ville, Prevosté, & Vicomté de Paris, ou droict civil parisien*. Paris: P. Mettayer, 1613.

Le Maistre, Antoine. *Les plaidoyez et harangues de Monsieur Le Maistre, cy-devant advocat au Parlement et conseiller du Roy en ses conseils d'estat et privé. Donnez au public par Monsieur Issali advocat au Parlement*. Paris: Pierre Le Petit, 1657.

Le Roy Ladurie, Emmanuel. "Structures familiales et coutumes d'héritage en France au XVIe siècle: Système de la coutume." *Annales. Économies, Sociétés, Civilisations* 27, no. 4 (1972), 825–46.

Lebrun, Auguste. *La coutume: Ses sources—son autorité en droit privé. Contribution à l'étude des sources du droit positif à l'époque moderne*. Paris: Librairie générale, 1932.

Lee, Daniel. "'Office Is a Thing Borrowed': Jean Bodin on Offices and Seigneurial Government." *Political Theory* 41, no. 3 (2013), 409–40.

Lee, Daniel. "Roman Law, German Liberties and the Constitution of the Holy Roman Empire." In *Freedom and the Constitution of Europe*, Vol. 1: *Religious and Constitutional Liberties*. Edited by Quentin Skinner and Martin Van Gelderen, 256–73. Cambridge: Cambridge University Press, 2013.

Lee, Daniel. *Popular Sovereignty in Early Modern Constitutional Thought*. Oxford: Oxford University Press, 2016.

Lefebvre-Teillard, Anne. "Naissance du droit français: L'apport de jurisprudence." *Droits: Revue française de théorie juridique* 38 (2003), 69–82.

Lefebvre-Teillard, Anne. "Marriage in France from the Sixteenth to the Eighteenth Century: Political and Juridical Aspects." In *Marriage in Europe, 1400–1800*. Edited by Silvana Seidel Menchi and Emlyn Eisenach, 261–93. Toronto: University of Toronto Press, 2016.

Legrand, Pierre. "Jameses at Play: A Tractation on the Comparison of Laws." *American Journal of Comparative Law* 65 (2017), 1–132.

Lepointe, Gabriel. *Droit romain et ancien droit français: Régimes matrimoniaux, libéralités, successions*. Paris: Montchrestien, 1958.

Les Olim ou registre des arrêts rendus par la cour du roi sous les règnes de saint Louis, de Philippe le Hardi, de Philippe le Bel, de Louis le Hutin et de Philippe le Long, publiés par le Comte Beugnot membre de l'Institut. 4 vols. Paris: Imprimerie royale, 1839.

Lettmaier, Saskia. "Marriage Law and the Reformation." *Law and History Review* 35, no. 2 (2017), 461–510.

Lévy, Jean-Philippe. "Les preuves dans la *Très ancienne coutume* de Bretagne." *Annales de Bretagne et des pays de l'Ouest* 59 (1952), 39–59.

Leyte, Guillaume. "'Le droit commun de la France': Observations sur l'apport des arrêtistes." *Droits: Revue française de théorie juridique* 38 (2003), 53–67.

Leyte, Guillaume. "Le provincialisme juridique dans la France d'ancien régime: Quelques remarques." *Revue d'histoire des facultés de droit et de la science juridique* 23 (2003), 95–117.

Leyte, Guillaume. "Charondas et le droit français." *Droits: Revue française de théorie juridique* 39 (2004), 17–33.

L'Hommeau, Pierre de. *Deux livres de la iurisprudence françoise*. Saumur: Thomas Portau, 1605.

L'Hôpital, Michel de. *Poésies complètes du chancelier Michel de L'Hospital première traduction annotée*. Translated by Louis Bandy de Nalèche. Paris: Hachette, 1857.

L'Hôpital, Michel de. *Discours pour la majorité de Charles IX: Et trois autres discours*. Edited by Robert Descimon. Paris: Imprimerie nationale, 1993.

L'Hôpital, Michel de. *Michel de L'Hospital et ses discours (1559–1562): La plume et la tribune*. Edited by Loris Petris. Geneva: Droz, 2002.

L'Hôpital, Michel de. *Michel de L'Hospital, discours et correspondance: La plume et la tribune II*. Edited by Loris Petris and David Amherdt. Geneva: Droz, 2013.

L'Hôpital, Michel de. *Carmina: Livre I. Michel de L'Hospital*. Edited by Perrine Galand and Loris Petris. Geneva: Droz, 2014.

L'Hôpital, Michel de. *Carmina: Livre II. Michel de L'Hospital*. Edited by David Amherdt, Laure Chappus Sandoz, Perrine Galand, and Loris Petris. Geneva: Droz, 2017.

Library of Congress European Law Division. *The Coutumes of France in the Library of Congress: An Annotated Bibliography*. Edited by Jean Caswell and Ivan Sipkov. Washington, DC: Library of Congress, 1977.

Lloyd, Howell A. *The State, France, and the Sixteenth Century*. London: G. Allen & Unwin, 1983.

Lloyd, Howell A. "Constitutional Thought in Sixteenth-Century France: The Case of Pierre Rebuffi." *French History* 8, no. 3 (1994), 259–75.

Loisel, Antoine. *Institutes coustumières ou Manuel de plusieurs et diverses reigles, sentences, et proverbes, tant anciens que modernes, du droict coustumier et plus ordinaire de la France*. Edited by Michel Reulos. Paris: Recueil Sirey, 1935.

Lorenzen, Ernest G. "The French Rules of the Conflict of Laws." *Yale Law Journal* 38, no. 2 (1928), 165–92.

Louis-Lucas, Paul. *Étude sur la vénalité des charges et fonctions publiques*. 2 vols. Paris: Challamel et Thorin, 1882.

Loyseau, Charles. *Traité des seigneuries*. Paris: Abel L'Angelier, 1608.

Loyseau, Charles. *Les œuvres de Maistre Charles Loyseau... contenant les cinq livres du droit des offices, les traitez des seigneuries, des ordres & simples dignitez, du déguerpissement & délaissement par hypothèque, de la garantie des rentes, & des abus des justices de village. Nouv. éd., suivant la correction & augmentation de l'auteur*. Lyon: La Compagnies des libraires, 1701.

Major, J. Russell. *Representative Government in Early Modern France*. New Haven: Yale University Press, 1980.

Major, J. Russell. *From Renaissance Monarchy to Absolute Monarchy: French Kings, Nobles, & Estates*. Baltimore: Johns Hopkins University Press, 1994.

Marion, Marcel. *Dictionnaire des institutions de la France aux XVIIe et XVIIIe siècles*. Paris: Picard, 1923.

Martin, Victor. *Le gallicanisme et la Réforme catholique: Essai historique sur l'introduction en France des décrets du Concile de Trente (156–1615)*. Paris: Picard, 1919.

Martin, Xavier. *Le principe d'égalité dans les successions roturières en Anjou et dans le Maine*. Paris: Presses universitaires de France, 1972.

Martin, Xavier. "L'unité du droit français à la veille de 1789: Une aspiration modérée?" *Pensiero Politico* 19 (1986), 319–28.

Martin, Xavier. "Vie et destinée des coutumes françaises, 1454–1804: Essai de synthèse." *Revue historique de droit français et étranger* 93, no. 4 (2015), 529–58.

Martin-Sarzeaud, G. *Recherches historiques sur l'inamovibilité de la magistrature*. Paris: E. Duchemin, 1883.

Masferrer, Aniceto. "The Decline and Displacement of Custom in Early Modern Spain." *Tijdschrift voor Rechtsgeschiedenis* 87 (2019), 1–46.

Maugis, Édouard. *Histoire du Parlement de Paris de l'avènement des rois Valois à la mort d'Henri IV*. Paris: Picard, 1913.

Mautner, Menachem. "Three Approaches to Law and Culture." *Cornell Law Review* 96, no. 4 (2011), 839–67.

May, Larry. "Custom, Opinio Juris, and Consent." In *Philosophy of Law: Classic and Contemporary Readings*. Edited by Larry May and Jeff Brown, 54–69. Malden: Wiley-Blackwell, 2010.

Mayali, Laurent. "La coutume dans la doctrine romaniste au Moyen Âge." In *La coutume Custom*, Vol. 2: *Europe occidentale médiévale et moderne*. Edited by Jacques

Vanderlinden, 11–31. Recueils de la Société Jean Bodin 52. Brussels: De Boeck-Wesmael, 1990.

Mayali, Laurent. "*Ius civile* et *ius commune* dans la tradition juridique médiévale." In *Droit romain, jus civile et droit français*. Edited by Jacques Krynen, 201–17. Toulouse: Presses de l'Université des sciences sociales de Toulouse, 1999.

Merlin, Philippe-Antoine. "Coutume." In *Recueil alphabétique des questions de droit qui se présentent le plus fréquemment dans les tribunaux*. 4th ed., vol. 2. Paris: Garnery, 1827.

Merryman, John Henry. *The Civil Law Tradition: An Introduction to the Legal Systems of Western Europe and Latin America*. Stanford: Stanford University Press, 1969.

Merryman, John Henry. "The French Deviation." *American Journal of Comparative Law* 44 (1996), 109–19.

Mesnard, Pierre. "François Hotman (1524–1590) et le complexe de Tribonien." *Bulletin de la Société de l'histoire du protestantisme français* 101 (1955), 117–37.

Meynial, Édmond. "Remarques sur le rôle joué par la doctrine et la jurisprudence dans l'œuvre d'unification du droit en France depuis la rédaction des coutumes jusqu'à la Révolution, en particulier dans la succession aux propres." *Revue générale du droit, de la législation et de la jurisprudence en France et à l'étranger* 27 (1903), 326–35 (Part I) and 446–57 (Part II).

Michaud, Hélène. *La grande chancellerie et les écritures royales au seizième siècle (1515–1589)*. Paris: Presses universitaires de France, 1967.

Montaigne, Michel de. *The Complete Essays of Montaigne*. Translated by Donald M. Frame. Stanford: Stanford University Press, 1958.

Montaigne, Michel de. *Les Essais* (Édition de Bordeaux, 1595). Edited by Pierre Villey and Verdun-L. Saulnier. Paris: Presses universitaires de France, 1965.

Monter, William. *Judging the French Reformation: Heresy Trials by Sixteenth-Century Parlements*. Cambridge, MA: Harvard University Press, 1999.

Montesquieu, Charles-Louis de Secondat, baron de. *L'esprit des lois*. Paris: Lavigne, 1845.

Moote, A. Lloyd. *The Revolt of the Judges: The Parlement of Paris and the Fronde, 1643–1652*. Princeton: Princeton University Press, 2015.

More, Thomas. *Utopia*. Translated by Ralph Robinson. London: Blackie and Son, 1908.

Moréteau, Olivier, Aniceto Masferrer, and Kjell Å Modéer, eds. *Comparative Legal History*. Cheltenham: Edward Elgar, 2019.

Mousnier, Mireille, and Jacques Poumarède, eds. *La coutume au village dans l'Europe médiévale et moderne: Actes des XXe journées internationales d'histoire de l'Abbaye de Flaran, septembre 1998*. Toulouse: Presses universitaires du Mirail, 2001.

Mousnier, Roland. *La vénalité des offices sous Henri IV et Louis XIII*. 2nd ed. Paris: Presses universitaires de France, 1971 [1946].

Mousnier, Roland. *The Institutions of France under the Absolute Monarchy, 1598–1798*. Translated by Brian Pearce and Arthur Goldhammer. 2 vols. Chicago: University of Chicago Press, 1979 and 1984.

Oberman, Heiko A. *The Harvest of Medieval Theology: Gabriel Biel and Late Medieval Nominalism*. Cambridge, MA: Harvard University Press, 1963.

Ōkawa, Shirō. "16 seiki Furansu kanshūhō kōshiki hensan ron: Sharuru Deyu Mūran (1500–1566) no 'Furansu kanshūhō tōitsu ron' o sozai ni shite" [The Theory of the Official Compilation of French Customary Law in the Sixteenth Century: Charles Dumoulin's 'Theory of the Concord of French Custom']. *Hōkyō ronshū* (Aichi Daigaku Hōgakubu) 175 (2007), 1–55.

Ōkubo, Yasuo. "Furansu chūsei ōken to Rōma hō" [Royal Power in Medieval France and Roman Law]. *Hōsei shi kenkyū* 23 (1973), 29–71.

Olivier-Martin, François. "Un coutumier du Châtelet de la fin du XVe siècle," *Travaux juridique et économiques de l'Université de Rennes* 1 (1907), 411–32.

Olivier-Martin, François. "Un document inédit sur les travaux préparatoires de l'ancienne coutume de Paris." *Nouvelle revue historique de droit français et étranger* 42 (1918), 192–227.

Olivier-Martin, François. *Histoire de la coutume de la prévôté et vicomté de Paris*. 3 vols. Paris: Éditions Cujas, 1922–1930.

Olivier-Martin, François. "Les manuscrits de Simon Marion et la coutume de Paris au XVIe siècle." In *Travaux juridiques et économiques de l'Université de Rennes* 8 (1923), 135–40.

Olivier-Martin, François. *La coutume de Paris: Trait d'union entre le droit romain et les législations modernes*. Paris: Recueil Sirey, 1925.

Olivier-Martin, François. *L'organisation corporative de la France d'Ancien Régime*. Paris: Recueil Sirey, 1938.

Olivier-Martin, François. "Le roi de France et les mauvaises coutumes au Moyen Âge." *Zeitschrift der Savigny-Stiftung für Rechtsgeschichte. Germanistische Abtheilung* 58 (1938), 108–37.

Olivier-Martin, François. *Précis d'histoire du droit français*. 2nd ed. Paris: Dalloz, 1945.

Olivier-Martin, François. *Histoire du droit français: Des origines à la Révolution*. Paris: Éditions du Centre national de la recherche scientifique, 1984.

Olivier-Martin, François. *Les lois du roi*. Paris: Librairie de droit et de jurisprudence, 1997.

Oosterhuis, Janwillem. *Specific Performance in German, French and Dutch Law in the Nineteenth Century: Remedies in an Age of Fundamental Rights and Industrialisation*. Leiden: Brill, 2011.

Osler, Douglas J. "Budaeus and Roman Law." *Ius Commune* 13 (1985), 195–212.

Osler, Douglas J. "The Myth of European Legal History." *Rechtshistorisches Journal* 16 (1997), 393–410.

Ourliac, Paul. "Législation, coutumes et coutumiers au temps de Philippe Auguste." In *La France de Philippe Auguste, le temps des mutations*. Edited by Robert Henri Bautier, 471–88. Paris: Centre nationale de la recherche scientifique, 1982.

Ourliac, Paul. "Réflexions sur l'origine de la coutume." *Études d'histoire du droit médiéval en souvenir de Josette Metman, Mémoires de la Société pour l'histoire du droit des anciens pays bourguignons, comtois et romand* 45 (1988), 341–45.

Ourliac, Paul, and Jean-Louis Gazzaniga. *Histoire du droit privé français de l'an mil au Code civil*. Paris: Albin Michel, 1985.

Ourliac, Paul, and Henri Gilles. *La période post-classique (1378–1500)*, vol. 1: *La problématique de l'époque, les sources* (vol. 13 of *Histoire du droit et des institutions de l'Église en Occident*). Paris: Éditions Cujas, 1971.

Ourliac, Paul, and Jehan de Malafosse. *Histoire du droit privé*. 3 vols. Paris: Presses universitaires de France, 1968.

Palmer, Vernon Valentine. "From Embrace to Banishment: A Study of Judicial Equity in France." *American Journal of Comparative Law* 47, no. 2 (1999), 277–301.

Palmer, Vernon Valentine. "Historical Notes on the First Codes and Institutions in French Louisiana." In *Essays in Honor of Saúl Litvinoff*. Edited by Olivier Moréteau, Julio Romañach, and Alberto Luis Zuppi, 231–54. Baton Rouge: Claitor's Publishing, 2008.

Pansey, Pierre-Paul-Nicolas Henrion de. *Traité des fiefs de Dumoulin, analysé et conféré avec les autres feudistes*. Paris: Valade, 1773.

Paradis, Olivier. "Michel de L'Hospital: Du Palais d'Aigueperse à la chancellerie de France." *Sparsae* [Association culturelle d'Aigueperse et ses environs] 57 (2006), 15–34.

Parker, David. *The Making of French Absolutism*. London: Arnold, 1983.

Parker, David. "Sovereignty, Absolutism and the Function of the Law in Seventeenth-Century France." *Past & Present* 122 (1989), 36–74.

Parker, David. *Class and State in Ancien Régime France: The Road to Modernity?* London: Routledge, 1996.

Parker, David. "Absolutism, Feudalism and Property Rights in the France of Louis XIV." *Past & Present* 179 (2003), 60–96.

Parrow, Kathleen A. "Provincial Estates and the Revision of Customary Law in Medieval and Early Modern France: Evidence from the *Procès-Verbal* Narratives." *Parliaments, Estates & Representation* 21 (2001), 57–71.

Parsons, Jotham. *The Church in the Republic: Gallicanism and Political Ideology in Renaissance France.* Washington, DC: Catholic University of America Press, 2004.

Pascal, Robert. "The Sources of Civil Order according to the Louisiana Civil Code." *Tulane Law Review* 54 (1980), 916–41.

Pasquier, Étienne. *Les œuvres d'Estienne Pasquier: Contenant ses Recherches de la France.* Amsterdam, 1723.

Pasquier, Étienne. *L'interprétation des Institutes de Justinian: Avec la conférence de chasque paragraphe aux ordonnances royaux, arrestz de parlement et coustumes générales de la France.* Edited by Étienne-Denis Pasquier and Charles Giraud. Paris: Videcoq ainé, 1847.

Pattou, Étienne. "Généalogie de la Maison de Thou." 2004. http://racineshistoire.free.fr/LGN/PDF/de-Thou.pdf.

Peach, Trevor. "Le droit romain en français au XVIe siècle: Deux Oraisons de François de Némond (1555)." *Revue historique de droit français et étranger* 60 (1982), 5–44.

Peguera Poch, Marta. *Aux origines de la réserve héréditaire du Code civil: La légitime en pays de coutumes (XVIe–XVIIIe siècles).* Aix-en-Provence: Presses universitaires d'Aix-Marseille, 2015. https://books.openedition.org/puam/885.

Perreau-Saussine, Amanda, and James B. Murphy. *The Nature of Customary Law: Legal, Historical and Philosophical Perspectives.* Cambridge: Cambridge University Press, 2007.

Peter, Rodolphe. "Le 'Tigre' de François Hotman: Une énigme bibliographique résolue." *Bulletin de la Société de l'histoire du protestantisme français* 124 (1978), 113–18.

Petigny, Jules de. "Testament de François de Vendôme, vidame de Chartres, 1560." *Bibliothèque de l'École des chartes* 11 (1850), 327–42.

Petitjean, Michel. *Essai sur l'histoire des substitutions du IXe au XVe siècle dans la pratique et la doctrine spécialement en France méridionale.* Dijon: Centre de recherches historiques, Faculté de droit et de science politique, 1975.

Petit-Renaud, Sophie. "Le roi, les légistes et le parlement de Paris aux XIVe et XVe siècles: Contradictions dans la perception du pouvoir de 'faire loy'?" *Cahiers de recherches médiévales (XIIIe–XVe siècles)* 7 (2000). http://journals.openedition.org/crm/889.

Petit-Renaud, Sophie, and Anne Rousselet-Pimont. "Histoire des normes: L'émergence de la loi moderne." In *L'histoire du droit en France: Nouvelles tendances, nouveaux territoires.* Edited by Jacques Krynen and Bernard d'Alteroche, 223–35. Paris: Classiques Garnier, 2014.

Petot, Pierre. *Études d'histoire du droit privé offertes à Pierre Petot.* Paris: Libraire générale de droit et de jurisprudence, 1959.

Petot, Pierre. "Le droit commun en France selon les coutumiers." *Revue historique de droit français et étranger* 37 (1960), 412–29.

Petot, Pierre, and Claude Bontems. *Histoire du droit privé français.* Paris: Loysel, 1992.

Petris, Loris. "'Toutes passions laissées et deposées': Hatred in Michel de L'Hospital's Poetry and Policy." *Renaissance Studies* 17 (2003), 674–94.

Piant, Hervé. *Une justice ordinaire: Justice civile et criminelle dans la prévôté royale de Vaucouleurs sous l'ancien régime.* Rennes: Presses universitaires de Rennes, 2006.

Picot, Georges. *Histoire des États généraux, considérés au point de vue de leur influence sur le gouvernement de la France de 1355 à 1614*. 4 vols. Paris: Hachette et cie, 1872.

Pignot, J.-Henri. *Un jurisconsulte au seizième siècle: Barthélemy de Chasseneuz, premier commentateur de la coutume de Bourgogne et président du Parlement de Provence, sa vie et ses œuvres*. Geneva: Slatkine Reprints, 1970.

Pihlajamäki, Heikki. "Merging Comparative Law and Legal History: Towards an Integrated Discipline." *American Journal of Comparative Law* 66 (2018), 733–50.

Pihlajamäki, Heikki, Markus Dirk Dubber, and Mark Godfrey, eds. *The Oxford Handbook of European Legal History*. Oxford: Oxford University Press, 2018.

Pintens, Walter. "Testamentary Formalities in France and Belgium." In *Comparative Succession Law*, Vol. 1: *Testamentary Formalities*. Edited by Kenneth G. Reid, Marius J. de Wall, and Reinhard Zimmermann, 51–70. Oxford: Oxford University Press, 2011.

Pissard, Hippolyte. *Essai sur la connaissance et la preuve des coutumes en justice, dans l'ancien droit français et dans le système romano-canonique*. Paris: Rousseau, 1910.

Planiol, M., ed. *Très-ancienne coutume de Bretagne*. Rennes, 1896.

Plessis, Paul J. du, and John W. Cairns, eds. *Reassessing Legal Humanism and Its Claims: Petere Fontes?* Edinburgh: Edinburgh University Press, 2016.

Pock, Max A. "The Rule against Perpetuities: A Comparison of Some Common Law and Civil Law Jurisdictions." *St. John's Law Review* 35, no. 1 (2013), 62–83.

Portalis, Jean-Étienne-Marie. *Discours préliminaire au premier projet de Code civil (le 21 janvier 1801)*. Bordeaux: Éditions Confluences, 2004.

Poudret, Jean-François. "Réflexions sur la preuve de la coutume devant les juridictions royales françaises aux XIIIe et XIVe siècles, notamment le rôle de l'enquête par turbe." *Revue historique de droit français et étranger* 65, no. 1 (1987), 71–86.

Poumarède, Jacques. "Défense et illustration de la coutume au temps de l'exégèse: Les débuts de l'école française du droit historique." In *La Coutume et la loi: Études d'un conflit*. Edited by Claude Journès, 95–112. Lyon: Presses universitaires de Lyon, 1986.

Poumarède, Jacques. "Olivier-Martin, François-Jean-Marie." In *Dictionnaire historique des juristes français (XIIe—XXe siècle)*. Edited by Patrick Arabeyre, Jean-Louis Halpérin, and Jacques Krynen. Paris: Presses universitaires de France, 2007.

Poumarède, Jacques. *Itinéraire(s) d'un historien du droit: Jacques Poumarède, regards croisés sur la naissance de nos institutions*. Edited by Jean-Pierre Allinne. Toulouse: CNRS-Université de Toulouse-Le Mirail, 2011.

Poumarède, Jacques, Anne Lefebvre-Teillard, and Société d'histoire du droit, eds. *Histoire de l'histoire du droit: Actes de journées internationales de la Société d'histoire du droit, Toulouse, 1–4 juin 2005*. Toulouse: Presses de l'Université des sciences sociales de Toulouse, 2006.

Poumarède, Jacques, and Jack Thomas, eds. *Les parlements de province: Pouvoirs, justice et société du XVe au XVIIIe siècle*. Toulouse: FRAMESPA, 1996.

Powis, Jonathan K. "Order, Religion, and the Magistrates of a Provincial Parlement in Sixteenth-Century France." *Archiv für Reformationsgeschichte* 71 (1980), 180–97.

Powis, Jonathan K. "Gallican Liberties and the Politics of Later Sixteenth-Century France." *Historical Journal* 26 (1983), 515–30.

Powis, Jonathan K. "Aristocratie et bureaucratie dans la France du XVIe siècle: État, office et patrimoine." In *L'État et les aristocraties (France, Angleterre, Écosse), XIIe-XVIIe siècle: Actes de la table ronde, 26 et 27 septembre 1986*. Edited by Philippe Contamine, 231–45. Paris: Presses de l'École normale supérieure, 1989.

Prest, Wilfrid R., ed. *Lawyers in Early Modern Europe and America*. New York: Holmes & Meier Publishers, 1981.

Prévost, Xavier. *Jacques Cujas (1522–1590), jurisconsulte humaniste*. Geneva: Libraire Droz, 2015.

Prévost, Xavier. "Reassessing the Influence of Medieval Jurisprudence on Jacques Cujas' (1522–1590) Method." In *Reassessing Legal Humanism and Its Claims: Petere Fontes?* Edited by Paul J. du Plessis and John W. Cairns, 88–107. Edinburgh: Edinburgh University Press, 2016.

Puchta, Georg Friedrich. *Das Gewohnheitsrecht: erster und zweiter Teil*. Erlangen: Palm, 1828–1837.

Puech, Marc, ed. *De code en code: Mélanges en l'honneur du doyen Georges Wiederkehr*. Paris: Dalloz, 2009.

Quilliet, Bernard. "La situation sociale des avocats au Parlement de Paris à l'époque de la Renaissance (1480–1560)." In *Espace, idéologie et société au XVIe siècle*. Edited by José Luis Alonso Hernández, 121–52. Grenoble: Presses universitaires de Grenoble, 1975.

Rahmatian, Andreas. "Friedrich Carl von Savigny's Beruf and Volksgeistlehre." *Journal of Legal History* 28 (2007), 1–29.

Regnault, Henri. *Les ordonnances civiles du chancelier Daguesseau*. 2 vols. Paris: Recueil Sirey, 1929–1938.

Reimann, Mathias, and Alain Levasseur, "Comparative Law and Legal History in the United States." *American Journal of Comparative Law* 46 (Supplement) (1998), 1–15.

Reimann, Mathias, and Reinhard Zimmermann, eds. *The Oxford Handbook of Comparative Law*. Oxford: Oxford University Press, 2006.

Rémy, Philippe. "Le rôle de l'exégèse dans l'enseignement du droit au XIXe siècle." *Annales d'histoire des facultés de droit* 2 (1985), 92–105.

Renoux-Zagamé, Marie-France. "Le droit commun dans l'histoire juridique européenne: Valeur et signification d'un héritage." In *L'Europa e il diritto*. Edited by Danilo Castellano, 17–37. Naples: Edizioni scientifiche italiane, 1989.

Renoux-Zagamé, Marie-France. "La méthode du droit commun: Réflexion sur la logique des droits non codifiés." *Revue d'histoire des facultés de droit et de la science juridique* 10–11 (1990), 133–52.

Reulos, Michel. *Étude sur l'esprit, les sources et la méthode des Institutes coutumières d'Antoine Loisel*. Paris: Recueil Sirey, 1935.

Reulos, Michel. "L'importance des praticiens dans humanisme juridique." In *Pédagogues et juristes; Congrès du Centre d'études supérieures de la Renaissance de Tours, été 1960*. Edited by Centre d'études supérieures de la Renaissance, 119–33. Paris: J. Vrin, 1963.

Reulos, Michel. "La notion de 'justice' et l'activité administrative du roi en France (XVe–XVIIe siècles)." In *Histoire comparée de l'administration (IVe–XVIIIe siècles): Actes du XIVe Colloque historique franco-allemand, Tours, 27 mars–1er avril 1977*. Edited by Werner Paravicini and Karl Ferdinand Werner, 33–46. Beihefte Der Francia 9. Munich: Artemis Verlag, 1980.

Reulos, Michel. "Vers la présentation coordonnée et logique du droit français." In *Pouvoir et institutions en Europe au XVIe siècle, vingt-septième colloque internationale d'études humanistes, Tours*. Edited by André Stegmann, 275–82. Paris: J. Vrin, 1987.

Reulos, Michel. "L'action législative d'Henri III." In *Henri III et son temps: Actes du colloque international du Centre de la Renaissance de Tours, octobre 1989*. Edited by Robert Sauzet, 177–82. Paris: J. Vrin, 1992.

Ricard, Jean-Marie. *Traité des donations entre-vifs et testamentaires: Le traité de la révocation des donations par la naissance & survenance des enfans*. Riom: M. Dégoutte, 1783.

Richet, Denis. *La France moderne: L'esprit des institutions*. Paris: Flammarion, 1973.

Richet, Denis. "Élite et noblesse: La formation des grands serviteurs de l'État (fin XVIe–début XVIIe siècle)." In *De la Réforme à la Révolution: Études sur la France moderne*. Edited by Denis Richet, 143–54. Paris: Aubier, 1991.

Rigaudière, Albert. "Législation royale et construction de l'État dans la France du XIIIe siècle." In *Renaissance du pouvoir législatif et genèse de l'État*. Edited by André Gouron and Albert Rigaudière. Montpellier: Société d'histoire du droit et des institutions des anciens pays de droit écrit, 1988.

Rigaudière, Albert. "Loi et État dans la France du bas Moyen Âge." In *L'État moderne: Le droit, l'espace et les formes de l'État, actes du colloque tenu à la Baume, 11–12 octobre 1984*. Edited by Noël Coulet and Jean-Philippe Genet, 33–59. Paris: Éditions du CNRS, 1990.

Roberts, Penny. "Royal Authority and Justice during the French Religious Wars." *Past & Present* 184, no. 1 (2004), 3–32.

Robinson, Olivia F., T. David Fergus, and William M Gordon. *European Legal History*. London: Butterworths, 2000.

Roelker, Nancy L. *One King, One Faith: The Parlement of Paris and the Religious Reformations of the Sixteenth Century*. Berkeley: University of California Press, 1996.

Roemier, Florent. "Avocat général et coutumes." In *Le juriste et la coutume du Moyen Âge au Code civil: Actes du colloque international organisé à Nancy, les 1er et 2 juillet 2010*. Edited by Antoine Astaing and François Lormant, 140–69. Nancy: PUN-Éditions universitaires de Lorraine, 2014.

Roland, Henri, and Laurent Boyer, eds. *Adages du droit français*. 2nd ed. Lyon: L'Hermès, 1986.

Root, Hilton. "Tying the King's Hands: Credible Commitments and Royal Fiscal Policy during the Old Regime." *Rationality and Society* 1 (1989), 240–58.

Ross, Alf. *Theorie der Rechtsquellen: Ein Beitrag zur Theorie des positiven Rechts auf Grundlage dogmenhistorischer Untersuchungen. Akademische Abhandlung*. Leipzig: Linz, 1929.

Ross, Alf. *On Law and Justice*. London: Stevens, 1958.

Rousseau, Jean-Jacques. *Considérations sur le gouvernement de Pologne, et sur sa réformation projettée*. London, 1782.

Rousselet-Pimont, Anne. *Le chancelier et la loi au XVIe siècle: D'après l'œuvre d'Antoine Duprat, de Guillaume Poyet et de Michel de l'Hospital*. Paris: De Boccard, 2005.

Rousselet-Pimont, Anne. "Une générosité suspecte: Les libéralités aux proches parents des conjoints d'après la jurisprudence du Parlement de Paris aux XVIe–XVIIe siècles." *Revue historique de droit français et étranger* 83 (2005), 183–213.

Royer, Jean-Pierre. *Histoire de la justice en France: De la monarchie absolue à la République*. Paris: Presses universitaires de France, 1995.

Rückert, Joachim. "The Invention of National Legal History." In *The Oxford Handbook of European Legal History*. Edited by Heikki Pihlajamäki, Markus Dirk Dubber, and Mark Godfrey, 22–83. Oxford: Oxford University Press, 2018.

Saint-Bonnet, François. "Le Parlement, juge constitutionnel (XVIe–XVIIIe siècle)." *Droits: Revue française de théorie, de philosophie et de culture juridiques* 34 (2001), 177–98.

Saint-Bonnet, François. "L'intérêt général dans l'ancien droit constitutionnel." In *L'intérêt général, norme constitutionnelle*. Edited by Bertrand Mathieu, Michel Verpeaux, Josseline de Clausade, and Michel Charasse, 9–21. Paris: Dalloz, 2007.

Saleilles, Raymond. "École historique et droit naturel d'après quelques ouvrages récents." *Revue trimestrielle de droit civil* 1 (1902), 80–112.

Salmon, John H. M. "Venality of Office and Popular Sedition in Seventeenth-Century France." *Past & Present* 37 (1967), 21–43.

Salmon, John H. M. "Bodin and the Monarchomachs." In *Jean Bodin: Verhandlungen der internationalen Bodin-Tagung in München*. Edited by Horst Denzer, 359–78. Munich: C. H. Beck, 1973.

Salmon, John H. M. *Society in Crisis: France in the Sixteenth Century*. New York: St. Martin's Press, 1975.

Salmon, John H. M. "Storm over the Noblesse." *Journal of Modern History* 53, no. 2 (1981), 242–57.

Salmon, John H. M. "France." In *The Cambridge History of Political Thought 1450–1700*. Edited by J. H. Burns and Mark Goldie, 458–97. Cambridge: Cambridge University Press, 1991.

Salmon, John H. M. "Renaissance Jurists and 'Enlightened' Magistrates: Perspectives on Feudalism in Eighteenth-Century France." *French History* 8, no. 4 (1994), 387–402.

Salmon, John H. M. "The Legacy of Jean Bodin: Absolutism, Populism or Constitutionalism?" *History of Political Thought* 17, no. 4 (1996), 500–22.

Sauvel, Tony. "Histoire du jugement motivé." *Revue du droit public et de la société politique en France et à l'étranger* 71 (1955), 5–53.

Sauvel, Tony. "Les demandes de motifs adressées par le conseil du roi aux cours souveraines." *Revue historique de droit français et étranger* 34 (1957), 529–48.

Savigny, Friedrich Carl von. *Of the Vocation of Our Age for Legislation and Jurisprudence*. Translated by Abraham Hayward. London: Littlewood, 1831.

Savigny, Friedrich Carl von. *System des heutigen römischen Rechts*. Berlin: Veit, 1840–1849.

Schiffman, Zachary Sayre. "An Anatomy of the Historical Revolution in Renaissance France." *Renaissance Quarterly* 42 (1989), 507–33.

Schmitt, Carl. *Political Theology: Four Chapters on the Concept of Sovereignty*. Translated by George Schwab. Chicago: University of Chicago Press, 2005 [1922].

Schnapper, Bernard. "Le naufrage du droit pénal coutumier." In *Voies nouvelles en histoire de droit: La justice, la famille, la répression pénale, XVIème–XXème siècles*, 177–85. Paris: Presses universitaires de France, 1991.

Schneider, Zoë A. *The King's Bench: Bailiwick Magistrates and Local Governance in Normandy, 1670–1740*. Rochester: University of Rochester Press, 2008.

Schönfeld, Karel Menzo. *Montesquieu en "la bouche de la loi"*. Leiden: New Rhine Publishers, 1979.

Seidel Menchi, Silvana, and Emlyn Eisenach, eds. *Marriage in Europe, 1400–1800*. Toronto: University of Toronto Press, 2016.

Seligman, Edmond. *La justice en France pendant la Révolution*. Vol. 1. Paris: Plon-Nourrit et cie, 1901–1913.

Seyssel, Claude de. *La grande monarchie de France*. Paris: Galiot du Pré, 1557.

Shennan, Joseph H. *The Parlement of Paris*. Ithaca: Cornell University Press, 1968.

Shennan, Joseph H. *Liberty and Order in Early Modern Europe: The Subject and the State, 1650–1800*. London: Longman, 1986.

Shklar, Judith N. *Montesquieu*. Oxford: Oxford University Press, 1987.

Skinner, Quentin. *The Foundation of Modern Political Thought*. 2 vols. Cambridge: Cambridge University Press, 1978.

Skoda, Hannah. "Legal Performances in Late Medieval France." In *Legalism: Anthropology and History*. Edited by Paul Dresch and Hannah Skoda, 279–306. Oxford: Oxford University Press, 2012.

Slongo, Paulo. "Genealogie della consuetudine nell'epoca delle guerre di religione in Francia." *Scienza & Politica* 30, no. 58 (2018), 155–76.

Smail, Daniel Lord. *The Consumption of Justice: Emotions, Publicity, and Legal Culture in Marseille, 1264–1423*. Ithaca: Cornell University Press, 2003.

Smedley-Weill, Anette, and Simone Geoffroy-Poisson. "Les assemblées d'états et la mise en forme du droit." *Les cahiers du Centre de recherches historiques* 26 (2001), 31–56.

Soboul, Albert. *La Révolution française*. Paris: Éditions sociales, 1982.

Société d'histoire du droit. "Société d'histoire du droit, 1983–1984." *Revue historique de droit français et étranger* 62 (1984), 693–724.

Société d'histoire du droit des pays flamands, picards et wallons. "Journées d'histoire des institutions tenues à Bruxelles et Malines, les 4, 5 et 6 juin 1949." *Revue du Nord* 31 (1949), 219–40.

Société de l'histoire de France. "Liste: Des bailliages et sénéchaussées de France, distribués par provinces et par pays, conformément à un ancien tableau de la superficie du royaume." *Annuaire historique pour l'année* 14 (1850), 27–52. https://www.jstor.org/stable/23399394.

Sperling, Jutta. "Marriage at the Time of the Council of Trent (1560–70): Clandestine Marriages, Kinship Prohibitions, and Dowry Exchange in European Comparison." *Journal of Early Modern History* 8, no. 1 (2004), 67–108.

Stein, Peter. "Legal Humanism and Legal Science." *Tidschrift voor Rechtsgchiedenis* 54, no. 4 (1986), 297–306.

Stein, Peter. "The Civil Law Doctrine of Custom and the Growth of Case Law." In *Scintillae iuris: Studi in memoria di Gino Gorla*, vol. 1, 371–81. Milan: A. Giuffrè, 1994.

Stein, Peter. *Roman Law in European History*. Cambridge: Cambridge University Press, 1999.

Steinberg, Sylvie. "Au défaut des mâles." *Annales. Histoire, Sciences Sociales* 67, no. 3 (2012), 679–713.

Stewart, Iain. "'Customs in Common': The Old Emperor's Clothes." *Macquarie Law Journal* 6 (2009), 139–60.

Stocker, Christopher. "Office as Maintenance in Renaissance France." *Canadian Journal of History* 6, no. 1 (1971), 21–44.

Stocker, Christopher. "Office and Justice: Louis XI and the Parlement of Paris (1465–1476)." *Mediaeval Studies* 37 (1975), 360–86.

Stocker, Christopher. "Public and Private Enterprise in the Administration of a Renaissance Monarchy: The First Sales of Office in the Parlement of Paris (1512–1524)." *Sixteenth Century Journal* 9, no. 2 (1978), 4–29.

Storez, Isabelle. "La philosophie politique du chancelier d'Aguesseau." *Revue historique* 265 (1981), 381–400.

Storez, Isabelle. *Le chancelier Henri François d'Aguesseau, 1668–1751: Monarchiste et libéral*. Paris: Publisud, 1996.

Strauss, Gerald. *Law, Resistance and the State: The Opposition to Roman Law in Reformation Germany*. Princeton: Princeton University Press, 1986.

Swann, Julian. *Provincial Power and Absolute Monarchy: The Estates General of Burgundy, 1661–1790*. Cambridge: Cambridge University Press, 2003.

Swart, K. W. *Sale of Offices in the Seventeenth Century*. The Hague: M. Nijhoff, 1949.

Taillandier, Alphonse-Honoré. *Nouvelles recherches historiques sur la vie et les ouvrages du chancelier de L'Hospital*. Paris: Firmin-Didot frères et fils, 1861.

Tallon, Alain. *Conscience nationale et sentiment religieux en France au XVIe siècle: Essai sur la vision gallicane du monde*. Paris: Presses universitaires de France, 2002.

Tamanaha, Brian Z. "A Non-Essentialist Version of Legal Pluralism." *Journal of Law and Society* 27 (2000), 296–321.

Tamanaha, Brian Z. "Understanding Legal Pluralism: Past to Present, Local to Global." *Sydney Law Review* 30 (2008), 375–411.

Tardif, Ernest-Joseph, ed. *Coutumiers de Normandie*, 3 vols. Rouen, 1881–1903.

Testaud, Georges. *Des juridictions municipales en France: Des origines jusqu'à l'ordonnance de Moulins, 1566*. Paris: Libraire de la Société du recueil général des lois et des arrêts, 1901.

Thireau, Jean-Louis. *Charles du Moulin, 1500–1566: Étude sur les sources, la méthode, les idées politiques et économiques d'un juriste de la Renaissance*. Geneva: Droz, 1980.

Thireau, Jean-Louis. "Aux origines des articles 1217 à 1225 du Code civil: *L'extricatio labyrinthi dividui et individui* de Charles Du Moulin." *Tijdschrift voor Rechtsgeschiedenis* 51 (1983), 51–109.

Thireau, Jean-Louis. "L'enseignement du droit et ses méthodes au XVIe siècle. Continuité ou rupture?" *Annales d'histoire des facultés de droit et de science juridique* 2 (1985), 27–36.

Thireau, Jean-Louis. "Le comparatisme et la naissance du droit français." *Revue d'histoire des facultés de droit et de la science juridique* 10–11 (1990), 153–91.

Thireau, Jean-Louis. "Professeurs et étudiants étrangers dans les facultés de droit françaises (XVIe–XVIIe siècles)." *Revue d'histoire des facultés et droit et de la science juridique* 13 (1992), 43–73.

Thireau, Jean-Louis. "Lumières et ombres de la profession d'avocat au tournant des XVIe et XVIIe siècles d'après le dialogue des avocats au Parlement de Paris." *Revue internationale d'histoire de la profession d'avocat* 5 (1993), 51–67.

Thireau, Jean-Louis. "Le jurisconsulte." *Droits* 20 (1994), 21–30.

Thireau, Jean-Louis. "Hugues Doneau et les fondements de la codification modern." *Droits: Revue française de théorie, de philosophie et de culture juridiques* 26 (1997), 81–100.

Thireau, Jean-Louis. "Préfaces de Guy Coquille." *Revue d'histoire des facultés de droit* 19 (1998), 217–49.

Thireau, Jean-Louis. "L'alliance des lois romaines avec le droit français." In *Droit romain, jus civile et droit français*. Edited by Jacques Krynen, 347–74. Toulouse: Presses de l'Université des sciences sociales de Toulouse, 1999.

Thireau, Jean-Louis. "Le bon juge chez les juristes français du XVIe siècle." In *La conscience du juge dans la tradition juridique européenne*. Edited by Jean-Marie Carbasse and Laurence Depambour-Tarride, 131–54. Paris: Presses universitaires de France, 1999.

Thireau, Jean-Louis. "Humaniste (Jurisprudence)." In *Dictionnaire de la culture juridique*. Edited by Denis Alland and Stéphane Rials, 795–800. Paris: Presses universitaires de France, 2003.

Thireau, Jean-Louis. "Une vision du droit public romain au XVIe siècle: *Le Tractatus analyticus de dignitatibus, magistratibus et civibus romanis* de Charles du Moulin." In *Science politique et droit public dans les facultés de droit européennes (XIIIe–XVIIIe siècle)*. Edited by Jacques Krynen and Michael Stolleis, 393–410. Frankfurt am Main: Vittorio Klostermann, 2008.

Thireau, Jean-Louis. "Fondements de l'exclusion successorale des filles dotées dans l'ouest de la France." In *Mélanges en l'honneur d'Anne Lefebvre-Teillard*. Edited by Bernard d'Alteroche, Florence Demoulin-Auzary, Olivier Descamps, and Franck Roumy, 991–1006. Paris: Éditions Panthéon-Assas, 2009.

Thireau, Jean-Louis. "Les trois rédactions de la coutume de Touraine." In *La coutume dans tous ses états: Actes du colloque international des 15 au 17 juin 2010 à l'occasion de la célébration du 500e anniversaire de la rédaction de la coutume d'Auvergne Clermont-Ferrand-Riom*. Edited by Florent Garnier and Jacqueline Vendrand-Voyer, 111–34. Paris: Éditions La Mémoire du Droit, 2013.

Thirsk, Joan. "The European Debate on Customs of Inheritance, 1500–1700." In *Family and Inheritance: Rural Society in Western Europe, 1200–1800*. Edited by Jack Goody, Joan Thirsk, and E. P. Thompson, 177–91. Cambridge: Cambridge University Press, 1976.

Thompson, Martyn P. "The History of Fundamental Law in Political Thought from the French Wars of Religion to the American Revolution." *American Historical Review* 91, no. 5 (1986), 1103–28.

Thou, Jacques-Auguste de. *Histoire universelle depuis 1543 jusqu'en 1607*. 11 vols. Basel: Jean Louis Brand Muller, 1742; *Histoire universelle depuis 1543 jusqu'en 1607*. 16 vols. London, 1734.

Timbal, Pierre-Clément. "La succession testamentaire dans la coutume de Toulouse." *Extrait des Annales de la faculté de droit d'Aix-en-Provence*, Nouvelle série no. 43. Aix-en-Provence: Imprimerie d'Éditions provençales, 1950.

Tisset, Pierre. "Mythes et réalités du droit écrit." In *Études d'histoire du droit privé: Offertes à Pierre Petot*, 553–60. Paris: Montchrestien, 1959.

Vanderlinden, Jacques. *Le concept de code en Europe occidentale du XIIIe au XIXe siècle: Essai de définition*. Brussels: Édition de l'Institut de sociologie, 1967.

Veillon, Didier. "Quelques observations sur le droit commun coutumier français (XVIe–XVIIIe s.)." *Slovenian Law Review* 4, no. 1/2 (2007), 215–26.

Vellet, Christophe. "Portraits individuels, portrait de groupe: Antoine Duprat et quelques acteurs de la rédaction de la coutume d'Auvergne." In *La coutume dans tous ses états: Actes du colloque international des 15 au 17 juin 2010 à l'occasion de la célébration du 500e anniversaire de la rédaction de la coutume d'Auvergne Clermont-Ferrand-Riom*. Edited by Florent Garnier and Jacqueline Vendrand-Voyer, 61–78. Paris: Éditions La Mémoire du Droit, 2013.

Vendrand-Voyer, Jacqueline. "Réformation des coutumes et droit romain. Pierre Lizet et la coutume de Berry." *Annales de la faculté de droit et de science politique de Clermont* 18 (1981), 313–81.

Vergne, Arnaud. "Coutumes de France et droit romain selon Pierre Taisand, Claude-Joseph de Ferrière et Antoine Terrasson (1678–1750)." *Slovenian Law Review* 4, no. 1/2 (2007), 229–48.

Viollet, Paul. *Précis de l'histoire du droit français*. Paris: L. Larose et Forcel, 1886.

Viollet, Paul. *Histoire du droit civil français, accompagnée de notions de droit canonique et d'indications bibliographiques*. Paris: L. Larose et Forcel, 1893.

Viollet, Paul. *Histoire des institutions politiques et administratives de la France*. Paris: L. Larose et Forcel, 1898.

Viret, Jérôme-Luther. "Droit, usages et coutume sous l'Ancien Régime: L'exemple de la prévôté de Paris au milieu du XVIIe siècle." *Revue historique de droit français et étranger* 77, no. 4 (1999), 505–17.

Viret, Jérôme-Luther. "La reproduction familiale et sociale en France sous l'Ancien Régime: Le rapport au droit et aux valeurs." *Histoire & sociétés rurales* 29 (2008), 165–88.

Voltaire, François Marie Arouet de. *Recueil des lettres de M. de Voltaire, 1769–1771. Œuvres complètes de Voltaire*, vol. 61. Paris: L'imprimerie de la société littéraire-typographique, 1785.

Voltaire, François Marie Arouet de. *Dictionnaire philosophique. Œuvres complètes de Voltaire*, nouvelle édition, vols. 35–36. Paris: Thomine et Fortic, 1821.

Voltaire, François Marie Arouet de. "Dialogue entre un plaideur et un avocat (1751)." In *Œuvres complètes de Voltaire*, vol. 24, 317–19. Paris: Libraire Hachette, 1892.

Waelkens, Laurent. *La théorie de la coutume chez Jacques de Révigny: Édition et analyse de sa répétition sur loi De quibus (D. 1, 3, 32)*. Leiden: Brill, 1984.

Waelkens, Laurent. "L'origine de l'enquête par turbe." *Tijdschrift voor Rechtsgeschiedenis* 53, no. 3 (1985), 337–46.

Wanegffelen, Thierry. *Ni Rome, ni Genève: Des fidèles entre deux chaires en France au XVIe siècle*. Paris: Honoré Champion, 1997.

Wanegffelen, Thierry. *L'édit de Nantes: Une histoire européenne de la tolérance du XVIe au XXe siècle*. Paris: Le Livre de poche, 1998.

Wanegffelen, Thierry, ed. *De Michel de L'Hospital à l'édit de Nantes: Politique et religion face aux églises*. Clermont-Ferrand: Presses universitaires Blaise-Pascal, 2002.

Warembourg, Nicolas. "Guy Coquille et le droit français: Le droit commun coutumier dans la doctrine juridique du XVIe siècle." Thèse de doctorat en Droit, Université de Lille 2, 2005.

Warembourg, Nicolas. "Romanisation du droit privé français (XIIe–XVIIe siècle)." In *L'Histoire du droit en France: Nouvelles tendances, nouveaux territoires*. Edited by Jacques Krynen and Bernard d'Alteroche, 45–67. Paris: Classiques Garnier, 2014.

Warembourg, Nicolas. "La notion de 'droit commun' dans l'ancienne France coutumière: Point d'étape." *GLOSSAE. European Journal of Legal History* 13 (2016), 670–84.

Watson, Alan. "An Approach to Customary Law." *University of Illinois Law Review* 3 (1984), 561–76.

Watson, Alan. "The Evolution of Law: Continued." *Law and History Review* 5 (1987), 537–56.

Watson, Alan. *The Evolution of Law*. Baltimore: Johns Hopkins University Press, 1989.

Watson, Alan. *Legal Transplants: An Approach to Comparative Law*. Athens: University of Georgia Press, 1993.

Watson, Alan. *The Evolution of Western Private Law*. Baltimore: Johns Hopkins University Press, 2001.

Wetter, P. van. "Le droit romain et Beaumanoir." In *Mélanges Fitting*. Edited by Walther Holtzmann, vol. 2, 534–82. Aalen: Scientia Verlag, 1969 [1907].

White, Stephen D. "Bad Custom (*malae consuetudines*) in Eleventh-Century France." In *Custom: The Development and Use of a Legal Concept in the Middle Ages*. Edited by Per Andersen and Mia Münster-Swendsen, 51–66. Copenhagen: DJØF Publishing, 2009.

Whitman, James Q. "Why Did the Revolutionary Lawyers Confuse Custom and Reason?" *University of Chicago Law Review* 58, no. 4 (1991), 1321–68.

Whitman, James Q. "Western Legal Imperialism: Thinking about the Deep Historical Roots." *Theoretical Inquiries in Law* 10 (2009), 305–32.

Wijffels, Alain. "Qu'est-ce que le ius commune?" In *Le Code civil entre ius commune et droit privé européen*. Edited by Alain Wijffels, 643–61. Brussels: Bruylant, 2005.

Wijffels, Alain. "Ancien Régime France: Legal Particularism under the Absolute Monarchy." In *The Laws' Many Bodies: Studies in Legal Hybridity and Jurisdictional Complexity, c1600–1900*. Edited by Seán Patrick Donlan and Dirk Heirbaut, 81–107. Berlin: Duncker & Humblot, 2015.

Wijffels, Alain. "Une très brève histoire du droit dans la civilisation occidentale (1000–2000)." *Annales de droit de Louvain* 77 (2017), 397–411.

Williams, Ivy. *The Sources of Law in the Swiss Civil Code*. London: Oxford University Press, Humphrey Milford, 1923.

Wolodkiewicz, Witold. "Livre préliminaire 'titre Préliminaire' dans le projet et dans le texte définitif du Code Napoléon." *Revue historique de droit français et étranger* 83, no. 3 (2005), 441–55.

Yabumoto, Masanori. "*Voluntas domini regis in suo regno facit jus*: 'Toruzu kanshū-hō' ni miru Kape cho nanfutsu shihai no jissō—Kanshū-hō o baikai to suru rippō zettai shugi no kakuritsu" [The Image of 'Roi législateur' in the Coutumes de Toulouse under the Capets in the Midi—The Establishment of Legislative Absolutism through Customary Law]. *Hōgaku seijigaku ronkyū* 73 (2007), 77–108.

Yardeni, Myriam. *La conscience nationale en France pendant les guerres de religion, 1559–1598*. Leuven: Béatrice-Nauwelaerts, 1971.

Yver, Jean. *Les caractères originaux de la coutume de Normandie*. Caen: Imprimerie de C. Le Tendre R. Bigot, 1952.

Yver, Jean. *Égalité entre héritiers et exclusion des enfants dotés: Essai de géographie coutumière*. Paris: Sirey, 1966.

Yver, Jean. "L'État des études d'histoire du droit privé en France." *Revue historique de droit français et étranger* 45, no. 4 (1967), 708–11.

Yver, Jean. "La rédaction officielle de la coutume de Normandie (Rouen, 1583): Son esprit." *Annales de Normandie* 36 (1986), 3–36.

Yver, Jean. "Le président Thibault Baillet et la rédaction des coutumes (1496–1514)." *Revue historique de droit français et étranger* 64 (1986), 19–42.

Zaki, Magdi Sami. "Définir l'équité." *Archives de philosophie du droit* 35 (1990), 87–118.

Zimmermann, Reinhard. "Savigny's Legacy: Legal History, Comparative Law and the Emergence of a European Legal Science." *Law Quarterly Review* 112 (1996), 576–605.

Zink, Anne. *L'héritier de la maison: Géographie coutumière du Sud-Ouest de la France sous l'Ancien Régime*. Paris: Éditions de l'École des hautes études en sciences sociales, 1993.

Zink, Anne. "Les éditions de coutumes à France à l'époque moderne." *Ivs Fvgit* 15 (2007–2008), 467–92.

Zoltvany, Yves F. "Esquisse de la coutume de Paris." *Revue d'histoire de l'Amérique française* 25, no. 3 (1971), 365–84.

Index

Note: Figures are indicated by an italic "*f*", respectively, following the page number.

For the benefit of digital users, indexed terms that span two pages (e.g., 52–53) may, on occasion, appear on only one of those pages.

9 780192 845498

Made in the USA
Las Vegas, NV
19 September 2026

d942b5ca-3720-4db5-b86c-53c04963f08fR01